SUPPORTING WORK TEAM EFFECTIVENESS

SUPPORTING WORK TEAM EFFECTIVENESS

Best Management Practices for Fostering High Performance

Eric Sundstrom and Associates

Jossey-Bass Publishers • San Francisco

Jossey-Bass books and products are available through most bookstores. To contact Jossey-Bass directly, call (888) 378-2537, fax to (800) 605-2665, or visit our website at www.josseybass.com.

Substantial discounts on bulk quantities of Jossey-Bass books are available to corporations, professional associations, and other organizations. For details and discount information, contact the special sales department at Jossey-Bass.

For sales outside the United States, please contact your Simon & Schuster International Office.

 Manufactured in the United States of America on Lyons Falls Turin Book. This paper is acid-free and 100 percent totally chlorine-free.

Library of Congress Cataloging-in-Publication Data

Sundstrom, Eric D.
   Supporting work team effectiveness : best management practices for fostering high performance / Eric Sundstrom and associates. — 1st ed.
      p. cm. — (The Jossey-Bass business & management series)
   Includes bibliographical references and index.
   ISBN 0-7879-4322-3 (acid-free paper)
   1. Teams in the workplace. 2. Management. I. Title. II. Series.
HD66 .S85 1998
   658.4'02—ddc21   98-25474

FIRST EDITION
HB Printing   10 9 8 7 6 5 4 3 2 1

The Jossey-Bass Business & Management Series

CONTENTS

PART FOUR
Best Management Practices for High-Performance Teams

PREFACE

MORE AND MORE organizations are using work teams to meet today's global competition and rising customer expectations. Work teams test products, deliver services, assemble components, design new systems, deal with emergencies, and manage entire businesses. Some companies publicize stunning successes with teams, while others struggle to follow their lead.

As work teams become more common, so do books about them. You can find more than a dozen good guidebooks about working effectively in teams, leading teams, making work teams cohesive, solving problems in teams, and so on. The basics are well documented.

This book takes the next step: it describes how managers can provide support from *outside* the team to promote high performance. It documents the management practices that lay the proper foundation for a successful, team-based organization, by establishing a context that promotes effective teams.

Supporting Work Team Effectiveness focuses on nine essential support systems for work team effectiveness: team structure; leaders' roles; facilities; and systems for staffing, communication, measurement, information, training, and rewards. You can find books about the current state of the art in all of these management support systems. You even can find books about how some of them apply to work teams. Until now, though, you could not find one that discusses how all nine support systems apply to work teams.

This book is for managers involved with teams and familiar with the basics of teamwork. If you plan, develop, implement, supervise, facilitate, or administer systems that use work teams, then you will find *Supporting Work Team Effectiveness* written for you. If you lead a team, manage several teams, or work in a team-based organization, this book tells what you need to know about supporting work teams.

Intended readers include managers of personnel, human resources, operations, organizational development, information systems, communication technology, and facilities. This book is also for students in college and university courses on personnel management, human resource management, human resource planning, personnel psychology, organizational psychology, and organizational behavior.

Supporting Work Team Effectiveness differs in four ways from other books about work teams now on your bookshelf.

First, this book deals with the environment of work teams more than with interpersonal dynamics of teams and team meetings. Whereas other books discuss how team members interact with one another, this one addresses how teams interact with their organizations.

Second, *Supporting Work Team Effectiveness* discusses different kinds of work teams. It addresses six common types—production, service, management, project, action, and parallel work teams—and their varying needs for external support from management. Some books treat work teams as generic or discuss just one type. Here we describe the specific needs of six kinds of teams.

Third, this book combines a practical approach with grounding in research. Some books focus mainly on research and theory about groups; others emphasize case examples and anecdotes. We draw from both, using case examples to illustrate best management practices and evaluating them against available research evidence. Recognizing that practice has moved ahead of research in many areas, we also discuss practices that appear promising though untested. (If this were a book about medicines, it would include herbs and vitamins as well as government-approved medications.) However, compared with academic books on teams, we give little space to the details of the research or the theories behind it. Compared with management books on teams, though, we probably cite more research studies and journal articles (but we do so out of the way of the text, in chapter notes and the reference list). We have sought to write a practical book with a solid but unobtrusive foundation in research.

Fourth, *Supporting Work Team Effectiveness* offers a unified collection of chapters by leading experts on the team support systems. The chapters are as diverse as the systems. To give the book coherence, we incorporate three integrative devices in each chapter: an extended case example to illustrate the support system, a discussion of differences among six kinds of teams, and a summary of best management practices or guidelines for applying the support system. Compared with other volumes having multiple authors, this book is probably more integrated; and compared with books in which one author team wrote all the chapters, this one probably has more authors—the count is twenty.

Supporting Work Team Effectiveness has eleven chapters. After an introductory chapter come nine chapters on specific support systems.

Initially we hoped to present the chapters of *Supporting Work Team Effectiveness* in the same sequence that a manager would use in establishing work teams, but quickly realized that no one sequence would apply in all situations. So we organized the eleven chapters into logical groups that constitute the four parts of the book. Part One has three chapters on laying the foundation for high-peformance teams, including an introduction to the challenges of team effectiveness (Chapter One), a discussion of organizing a structure for teams (Chapter Two), and an analysis of team staffing (Chapter Three). Part Two concerns four specific support systems for work team effectiveness: leaders' roles (Chapter Four), training (Chaper Five), performance measurement (Chapter Six), and pay systems (Chapter Seven). Part Three deals with infrastructure, including the information system (Chapter Eight), communication technology (Chapter Nine), and the facility (Chapter 10). The last part consists of just one chapter that summarizes the best management practices offered throughout the book for supporting work team effectiveness.

Here is a preview.

Chapter One outlines current trends concerning work teams and introduces three challenges of supporting work team effectiveness: defining the team and what it means for it to be effective, providing the external support needed for best performance, and tailoring the support systems to the type of team. It distinguishes the six kinds of teams discussed in the other chapters.

Chapter Two describes the process of organizing teams and building a team structure. It uses the case of an electric motor plant of "MotorCo" (not the company's real name) to illustrate the process of designing a team-based manufacturing organization. It discusses the necessary elements of a team charter, the processes that help teams get started, and guidelines for giving teams just enough structure while allowing discretion for members to apply their expertise to their work.

Chapter Three illustrates the process of staffing teams through the example of filling an opening in a project team at a company we call "Software, Inc." The chapter contrasts practices of selection for individual jobs versus team-based organizations. It presents a staffing process based on an individual-in-team approach that includes teamwork analysis, and it examines resources for screening, assessment, and selection decision processes and variations for the six kinds of teams.

Chapter Four addresses leaders' roles related to teams, using the case of Boeing's 777 project to illustrate the increasing expectations of leaders in team-based organizations. This chapter describes key elements of leaders' roles, including direction setting, coordination, and liaison with the team's counterparts. Variations in leadership roles are examined at different levels and for the six kinds of teams.

Chapter Five examines training for work teams, using the example of a transition to teams at an established production facility, a copper mill of Phelps Dodge. The case illustrates the powerful role of training in an organization that relies on "natural teams" (based on existing reporting relationships). It demonstrates the sequence of assessing training needs, designing, delivering, and evaluating training. It also illustrates a common feature of teamwork training today: partial reliance on external contractors.

Chapter Six addresses performance measurement and feedback for work teams. It uses the case of a production team at a factory operated by "Electric Components Co." (not the company's real name) to illustrate the step-by-step process of building a set of performance indicators that reflect both the organization's business strategy and the team's unique situation. It reviews practices for developing measurement systems for various kinds of teams and for delivering feedback to teams such that constructive response and follow-up are ensured.

Chapter Seven examines reward systems for work teams. It uses the example of Solectron (the actual company name), an award-winning, team-based electronics manufacturer, to illustrate the impact of pay systems on team performance. It describes possible components of pay systems: base pay; skill-based pay; merit pay; and performance-based pay involving gain sharing, profit sharing, and employee ownership. The crucial question of balance among pay system components for teams is examined for the different types of teams.

Chapter Eight looks at information technologies for work teams, focusing on exchange of information between teams and their counterparts such as customers and managers. The chapter describes a high-tech project team at a small company, Digital Evolution (not a pseudonym), whose products include information systems. Pointing out that teams have converged with information technologies, the chapter discusses information needs of different kinds of teams and innovative information practices that make all teams effective.

Chapter Nine describes the rapidly evolving communication technologies that support virtual team meetings from geographically dispersed locations, as in the case of a project team's videoconference for an international banking firm we call "FirstGlobal" (not the organization's real name). The chapter discusses technologies for virtual team meetings by people in different cities. Management practices for group support systems in specially equipped conference facilities are also discussed, along with the kinds of communication technology appropriate for each type of team.

Chapter Ten describes facilities that support teams whose members work in the same building. A case example of the engineering offices at a Ford automobile assembly plant illustrates the role of facility design in creating opportunities for informal, face-to-face interaction across functional lines. This chapter analyzes the layout of team working areas for intrateam communication and regulation of external interactions, and it addresses the requirements for supportive physical environments for the six kinds of teams.

Chapter Eleven summarizes the management practices for fostering team effectiveness suggested in the preceding chapters and condenses them into checklists. It points out the most important support systems for each type of team, identifies current trends in teams and their support, and describes the challenges ahead.

This book is the product of a virtual project team aided by as many of the support systems as we could arrange. From offices in nine states—Arizona, California, Connecticut, Illinois, Indiana, Missouri, Tennessee, Texas, and Virginia—we collaborated via mail, telephone, e-mail, and sometimes even face-to-face meetings (though some of us still have never met in person). Most of the chapters traveled several times via the Internet and Federal Express, today's essential support systems. We tried to follow the advice outlined in the book, and we succeeded more often than not. We hope the product of our virtual project team helps make your work teams more effective.

For Alexander and Claire

ACKNOWLEDGMENTS

THIS BOOK BENEFITED from contributions by many people besides the virtual project team of twenty chapter authors. It was conceived in San Diego at the 1996 conference of SIOP, the Society for Industrial and Organizational Psychology, whose members continue to be sources of inspiration. Presentations by several SIOP members, including Susan Cohen, Jerry Ledford, and Janis Cannon-Bowers, pointed to the importance of support systems for work teams. Other SIOP members, such as Ann Howard and Richard Hackman, served as examples of best practice for book editors. Special thanks go to Bill Hicks of Lexington Press, who gave encouragement when the book was barely an idea; and to Susan Cohen, Steve Jones, and Richard Klimoski for conversations that helped move the book from an idea to a proposal.

The Jossey-Bass project team for this book exemplifies the teamwork and effectiveness discussed in the chapters. Cedric Crocker, business and management editor, provided expert advice and guidance from the outset and chose team members well suited to the project. Among the many insights about editing a book that he passed along to this new book editor is the importance of "guilt management."

Julianna Gustafson managed to convey smiles on the telephone as she efficiently handled contracting and distribution of first drafts for review. (We also owe thanks to four anonymous reviewers for their helpful comments.) Julianna cheerfully coordinated other details as well, including permissions and artwork. Katie Crouch, marketing coordinator, showed patience with a book editor unused to Jossey-Bass's ways and managed the development of an excellent marketing plan. Editor Byron Schneider demonstrated the ideal combination of professional attention to detail and give-and-take as the book took shape.

In Knoxville, Tennessee, Terry Halfhill, Emily Nelson, and Kristi Rutherford helped with library research. Linda Duffey worked diligently on the references.

Thanks go to Ed Lawler for suggesting our team reward system, based on royalty sharing.

When the manuscript finally went to Jossey-Bass production editor Sophia Ho, her experience was evident at every step. Tom Finnegan's able copyediting usually left us asking, "Why didn't we think of that?" We appreciate the artwork by illustrator Richard Sheppard, and the cover design by Richard Adelson.

THE AUTHORS

Tora K. Bikson is a senior scientist at the RAND Corporation, recognized for her research on the introduction of advanced communication and information technologies and their effects in varied social contexts. She recently carried out a study of the feasibility and societal implications of universal access to electronic mail in the United States. She is working on a project to define organizational needs and identify best practices for creating, managing, and distributing electronic documents among United Nations organizations based in Europe, North America, and South America. In previous projects for clients that include the National Science Foundation, the World Bank, the OECD, the United Nations, the Markle Foundation, and others, she has addressed such issues as the factors affecting successful institutionalization of new interactive technologies in communities of practice, how these innovative media influence intraorganizational and interorganizational structures and group processes, their impact on task performance and social outcomes, and their policy implications. She holds Ph.D. degrees in philosophy (University of Missouri) and psychology (UCLA) and has coauthored three recent books related to introducing networked digital technologies in governmental and business settings. Her research is also represented in numerous journal articles, books, and chapters of edited volumes.

Robert O. Briggs is a research scientist at the University of Arizona's Center for the Management of Information, where he conducts theoretical and empirical research on applications of group support technology to improve team productivity and enhance learning. He earned B.S. and B.A. degrees (graduating summa cum laude) as well as his master's degree in information and decision systems from San Diego State University, where he won the 1989 Outstanding Faculty award. He was awarded a National Doctoral Fellowship and received his Ph.D. from the University of Arizona in 1994. His research has addressed application of information and communication technology to support teams of military decision makers. His current research focus is on supporting geographically separated decision makers who need access to multiple sources of information and expertise.

Susan G. Cohen is an associate research professor at the Center for Effective Organizations, Marshall School of Business, University of Southern California. She has done research and consulted on a variety of approaches to improving organizational effectiveness, including group empowerment and effectiveness, employee involvement, organization development and change, participative management, performance management, and implementation of information technology. She has done extensive research on self-managing teams and team effectiveness, particularly in knowledge-work settings. She is the author of numerous articles and chapters about teams and teamwork, employee involvement and empowerment, and human resource strategies. She is coauthor of *Designing Team-Based Organizations: New Forms for Knowledge Work* (Jossey-Bass, 1995) and *Teams and Technology.*

Dee Hoffman is an organization consultant with Competitive Human Resources Strategies and also works with Times Mirror Training International. She previously worked as an internal organization development consultant with General Electric, focusing on employee involvement and self-regulating work teams, training, and empowerment. She currently works in the United States, Canada, and the United Kingdom, specializing in work design; work team implementation; and individual, team, and organization assessment and development. Other areas of expertise include labor-management partnership implementation and gainsharing support. She has made presentations at various conferences on topics such as team leadership and team reward systems. She received her doctorate in industrial-organizational psychology from the University of Tennessee.

Steve Jones is associate professor at Middle Tennessee State University and member of a self-directed work team with the industrial-organizational psychology program faculty. His Ph.D. is from the University of Houston (1986). He has measured team performance in manufacturing, health care, retail, insurance, and military organizations, as well as his current university. A certified Zenger-Miller trainer, he conducts workshops in team performance measurement, team leadership, and team building.

Richard J. Klimoski is professor of psychology, director of the Center for Behavioral and Cognitive Studies, and director of the applied/experimental program in psychology at George Mason University. His research interests and consulting practice involve the interface between human resource policy and design and implementation of effective teams. He received his Ph.D. from Purdue University (1970) in psychology and management. His research has appeared in a number of journals, and he has coauthored the book *Human Resource Management*. He has served on the editorial boards of several journals and was editor of the *Academy of Management Review* from 1990 to 1993. He has worked with a variety of organizations, both public and private, dealing with such issues as human resource management systems, job-related stress, and quality of work life.

Edward E. Lawler III is a professor of management and organization in the Marshall School of Business at the University of Southern California. He joined USC in 1978 and in 1979 founded and became director of the university's Center for Effective Organizations. He has been honored as a top contributor in the fields of organizational development, organizational behavior, and compensation. He is the author of more than two hundred articles and twenty-five books. His most recent Jossey-Bass books include *Strategic Pay* (1992), *The Ultimate Advantage* (1992), *Organizing for the Future* (1993), *Creating High-Performance Organizations* (1995), *From the Ground Up: Six Principles for Creating the New Logic Corporation* (1996), and *Tomorrow's Organization* (1998).

Don Mankin is dean of the College of Organizational Studies at the California School of Professional Psychology, Los Angeles campus. His primary areas of expertise are team effectiveness, information systems development and implementation, and change management. He has a B.S. in electrical engineering from Drexel University and M.A. and Ph.D. from Johns Hopkins University, concentrating in engineering psychology. He has held faculty positions at Lehigh University, the University of Houston, and the University of Maryland and has served as visiting fellow and research consultant at the RAND Corporation. He recently coauthored *Teams and Technology*. He has authored numerous articles and chapters, made academic and professional presentations in the United States, Asia, and Latin America, and has served as a consultant to corporate clients.

Michelle A. Marks is assistant professor of psychology at Florida International University. She received her Ph.D. (1998) in industrial-organizational psychology from George Mason University. Her research interests are team cognition, training and effectiveness, leadership, and mentoring relationships. She is currently designing the Florida International Team Effectiveness Center, where studies of team-related issues will be conducted.

Daniel Mittleman is an assistant professor in the School of Computer Science, Telecommunications and Information Systems at DePaul University. He holds a Ph.D. from the University of Arizona in management information systems. His research focuses on group support systems (GSS) and collaboration technologies; projects include investigation of local and virtual collaboration aboard U.S. Navy ships; development of GSS processes to support architectural planning, collaborative writing, and brainstorming; and design of technology-supported collaboration facilities. As a facilitator, he has guided more than five hundred strategic planning, documentation, and requirements elicitation meetings over the past nine years for industry, government, and educational organizations.

Richard G. Moffett III is assistant professor and member of the industrial-organizational psychology program at Middle Tennessee State University. He received his M.S. degree in clinical psychology from Valdosta State College (1979) and Ph.D. in industrial-organizational psychology from Auburn University (1996). He has worked as a psychological evaluator, training program developer, and human resource program consultant. His most recent work has been in conducting large-scale survey feedback to help an organization transform itself into a team-based organization. He is a certified Zenger-Miller trainer and conducts training workshops on group decision making and problem solving.

Linda Moran is a senior consultant with Zenger-Miller and an active team consultant and trainer. She is coauthor of numerous articles and *Self-Directed Work Teams*. Her most recent book is *Keeping Teams on Track*.

Margaret Gilchrist Serrato is a student in the doctoral program in architecture at Georgia Institute of Technology. Her research background includes field studies in group workspace and communication evaluation. She practices architecture at the firm of Lord, Aeck, Sargent in Atlanta.

Jerry L. Smolek is an organizational consultant with Competitive Human Resources Strategies and is president of Smolek Associates. He works with clients throughout the United States on planning and implementing cultural change. He has extensive experience at union and nonunion manufacturing sites and white-collar environments within pharmaceutical, utility, automotive, financial, and building-product industries as well as government organizations, working with leadership, product design, problem-solving, and work teams. He holds a bachelor's degree in business economics and a master's degree in industrial relations from Purdue University. He has worked for almost twenty-five years in human resources, including five years with Zenger-Miller as an executive consultant and eighteen years with General Electric, where he was recognized for his expertise in developing high-performance teams. As a pioneer in planning and implementing high-performance work systems, he is a featured speaker at regional and national symposiums and conferences.

Michael J. Stevens is director of consulting at Psychological Associates, a consulting firm based in St. Louis. His primary areas of expertise include improving organizational performance through empowerment and teamwork systems, training and change management, staffing and selection (especially for teams), and employee motivation and reward systems. He received his Ph.D. from the Krannert School of Management at Purdue University and won the Ralph G. Alexander Best Dissertation Award from the Human Resource Division of the Academy of Management. He has published articles in highly respected management journals and regularly gives presentations at professional conferences and meetings. He is principal author of The Teamwork-KSA Test, an employment test used in industry to measure an individual's aptitude for working successfully in a self-directed team environment. He is active in professional organizations and has held management positions in industry, government, and nonprofit organizations.

Eric Sundstrom is professor of psychology at the University of Tennessee, with research interests in work team effectiveness and the work environment. His B.A. is from the University of California and M.A. and Ph.D. (1973) from the University of Utah. His 1986 book *Work Places* was published in Japanese in 1992. He has more than sixty professional publications and serves on the editorial board of the journal *Group Dynamics*. His consulting practice has focused on organizational development, team effectiveness, and workplace design. He has provided consultation to major corporations, including AT&T, ALCOA, Chrysler Corp., Exxon USA, Lockheed-Martin, M & M/Mars, Maraven (Venezuela), Nortel, PepsiCo, United Technologies Corp., and Weyerhaeuser, and such government organizations as the South Carolina Department of Mental Health, Tennessee Department of Human Services, and U.S. Department of Energy.

Jean Wineman is associate professor and director of the doctoral program in the College of Architecture at Georgia Institute of Technology.

Her scholarship, research, and teaching explore the links between visual and spatial properties of architecture and behavioral and educational outcomes. Her research interests include museum and exhibit design, design of work settings to enhance productivity, and design for special populations. She is the editor of *Behavioral Issues in Office Design* and two special issues of *Environment and Behavior.* Her most recent publications include an article on spatial configuration within buildings in *Environment and Planning.*

Michael Yarish is engineering manager for Phelps Dodge Refining in Texas. After serving in the U.S. Air Force, he completed his B.S. in metallurgical engineering at the University of Texas at El Paso and joined Phelps Dodge in 1980. He is a past chairman of the local chapter of the American Institute of Metallurgical Engineers and was named Science Advisor of the Year for 1996–97 by the Texas Alliance for Minorities in Engineering. He entered graduate school at the University of Texas at El Paso and received his M.B.A. in 1997.

Stephen J. Zaccaro is associate professor of psychology and associate director of the Center for Behavioral and Cognitive Studies at George Mason University; he has held positions on the faculties of Virginia Polytechnic Institute and State University and College of the Holy Cross. He received an M.A. (1980) and Ph.D.(1981) from the University of Connecticut, specializing in social psychology. He has published numerous articles and chapters on work stress, leadership, group processes, and team performance and coedited *Occupational Stress and Organizational Effectiveness* and three special issues of *Leadership Quarterly* on individual differences and leadership. He has directed funded projects in the areas of team performance and shared mental models, leadership training, cognitive and metacognitive leadership capacities, and executive leadership.

Lori B. Zukin is a doctoral candidate in industrial and organizational psychology at George Mason University. She received her M.A. degree from Columbia University in 1993. Her primary research interests are team selection, vision in top management teams, and individual differences as they predict individual-in-team performance. Her consulting experience is in development of promotional exams and structured interviews.

SUPPORTING WORK TEAM
EFFECTIVENESS

PART ONE

LAYING THE FOUNDATION FOR HIGH-PERFORMANCE WORK TEAMS

I

THE CHALLENGES OF SUPPORTING WORK TEAM EFFECTIVENESS

Eric Sundstrom

SLIGHTLY MORE THAN a decade ago, a well-known management expert advised, "Organize *every function* into ten-to-thirty-person, largely self-managing teams."[1] At the time it was a controversial suggestion, and to some managers it probably seemed radical. Not any longer. Now work teams are commonplace, as more and more managers follow the advice.

Many organizations use work teams for management, production, service, problem solving, projects, and other work. Among large companies relying on work teams are AT&T, Boeing, Eastman Chemical, Hewlett-Packard, Motorola, Federal Express, Saturn, and Xerox. Of these, half have won Malcolm Baldrige National Quality Awards, and all continue to make a profit.[2] It is not surprising to see organizations of all kinds—large and small, public and private, manufacturing and service—follow their lead.

Work teams are integral to a new breed of high-involvement organization, evolving in an environment of global competition, rapidly evolving technology, and rising customer expectations.[3] They stay competitive by improving the quality of their products and services while reducing costs, offering faster service, and getting to market ever more quickly with new products. Achieving these advances has meant capitalizing on the talents, ideas, and energy of employees at all levels.

Properly designed and supported, work teams offer exactly what is needed: a platform for promoting creativity, motivating extraordinary performance, and enabling fast, flexible response to customers' needs. Work teams allow "flat" organizational structures, with few hierarchical levels and maximum authority at the lowest levels. They give employees the opportunity to exercise responsibility and authority—or *empowerment*.[4] At the same time, work teams allow and require employees to develop new skills while working, a source of both satisfaction and challenge. A team-based structure links each work team to the organization's leaders and serves as both a vehicle for alignment with the organization's strategy and the means of fostering employee involvement.[5]

Companies continue to report stunning successes with work teams: tenfold reductions in error rates and quality defects, productivity gains of 200 percent and more, 90 percent reductions in response time, process steps reduced in number to one-tenth what they were; product-to-market cycle cut by half.[6] Such examples continue to multiply. In view of such impressive results, few managers question the potential benefits of work teams.

Today's question—and the topic of this book—is *how* to foster effective teams. An answer based on decades of experience and research is *to give them the necessary management support*. To be effective, work teams need several kinds of support, including a structure compatible with teamwork; leaders' roles that foster cooperation; complementary systems for selection, measurement, information, training, and compensation; and facilities with communication technology that facilitates needed interaction within and among teams.

The primary goal of this book is to identify the best management practices for supporting effective work teams. Meeting this goal calls for reviewing current literature on management practices. It also calls for drawing on the experience of managers and consultants who have worked with teams in a variety of settings, as have the authors of the chapters. It means documenting practices that have not yet appeared widely in print.

A second goal of this book is to evaluate current management practices for promoting team effectiveness against available research evidence. For well-established practices, such as procedures for personnel selection, ample evidence exists. Other practices are too new to have been tested but have enough support from case examples to be widely accepted. We intend to give you the best possible basis for deciding whether or not to try the management practices in your own organization.

A guiding theme of this book is that various kinds of work teams have differing needs. A team that assembles automobile transmissions at the Saturn plant in Spring Hill, Tennessee, for instance, needs up-to-the-minute information on current supplies of transmission parts. A product development team at the 3M electronics operation at Austin, Texas, needs information with less time urgency and from many more sources.

Six kinds of work teams—production, service, management, project, action, and parallel—have diverse requirements. Within types, each team has unique needs. The management challenge is to design, implement, and maintain organizational support systems to meet the needs of the type of team, with flexibility to accommodate each team's unique features.

Adequate support for work teams becomes increasingly urgent as organizations introduce work teams at an ever-increasing pace. Today it may be difficult to find an organization *not* using work teams, at least experimentally. A national survey repeated three times by a research team from the University of Southern California's Center for Effective Organizations shows the trend.[7] Researchers contacted representatives of Fortune 1000 companies in 1987 and asked, among other things, how many employees were involved in "employee participation groups other than quality circles" and in "self-managing work teams." They asked again in 1990 and 1993. Figure 1.1 shows percentages of organizations whose representatives said at least some employees were involved. The most common answer at all three times was "almost none" (1 percent to 20 percent), so the trend in this histogram represents limited use of teams. Even so, by 1993 more than two-thirds of responding companies reported having at least some self-managing teams. The histogram shows an increase of about 40 percent over six years, an annual gain of more than 6 percent. If the use of self-managing teams continues at the same rate, it should approach 100 percent by the time you read this.

This opening chapter describes three fundamental challenges facing managers who intend to support work teams:

1. Defining work teams clearly enough to give them identity as work units
2. Preparing nine essential support systems for fostering effective teams
3. Tailoring the support systems to the type of team

The chapter has three sections, one for each challenge.

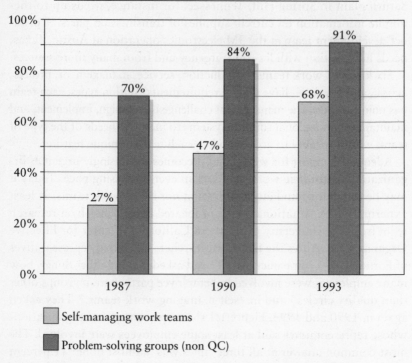

Figure 1.1. Use of Work Teams Reported
by Fortune 1000 Company Representatives.

☐ Self-managing work teams

■ Problem-solving groups (non QC)

Source: Adapted from Lawler, Mohrman, and Ledford (1992, 1995).

CHALLENGE NUMBER ONE: DEFINING WORK TEAMS

The challenge of defining work teams has three parts: (1) making sure there are actually work teams to support, (2) defining them clearly enough that they become viable work units, and (3) specifying what it means for them to be effective. Some managers have discovered through experience that it is not enough to simply announce to a group of employees that they are now a team and should act accordingly. Such "teams" fail for many reasons, especially the most basic one: the employees do not even meet the minimum definition of a work team. If they do, they may need to exceed the minimum definition to have realistic prospects of being effective in their organization. It definitely helps if they know exactly what it means for them to be effective.

Minimum Definition of a Work Team

A *work team* consists of "interdependent individuals who share responsibility for specific outcomes for their organization."[8] The minimum defining features are shared responsibility and interdependence.

Individuals are interdependent if each depends on the others to carry out his or her role, to accomplish goals, or create cooperative outputs. Members of a manufacturing plant management team are usually interdependent in all three ways. First, they have *role interdependence*: the operations manager, for example, depends on daily information from the sales manager on how much of each product was sold; the sales manager depends on information about production to know when orders can be promised. Second, they may have *goal interdependence*: the production manager can only meet certain production goals with the support of sales, and vice versa. Third, they have *outcome interdependence*: advancing their careers within the company depends on success achieved through cooperation. If they work on a gainsharing plan, their checks depend on the gains they realize together. If they own company stock, their returns depend partly on how well they manage the plant.

Without some form of interdependence, people have no reason to cooperate, even if others think of them as a team. An example is a so-called sales team at a midwestern farm equipment sales and leasing company. The eight sales agents have separate territories and are paid on commission. Their manager hopes that calling them a team encourages teamwork (the idea sounded good, anyway). Unfortunately, they almost never see one another and have no joint duties. Even if they like the idea of being a team, they cannot hope to do so without some form of interdependence. They represent what some have called a "pseudo team,"[9] a group that has no shared duties, no joint performance goals, and no motivation to cooperate.

In brief, the first step in supporting a work team is to be sure that the people in question have the critical ingredients of a work team: shared responsibility and at least one form of interdependence. If they do not, they are not a work team.

Features That Strengthen Team Definition

Besides some form of interdependence, a work team may need more definition to have realistic prospects of success. Features that strengthen team definition are additional forms of interdependence, reporting to the same manager, sharing a workplace (co-location), small group size, seeing themselves as a team, and stable membership.[10] The more of these features a group has, the clearer its definition as a work team. A manager can reinforce a team's identity and increase its prospects of being effective by arranging for it to have as many of these features as possible.

INTERDEPENDENT ROLES. Work teams sometimes incorporate complementary, interdependent roles linked to technology, as in hospital operating room teams, military tank crews, and cockpit crews.[11] However, even individual roles, such as sales agent or customer service representative, can be made interdependent if individuals have shared responsibility for such tasks as scheduling work, making assignments, and covering absences.

INTERDEPENDENT GOALS. One basis for defining a work team is to have collective goals achievable only through cooperation, as in many cross-functional project teams. Research shows that such commonly held "superordinate goals" promote cooperation.[12] Team assignments can lead to shared performance goals that work the same way.

INTERDEPENDENT OUTCOMES OR SHARED FATE. Members of a work team who share the results of cooperative effort, such as the credit for a new piece of software or the royalties from its sales, have a definite incentive to cooperate. Members of management teams at Federal Express, for instance, receive annual bonuses worth more than a quarter of their salaries if team performance reaches certain targets based on such measures as the percentage of packages delivered late. Shared outcomes can come from a team reward system.

REPORTING TO THE SAME MANAGER. Team definition can be reinforced through the organization chart: whoever reports directly to the same supervisor or manager is part of the same "natural team." In a matrix organization like Boeing's, for example, members of cross-functional project teams each report to a project manager and a functional manager and belong to two natural teams. Whether such supervisor-supervisee groups act like teams depends on leaders' skill at encouraging participation in decisions, inviting employee involvement, and generally acting more as facilitator and coach than commander and disciplinarian.[13]

CO-LOCATION OR SHARED WORKPLACE. A well-accepted way of reinforcing team definition is to assign people to the same work area, ideally in adjacent workstations. Such co-location is common for project teams whose members sometimes share team rooms or labs that symbolically reinforce team identity. The work site creates opportunities for face-to-face conversation among members, both task-oriented and informal, which in turn bolsters group cohesion.[14] A group in an isolated site may develop self-sufficiency by taking on responsibilities that traditionally belong to managers, such as work assignments, quality checking, and troubleshooting.[15]

SMALL SIZE. In a group that is too large, members have trouble maintaining personal relationships with each other. Although it is difficult to know exactly how many is too many, experts say it is best to keep a work team's size as small as possible.[16] Some successful work teams have relatively large numbers of members: in the sixty-person crew of one California offshore oil-drilling platform, members claim they regularly interact with practically all of the others and say they work as one large team. But unless a team lives together around the clock for ten days at a time in its workplace as these people do, it is best to keep the size much smaller. The ideal team size seems to be five to nine members.

MEMBERS SEE THEMSELVES AS A TEAM. Social psychologists say that a team exists when individuals see themselves as one. Team identity can be reinforced by forming teams of individuals who have a history of working together or are friends. Another way is to formally identify the members in a team roster and make it available to the team and others in the organization.

STABLE MEMBERSHIP. A team's definition is clear to members and nonmembers alike if the membership is stable over time. Today's teams increasingly consist of specialists who come and go as the work evolves.[17] Some kinds of work teams exhibit better performance when their membership remains stable.[18]

Expectations for Effectiveness

The third part of the challenge of defining a work team calls for specifying what it means for the team to be effective. Effectiveness starts with meeting the performance expectations of those who receive, use, or review the team's output.[19] This usually means meeting the expectations of a manager, customers inside or outside the organization, and possibly others. Effectiveness also includes something more: meeting members' own expectations of satisfying work and working relationships in the team. As long as members' expectations and needs are met, the team retains its viability as a work unit.[20] If a team allows divisive interpersonal conflict, its members may burn out and want to leave.[21] Therefore, a practical definition of *team effectiveness* is *the extent to which a work team meets the performance expectations of key counterparts—managers, customers, and others—while continuing to meet members' expectations of working with the team.*

For a manager, the challenge of defining the team is to identify its key counterparts and clarify their expectations. These include the customer's expectations, the manager's own requirements, those of other counterparts (such as suppliers, peers, members of professional organizations, regulators, and subordinates), and the reasonable expectations of the members themselves.

CUSTOMERS' EXPECTATIONS. Work teams usually deliver to their customers one of four kinds of output:

1. Tangible objects (automobile parts, new product prototypes, written reports)

2. Decisions or recommendations (which candidate to hire, whether to construct a building or rent, whether to acquire another company)

3. Completed service transactions (a repaired diesel engine, processed insurance claim, argued legal case, completed heart bypass surgery, airline flight arriving in Chicago)

4. Performance events (concerts, presentations, new product demonstrations)

Customers judge team output in terms of quantity, quality, timeliness, cost, and responsiveness of service. Today's customers usually have multiple requirements, and the manager's job is to make them explicit for the work team. Realize, too, that a work team's only customer might be the manager who convened it.

MANAGERS' EXPECTATIONS. For managers, especially those who are stakeholders (with a financial interest in the business), meeting customers' expectations represents a primary performance requirement of work teams. Other performance expectations deal with productivity[22] or the output in relation to the resources required to generate it. Among other things, productivity requirements involve timeliness and quantity as well as efficiency with respect to resources used, such as employees' time and the costs of space, raw materials, equipment, energy, training, security, and staff. A wise manager also has expectations about maintaining and enhancing the organization's capacity, including the viability of the team and its members' individual skills.

OTHER COUNTERPARTS. Counterparts of a work team include subordinates or staff members who report to those in the team; peers who maintain professional norms or methods, databases, standards, or technologies that apply to the team's work or outputs; suppliers who provide information, materials, parts, supplies, services, or consultation; and, perhaps, external regulators. Depending on which external relationships apply, what it means to be effective may be defined by multiple sets of expectations besides those of managers and customers.

MEMBERS' EXPECTATIONS. For a work team to be a viable unit, members need motivation to commit their effort and ideas to achieving team goals, and a sufficiently satisfying experience that they want to continue working with the team or one like it. Team members can reasonably expect their managers to provide the help and resources necessary to maintain conditions conducive to the work and congenial relations among coworkers. As any manager knows who has worked with teams, this can be difficult and complicated;[23] still, it is achievable given time, attention, and energy. For a manager, the key point is that members' expectations of working with the team need to be understood and addressed, as customers' expectations are.

Fortunately, teams have learning curves[24] and require less external support as they develop increasing self-sufficiency over time. With guidance and support at the beginning, members of a work team gain individual and collective confidence in their capacities. Managers who provide early support can promote cycles of increasing confidence and perceived self-efficacy in work teams,[25] which contribute to both self-sufficiency and performance. The question of support leads to the next challenge.

CHALLENGE NUMBER TWO: PROVIDING ESSENTIAL SUPPORT SYSTEMS

The second challenge in supporting work team effectiveness is to provide nine essential support systems:

- Team structure
- Leaders' roles
- Team staffing
- Training
- Measurement and feedback
- Reward system
- Information system
- Communication technology
- Facility

The nine support systems all have direct links to a work team's potential effectiveness. As an illustration of their impact, consider the example of a production team at the Saturn plant in Spring Hill, Tennessee. A Saturn production team consists of about ten people permanently assigned to work together in the same production area on the same shift.

Team Structure: Responsibilities, Authority, Resources, Accountability

A team's role within the organization establishes the fundamental expectations that provide the basis for evaluating its effectiveness. The role specifies the team's primary duties, outputs, external workflows, and reporting relationships in the hierarchy of authority—in other words, the team's place in the organization's structure—as well as its size; composition; resources; life span; and counterparts such as suppliers, customers, and support personnel. In turn, the team's role establishes the collective knowledge, skills, and abilities required of the members. Clarity of the role—and the extent to which it is understood in the same way by members, managers, customers, and other counterparts—may determine the extent to which a team focuses on the work instead of spending its time finding out what is expected or dealing with conflicting expectations.

A Saturn production team has a permanent assignment. Its main responsibility is to assemble a major component, such as front disc brakes, and to install it. A production team also conducts preventive maintenance, maintains a stock of tools and supplies, does housekeeping, handles work assignments, checks the quality of the work, schedules training, and coordinates with suppliers and internal customers. In brief, a Saturn team has responsibility for many management tasks as well as production.

A team's performance expectations also specify results for which members are held jointly accountable through the reward system. Teams may be accountable for costs, timeliness, output, service quality, customer satisfaction ratings, and other results. Clear expectations are critical to team effectiveness, and making them explicit is part of the leader's role.

Leaders' Roles

In a team-based organization, leaders' roles differ from those in traditional hierarchies, where leaders use a command-and-control style. With teams, the roles explicitly call for soliciting employee involvement, participation, and ideas as well as facilitating group decisions, promoting self-direction, and encouraging individual development.[26]

A work team usually has one of two leader role configurations. A *supervisor-led team* includes a higher-ranking supervisor to whom team members formally report, who works with the team, directs its activities, and reports personally to a higher-ranking manager. Examples today include most military units and coal-mining crews. A second pattern appears in a *semiautonomous team,* consisting of members who have the same rank, one of whom is an appointed or elected leader reporting to an external manager responsible for coordinating several teams. Examples include many production and service teams. The same leader role configuration applies to *self-directed* or *self-managing* teams, whose members have more of the responsibilities that traditionally belong to managers, such as scheduling work, making work assignments, coordinating training, handling safety, and others.[27]

Production teams at Saturn report to an external coordinator, who supports multiple teams. Each team is also accountable to a representative of the local United Automobile Workers, whose job is to ensure that team members are complying with the labor agreement. The union rep works as a partner with the production coordinator, and the two share responsibility for the same teams. Each team has an appointed internal leader, who keeps the coordinator and union representative informed of the team's work.

Leader roles are critical to Saturn's production teams, especially the role of coordinator. As the manager of multiple teams, a Saturn coordinator has little time to micromanage. Primary tasks are to make sure the teams have information and resources needed for their work; help teams stay synchronized with the production schedule; keep everyone informed of engineering changes, safety bulletins, and other news; and manage the flow of information to higher levels of management. The coordinator serves as a communication link among teams and with management. The role is particularly important in encouraging decision making, initiatives, and input by production teams, who are the primary source of suggestions for improvement.

Team Staffing

Staffing is an important aid to team effectiveness because it ensures that team members have the requisite mix of knowledge, skills, abilities, and other attributes (KSAOs) for the work. The staffing system typically consists of people in the human resource department who handle recruitment, screening, selection, hiring, and placement of employees in positions in the organization. When providing personnel for teams, the staffing system has to recruit and select people who have teamwork skills, and to make assignments that take account of the necessary mix of skills and expertise needed for the team's work.[28]

At Saturn, applicants for production jobs are recruited from among union members and invited to take part in onsite testing, assessment center exercises, and interviews. Applicants complete tests of basic abilities and assessment center exercises to evaluate teamwork skills. Those who meet the criteria participate in structured interviews. Since the initial selection of employees for the newly constructed plant (often called a "green field" site), production teams have had a significant part in selecting their own members and interviewing applicants themselves. As a result, production teams at Saturn include new members compatible with the team besides having the job-related abilities and skills.

Training

The organization's system for training and development helps employees acquire skills and knowledge needed for their jobs after they are hired. Training has been important in companies adopting team-based structures (such as Motorola and Xerox[29]), and today team training is widely used.[30]

Saturn has been a team-based organization from inception. The six-week employee orientation training includes an introduction to teamwork skills and practices as well as the usual introductions to safety procedures, plant operations, and production processes. Once on the job, Saturn production employees are expected to obtain ninety-two hours of training each year. Teams have individual "point roles," assigned to members for one year, specific jobs such as training representative and safety coordinator. (The point role system itself is a form of on-the-job training.) Each team's training representative monitors training programs, forwards requests for topics to human resources, keeps members informed about upcoming training opportunities, stays familiar with training histories and training needs, and schedules appropriate training for members. Saturn employees use training to develop new skills as their work and technology evolve. Without it, the teams would have difficulty meeting their performance goals.

Measurement and Feedback

Research demonstrates that team effectiveness benefits if members have access to objective measures of their performance, especially if the team has established goals on the measures.[31] Within the past two decades, organizations have increasingly used objective measures of production for evaluating performance, often during adoption of total quality management (TQM).[32] Objective measurement as a basis for evaluating employee performance contrasts with the traditional practice of using supervisors' evaluations in periodic performance appraisals. Instead, team-based organizations tend to rely increasingly on objective measures of performance wherever possible.

Saturn's production teams monitor their own performance on multiple measures of output and operations, which are instantly accessible via computer terminals in their work areas. The same data go to production coordinators, managers, and other teams. The coordinator discusses performance data with each team and ideas for improving. Such feedback and how it is delivered and discussed have a substantial influence on team members' motivation to make improvements.

Reward System

An organization's pay-and-recognition system has a major influence on team performance.[33] Analyses of team effectiveness note that individual motivation to expend effort on behalf of a team depends on individual incentives, or expectations of receiving valued outcomes as a result of the effort. Team members may be motivated by intrinsic factors, such as an interesting job or autonomy in carrying it out. However, the evidence clearly indicates that extrinsic motivation is necessary for sustained performance by most kinds of work teams.

Saturn uses a pay-for-skill system in which hourly wages increase as employees achieve certification on new job skills. Members of production teams also receive a gainsharing bonus based on the amounts by which the plant exceeds certain production targets. (In the early 1990s, team members received annual bonuses of about $10,000.) As a result, teams have a powerful incentive not only to perform well but to cooperate and find ways of improving production.

Information System

Team effectiveness depends on having up-to-date information about technology, work processes, supplies, customers, and other critical data. Teams must also inform managers and counterparts about their output, resource requirements, use of resources, and details of their work and plans. These depend on the organization's information technology.[34]

Today, *information system* often translates as "computer network." Organizations of all sizes use networked terminals or PCs for storage and communication of management information. Work teams must decide which information is important, a task complicated by the need for basic computer skills to gain access to the information.[35]

Saturn production teams tap a huge array of information through computer terminals in their work areas. Team members look up data on parts supplies, production schedules, production by upstream and downstream teams, delivery schedules, and other topics. Production teams receive information on their own production and the extent to which the team is meeting the expectations of management and customers.

Communication Technology

New communication technology gives work teams a variety of ways to communicate besides face-to-face conversation: telephone, fax, teleconference, computer conference, voice mail, e-mail, and videoconference. New technologies also aid group collaboration through "group support systems" (GSSs), such as conference rooms containing whiteboards that print copies of their contents and networked computers with software that allows multiple users to simultaneously enter text in the same file displayed for all to see.[36]

New communication technologies have created the possibility of "virtual teams," whose members collaborate from different cities—even different continents—using electronic media.[37] The same technologies allow fast communication with suppliers, customers, and peers in distant locations.

Saturn production teams work at the same facility, so members of production teams can rely on face-to-face conversation for communication. Team coordinators also carry phone pagers. Production teams rely on their networked computer terminals for access to local databases as well as remote ones (including those of the larger organization, General Motors) and use electronic media to stay in touch with suppliers. As in many other teams, these technologies have become integral to their work.[38]

Facility

The physical working environment is easily overlooked as a potential source of support for effectiveness of work teams, yet it may be as important as any other factor. For teams whose members work at the same facility, the physical layout of workstations either facilitates or inhibits face-to-face conversation among members. The many features of working environments related to ease of conversation among team members include proximity of workstations, access to conference rooms, and access to central gathering places.[39]

Saturn's production teams work in a facility that integrates teams with a complex production process. Each team has a defined working area with workstations located according to the dictates of the production process. The distance between individual workstations and the level of background noise do not always allow face-to-face conversation between members. However, teams have access to small conference rooms, of which the plant has several kinds. The physical facility supports production teams by aiding communication among team members and workflow between teams and their counterparts.

In brief, Saturn's production teams receive support from their organizations from nine essential support systems: team structure, leaders' roles, facility, staffing, communication technology, measurement and feedback, information systems, training, and rewards. Although these support systems are necessary for an environment in which production teams can be effective, they are not sufficient to ensure the success of the organization. When Saturn's employees renewed their union labor contract in March 1998, the market for its small cars had shrunk while the demand for larger vehicles was expanding. Dealing effectively with the question of whether to expand the Saturn product line to meet the changing market represents a task for the GM executive team. The kind of support needed for effectiveness in executive and other management teams differs from what is required for production teams. Indeed, supporting work team effectiveness is largely a matter of tailoring the support systems to the needs of the specific type of team. This is the third challenge.

CHALLENGE NUMBER THREE: TAILORING SUPPORT SYSTEMS TO THE TYPE OF TEAM

Numerous kinds of work teams exist today. Some are more self-managing than others. Some work in the same place, and others are virtual and collaborate from a distance. Some are permanent, others temporary. However, for managers probably the most important difference among work teams concerns the work they do. Seen this way, at least six kinds of teams can be distinguished:

1. Production teams
2. Service teams
3. Management teams
4. Project teams
5. Action or performing teams
6. Parallel teams[40]

This section discusses their differences and commonalities; the six kinds of teams are discussed in other chapters.

Management Teams

Management teams consist of managers and their direct reports. Each team has responsibility for coordinating the work of units under its purview. Shared duties include planning, policy making, budgeting, staffing, and coordination. These teams usually have the highest rank and greatest authority. They organize their working arrangements in whatever way their leaders allow and may be regarded as self-designing.[41] Typically treated as permanent, in practice they may have frequent changes of membership as managers are promoted and transferred. Members of management teams are usually interdependent with one another in some ways, and as teams they are interdependent with the work units they coordinate. The time urgency of their interactions varies to extremes, from emergency decisions required in minutes to long-range plans that take months. Management teams are moderately specialized; usually no other team in the organization does exactly the same thing, though some organizations have dozens of management teams with similar management responsibilities for different work units. Specialization within the team also varies in that managers may have different specialties, though they share similar duties with respect to their units. Examples are corporate executive teams and middle-management teams.

Project Teams

Also called *task forces*,[42] project teams have specific tasks to do within definite time periods; they disband after finishing. Usually cross-functional, their members represent different job functions or parts of the organization.[43] Membership consists of experts selected for specialized skills and contributions to the team's collective expertise. Each project team has a highly specialized task to accomplish, such as developing a new product, writing a computer program, building a prototype, or designing a component. Authority of project teams varies; some consist of low-ranking frontline employees, while others comprise high-ranking professionals or managers who have their own staffs. Examples of project teams are the engineering teams at Boeing that designed components for the new 777 airliner[44] and programming teams at Microsoft that write parts of new software packages.

As recently as a decade ago, project teams worked independently, relying on their leaders for necessary information and otherwise remaining isolated from their organizations. The well-chronicled "Eagle team" at a large computer manufacturer in the 1970s, Data General, developed a prototype computer this way; the team was deliberately separated as much as possible from the rest of the organization. It concentrated single-mindedly on its project, with relatively little outside contact.[45] Today, however, a project team cannot work effectively in isolation; instead, it must maintain close contact with peers, customers, other project teams, and its managers.[46] New communication technologies enable project teams to maintain external liaison in many ways, while at the same time allowing for virtual project teams whose members collaborate electronically without ever meeting in person.[47]

Production Teams

Like the Saturn teams, production teams in general consist of frontline employees who repeatedly produce tangible outputs of a particular kind. They usually have low rank and sharply limited authority. Membership tends to be indefinite, and some production teams remain stable for years. Depending on the complexity of the work, members may be expected to participate in cross-training to learn one another's specialized skills and job rotation to master all of the specialized tasks done by the team. Their work is only moderately specialized; many production teams in the organization may do very similar work.

A self-managing production team usually reports through an elected or assigned team leader to a manager or coordinator to whom several other teams also report. Members of a self-managing production team have duties traditionally done by supervisors: they schedule their work, order supplies, handle housekeeping, maintain their equipment, and conduct business with customers. They may even participate in decisions about budgets, performance appraisals, training, and personnel selection.[48]

A typical production team is interdependent and tightly linked with other production teams producing parts of the same larger product.[49] Work relies on complex equipment, timely information, and reliable flow of components provided by upstream suppliers.

Service Teams

Like production teams in many ways, service teams consist of employees who conduct repeated transactions with the organization's customers; these transactions may take only a few minutes or may last several weeks or months. These teams usually occupy the lowest echelons of their organizations, like production teams, and may be self-managing.

Work done by service teams varies in complexity. Examples of service teams are telecommunications sales and service teams,[50] operating-room support teams, hospital patient care teams, airline attendant teams, and maintenance teams.[51]

Assignment to a service team is permanent or temporary. Some teams of employees of the Tennessee Department of Human Services, for example, have worked together to administer family assistance services for more than five years. In contrast, the flight attendant teams for some airlines change composition for every flight, so the life span of any one team may be measured in hours.

Action and Performing Teams

Teams in the category of action and performance conduct complex, time-limited engagements with audiences, adversaries, or challenging environments in "performance events" for which teams maintain specialized, collective skill.[52] These teams consist of highly trained professionals, who tend to occupy the lower or middle echelons of their organizations. Work output often consists of intangible events. Action teams also confront sudden, unpredictable behavior in their work environments that demands quick and sometimes improvised response. Examples of action and performing teams are surgery teams, investigative units, rescue units, spill containment teams, cockpit crews, athletic teams, sales teams, law-enforcement teams, firefighting teams, military units, intelligence teams, government regulatory teams, professional musician ensembles, military units, legal teams, negotiation teams, and expeditions.

A hallmark of action teams is the requirement for coordination among specialized roles; it can take years to master. Individual members must not only maintain special technical skills but also the teamwork skills needed to synchronize their own performances with those of their counterparts. Teams might perform well only after members learn to adjust to coworkers' idiosyncrasies. Cross-training and job rotation may be impractical for action and performing teams, in light of the time required for mastery of any one specialized role.

Under ideal conditions, the members of an action or performing team have indefinite or permanent assignments, with little turnover in team makeup. Extended team life span allows development and maintenance of smoothly coordinated, collective performances. For example, professional string quartets may take years to learn to play together.[53]

Many action and performing teams are quite temporary, being newly composed for each performance event. Examples are some negotiation teams, legal teams, investigative teams, and sales teams. Unable to practice together in advance, their capacity to perform depends on the teamwork skills of individual members, who must adjust quickly to one another. Quick adjustment depends on standardization of the skills of the individual and specialized roles, as well as relying on individual teamwork skills. For example, the cockpit crews of one U.S. airline are reconstituted for each flight but are still able to perform with only a few minutes together before taking off, as each works with the knowledge that counterparts have thoroughly mastered certain standard routines always done in the same way.[54]

Action and performing teams typically are highly specialized and may be unique at their sites in executing their particular performance events. At the same time, they usually depend heavily on external support, often relying on multiple suppliers from inside and outside the organization. Surgery teams, professional sports teams, and expeditions represent extreme examples of external linkage.

Parallel Teams

Parallel teams sometimes qualify only barely as work teams, and sometimes they do not. Parallel teams work outside of—and in parallel with—the primary production, service, performing, or research-and-development processes of the organization.[55] They consist of temporary, ad hoc committees appointed by managers to make suggestions or recommendations. Parallel teams have no authority beyond their specific mandates. Membership often includes a cross-section of relevant constituencies to provide for broad representation. Examples are selection committees, advisory councils, employee involvement teams, and the "quality circles" of the 1980s.[56]

Parallel teams are, by definition, isolated from the primary processes of the organization, so they have limited external linkage. At the same time, they may have few requirements for specialized knowledge, skills, and abilities other than those required for constructive participation in the committee's work. A manager forming a team of this type, such as a selection committee, may give more thought to the job titles and work areas represented on the committee than to potential members' specialized expertise. Individual members are generally readily interchangeable. Parallel teams usually are not as specialized as project teams or action and performing teams.

SUMMARY: KINDS OF WORK TEAMS

The six kinds of work teams differ in several ways, as shown in Table 1.1. The table gives examples of each kind of team and displays the differences in five characteristics: authority, temporary versus permanent, external linkage, whole-team specialization, and specialization within the team. The table might include other features as well.

Just in terms of these features, you see that teams differ substantially by type. For example, project teams are almost always temporary, and production teams are usually permanent. If you scan across the profiles of the six kinds, you find no two alike.

The challenges of tailoring support systems to the kind of team differ for each support system essential for work team effectiveness. The next nine chapters each discuss one support system and how to tailor it to the types of teams.

Table 1.1. Six Kinds of Work Teams: Examples and Typical Features.

KINDS OF WORK TEAMS	EXAMPLES	TYPICAL FEATURES				
		Team authority	Temporary/ permanent	External linkage	Whole-team specialization	Within-team specialization
Management	Executive team Management team	Moderate to high	Permanent	High	Moderate	Varied
Project	New-product team Design team	Varied	Temporary	High	High	High
Production	Assembly team Coal-mining crew	Low	Permanent	High	Low to moderate	Low
Service	Retail sales team HR training team	Low	Permanent or temporary	High	Low to moderate	Varied
Action and performing	Negotiation team Rescue team	Low to moderate	Permanent or temporary	High	High	High
Parallel	Quality circle Selection committee	Low to moderate	Temporary	Low	Varied	Low to moderate

ORGANIZING TEAMS FOR SUCCESS

Jerry Smolek, Dee Hoffman, Linda Moran

If teams are the answer, what was the question?

IN THE LAST TWENTY YEARS, foreign and domestic competition has raised the performance bar for virtually every organization. No longer are high quality, productivity, and fast delivery just desired; they are expected. No country, no industry, and no service is immune. No one.

Leadership continuously searches for ways to meet these challenges in this ever-changing milieu. One of the most visible means has been the use of teams. The benefits of teams are well documented. Teams can be creative, responsive, more productive, and more efficient and effective. Employees frequently report that in teams their work is more satisfying and motivating.[1]

The proof is there. Teams can and do work. So why then, do so many team efforts fail? Why are so many employees frustrated with poor results and managers complaining that teams are not held accountable?

We believe lack of knowledge and systematic attention to how teams are put together and integrated with the rest of the organization, or *structure,* is a key reason for underperformance or even outright failure of teams. We have seen all kinds of teams without a clearly defined and shared purpose, with unclear roles, with too many members. We have seen some without the required knowledge, information, and skills. We have seen teams that were set up well but did not have an organizational infrastructure to support them. Without attention and clarity around these issues, employees usually stick with what they know. As a result, there is little change in how work gets done other than weekly attendance to a quote-unquote team meeting. Nothing really changes but the name and an increase in cynicism about organizational change efforts. People describe the team effort as just another way to cut heads, and *team* becomes just another four-letter word.

A second reason for poor implementation of teams is that they are sometimes given too much or too little structure.[2] In this instance, the organization may understand there is a need for clarity of purpose, clear roles, effective work processes to get the work done, and norms and values to drive team behavior. But managers are uncertain about how much or how little structure to give the team. The structure may be overspecified, thus creating lower levels of commitment and less adaptability. Others impose too little structure, which creates confusion and chaos. Both approaches create greater resistance to the team effort. Teams need *just enough structure* to decrease confusion while at the same time increasing adaptability and commitment.

Third, we also believe the *process* for creating teams is frequently flawed. This is especially common when creating service and production teams, since these teams are often overlaid onto poorly designed work processes. Members do not know what the team is supposed to accomplish. They do not know what they can and cannot decide. Supervisors and managers do not understand their roles in developing and helping teams. Neither do the support people in engineering, human resources, or accounting. It has been our experience that designing implementation processes to create clarity, understanding, commitment, and ownership among these key stakeholders leads to more successful production and service teams.

In this chapter, we focus on team structure and the elements necessary to successfully organize different types of teams. We review considerations in determining how much structure to provide and how much teams should create for themselves. Finally, we discuss processes for implementing production and service teams.

CASE EXAMPLE: ORGANIZING TEAMS FOR MANUFACTURING MOTORS

The electric motor business was nearly a hundred years old—hardly high-tech. Thus "MotorCo" (not the company's real name) found itself in a highly competitive commodity business. There were about fifty competitors making motors for large applications; only two were making money. MotorCo was not one of the "elite two." It had been downsizing for nearly a decade. Indeed, a look at an organization chart suggested that the only ones left were managers and supervisors. There was a dearth of technical support people: engineers and technicians. The plant and equipment were deteriorating rapidly. The situation could only be described as bleak.

There was the dilemma. MotorCo's cost structure was too high for it to be competitive. Base costs—a euphemism for salaried personnel—needed to be reduced. More technical people were needed to refurbish the plant and equipment—and just keep it running. With the support of the director of human resources, the director of manufacturing began exploring alternatives. They were amazed to discover manufacturing plants in other industries with no supervisors. They read articles and books; they visited innovative work sites. They decided it was worth the risk to drastically reduce the number of supervisors while adding technical support people. The suggested approach would be to totally rethink the work to use production teams.

The director of manufacturing presented the idea to the nine manufacturing plant leadership teams. Each of these teams consisted of the plant manager and managers of operations, manufacturing engineering, quality, production control, human resources, and accounting. They were challenged to reduce their salaried cost further, while protecting technical expertise. They were presented with the alternative concept: self-managed work teams. Members of the plant leadership teams asked if they had to implement self-managed teams. The manufacturing director responded, "No. However, you must reduce the number of salaried employees and protect your technical expertise."

The business need was clear. Cost had to be reduced further to remain in business. The direction was clear: leaner management staffs using production teams to plan and monitor their performance.

Headquarters began offering education to help the plants prepare for the change. A couple of people from each plant—often the managers of operations and HR—would attend a planning session at headquarters. Designed by external consultants but delivered by HR and manufacturing executives, the sessions would provide direction and planning tools and techniques. The attendees would be instructed to return to their plants and work with the plant leadership team to develop

- A vision
- A value statement
- A description of the "felt need" for change

- A description of the roles and responsibilities
- A communication plan
- A training plan
- A plan to make revisions to plant practices, policies, and procedures

With the guidelines in hand, the plant representatives would return to their plants.

At MotorCo, these emissaries for the new culture had a couple of advantages: successful parallel teams (quality circles) and work cells. Both helped create a foundation vital to the success of teams at MotorCo.

Experience with quality circles (parallel teams) had given people experience and training in the structures and behaviors necessary for good teams. The quality improvements and cost savings resulting from the teams had benefited the business, and teams were seen as valuable. This was true even though the enthusiasm for the quality circles was waning.

Workers were frustrated with the parallel teams because they could not submit ideas to improve productivity, costs, or safety, which were outside the scope of quality improvement. These parallel teams were implementing ideas adversely affecting workers on other parts of the line without first getting their support. Support personnel, strapped for time, facing demands from their managers, dealing with technical problems, and caught up in "firefighting," began to give parallel team ideas a lower priority.

Still, this experience was an advantage for the emissaries. As a result of using parallel teams, a core group of people had received problem-solving and facilitation training. In addition, as a result of participating on the teams, workers knew what to expect from teams, had a more mature sense of how to make teams work, and had developed a better understanding of the business. They were ready for more.

The second major advantage the emissaries had was that the plant was already being redesigned into manufacturing cells. These cells gave small groups of people the responsibility for completing a larger segment of the work, and delegation of decision making was a logical next step in redesigning the work.

The plant was ready for the change.

Fresh with new information and knowledge, the emissaries worked with the plant leadership team. The leadership team developed a vision, a value statement, and a description for the need for change. The need for change was pretty easy to describe, because there was a constant flow of communications about competitive realities. In a sister plant, the realities were so well understood that employees could and did articulate to news reporters that what they made had to be produced in a cheaper labor market in a far-off country. At headquarters and in the plants, people understood what was going on in the marketplace. They knew what competitors were doing. They knew what customers expected. Open, candid communications helped create this business knowledge.

The leadership team members took it upon themselves to map out the roles, responsibilities, measures, and accountabilities required in the new organization. There would be production coordinators who would take on more than traditional supervision: team development, production control, communications, training, work methods, and discipline, among other tasks. There would be technical support people—engineers and maintenance personnel—who would split their time between providing day-to-day support and working on long-term technical projects. Some responsibilities would be eliminated. Some would emigrate to lower levels within the organization, to team leaders and team members. The leadership team tried to minimize the number of responsibilities that would evaporate, disappearing over time if people did not have time to get them done.

Measurements proved to be a challenge. There was agreement on the critical measures of quality, cost, and productivity, but the information systems had not been created with teams in mind. The system was designed so department and individual—not team—performance could be tracked and monitored. In addition, performance reports were untimely. Data were entered daily in the form of labor vouchers, and a week or so later the information was available to management. It seldom made it to the team level.

Another measurement challenge was the complexity of the productivity measurements. The local guru of measurements, the plant accountant, explained that only he understood the measurements. Someone asked, "What good are they, then?" Since most of management could not explain the productivity numbers, it was safe to assume team members did not have the wherewithal to evaluate the numbers and make adjustments to improve productivity.

Simpler, more timely measures were developed.

The vision, the values, and the need for change were presented to the entire plant by the plant manager. Small group sessions were conducted by the operations and HR managers. Everyone attended, including the production coordinators. The team concept was presented, and people expressed their reactions. Among other things, they wondered who was going to be on which teams, what their responsibilities were going to be, who was going to select leaders, and when they would start. Their questions and comments helped identify areas of immediate concern to the people on the floor, and these became planning priorities. The vast majority of the meeting participants agreed that they would individually support the change, but their coworkers were less likely to do so!

Each member of the plant leadership team reviewed the roles, responsibilities, measures, and accountabilities with the direct reports. They changed the organization design, adding responsibilities that were missed. They moved some people to the team and eliminated others. The meetings were very effective. One manager looked at the wallchart describing the new organization, shook his head, and said, "You think you've got troubles? I've been in supervision twenty-five years. I've got to learn everything over."

Another participant in the review sessions challenged the plant leadership team. She said, "If you think you're going to be able to announce this thing in a plantwide meeting in the cafeteria and have everyone understand and accept it, you're crazy." (Open, clear communication was the norm!) Plant leadership resisted. They said they did not have time to meet with everybody in the plant. Undeterred, she responded, "We do."

The newly appointed production coordinators embarked on the mission of explaining the new organization, asking for ideas, modifying the design where they were empowered to do so, and bringing ideas and concerns back to the plant leadership team. During these dialogues, teams reconfigured themselves. Based on their knowledge of the work processes, they decided which jobs needed to be on which teams. In some cases, they consolidated teams because the work processes were nearly identical and they were working off the same schedule and conveyor. In other cases, they shifted one or two people to different teams. These sessions resulted in changes to the overall design.

The role agreed upon for the team leader was to ensure that the team was producing quality parts, treat team members fairly and equally, and discuss team performance with production coordinators. A sampling of specific responsibilities included overall schedule attainment, schedule distribution, work assignments, compilation of team production status, member training, expedition, coordination of meetings, and requests for maintenance support. Because team leaders were to accomplish these additional responsibilities and their "real" jobs within a nine-hour day, most leaders chose to spend less than the allotted hour, because they did not want to work overtime.

In defining their roles, team members were to meet quality expectations, maintain effective work habits, meet productivity requirements, and work together as a team. Within the definition, team members had input in appraising the leader and inputs regarding team discipline. In addition, they were to maintain their own time cards, identify overtime needs, approve withdrawal of tools and supplies, attend group meetings, and ensure communication among members. Team member roles were redesigned by the teams; for instance, team members added approval for withdrawal of tools and supplies to the list. They thought it was a waste of time to go to a production coordinator to obtain approval for checking out a twenty-nine cent pair of work gloves.

Although the organization structure was clear and being put in place, it took five months to design the team structure before it was implemented. Then, while the team structure was being defined and refined, critical policies and procedures were developed or modified. Volunteers examined issues of leader selection, leader pay, bumping procedures, and the like. The sessions were conducted across shifts. These volunteers made interesting choices, stipulating a minimum amount of time that the leader had to serve. They concluded the person had to stay long enough to learn the job and contribute. They chose not to pay the leader a premium, recognizing that a premium would place the leader in a different class—that of a supervisor.

Some things were left to the teams themselves. For example, teams developed the criteria for selecting leaders, and they carried out the selection themselves.

The design was complete. The teams were launched throughout the *entire plant* about seven months after the plant leadership team learned of their challenge to rethink how work was done at MotorCo. From all the communications during the implementation process, teams knew why they were being formed. They knew where their work began and ended; they played a major decision-making role in determining their boundaries. They knew who was on the team, and they understood the roles of team leader and member. They knew the role of the production coordinator was different, since they had helped design it also. They knew what their measurements were. They knew to whom to communicate results and where to ask for help, because it was explained to them fully.

The training demands were real, since new administrative and interpersonal skills were required. Fortunately, the earlier quality-circle training had helped develop problem-solving, decision-making, and facilitation skills. The plan was to begin with interpersonal skill training, with the production coordinators and team leaders to codeliver the interpersonal skill training. Team leaders and members quickly adjusted the priorities, thinking the administrative skill training needed to come first. They wanted to make sure the paperwork they were completing was being done properly. Staff members delivered the administrative training, working hard at explaining why the information was needed. The process of staff members delivering the training did seem to send a message that they cared, they thought people could understand, and that they (the staff members) wanted the new system to work. Once the administrative training was completed, the interpersonal training resumed.

Teams developed differently. Some soared; others struggled. Unfortunately, there was no systematic gathering of data to try to determine what worked and what did not. Some teams achieved quality levels only dreamed of before the transition to teams. A production coordinator went to the HR manager to exclaim about a team in his area. It had set a goal of 4.0 percent rejects. Although that didn't sound stellar, historically the numbers were in the 15 percent range. The production coordinator had never been willing to commit to anything lower than 9.9 percent to the man in the corner office—the plant manager. Within six months, the team beat the 4.0 percent goal and was setting constantly better goals. The production coordinator was elated.

Another team attained the zero-defect level for the first time in the history of their work area. The team leader chose to reward the people with cake and coffee during their break. On the other hand, the same coordinator related a story about a team that wanted to share extra personnel with one needing some help meeting its own goal. Instead, the coordinator's advice was to ignore the other team's needs and work on cross-training within their own team. The coordinator clearly needed coaching on interteam cooperation; the team was out ahead of the coach.

Team leadership was another hotbed. Some leaders got frustrated and wanted to get out of that position and allow others the "opportunity" to lead and walk in their shoes. Other teams wanted their leaders to step down because the members did not want to follow them. Teams were usually given the opportunity to work out these issues. A common solution was to rotate leaders. As teams demonstrated maturity—and many did very early—they were allowed to decide these things for themselves team by team.

There were exceptional operational gains. Manufacturing costs were reduced $870,000. The manufacturing plant went on to operate at 9.3 percent below budget over a three-year period, in a flat market. Internal quality costs (line rejects) were reduced 8 percent. External quality costs (customer rejects) were down 22 percent. Salaried costs were down $700,000 over two years.

The team initiative was a success by all measurements. In the past, the plant had invested more money in equipment than they did in teams and achieved far fewer results.

ELEMENTS OF STRUCTURE ESSENTIAL TO EFFECTIVE TEAMS

Team structure refers to the building blocks that must be laid out for, or by, a team to maximize the probability of success, regardless of the type of team. The most relevant consideration in structuring teams is to clarify purpose and goals, roles, resources, team processes, and interpersonal expectations. If teams are going to get results, these need to be set up properly and clearly understood by all members. In addition, the teams need a supportive infrastructure to succeed.

Designing a team structure involves thoughtful delineation of expectations about what teams and team members do, how they work, and how they get support. This process should not be rushed. In MotorCo, it took seven months before the team-based organization was launched. (We have worked with others who needed even longer to develop adequate plans.)

In summary, goals, roles, processes, and interpersonal relationships are critical to any successful team, whether management, project, production, service, action, or parallel. Each type of team needs a supportive infrastructure. In the following section, we address specific issues and concerns within each of these elements.

Purpose and Boundaries

There are several issues to address when clarifying the context for a team. These include the team's purpose, measures, and boundaries.

PURPOSE. The initial challenge for designing the structure of a team is to identify a clear reason for existence: its purpose. This is the most critical element for structuring teams. A team without a clearly stated purpose is simply a collection of people who would probably much rather be doing something else! They would be justified in that feeling; it is patently unfair to hold such a team accountable. Indeed, most organizations think they address this issue.

One of us was called in to work with just such an underspecified team in a reinforced-plastics organization. The team had floundered for six months on just what they were supposed to accomplish. There were disagreements and conflicts; management's view was that the team members were in need of interpersonal skills training. Upon brief examination, it became very obvious that the team had not been structured with a focused purpose. Team members held conflicting views of their purpose and were at an impasse. They were reluctant to ask management for clarification, feeling that it would reflect poorly on them. Once we interceded and asked management to clarify the purpose, the interpersonal issues disappeared. Closer and more specific attention to the purpose would have helped avoid an enormous waste of time.

The purpose of the earlier parallel teams at MotorCo was to develop recommendations to improve quality. The purpose of the production teams was to meet production schedules while monitoring and improving cost, quality, and productivity. These were made very clear to the teams.

Clarity of purpose provides focus and enables members to align their energy. Time is not wasted by complaining "Why are we here?" Instead, members are free to focus creatively on methods to fulfill the purpose. Among all the potential structural flaws, forming a team without a clear purpose is almost always fatal.

MEASURES. Measures are key indicators, describing results or outcomes or steps along the way. They can be quantitative or qualitative. Measures are often developed for quality, customer satisfaction, cycle time, productivity, and cost. Meeting budgeted expenditures and project schedules are frequently used measures as well.

Measurements are used to enable the team in tracking, monitoring, evaluating, and improving its own performance; allowing the team and management to evaluate whether or not the team is meeting expectations; and linking team performance directly to strategic measures to ensure the team is contributing to the organization's success.

Why measurements are essential elements for a team is simple. Without measures, there can be no accountability. Any team needs to have the tools to track, monitor, and evaluate its own performance if it is going to be held accountable for performance.

Measures should be chosen carefully and aligned with the overall organization. Poorly selected measures may actually result in suboptimization of the organization. Chapter Six discusses measurements in detail.

BOUNDARIES. Clear purpose and measures should be accompanied by a description of the boundaries of the team. These are defined by identification of the team's scope, responsibilities, authority, and resources—in other words, what they can and cannot do, and what they have to do it with.

Scope

The first boundary to identify is the scope of the team. Basically, this may be considered the work that is owned by the team: what work is theirs, and just as important, what work is not.

The rationale for setting the scope of the work to be performed by a team is based on several variables. Chief among these are time, territory, and technology.[3] Teams need to spend *time* together to accomplish their task. As a result, team boundaries are often created along the lines of work shifts. The second variable, *territory* or geographic proximity, refers to physical location of the work in determining boundaries. With the advent of electronic mail, teleconferencing, and other electronic media, teams can overcome time and territory issues. *Technology* refers to machinery, techniques, and skills. It is generally preferable to set the boundaries where there are significant changes in the technology. In a manufacturing team, this may be where the process changes from chemical to mechanical. In service teams, it may be where skills required by the overall work change significantly. It is also critical that the boundary of the team encompass a significant and meaningful piece of work.

A fourth variable is *task interdependence,* with the operative word being "interdependence." The interdependence most conducive to team work lies in the task itself; it can be created. At MotorCo, a cellular manufacturing system helped do so. Lathe operators performing the cutting operations on shafts were marginally dependent on their fellow lathe operators. When cells were created grouping lathe operators with milling machine operators, there was more interdependence. The milling operator could not perform her job unless the lathe operator, now in the same work group, properly performed his. When task interdependence is a stretch, it can be augmented with goal-and-outcome interdependence. It is important to note, however, that if there is no way to create a team boundary that encompasses interdependent work then you must reconsider the very value of creating a team.

Scope may seem cut and dried, but it is not unusual to have conflict over who "owns" a particular piece of work. For example, in a paper mill in the United Kingdom the stacked wood pile between the wood yard area and the pulp area was not assigned to either of the teams. As a result, there could be no accountability and there was often conflict over whose responsibility it really was to move the wood pile to the pulp grinding equipment. Consequently there were times the wood pile was not moved, and inefficiency and downtime occurred. Note how a poorly defined structural element can lead to "interpersonal problems."

Responsibilities

A second boundary to set for teams is to know what responsibilities belong to the team. *Responsibilities* refer to the tasks and duties required to get the work done. Clearly, once a team's scope is defined, the technical responsibilities become clearer. If a machine process is within the scope of the team, then it is likely the team members are responsible for running it. There are some responsibilities associated with a machine process, however, that may not be theirs. For example, it may not be their responsibility to set it up. Or it may be their responsibility some day, but not now.

It is critical to define responsibilities to avoid drops, misses, and "Oops, I thought *they* were doing that" events. This is particularly crucial if the organization is in the process of empowering employees with responsibilities formerly held by support organizations such as maintenance, quality, or personnel. The transition period needs to be managed carefully and duties constantly reclarified.

Numerous questions about team responsibilities need to be answered. What are the core tasks the team members must do to fulfill the team's purpose? What are the tasks formerly done by other functions that they should now do? Do they clean their work area? Do they do preventive maintenance? Do they do their own rework? If they do not do any of these things, when might they? Soon? Never?

Authority

The third boundary is set by level of authority. This is closely related to responsibilities. Teams need to know what decisions they can and cannot make. In particular, this includes decisions formerly made by managers but now transferred to employees. Can they shut a line down? Can they set their own work schedules? Can they call a customer? Can they offer a discount on the spot? Can they approve a check? Can they sign out a pair of twenty-nine cent gloves?

If team members do not know the answers, they often revert to old habits. Managers are called and time is wasted. At times, customers are irritated—just as they are when the retail store clerk has to hold, delay, or stop the line to get a manager to make a decision when a minor problem arises.

Resources

The fourth boundary is set by the resources. This includes what is available in terms of money, space, equipment, time, and personnel. The resources should be defined and reasonable. If this is not done, problems arise. For example, one engineering team had no description of resources available to them. They assumed there were none, and this severely limited the effectiveness of their final solution. When questioned during their final presentation as to why they had not taken a certain action, they responded, "We thought it would be too expensive!"

Another organization, an appliance manufacturer, did define the resources clearly for its labor-management partnership teams. But the resource allocation was viewed as totally unreasonable, and as a result team members were cynical about the commitment of management. The team was severely restricted by its allotted meeting time; the time frame was very tight. There was no money available for any improvements. Upon review, many managers did agree that the resources were inappropriately meager and agreed to change the boundary. As a result, the teams felt they had a fighting chance at being successful.

Resource questions center on money, space, and the like. What is their budget? How much money can the team spend without seeking higher approvals? Do the teams need common space within which to work? Where can they meet? Do they have the equipment they need? The software? How much time are they to spend with another team performing work they need? Which people in the organization are resources available for the team to use? Defining this boundary saves precious time down the road.

Roles

Once the goals and associated boundaries are defined for a team, it is possible to identify roles needed to support the team. There are three types of roles on teams. First, there are the task roles, which represent the core activities that must be completed to accomplish the desired outcomes. Second, there are the leadership roles, the activities providing the direction and coordination necessary to accomplish objectives and output. Third, there are the process roles: activities undertaken to enable the team to function as a harmonious, open, energetic, and effective unit. Facilitation and recordkeeping are typical process roles filled within effective teams.

Task roles that require specialized expertise not easily amenable to cross-training must be identified before the team members are selected. Then selecting members to fill the roles becomes a matter of team staffing (Chapter Three).

In many organizations, the *leadership role* is often assigned to an individual. It usually includes responsibilities such as ensuring overall direction for the team, coordinating completion of task assignments, maintaining external-internal interfaces, securing additional resources, ensuring that the team monitors its own performance and adjusts accordingly, and generally keeping the team focused. This was the role of the team leader within the teams at MotorCo.

There are benefits as well as drawbacks to the single-leadership approach. A single leader often requires less extensive training support, and most teams have a natural leader who readily fits the role. However, use of one leader frequently creates dependency on the part of other team members. It becomes easier to rely on this individual and let him or her do all the "extra" work. It is also not unusual for a single leader to be seen as a minisupervisor, and this may create resentment in others. To a certain extent, rotating the role helps address these issues.

Sometimes, however, the leadership role is shared. Selecting task force cochairs is a common example. The leadership roles outlined above can be divided between cochairs to suit the individuals' strengths and needs. In some cases, the leadership role is more extensively divided; some production teams use shared leadership, with two, three, or more people holding a leadership role. Each role encompasses a major area of responsibility (operations, quality, HR, resources, communications, safety, and so on); these roles may also be rotated.

Shared leadership is an appealing approach. It offers a way to avoid the dependence often placed on a single leader. It also helps avoid the minisupervisor issue. However, this approach may demand significant investment in training. There is also a problem in the willingness of team members to take on one of the roles.

The third type of role, *process roles,* includes such activities as maintaining agendas, developing objectives, encouraging participation, staying on track, ensuring development of team norms, monitoring team dynamics, conducting process checks to determine if they are functioning effectively as a team, and providing tools and techniques to help the team function more effectively. Another process role is documentation. If all of this reads like facilitation, that is because it is.

In summary, the team needs to be sure that each member's part in filling the leadership, task, and process roles on the team is clear. Additionally, they must also be clear on the expectations of other members in terms of actions and timing.

Work Processes

Another important structural element is process. *Processes* are particular methods of doing something, whether it be making decisions, transforming product, conducting meetings, or a host of other organizational necessities. Among the most important ones to clarify are decision making, meetings, communication, and feedback. Additionally, processes associated with a team's core work may need to be specified—particularly in manufacturing work teams.

CORE WORK PROCESSES. Core work processes include those necessary to create the product or service of the team. There are two types of work processes: linear and nonlinear.[4]

Linear work follows a routine sequence of steps necessary to produce the team output. Most manufacturing teams have linear work. It is particularly necessary to clearly define each step and its requirement, to maintain repeatability and quality. In fact, quality certifications such as ISO 9000 require these steps to be exceedingly well documented.

Nonlinear work, on the other hand, does not follow a prescribed routine. It is unprogrammed. In fact, many times the next step is determined only after the preceding one is taken. Nonlinear work is sometimes referred to as knowledge work.[5] Most of the work performed by executive teams is nonlinear; similarly, project teams often work on nonlinear tasks. For example, a product development team in the health care industry is required to design and conduct tests, evaluate results, prepare submissions for government approval, and develop and implement a marketing plan. These are all nonlinear tasks. When designing nonlinear work processes, it is important to clarify criteria for decisions and accountability for actions.

DECISION-MAKING PROCESSES. Decision-making processes represent how information is evaluated against selected criteria to assess options that enable decisions. There are a number of decision-making alternatives: leader, expert, majority, consensus, and unanimity. No one type is right for every situation. Groups often determine which type of decision is consonant with their needs and the decision at hand.

A faulty decision-making structure often manifests itself in delays, conflict, and mistrust. For example, if the decision-making criteria are not clear, additional data may be required, causing delays. If people do not agree upon criteria up front, suspicions and mistrust develop around the criteria being used. As decisions get delayed, agreements cannot be reached, and conflict develops.

When choosing the type of decision, effective teams usually select the best one for the decision to be made. It is basically a matter of balancing time and commitment. On one extreme, decisions that require clarity, commitment, and ownership need consensus. Other decisions that necessitate speed may require a leader or an expert to make the decision.

EFFECTIVE MEETING PROCESSES. Effective meeting processes describe how meetings are to be conducted. Even though meetings are the bane of corporate culture, they continue to be the primary medium for planning, problem solving, decision making, and communication. Ineffective meetings result in slow decision making, wasted time, low attendance (requiring repetitious communication), and conflict. Effective meetings are a basic process without which teams flounder. It is worth the effort to define the desired outcome of the forums and to create a relatively structured approach for meetings.[6]

INFORMATION PROCESSES. Teams need timely information to accomplish their tasks efficiently and effectively. They need background information to help understand the task at hand, and to evaluate their position and progress.

Teams need information on what is known about the task or work to be done. As one example, the leadership team at MotorCo demanded a lot of information about the process of organizational change and the concept of production teams as they began the process of redesigning the plant. In another illustration, a project team charged with increasing global market share needs to spend time describing the global market, competitive strengths and weaknesses, competitive strategies, and product characteristics and applications before they develop a strategy for growth.

Another major source of information is measurements. Production teams at MotorCo wanted to know if they were successful during and at the end of the day. Two-week-old computerized labor efficiency reports were not helpful; process control charts were better.

Another informational need is internal and external customer feedback. With the formation of manufacturing cells at MotorCo, information flowed more freely as internal customer chains were more likely to be located near one another. Free flow of *timely* information is at the heart of most successful teams.

There are many processes that occur within teams. We have mentioned the most common and what we feel are most critical. Each organization has additional ones important for its own success. These should also be defined carefully as much as possible.

Interpersonal Relations

Solid team structure reduces the level of interpersonal conflict. It does not, however, eliminate it! The last building block for the teams is to set expectations for interpersonal conduct. These are often referred to as ground rules or guidelines and consist of statements reflecting the expected behavior of team members (such as *Focus on issues, not on personalities; Be on time; Stay on the topic*).

Ground rules should be discussed, agreed upon, and posted in a prominent location. It should then be the responsibility of all team members to refer to them if they feel the rules are being violated. This increases team accountability and reduces the need for the facilitator to be drill sergeant. The ground rules are to be reviewed along with the team's performance measures.

Organization Infrastructure

Teams are part of an organizational community that includes support and management groups as well as other teams. As such, attention should be paid to this environment as well, to align it with the needs of the team. Unfortunately, this is an oft-neglected feature of team design. We repeatedly find teams embedded in traditional, autocratic organizations. Putting one or two teams in the midst of a wider, very traditional organization is like planting one or two soybean plants in a twenty-acre field of corn. The corn grows, and even though the soybean plants start out well, they are ultimately fruitless. If teams are to survive, they have to be put in a supportive context.

The need for developing an infrastructure supportive of teams is central to this book. Compensation, selection, training, measures, and information systems all need to be aligned with a team-based system. Other infrastructure needs include management structure, communication and problem-solving forums, and special roles. At MotorCo, for example, a business unit team with management, engineering, production scheduling, and quality skills led and supported the production teams. Cross-functional executive teams often support major product development teams.

Simpler infrastructure issues are forums set up to link, communicate, and solve problems. The forums can be as simple as paper or computer forms created to ensure communication across shifts. Or they can be meetings. At the end of the shift at MotorCo, the team leaders within a business unit meet with their business unit teams to discuss production status and other issues. Some forums are quite creative; at one manufacturing facility requests for support by production teams were catalogued publicly on easels. The nature of the request, the date of the request, who the request was made of, and the status and date of completion were publicly displayed for all to see.

Indeed, communication is a recurring infrastructure need. Complex project teams such as those product development teams found within the pharmaceutical and automotive industries may present the biggest challenge. They often consist of members from multiple functions within global businesses. If communication problems are related to people geographically distant because they work in different functions, co-location can help solve them (see Chapter Ten).

Co-location may be possible for high-profile major product design teams. Other project teams might not be able to be co-located and might need to resort to alternative means. Technology plays a major role. E-mail and the Internet make it easy to transfer data and information. Articles and chapters can be coauthored (without investing heavily in Fed Ex or UPS). Conference calls and videoconferencing are available for global teams trying to conduct business (see Chapter Nine). Then there are more mundane methods such as meeting notes, follow-up calls, and the like to further understanding and clarity.

Teams with a clear set of expectations, understandable information, performance feedback, and effective communication mechanics are more likely to function effectively.

Sometimes the infrastructure needs to take the form of special resource roles, such as sponsoring and mentoring or process facilitation.

Creating a sponsor role is another approach to integrating teams that span functions. The sponsor is frequently not a member of the team but serves as a connecting link, supporting the team vertically with higher-level executives and laterally with managers of team members who report to different managers.

Regarding facilitators, some organizations maintain a cadre of people to fulfill the process role for a number of teams. Facilitators often have other jobs and work part-time with teams as needed, as in the quality circles used early on at MotorCo. Other organizations try to develop facilitation skills within the teams, as in MotorCo's self-managing production teams. We strongly recommend when implementing production and service teams that the facilitation role be integrated into the team.

In summary, our experience indicates that purpose, boundaries, roles, measurements, skills, information, communication, and a supporting management infrastructure are all critical. Unfortunately, many organizations are lax in clarifying purpose, roles, resources, and processes for teams (that is, the team structure). Instead they place initial emphasis on building or "fixing" interpersonal relationships. Perhaps this stems from the team-building emphasis of the 1970s. Ironically, addressing goals, roles, and process capabilities *first* helps avoid many of the interpersonal conflicts and issues that team building is meant to address!

One challenge is to be sure the essential elements are in place. Another challenge is to provide the right degree of detail. Finding the right amount of detail is difficult because the needs depend upon several factors, among them the type of team.

JUST ENOUGH STRUCTURE

Elements of team structure such as purpose and boundaries, roles, and processes can be defined broadly or in great detail. For example, team members may be required to rotate tasks; this is a generally defined specification. The team itself would be responsible for determining how often to rotate and among which jobs. On the other hand, a team required to rotate tasks hourly and in a prescribed order faces a detailed specification. The team has very little latitude to make decisions about how to rotate. Those decisions have been made for them.

A question frequently asked is, "Who defines the details?" Does the start-up team develop the detailed design? Does a steering group of managers and union officials flesh out the details? Or is it done by a design team made up of a cross-functional, diagonal slice of the organization? Does the top executive provide the specific details when she asks the functional leaders to develop a corporate policy as a team? Regardless of who is in the design group, the question is whether structural details are the responsibility of a design group, or of the teams.

Minimum critical specification, often used as a guideline, refers to the idea of specifying the fewest details possible to create work units or teams—just enough structure.[7] The goal is to leave as many design decisions as possible open for the teams to decide. If the design group specifies only what is absolutely necessary, teams are better able to make their own adaptations and adjustments as they gain experience. It creates an ownership that cannot be dictated. Whenever possible, it is best to allow teams to define how they work.

But what is absolutely necessary to define? Most people involved in structuring teams understand and quickly endorse the concept of minimum critical specification. They want the teams to have elbow room in designing how they work. However, what constitutes *just enough structure* for their specific organization is not always clear. Design groups struggle with how much detail is too much. In their quest to give teams as much self-determination as possible, they sometimes underspecify the structure. This can result in floundering, frustrated teams. One production employee at a small appliances plant exclaimed, "When they started us, we felt like they just waved a wand and said 'Thou art a team.' We didn't have a clue of what we were about, other than to be a team—whatever that meant!"

At other times, design groups err on the side of too much detail. As a result, team members feel overconstrained. They may even lack the flexibility to make needed changes and adaptations. One warehouse employee explained, "We had no real say. The roles didn't work for us, we didn't get to set our goals, and don't even get me started on the measures!"

Factors to Consider in Specifying Team Structure

There is no magic formula that determines how much detail and structure to give teams and how much leeway they should have for self-design. Considering certain key factors helps in making that determination: group specialization, external linkage, and changing membership. None of these alone necessarily determines the degree of specificity needed, since it also depends on the unique circumstances of the organization.

SPECIALIZATION. Chapter One identified two kinds of specialization. A whole team can be specialized, as in an oil well or firefighting crew. Or within teams, the members can do highly specialized tasks, as in a product development team.

When determining the degree of structure required, specialization within the team is most relevant. High specialization means the work of the team is subdivided into unique task roles, which vary on complexity. Complex and highly specialized task roles are found in such groups as a cockpit crew, made up of, say, pilot, copilot, and navigator. In a case like this, cross-training may be unrealistic. Usually such roles are defined before the team is created, and members with the needed qualifications are selected to fill the specialized roles.

Less complex, specialized task roles are found in some service teams, such as an insurance claims group. Most team members, with training, can successfully perform roles such as liability claims adjuster, storm and flood adjuster, and fire adjuster. In such cases, the design group allows the team to define task roles, make assignments, and develop cross-training plans.

EXTERNAL LINKAGE. A team needs to be linked to external individuals or groups. The linkage can be as simple as that required between shifts, or it can be as complex as a product development team trying to mesh customer needs, engineering designs, production capability, and product introduction strategies. A major task is to identify key counterparts and then create links to each, as outlined in Chapter Eight.

Teams vary in their needs for linkage. The degree of structure afforded the team depends upon the complexity of the linkage. It also depends upon the effect of the linkage on the performance of the larger organization.

Suppose a first-shift team and a second-shift team need to be linked. This is not complex. It is simply a connection between one team and another. In this case, a design group recommends that the two teams meet to determine their own methods to link. The two teams adapt an appropriate linkage to meet their needs.

On the other hand, consider the linkage between a cockpit crew and maintenance crews, which is complex. The cockpit crew deals with a different maintenance crew at each airport; similarly, a maintenance crew deals with many cockpit crews. Further, there are many specialty roles within each crew. Safety is a primary concern, and poor linkage has great potential impact on the rest of the organization—not to mention the passengers and crew themselves. In this case, it would be best for a design group to develop a detailed and consistent method for linking these two groups at all airports.

Linking Mechanisms

Four ways of linking teams are available: linking roles, sponsor roles, linking infrastructures, and common processes.

Common *linking roles* are those required and defined for *each* team. These people serve as a single point of contact for the team in some defined area. Some examples of these are quality coordinator, safety coordinator, or team leader. These common roles clarify whom to contact on each team about significant issues. For example, a quality engineer wishing to give a team some feedback would know to work through the quality coordinator. A safety coordinator on a team knows to contact the safety coordinator on another team about any safety issues. A pilot knows to contact the hydraulics coordinator on the maintenance crew.

Another approach to integrating teams with those outside is to create the role of a *sponsor.* Usually, the sponsor is not a member of the team but is instead a supervisor or manager serving as a connecting link. The sponsor supports the teams vertically with higher-level managers and laterally with other sponsors.

Linking infrastructures may be created to provide a forum for linking teams. For example, in one appliance organization the design provided for weekly meetings of quality coordinators from each team. Another manufacturing organization created a "team of teams" whose membership consisted of the team leaders from each group across the plant, for communication and problem solving. Forums such as these greatly assist linkage.

Finally, teams or team members often work with members of other teams or functions to solve problems or do other work. Identifying standard organizational *common processes* for such things as problem solving, meetings, and decision making significantly speeds up such work.

CHANGING MEMBERSHIP. Some teams retain stable membership for relatively long periods of time. For example, quality circles at MotorCo stayed together for years. Service teams at an insurance company were considered permanent. Such teams have the time to develop and adapt their own structures. They may require little specificity from a design group.

Other teams are frequently reconstituted. Production, service, and even management teams have to deal with new members because of promotions during periods of growth or layoffs during periods of decline. Like newly created teams, those with frequent changes in membership benefit from a relatively detailed design.

Some ways to address the challenge of rapidly changing membership include common roles, standard operating procedures, new-member socialization, and ground rules.

A standard set of *common roles* allows for a common language and common approach throughout the organization. For example, in production teams identified roles may be those of facilitator, materials coordinator, and safety leader. Standard roles on a surgical team include surgeon, anesthesiologist, and nurse. Members moving into the team do not need to learn a new team structure. This clear knowledge significantly decreases the amount of time it takes for a new team to function well.

Identifying *standard operating processes* for all teams assists newcomers or new teams in getting off the ground quickly. This includes using the same problem-solving process, decision-making tools, and meeting processes. For example, flight crews, which frequently change membership, are given team structure in great detail. They are given detailed, documented work instructions and decision-making and problem-solving processes.

Design groups can deal with movement issues through *new-member socialization* processes, which require teams to share their mission, vision, goals, and behavioral expectations with prospective or new team members. This helps establish a set of clear expectations.

Teams are often asked to develop a set of written behavioral expectations, or *ground rules,* consistent with the organization's values. Explaining the ground rules to new members helps them become quickly familiar with how the team works; it helps the team maintain consistent norms through membership changes.

Structure for Different Types of Teams

Every team needs structure—not too much and not too little. At a minimum, every team must receive a clear description of its purpose, deliverables, measures, and boundaries. However, the need for other elements of structure varies with the type of team.

MANAGEMENT TEAMS. Purposes, measures, and boundaries of management teams are sometimes established by the organization design; their requirements for external linkage are extraordinarily high. Otherwise management teams tend to be self-designing and determine much of their own structure.[8]

Management teams usually have specialized members who spend much of their time leading functional groups, project teams, or divisions of the organization. Even so, they must sometimes cooperate as a team themselves. The leadership team at MotorCo, for instance, had to redesign the plant's organization to reduce salaried costs while protecting the technical skills needed to run the plant. To accomplish the task, they defined task, leadership, and process roles. They created decision-making and meeting processes, ground rules, and an infrastructure for communication. They structured their own team to redesign the organization while continuing to lead and manage their parts of the organization.

Management teams have high requirements for external linkage, some of which is dictated by the organization. Reporting relationships, performance measures, and performance reviews represent some of the links.

The linkages vary when the management team needs to function as a team to accomplish a task. The MotorCo leadership team had to design ways to communicate with leaders, customers, and the whole plant organization. Managers took the time to review new assignment of roles, responsibilities, tasks, accountabilities, and measures with each of the groups they were leading. They sought and shared feedback, reaction, and changes. The leadership team self-designed linkages required to meet their goal.

Management teams often have changing membership. If managers do their jobs well, they have opportunities to do bigger and better things as a reward. Having a process for assimilating new members helps. Although changing membership has an impact on all teams, it has a potentially greater impact on the entire organization if the change is at the top. Organizations trying to create team-based systems need to have a management team that is supportive of the concept and that models the behavior. When changing members on the leadership team, special attention needs to be given to the selection criteria and process. Consider a selection process that includes team members.

Although management teams are self-designing, they need to be attentive to the amount of structure they create for themselves to function as a team.

PRODUCTION AND SERVICE TEAMS. This kind of work team, such as assembly and customer service teams, has repetitive tasks and some within-team specialization. Many teams can determine their own task roles (who does what) instead of having them specified by a design group. At MotorCo, the team members discussed and decided who would do what; often, they decided to rotate duties. In a credit card customer-service team, members divided special task roles daily.

When team members design their own task roles, their ownership and adaptability usually increase. Typically, they have a high need for external linkage with other teams and support functions such as material or quality. Most production and service teams have high need for external linkage to internal and external customers, suppliers, and peer teams. Methods to achieve linkage should generally be created by the design group since they apply to all of these teams. Design solutions involve linking mechanisms: common roles, sponsor roles, infrastructures, and common processes.

Membership change on production teams varies. Some organizations have a great deal of bidding and bumping from team to team. Others have seasonal layoffs and recalls. Both situations call for commonality and consistency across teams to allow new members to assimilate quickly. It is important for the design group to specify common roles, standard operating processes, and new-member socialization.

In organizations where there is little movement across production or service teams, there may be less need for consistency and commonality of design. In those cases, the design group does not attend to as much detail. In other words, the teams design or even evolve their own unique sets of roles, processes, and ground rules.

Other issues enter into decisions about the degree to which production and service teams are structured by a design group or by themselves. These include experience in employee involvement, business knowledge, presence of a union, reward system, and regulatory requirements.

Where employees are accustomed to self-determination, there is relatively little need to specify a detailed design. For example, a metal cutting tool insert company had a long history of working in teams. Deciding to increase the level of employee involvement in the organization, they formed eight teams to redesign the work. Because of their experience, they could work quickly with little time spent on start-up or training. In turn, the design teams created work designs that gave the people on the floor a lot of latitude about how they would operate in teams.

Less *experience with employee involvement* means more structure. The design team may have to identify key competencies and common processes to be used across all teams. These include problem-solving processes, planning tools, decision-making tools, meeting processes, and conflict resolution. Training should be provided in these areas. In addition the design group needs to clearly define roles, responsibilities, and measurements for the supporting infrastructure. This is especially true of supervisors who have spent their entire careers in traditionally run organizations. These people require training and supportive coaching by their managers.

Without *business knowledge,* it is difficult for employees to make informed decisions about how their team can best contribute to resolving customer needs. For example, in a paper mill employees in the packaging team resisted cross-training, seeing no business need. It might have helped for the design team to clarify the need and detail the process. In any high-involvement organization, development of business knowledge should be undertaken before implementing teams.

Measurements for production and service teams should be established that link to strategic goals and marketplace needs. The process for allocating people and monetary resources needs to be explained in some detail in those organizations with little business knowledge. As the level of business knowledge increases, teams can be expected to link their outputs to business needs and measure themselves accordingly.

As for *union considerations,* the roles and tasks performed by production and service teams are often clearly prescribed by the contract. It is critical to integrate the concerns of the union in determining which tasks are performed by union members. The design group, which must include union members, should carefully specify roles within the boundaries of the contract or, at times, make arrangements to open the contract.

There are a variety of innovative *reward systems* being created and used by organizations, including profit sharing, gainsharing, and other approaches to paying for skills, learning, or performance (Chapter Seven). Profit sharing and gainsharing have little impact on the level of detail in the team structure. On the other hand, skill-based pay has a great impact on the level of detail to be defined in task responsibilities.

Pay-for-skills reward systems are most often seen in production teams and some service teams. Development of this type of reward system requires a high degree of specificity about desired tasks and behaviors, including technical, team member, and leadership tasks. Each desired task is analyzed for the knowledge, skills, and abilities required for performance. A monetary value is placed on a task or cluster of tasks. Frequently, training and certification programs are developed to support acquisition of skills.

All of this means that the design group has to clearly specify a significant level of detail to allow development of a pay-for-skills plan and its inherent support systems. With pay-for-skills, work teams have less leeway to change or add tasks unless they are willing to do so without compensation or wait until the pay plan is adjusted.

Organizations are subject to varied *regulatory presence*. Some, such as ISO 9000, are driven by the marketplace. Others are driven by government regulatory agencies, such as good manufacturing practices (GMPs) within the pharmaceutical industry. Other regulations are created to defend against lawsuits.

In organizations operating within a regulatory environment, the design group must provide enough detail to ensure that teams abide by the regulations. The group can do this by providing enough information, knowledge, documentation, and training for the teams to act within the regulations.

PROJECT TEAMS. There are a broad range of teams described as project teams. They are as simple as a group of people brought together to plan the annual picnic or as complex as a pharmaceutical product development team charged with getting a new drug tested, approved, and introduced into the global marketplace. This wide variation in what constitutes a project team entails corresponding variety in the amount of structure to impose on this category.

There is little specialization with the picnic planning team. Consequently, the design group can pretty much leave it up to them to determine the roles, group processes, and ground rules. In the product development team, roles are highly specialized. In this situation, task and leadership roles are defined by the design group, and people with the necessary talent are selected to fill the roles.

A product development team has a high need for linking with stakeholders outside the team, perhaps with test sites throughout the world. They need to link with the executives at the highest level to keep them informed of progress, barriers, and issues so that the top executives can keep investors informed. They must gradually build support for the new product with user groups. They have to link with governmental bodies to ensure that testing and analysis are conducted to meet the needs of the regulatory agencies. They need to link with the functions to be certain that needed resources are made available.

It is essential that the design group provide a high degree of structure. They must make sure the linking roles are embedded in the team. Sponsoring roles should be defined and filled by individuals with high internal and external credibility. There should be linking infrastructures such as periodic product development team review meetings with the top executives. The design group may have to make certain that communication technology meets the teams' needs. For example, teleconferencing, videoconferencing, and e-mail may be necessary to support their global communication requirements.

There is little need for external linkage for the picnic planning team. What need there is can generally be designed by the team itself. The design group may even relinquish this job of establishing linkage to the team. There is usually little change in the membership of teams with relatively simple tasks to be completed in short periods of time. This would be true of the picnic planning team, so the design group does not have to plan for this contingency.

The product development team is another case. Over the duration of the project, different skill sets are often required. For example, when developing and implementing test protocols, there is much need for information system resources and a relatively low need for report writers and editors. However, when preparing the analysis for government approval, the need for writers and editors increases while the need for people to design the system used to crunch the data diminishes. In neither case does need go to zero, but it does fluctuate and as a result membership on the team varies widely.

The design group might create a core leadership group, assigned to the team for its duration, to maintain continuity. The group may define guidelines and insist that the team develop documented, standardized operating processes to ease the transition for new members. It may create a role on the team to develop processes for assimilating new members. Because people enter and leave the team between appraisal cycles, the design group may require the appraisal process to integrate performance on the team with performance within the respective functions from which they came.

An additional consideration relevant to project teams is experience in employee involvement. With little such experience, project teams need more detailed team structures, including training on team skills and competencies. The design group can identify common processes, such as problem solving, planning, or decision making, to be used across all teams. This includes problem-solving processes, planning tools, decision-making tools, meeting processes, and conflict resolution. Training should be provided in these areas.

PARALLEL TEAMS. Problem-solving groups such as the quality circle teams at MotorCo tend to be homogenous. The primary challenge of the design group is to ensure the teams have necessary skills for efficient meetings. It may choose to develop facilitation skills within the teams or create a central pool of facilitators.

Linkage on parallel teams tends to be limited. MotorCo quality circles in an area on one shift would implement an idea affecting people in the same area on another shift. The team could figure out how to handle the situation by working directly with the other shift. The quality circles would also implement ideas that adversely affected work groups far from their own and downstream in the production process. The design group set it up so that these issues were to be assigned to the first line supervisor, or the team facilitator assigned their boundary management role. If still unresolved, a steering group made the decision on whether or not the idea had an overall positive or negative effect on plant operations.

Unless there are wide fluctuations in employment levels, team membership stays largely intact. This was true at MotorCo, where the team design included common roles across teams, common boundaries, and common meeting and problem-solving processes. These helped teams assimilate new members and cope with any turnover.

There is a paradox of sorts with team membership experiencing low turnover, especially when combined with the longevity of teams. They may conclude they have exhausted their ideas for improvement, lose energy, wither, and become ineffective. They may experience a series of failures and stop functioning effectively as a team. The design group might have to get involved, reexamining the structure and expanding the scope and boundaries of the team, or setting up a process for disbanding dysfunctional teams and moving members to other teams.

ACTION TEAMS. The design of action teams is embedded in the organization design, policies, and procedures, as in the examples of firefighting crews, cockpit crews, and surgical teams. They often have highly specialized tasks, significant external linkage, and sometimes rapidly changing membership.

Action teams tend to have highly specialized tasks, as with surgical teams and flight crews. Imagine watching your surgery while under a local anesthetic and seeing a discussion about who wants to cut where today. Imagine watching a fire crew trying to develop a consensus on who is going to drive what while your house is burning. Imagine getting onto a plane and observing a discussion among the flight crew about who is going to fly the plane. Design groups go to great lengths to define competencies required to perform the work. Whenever possible, people with the skills are selected to fill the roles, as with pilots and surgeons. If the skills are not readily available in the marketplace, extensive skill training is designed into the system; an example is firefighting skill training.

There is some variation in external linkage among action teams. Flight crews, for example. need to be linked with maintenance, air traffic control, and other flight crews. It is a key part of completing their respective tasks. Fire crews need to be linked with paramedics, police, other fire crews, and the people needing help.

The design group often identifies detailed linking infrastructures and common processes to provide the linkage. For example, the cockpit has a well-defined set of protocols to follow before taking off. The team members complete detailed checklists, including communications with external support groups. The surgical team has well-defined roles and protocols to follow, as does the fire crew. These teams also have a common set of processes from which to work. The easiest to see is the decision-making processes; decisions lie with the pilot and the surgeon. Within the team design, it is made clear to all team members how decisions are made and who calls the shots.

These teams deal often with life-and-death matters. It is most interesting that there is frequently changing membership. The best example is flight crews, which change frequently. People who fly regularly may observe crew members introducing themselves to each other. Yet, these teams formed on the spot are still able to provide safe and efficient air travel. The design group structures in great detail the roles of the pilot, copilot, and navigator. People selected to fill the roles meet a stringent set of criteria. Operating procedures and processes are standardized and documented to the full extent feasible. Decision-making processes are carefully prescribed, and protocols are carefully defined.

There may be no other type of team given so much structure as the action teams. Here, the team is so integral to accomplishing the work that the organization embeds many of the elements essential to effective teams when the organization itself is created.

We have identified several key considerations to help in determining how much structure to create for various teams. Each design group should take care to consider these and any unique factors in their own organization when making the decision of what is just enough structure.

THE PROCESS OF CREATING A TEAM

On a micro level, there are two basic steps to ensuring that a team is effectively structured. One is the *charter,* and the other is the *mission.* The charter is the responsibility of the chartering group, while the mission is the responsibility of the team itself. The two are intertwined with the process of dialogue.

A charter is important for most types of teams. Even the leader of an executive team needs to spell out what she expects her staff to accomplish as a team. With permanent action teams such as airline crews or surgical teams, the charter is actually embedded within the job codes, and understanding is developed through very thorough training on well-documented processes. Of course, a charter provides direction. It also minimizes the confusion inherent in the earlier stages of team development; we think it reduces the learning curve for the team.

A charter goes a long way toward developing the essential elements of an effective team. It offers background to clarify the purpose and needed information. It establishes expectations by defining overall outcomes, goals, and measurements. It helps clarify roles assigned to or needed by the team, establishing the depth and breadth of the team's charge by delineating boundaries. A charter outlines the process for communication with the chartering group.

The charter spells out what the chartering group—usually management—expects of the work team. The degree of structure depends upon factors described earlier. For example, at MotorCo the earlier parallel teams had a clear set of expectations, established roles, and boundaries narrowly defining the scope of their problem solving. With the transition to production teams, the production employees played a greater role in establishing their boundaries, setting goals, creating roles, declaring information needs, and addressing communication needs. The earlier initiative enabled the teams to develop more on their own.

Here are questions to consider in developing a charter:

- Purpose: Why is the team being formed? For what purpose? What is its goal? How does the task affect our ability to compete more effectively in the marketplace, to serve our internal and external customers better?

- History: What background is relevant to this project? Does it affect quality, speed, value, costs, or people? Are there data (hard or soft) that the team needs? What has been tried before? In what ways were earlier efforts successful? Unsuccessful? Why?

- Boundaries: What is the level of decision-making authority (recommend, decide, plan, implement)? What financial resources does the team have (budget, benchmarking, travel expenses, consultants, seminars)? What people resources are available (administrative, information systems, facilitation, communication specialists)? How much time can they devote to the task (what percent, in meetings, in preparation for meetings)?

- Roles on the team: What roles are to be filled within the team (leadership, facilitation)? How are the roles to be filled (by the charterers, by the team)? What roles are identified but remain outside the team (financial analysis, information systems support, team sponsors)?

- Definition of success: What does the chartering group want to see as a result of the team's work? What would they consider success? (Try to be specific.)

- Measurement: What are key milestones for the project (budgets, product or service measurement objectives)? What are the key operating measures (quality, costs, cycle time)?

- Communication expectations: How do the charterers want to be kept informed of the team's progress, barriers, and successes (staff meeting updates, written summaries, how often)? Who else needs to be kept informed of the team's decisions and actions? Who needs to provide input?

A pitfall of many chartering processes we have observed is that they regard the charter as the end of the process. The charterers walk away from the team confident that its members know exactly what is expected and that they should be able to function effectively. With most teams, it is far better to use the charter as the beginning of a dialogue, as a kind of structured active listening process.

An effective dialogue begins by asking the team to develop a mission. This is the initial step in making a team out of a diverse group of individuals. The *mission* describes the team members' understanding of the purpose of the team: "Why does the team exist?" Of course, the mission must fit, or be congruent with, the greater organizational mission. Obviously, it must fulfill the needs of the charter. It should describe the

ead it as part of a political science course in college, it did not
particularly applicable to a career in business. After all, it is
theories being introduced into the scientific community and
by logical scientists. To take an example, Alfred Wegener in-
he theory of continental drift at the beginning of the twenti-
. He examined the data and noticed, as had many before him,
stern coastlines of the Americas seemed to mesh with the west-
ines of Africa and Europe. He noticed the newness of the
ranges on the western coasts of the Americas—mountain
had to be created by huge forces. It also became known fairly
ugh the study of paleontologists, that there were fossils of
animals indigenous to only the western coastline of Africa
stern coastline of South America. He concluded the continents
one large land mass and had been drifting apart ever since,
mericas drifting westward. The evidence was there. It piled
middle of the century—approximately fifty years later—it be-
ccepted theory. Why did it take so long?

rgue that even among scientists, who are logical and data-
re is resistance to changing their *paradigm* of how things are.
natural. Scientists build careers based upon accepted models
ings are. When the model changes, a life's work can seemingly
the drain. At a minimum, a life's work might have to be
based on a whole new set of assumptions. Scientists seek po-
h institutions to conduct research—institutions populated by
have based their careers on a different paradigm than the one
fered. It is little wonder they resist new theories.

that managers, professionals, union leaders, and employees as
difficult to accept new schemes of management, new ways of
, shifts in the traditional division of labor, and so on. Although
to see the measurable, operational results, the reality is that—
e geologists in the early twentieth century—it does not matter.
ed organization within organizations created by rugged indi-
represents a major shift in paradigm, and a major shift in what
to succeed.

uently, the transition to production and service teams is diffi-
more difficult than starting up a new plant, or introducing a
ce or product line, or installing new lines of equipment. The
em—including behaviors—has to change.

nge process the organization uses must be different when in-
production and service teams. (Indeed, it may also need to be
when introducing complex project teams such as product
nt teams.) It should be designed for learning. It should be de-

product or service the team has been cr
the expectations of customers, team mer
managers. Here are two examples, the fi

> Our mission is to establish a master pla
> velopment, and support of strategically j
> medical division. This plan will incorp
> tion, empowerment, ownership, and acc
> ensure quality, speed, and value of equi
> tory, and marketing support for both int
> Our teams will positively contribute to t
> U.S. affiliate and thus the continued suc

The second is from a new-business co

> To identify and select markets, applicati
> ucts to generate significant growth for c
> ble technology.

Each member of a newly formed team
we here? Why do I need to be here? Tear
mance until they answer these questions
tively. Developing a mission statement, a
the hazards of each individual's forming
purpose. Pursuing different agendas, tean
working at cross-purposes or against the

The dialogue between the chartering g
the team establishes goals, makes plans,
These conversations should be focused c
lationship so the team can optimize its cl

The team also has internal needs. Reg
ternal dialogue is essential in creating a
norms to define mutually expected beha
roles, and monitoring performance to c
rective action where necessary.

A PROCESS FOR TRANSITI
TO A TEAM-BASED ORGAN

In implementing the transition to produ
most useful model for understanding the
The Structure of Scientific Revolutions by

one of us
seem to b
about ne
resistance
troduced
eth centu
that the e
ern coast
mountai
ranges th
early, thr
plants an
and the e
were onc
with the
up. In th
came an
Some
driven, th
It is quit
of how th
go down
rethough
sitions w
peers wh
being pro
So it is
well find
leadershi
some ask
as with t
Team-ba
vidualist
is needed
Conse
cult. It is
new serv
whole sy
The c
troducin
differen
developm

signed to answer questions. The process needs to reflect how decisions and actions are to be made in the future state. It needs to be open to ideas and challenges; it does not have to be perfect.

A process we have successfully used to guide the transformation is "explore, prepare, implement, and sustain." It is an iterative process that can be used for large changes, small changes, and continuous improvement.

Explore

The goal of the *explore phase* is to make an informed choice about the appropriateness of teams. In this phase, the organization takes the time to learn about teams. A cross-functional, diagonal slice of the organization is selected to conduct an analysis of teams, their uses, their effectiveness, their needs, effective change processes, and pitfalls. Often this group becomes the leadership team or steering committee, reading the literature, conducting site visits, and attending seminars. If pursuing production or service teams, the group is well served by asking for external evaluation of the likelihood of success in implementing teams. Upon reviewing a set of readiness factors, sometimes the consultant concludes it is a no-go. More often than not, the consultant offers a "conditional go": proceed only if you are willing to address certain issues.

There are excellent resources to provide practical and theoretical guidance to the overall change process.[9] Union environments require a unique change process.[10] Others elaborate on the magnitude and complexity of the challenge of leading transformational change.[11] Organization change affects individuals, creating individual transitions that have to be understood and managed.[12]

This is a stage in which support for the organizational transition is built. Management leaders, union leaders, and other shapers of thought can get questions answered, learn how issues are addressed, and understand what constraints have to be applied within their culture or environment. All too often, few people are involved in the exploration process. To worsen matters, management and union leaders move forward without allowing other leaders the opportunity to learn and have their questions answered. Resistance to change builds because people do not have the answers they need to support it.

Prepare

The goal of the *prepare phase* is to have an understandable plan that can be communicated and implemented. Like the perfect performance appraisal, it should contain no surprises.

Once an informed choice is made by the organization, the work has only begun. Building support among stakeholders while creating a flexible implementation plan is critical to a successful transition. The plan clarifies such issues as the type(s) of team being used, what the team is expected to achieve, the level of decision making the teams have, the roles and responsibilities of team members, the training necessary to develop certain skills, and the needed systems changes. If project, parallel, production, or service teams are the choice, a leadership team is often used to structure and lead the initiative. Complex project teams and production and service teams often need a design team to thoroughly examine the work being done and redesign the work if necessary. During the planning phase, supervisors and managers should prepare for their new roles in a team-based system.

The change process selected varies from organization to organization. Some organizations choose the steering committee or design team process.[13] Others choose an even more open change process.[14] Many resources exist for organizations wishing to redesign work.[15] For production and service teams performing repetitive, predictable tasks, sociotechnical analysis is appropriate.[16] Practitioners and theorists apply different models, tools, and techniques to nonlinear (knowledge) work, performed by service teams such as research teams and project teams.[17] For most organizations transitioning to teams, the leadership role changes drastically.[18]

There are two major pitfalls in the preparation phase. First, organizations frequently fail to prepare the managers and supervisors for their new role—a group whose support is critical to the change process. Loss of power and control are often cited as reasons for resistance. Our experience indicates that lack of knowledge of their new role, how to fulfill the role, and misalignment of measures are at least as important.

Second, the organization does not communicate adequately during the planning process. Absence of communication and dialogue usually leads people to focus on their fears and concerns rather than their hopes and dreams, and this becomes a powerful source of resistance.

Execute

The aim of the *execute phase* is to launch successful teams and make the changes necessary to ensure they stay successful. Teams need to be launched with clear goals, roles, and responsibilities. They need to have effective group processes and the ability to interact effectively. Teams must monitor their own progress. The leadership team, design teams, and frontline managers and supervisors should monitor the teams to determine if they have needs beyond what they are capable of providing for themselves. There are a number of tools and techniques on the market to use in designing interventions to support team development.[19]

The pace of change is important throughout the process. It is a major pitfall in the execution phase. Dropping tasks onto inadequately prepared teams is a formula for disaster. On the other hand, implementations that bog down in training at the expense of customer satisfaction have a tendency to fail. Teams that are denied responsibilities when they are ready are likely to become frustrated. Pace is the key, but applying the right pace is more art than science.

A pitfall in execution is eliminating first-line supervisors when implementing production and service teams. Use their knowledge of the workforce, knowledge of priorities, coaching skills, grasp of the bigger picture, and familiarity with decision-making processes to facilitate the undertaking. Curiously, some organizations conclude they are better off eliminating 10 percent of their supervisors than they are improving productivity by 10 percent. The focus should be on changing the role from one of monitoring and control to one of supporting the production and service teams.

Sustain

The aim of the *sustain phase* is to create a culture in which it is obvious to all that to succeed within the culture one has to know how to participate in and lead teams.

To sustain project, parallel, and production and service teams, extensive cultural change is required. The policies, practices, procedures, and systems that reflect the current culture need to be aligned with use of teams. Some of these changes should be made early in the planning phase, while others can be delayed. This is sometimes referred to as a "lag-lead" approach.[20] Obviously, measurement systems should be aligned early to provide the performance feedback necessary for teams to monitor and improve their own performance. Compensation may be a lead or a lag system. Individual, or piecework, systems should be eliminated before starting production and service teams. Other compensation systems such as gainsharing, designed to reward employees for their contributions in improving operating results, may be used to lead the cultural change. Gainsharing sometimes lags, to reward demonstrated behaviors.

The most frequent pitfall in implementation is failure to align the systems to the team-based organization. It is like planting an azalea in hard clay; there are beautiful blooms early on, but over the long haul the fragile root system does not support the plant and it withers and dies. An often-cited example is the organization that promotes the leader of budding cultural change, only to replace the person with an autocratic leader who does not have a clue as to how to lead the team-based environment.

The process is repetitive, but it tends to be less complex as the new organization matures. The process objectives of the transition are not to attain perfection; they are instead clarity, understanding, learning, commitment, and ownership of the vision. The process ought to enable a mature organization to address its imperfections.

BEST PRACTICES FOR TEAM STRUCTURE

Typically, teams have a high need for external linkage with other teams and support functions such as material or quality. What are the best practices in exploring, preparing, implementing, and sustaining teams? It is our view that best practices are ideas to be considered, not short-cuts to implementation. Dialogues on best practices create even better practices for the organization. Here are some of the best practices we have seen in structuring teams.

• *Inclusive design processes.* In exploring and planning for teams, the more inclusive the process the more likely the effort is to succeed. People are far more committed to change they have helped create than to that which is imposed. When done well, production and service teams have a clear idea of such areas as goals and roles before teams are launched, as was the case at MotorCo. If issues causing resistance are openly discussed and addressed, the launch tends to be more successful.

• *Change driven by the need to make a good situation better.* Prevailing thought seems to be that an organization needs to confront its own demise (as at MotorCo), but it has been our experience that successful companies are also more successful at sustaining change. It may be that they are successful because they do a better job of managing change, or perhaps they have the resources to make change a reality. Why would a successful organization implement change? It could be driven by the desire to make a great organization even better.

• *The need to use teams driven by operational objectives.* Using teams for the sake of teams is a waste of time, money, and credibility. If teams will enhance the performance of the organization, then, by all means, choose them. If not, choose another approach.

• *Early consensus on a definition of team success among the leadership team.* After a year or so, the question arises as to whether or not the teams have been effective. Although one year might be too short a time frame, it is fair to assess whether or not teams are meeting expectations. The challenge for the leadership team is to agree upon the criteria by which teams are evaluated. They can be designed to achieve desired objectives if the objectives are known ahead of time.

• *Extensive preparation of managers and first-line supervisors.* Help them. Do not eliminate them—unless they choose not to be helped. With the possible exception of permanent action teams such as flight crews and surgical teams, managers and supervisors need to be prepared for their new role, one that is different from what they have observed and filled in most traditional organizations. Resistance based upon job insecurity is because people do not know if they are able to fill the new role. Prepare them, in addition to the people who will coach them.

• *Union leaders from innovative work sites presenting their experience directly to union members at the site preparing to use teams.* Unions often need direct interaction with fellow union members to get their questions answered. Give them an opportunity to do so. Sometimes this is done through seminars and site visits, but a very efficient and cost effective way is to invite union leaders and members from innovative work sites to talk with local union leaders and members.

• *Work redesign.* When designing production and service teams, conduct a work redesign. The analysis alone often uncovers enough improvement opportunities to pay for the team implementation. In addition, it verifies the need for teams to achieve operational results.

• *Chartering to create a foundation for a dialogue to determine team goals and roles.* Chartering creates the basis for the existence of production, service, parallel, and project teams. It clearly elaborates the direction the charterers want the teams to take.

• *Developing teams with clear goals and roles and with effective team processes and relationships.* Many organizations focus on preparing teams with conflict-resolution skills, when the underlying cause for conflict is unclear goals, undefined roles, poor team processes, and nonexistent norms. Address these causes first as part of the design process.

• *Needs assessment and skill development.* This is quite obvious yet often ignored. Of course, the organization should determine what skills are necessary and what skills people have, and then offer the needed training to fill the gaps. Effective teams require significant training. Use resources wisely.

- *Measurements aligned with strategic objectives and designed to provide immediate feedback to team members.* If teams are going to help the organization meet marketplace demands, measurements must be closely linked to those demands. In addition, the measures must be timely so the team can monitor and improve its own performance. A side benefit of timely measurement feedback is that team members provide themselves with ongoing recognition as goals are achieved.
- *Aggressive implementation with a phasing-in of decision making.* Some organizations are able to use pilot teams effectively as a learning lab on how to create teams. This sometimes works with project teams. With production and service teams, the piloting process seems to reduce risk. However, it also reduces the likelihood of long-term success. A better practice with production and service teams is to implement broadly, while gradually but steadily empowering the teams to make decisions.
- *Co-location of project teams.* Bringing major project teams, such as product development teams, to a common location works wonders in terms of increasing team effectiveness. The primary benefits are focus on the task at hand and communication of needs and issues.
- *Distributive leadership on production and service teams.* Assigning leadership functions to various members of production and service teams minimizes leader dependence, yields a broader range of opportunities for team members to lead, and enables the organization to build the skills within the team more rapidly.

CONCLUSION

This chapter has identified the elements of structure necessary for successful work teams. We have discussed factors that help determine how much structure is just enough to give to teams, as opposed to how much structure they can create for themselves. Finally, we have described an implementation process for creating teams and team-based organizations.

Inattention to these issues is sure to result in disgruntled management, a cynical workforce, and a failed effort to introduce teams. We have seen this played out many times. If you pay attention to the structural elements, give just enough structure, and adapt the concepts for transition, will you be successful? Not necessarily. Even if the stars are in alignment and work teams are delivering the expected results, there is no guarantee teams will be implemented throughout the organization. To do so requires a paradigm shift. It requires that the organization aggressively develop a supportive context, as described in the rest of this book. It also requires the organization to provide a competitive product or service.

3

SELECTION AND STAFFING FOR TEAM EFFECTIVENESS

Richard J. Klimoski, Lori B. Zukin

SELECTING INDIVIDUALS to be members of a work team presents special challenges. Traditionally, a job analysis produced the information needed to determine the knowledge, skills, abilities, and other attributes (KSAOs) required to perform an individual job. However, staffing a team must also take into account the individual's responsibility, with other team members, for the whole team's performance. Team staffing requires more than individual job analysis; it calls for teamwork analysis. An added complexity is that these challenges vary, depending on the type of team.

This chapter discusses the impact of team type on staffing, while contrasting approaches to traditional organizational staffing with the new requirements for team-based work. It discusses a range of staffing situations, from selecting a single team member for a short-term committee assignment to choosing all members of a new project team. It addresses processes involved in moving from staffing traditional, individual jobs to filling positions on teams.

In doing this, we introduce the person-in-team performance model, a framework for teamwork analysis. It assists us in identifying the team's performance dimensions and, therefore, the knowledge, skills, and abilities as well as the selection practices for the team of interest. The framework also reveals the process that a person responsible for staffing a team might go through in determining the best approach to selecting (or placing) team members.

This chapter

- Explains why the best approach to staffing is contingent upon team type and the context in which the team functions
- Points out the similarities and distinctions between staffing at the individual and team levels
- Describes the steps a staffing specialist might take to analyze the team's function within the organization, the team functions as a team itself, and the individual members' functions within the team
- Presents examples of real-life team staffing strategies used by organizations today
- Clarifies the issues that come up when staffing a team in the green-field scenario
- Shares best practices for team staffing
- Provides a learning case study to illustrate the problematics that occur when attempting to staff a team

TEAM STAFFING IN TODAY'S ORGANIZATIONS

The goal of staffing teams resembles the goal of selecting individual employees: to find the best person to do the work. Any staffing effort begins by identifying the work context. This helps identify the KSAOs or worker requirements needed to be successful. For an individual, the KSAOs needed to perform a job are evaluated in terms of individual performance. For a work team, they are additionally evaluated in terms of group performance.

At both individual and team levels, several classes of requirements are the same. Although they may constitute a necessary set, the commonalities alone are not sufficient. In fact, the goal of early efforts at team staffing is to identify

- Generic worker requirements that any organization has for any employees (that is, such traits as conscientiousness and integrity)
- Company-relevant requirements to get at those skills necessary to work within the culture and the policies of the company (ability to take on shiftwork, willingness to work in a start-up company)

- Individual position requirements, referring to capabilities important for performing the specific tasks for which a person would be responsible, either as part of a team or in individual work (such as estimating costs, visual acuity to spot defects in parts)

- Team-relevant requirements, since for performance in a team environment we add further requirements that get at the individual's ability to interact with and work with others in a coordinated and collaborative fashion generally (skill in negotiation, attitudes toward team work), and those needed for the specific team context (say, operating on a team-based production system)

General Approach to Team Staffing

Team staffing approaches vary greatly depending on the type of team and the organizational context. However, there are some general similarities. Usually the human resource group works with the unit or group manager responsible for the team, as in starting up a new team or attempting to fill a vacancy in a current team. The KSAOs for the team leader are identified first. If the team is to have a formal leader (and most do), the team leader is then chosen. Following this, the HR group, working with the unit manager and the team leader, identifies the KSAOs necessary for the various team members. Occasionally, current team members participate in selecting newer members. However, even though the process of staffing teams has steps parallel to staffing individual jobs, the devil is in the details.

At Libbey-Owens Ford,[1] a glass manufacturing company in Toledo, Ohio, both team members and HR members conduct the assessment. The HR department recruits candidates and brings them in for an orientation to the company and then tests them on aptitude, motivation, and ability to spot defects in glass. Those who pass this hurdle are assessed—by way of small group discussions with team members, HR members, and other production representatives—on communication, cooperation, and problem-solving skills. After this step, HR staff and team members conduct interviews.

Team members are also involved in assessing candidates. A matching system, administered by HR, exists whereby candidates learn about the various teams and then indicate which one they would like to work on by placing their names on a job preference poster. Team representatives make offers based on their assessment of the candidate's match with the team.

Case Example: Filling a Vacancy on a Product Development Team

At "Software, Inc.," the pseudonym we give to a small firm that supplies automated manufacturing companies with software to run manufacturing robots, a new product development team has been working for over a year. To date, team members have been effective in terms of meeting goals and coordinating their efforts. The team is multifunctional; each member is highly dependent on the others' expertise. The project is moving along smoothly when Max, the representative from sales, announces to John, the project director, that he is leaving the organization.

PROBLEM. The team must deliver a briefing to the management executive council in two months. Max's role on the team has been critical for several reasons. First, his knowledge of customer needs has offered the team critical recommendations in terms of developing a customer-friendly product. Second, prior to Max's joining the team, it did not have a representative from sales. The move to include a member from sales was influenced by the perception that new products were not meeting the demands of the customers. For this reason, his role has become crucial to the team's success. Most, but not all, of the top management team members have come to value having a representative from sales on the team. The vacancy must be filled as soon as possible to meet the briefing deadline.

Mary, an internal staffing consultant, is charged with finding Max's replacement. Until now, the team's context within the organization has not been assessed with regard to staffing issues. Mary knows the urgency imposed by the team's deadline. Team staffing is new to her, but because of her experience with individual staffing she has some ideas regarding how she might find out the characteristics necessary in a good replacement for Max.

CONTEXTUAL AND TEAMWORK ANALYSIS. Because this organization is moving toward the regular use of teams to initiate new products, it is likely that vacancies such as this will need to be staffed again. Although Mary could improvise and expedite the process, she sets out to develop a staffing approach to serve as a prototype for future vacancies. She begins by clarifying for herself the specific tasks the team as a whole must do and those organizational entities with which they must interact. Using discussions with team members and the project manager (John), she develops a list of the functions that the team carries out for the organization:

1. Gathering and assembling information, opinions, and data, including consumer surveys and competitor analysis

2. Working with other organizational entities to identify the vision resources and constraints in developing the product

3. Identifying, anticipating, and conceptualizing the needs of customers

4. Transforming ideas, experience, and data on capacities, forecasts, customer surveys, and competitor analyses into an innovative new product that meets the customer's demands and is potentially profitable for the firm

5. Preparing and delivering a proposal that meets management's needs and expectations

In addition to these functions, Mary helps the team members and John identify the knowledge, skills, abilities, and other attributes (KSAOs) required of this position. To find out what those requirements are, and to verify that the team-level tasks are correctly understood, she holds a meeting with several team members. During this meeting, John informs her that knowledge of customer requirements, product knowledge, and functional knowledge (knowledge of sales and marketing) are absolute requirements for this team member. Current team members say that Max's replacement needs to effectively represent the sales department in terms of knowing the customer and understanding how the salesforce does its business.

The meeting is about to end when Jane, a member from engineering, addresses the need to schedule still another meeting of the team. An argument begins to brew regarding the time Jane and Tom, from marketing, have been putting into their work. They catch themselves and apologize to Mary, saying that their tempers are a bit short because they have given up so many weekends and evenings with their families to cover for those who have not been giving the project what it needs. This implies to Mary that the group simply is not as cohesive as she thought.

She makes a mental note that in addition to other skills, Max's replacement may need to command respect and have some process management skills to help get the team back on track.

Mary continues her quest to find out about the probable requirements of this position by speaking with some individuals within the company's sales department who have worked with Max and the team in the past. These interviews reveal to Mary that communication between sales and the product development team could be better. For example, changes made to product specifications have not been communicated promptly to the sales manager. This lack of communication results in a less promising product. Another thought registers with Mary: perhaps the replacement needs to be someone who can effectively act as liaison with other organizational units affected by the team's proposal.

Although Mary has not had much experience in team staffing, she seems to be on the right track as far as conducting teamwork analysis and identifying the context in which the team works. She has gathered information from experts, both within and outside the team, with regard to the tasks and KSAOs required of the position. Furthermore, she has used a critical incident (the conflict between Jane and Tom about putting in extra time) as input to determining the skills the replacement should have.

Mary is keeping a record of her discussions and of her analysis of the job. This makes the assessment process more defensible as she has a record of how the assessment tools and KSAOs are linked to the job (which is to say, her assessment has content validity). Whenever she faces a similar replacement problem in the future, she will have these as something to build upon. Moreover, in the course of a number of cases, doing this will end up providing the company with a set of worthwhile and workable procedures.

IDENTIFYING THE KSAOS. Although Mary has not yet been explicitly exposed to the person-in-team performance model, she has been thinking of KSAOs that go beyond simply the individual's task and include team-level requirements (that is, process management skills). She develops a draft list of KSAOs and then obtains feedback from both the team members and other organizational entities (including other product development teams within the organization). Her final list includes these KSAOs:

Product knowledge

Functional knowledge (knowledge of sales and marketing)

Knowledge of customer demands

Knowledge of organizational practices and policies

Oral communication skills

Ability to gather information

Ability to work in teams

Behavioral flexibility

Innovation

Analytical thinking

Skill in negotiation

Process management skills

Boundary spanning (networking) skills

DECISION ON INTERNAL VERSUS EXTERNAL STAFFING. Now that Mary has finalized the KSAOs for this position, there are several issues she must consider. First, should she recommend internal or external recruiting for this position? The considerations are that many of the KSAOs are specific to the organization (such as knowledge of customer requirements), the team must be staffed immediately, and the assignment will last only until the product is on the market (about one year).

One problem is that the organization is fairly new to the team method of getting work done. The transformation from individual to team-based work began only about two years ago. Thus, there are many people within the organization who simply are not used to teamwork. This implies that there may not be too many suitable candidates among the individuals now working in teams.

Mary decides to do some informal benchmarking on this issue. She identifies organizations that are similar to hers in terms of their stage in the transition to teams. Michael, an HR recruiter, tells her that he has experienced a similar problem of lack of experience in working with a team. He recommends that the Teamwork KSA Test[2] be used to assess individual ability to work on teams. This tool measures such teamwork skills as collaborative problem solving, communication, planning and task coordination, etc.

In addition, another contact suggests that best candidates might be identifiable through the rich human resource information system (HRIS) that Mary has at her disposal. For example, evidence of individuals with product knowledge, functional knowledge, innovation, analytical thinking, and knowledge of customer demands has most likely been assessed through performance reviews or feedback from customers and supervisors. Furthermore, such skills as behavioral flexibility, skill in negotiation, process management skills, and boundary spanning skills are likely to have been exhibited in previous interactions with organizational members and may be a matter of record.

From her experiences, Mary feels that other skills such as oral communication and ability to gather information could be assessed through a structured interview. Although the candidate may not have worked in an organizational team (remember, this organization is fairly new to the team method of doing work), he or she may have had past experience working with special committees, task forces, etc. A candidate can be asked about past experience working with teams, and how he or she acted when confronted with various interpersonal conflicts within those teams.

Mary is beginning to get a sense of how this process works. She knows she wants to hire internally, and she knows that an interview is necessary to assess many of the important KSAOs, especially ability to work in teams and process management skills.

POLITICAL ISSUES. Mary discusses her progress with John. Together they present their work to Stan, the executive vice president of human resources. Stan questions the need for a replacement, especially since the group will have its major work rolled out in two months. Because of the organizational cutbacks, Stan thinks that it may not be necessary to have a member from sales on this team. Although he has not sat in on their meetings, he has seen their progress reports. Stan believes the team has been working well together, regardless of their being down one person. He suggests this idea to Mary and John; but after all of their work analyzing the team and recognizing the importance of replacing Max, John and Mary disagree adamantly with Stan. Mary and John discuss their views and make two points. John argues for the need for a new team member with process skills. Mary then reminds Stan that Jan, the vice president of sales, has advocated having a sales representative on every product development team. Jan believes the quality of the product is greatly increased if a sales perspective is represented. Furthermore, although top management has not been in total agreement on this issue, they have sent down a statement that sales should be on this type of team. In the end, Mary and John are given permission to go forward with the replacement. Mary places the position on the company's computerized posting system.

The politics of staffing can be an issue. In this case, we see that not everyone agrees that the team should be staffed with certain members. Sometimes organizational members need to negotiate to compose the team as they feel is best for the organization. Sometimes it is important to fill the vacancy, while at other times the team effectively compensates for the loss.

WHO SHOULD BE INVOLVED IN SELECTING THE NEW MEMBER?
Mary posts the opening in accordance with company policy. She lists the KSAOs and asks that candidates express their interest in this position in the coming week.

Her benchmarking calls confirm that many people must be involved in the process of staffing this team: herself; Jan, the sales VP; the project director; HR; and at least one member of the team.

HOW TO DO THE ASSESSMENT? By deadline, Mary receives applications from five nominees. She and John look at the KSAOs and develop a test plan (Exhibit 3.1) that indicates which tools most effectively assess the candidates. The plan suggests that tools include a review of credentials (including references from current managers) and a structured interview.[3] It is reasonable to assume that some KSAOs (knowledge of customer needs, functional knowledge) are held by all candidates by virtue of the fact that they have worked in sales for some time. Thus, an assessment of these KSAOs is not critical at this time. However, it is important to know how the individual will handle the teamwork situation. It seems critical to assess such team level skills as negotiation, ability to work in teams, etc.

Interviews are conducted by John, another team member, and Mary. Interviewers rate how well the candidate answers each question, and they assign an overall rating. The interviewers come to consensus on the final score for each candidate. This information is then brought back to the team to make a final decision.

In the end, Joyce, a ten-year veteran of the sales office in the local region, is identified as the preferred candidate.

TEAM STAFFING PROCESS

The process of staffing teams varies greatly depending on the team and situation, but it involves some common steps. Figure 3.1 shows a typical sequence.

Contextual Analysis: What Is the Situation?

A contextual analysis is generally conducted to provide a framework for team staffing.

START-UP VERSUS REPLACEMENT. Depending on whether we are filling a vacancy, staffing a brand new team, or transforming the organization from individual to team-based work, our approach must differ. In filling a vacancy in an existing team, we are likely to have some idea already of the team's processes and know what the team's purpose and current performance needs are. Thus, we can concentrate on the individual and

Exhibit 3.1. Methods for Assessing KSAOs of Candidates for New Team Members.

KSAO	Teamwork test	Past performance	Interview
Product knowledge		X	
Functional knowledge (knowledge of sales and marketing)		X	
Knowledge of customer demands		X	
Knowledge of organizational practices and policies			
Oral communication skills			X
Ability to gather information			X
Ability to work in teams	X		X
Behavioral flexibility		X	
Innovation		X	X
Analytical thinking		X	X
Skill in negotiation	X	X	
Process management skills	X	X	
Boundary spanning (networking) skills	X	X	

the individual's role within the team. Unless there is some reason to question the status quo, we spend little effort on the team-level analysis. If, however, we are developing a new type of team, we have to stress such an analysis and investigate to identify the functions the team performs and how many people are needed to perform the tasks.

A modified form of this approach occurs when staffing a single team of limited direction (a task force, or a product development team). Finally, moving to team-based work while an organization is transforming itself from individual to team-based management systems calls for still another approach.[4] Here, teamwork analysis helps us reveal who

Figure 3.1. Getting the Right Person into the Team.

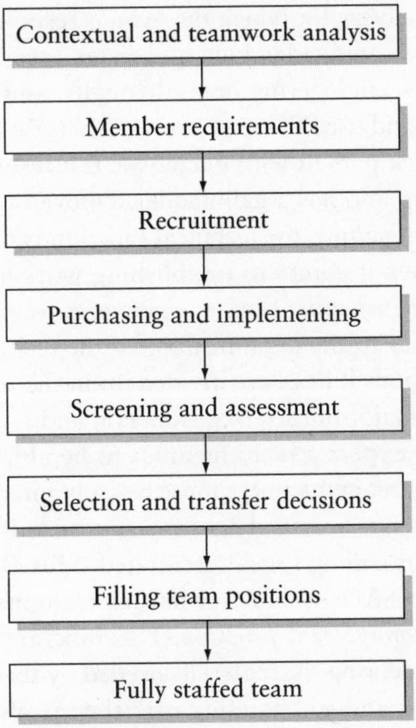

```
┌─────────────────────────────────────┐
│   Contextual and teamwork analysis  │
└─────────────────────────────────────┘
                  │
┌─────────────────────────────────────┐
│         Member requirements         │
└─────────────────────────────────────┘
                  │
┌─────────────────────────────────────┐
│             Recruitment             │
└─────────────────────────────────────┘
                  │
┌─────────────────────────────────────┐
│      Purchasing and implementing    │
└─────────────────────────────────────┘
                  │
┌─────────────────────────────────────┐
│      Screening and assessment       │
└─────────────────────────────────────┘
                  │
┌─────────────────────────────────────┐
│     Selection and transfer decisions│
└─────────────────────────────────────┘
                  │
┌─────────────────────────────────────┐
│        Filling team positions       │
└─────────────────────────────────────┘
                  │
┌─────────────────────────────────────┐
│          Fully staffed team         │
└─────────────────────────────────────┘
```

within the organization best meets the new HR requirements of the team as it is being formed or created.

Before beginning any team staffing process, it is critical to look at the type of team and the team's functions within the organization.

THE TEAM'S FUNCTION. A person staffing a team might begin by looking at the team's functions within the organization and then move inward to how the team itself must function as a unit. Then it is prudent to examine each individual member's functions in the team.

At the outset of a team staffing effort, it is necessary to consider the potential functions of the team. For example, just as departments have specific functions (such as production, adaptation, and management), so too do teams. An evaluation of these functions at the contextual analysis phase of the staffing process assists the staffer in identifying the larger issues the team must focus on as it does its work. This has implications for identifying and assessing the KSAOs necessary for effective team membership. Here are five examples of functions:[5]

1. *Productive/technical function.* This function has associated with it all the things that workers do together to add value to a product or to a phase of service delivery for which the team is responsible. To illustrate, a subassembly is created, added on, and tested (production team); customer preferences, engineering breakthroughs, and financial data are read, interpreted, and used to create a proposal for a new product (project teams); or a sick patient with diagnostic test results is "introduced" to a surgical group and has a gallbladder removed (action or performing team). To put it simply, the technical function is the raison d'être for a given team. When it comes to establishing worker requirements for hiring into a team, we must look at the extent to which the team has major responsibility to the organization for the technical function, and if so, how the responsibilities are divided up in the team. For example, in teams with the major burden of production and a variety of stages involved, we might expect a team member to be able to perform all of these stages. Thus, team members must be truly interchangeable. More commonly, however, team members are responsible for different aspects of the process, thus calling for differentiated skills. This has an impact on which specific KSAOs to look for in each team member.

2. *Boundary management function.* This function refers to activities associated with procuring the materials needed by the team or organization to do its work and to "handing off" the team's work product to someone else. In some contexts, this function is hardly an issue at all. For example, in most production contexts, as a result of engineering decisions team members automatically receive what they need (it may even be machine-delivered) and have little responsibility for worrying about where their work product goes next. To use a term introduced in Chapter One, there are high "external linkages" as a contextual feature. But in many other organizational settings, one or more of the team members is at least partially responsible for liaison activities, or boundary spanning. For instance, the team members themselves might have to procure a client, or a sponsor for capital, or raw material that is needed (inputs); similarly, someone may have to ensure that a customer gets the product once it is completed (outputs). This boundary spanning may include external spanning as well. As an illustration, teams at Johnsonville Foods, in Sheboygan, Wisconsin, read letters from customers so that they can respond to complaints (presumably to retain customers for their team's products).[6] Additionally, sometimes buffers must be built to protect the team. For example, an engineering executive might wish to protect a team from having to produce, on short notice, by influencing the marketing department to seek out customers with predictable needs. Making boundaries more

well defined to ensure a sense of identity and loyalty to the team, also known as bringing up the boundaries, is usually called for in boundary management as well.[7] But boundary management functions may be important for some teams and only some team members. Assessing the need for these functions and who should be tasked with carrying them out is essential in the staffing process.

3. *Adaptive function.* Adaptive functions refer to ensuring that the welfare of the team or organization is not threatened by forces around the immediate team (but outside its boundaries). Usually, activities associated with adaptation focus on learning as much as possible about the team's context, especially with regard to potential threats or opportunities. Is the company able to maintain the supply of resources needed? At the team level, are there other units that might take away from the team's importance?

Alternatively, other activities might be carried out to enhance the team's reputation in the company or its viability in the future. Promoting the team in the presence of top management and marketing the group's products or services to powerful constituencies are examples.

4. *Maintenance function.* In contrast to an external orientation, maintenance activities focus on what is going on internally to the team, especially regarding interpersonal relations. Generally speaking, teams, like systems of any sort, require collaboration and smooth coordination among the parts (the members). Interpersonal incompatibility, conflict, or differing goals are not desirable. Maintenance activities on the part of team members thus include those things that promote good and effective relationships. These range from establishing norms, honoring members for exemplary behavior, and modeling good team citizenship to being willing to help someone learn what must be done.

5. *Managerial/executive function.* Finally, in most systems decisions have to be made, arguments must be settled, and goals need to be set. These are considered managerial (or executive) subsystems functions. This is what Chapter One refers to as the notion of authority. Teams that are self-regulating, self-directed, or self-managing have one or more team members who do this. In contrast, for traditional teams a leader or a manager might be the one who is responsible.

These five functions are more or less needed in most organizations, and by extension in most work teams. Although all teams exist to fulfill some functional requirement, the extent that the other functions are needed or evident varies with several contextual factors, including most of those covered by various chapters in this book. For example, if team member training or compensation arrangements are carried out effectively by the organization, there is less need for team members themselves to perform maintenance activities. Similarly, in a company with a good information system, adaptive (scanning) activities also are not so necessary for team members.

In brief, a team might perform one of five broad functions: production, or a technical task that supports production; maintenance of smooth organizational operation; development of new products or information (adaptive function); conducting transactions across the organization's boundary; or management.

TEAMWORK ANALYSIS. To establish worker requirements, teamwork analysis involves interviewing or observing team members and analyzing team processes. It entails analysis of the team's role in the organization, its division of labor, and the function of each position.

1. *The team's role.* What are the team's primary responsibilities? To what degree is the whole team responsible for a subsystem of the organization? For example, a production team probably has the main responsibility for a productive or technical subsystem and little direct responsibility for the well-being of workers within the organization. This is largely the HR department's role. Though the example may seem obvious, in most cases a team's function for the organization may be complex or even ambiguous.

2. *Team division of labor.* To what degree is each team member responsible for fulfilling or contributing to the functions? For example, a production team has as its main function production of some output; yet some of its members also have to worry about maintenance, boundary spanning, and adaptive activities, etc., within the team. In fact some production teams have "expediters" who can solve problems at the "edge" of the team's domain. Note that we recommend a direct examination of the real situation as it relates to team member activities. We do not rely on any official document or statement about division of labor since it may be misleading or at the least too idealistic.

3. *The function of the position.* Much of team staffing involves filling a position within a team. Thus, we need to ascertain to what degree activities of each team subfunction are performed in the position having the vacancy. For example, in what is nominally a production-type team, not all members need to carry out the adaptive subsystem. It may be enough to have only one person attending to the organizational context of the team. (In fact, in hierarchical teams, this is often done as the team

leader attends key meetings, manages relationships with other teams, etc.) Once again, we recommend direct examination of the situation. When a vacancy occurs, ask just what the departing incumbent actually did for the team.

TEAM MEMBER REQUIREMENTS. In most work teams, it is unlikely that *all* team members perform the very same activities, nor does each team member have a unique set of duties. The typical case involves a mixture of specialized and general responsibilities. We refer to this situation as producing a person-in-team view of team member requirements.

Thorough teamwork analysis, as described above, should uncover the precise mixture of duties being demanded of a team member in a given context. However, in general the logic of the teamwork analysis can also be used to create a template; this helps most companies reach some conclusions regarding the crucial KSAOs needed in applicants for team assignments. Specifically, a person-in-team view based on a teamwork (functional) analysis leads us to recommend that any set of worker requirements be built around four categories:

1. *Individual position requirements.* As noted, these are the skills and abilities needed to perform the position assigned to the particular team member who is being replaced. Based on science and practice, position performance requirements are likely to be such things as cognitive ability (perhaps intelligence), task-specific knowledge, oral communication skill, and conscientiousness (as in willingness to put forth extra effort).

2. *Team task management requirements.* Most team members have some responsibility to assist one another in executing team tasks. At the most mundane level, this might involve coordinating individual effort (as members of a tug-of-war team must do). Most of the time, it involves thinking of the team's tasks and supplying information, effort, and skill when and where it is needed as the team goes about performing its business. Interpositional knowledge (the knowledge of both the team member's own tasks as well as those of other team members), ability to monitor and provide feedback to team members, and persuasive communication skills are some examples of this type of requirement.

3. *Team process management requirements.* These requirements are implied in our treatment of maintenance and management subfunctions. We have found that the needs and emotions of team members must be addressed in most teams. Differences of opinion and interpersonal conflict must be resolved. This subset of skills and abilities is required of all team members if such a resolution is to be done regularly and when

needed. Some specific requirements that have been identified as fitting this category are interpersonal competence (ability to interact well with others), communication skills, trustworthiness, and ability to lead by example.

4. *Team boundary management.* This category stems from the demands of boundary management and adaptive functions required by a team. As implied, most teams are open systems. This implies that the welfare of the team and its members is strongly influenced by factors and forces outside the immediate team's "space." Thus it seems that skills and abilities required for effective boundary management should also be expected of most new team members. Examples of team boundary management requirements include negotiation skill, conflict management skill, presentation skills, and knowledge of organizational strategy.

Determining the KSAOs for a specific job opening in a team—much less for a whole new team—requires some careful investigation. One might approach the task in terms of looking for the relative mix of these four sets of requirements.

Along with assessing member requirements comes the need to identify when, in the process, the team member must possess certain KSAOs. Must they be present at entry to the job, or can the organization expend the resources to train the new team member after hiring? Toyota used this strategy in determining that certain member requirements were necessary at entry to the job so as to train team members in the "Toyota way." The company purposely selected candidates who did not have manufacturing experience, to eliminate the need to change bad habits and cultural assumptions associated with traditional manufacturing.[8]

Recruiting: How to Locate the Right People

Context guides the recruiting process as well. Filling a vacancy on an existing team may not differ much from the individual case except that we usually look for some additional attributes. The replacement not only meets the requirements for individual job performance in the established setting but also requires some team-level skills.

In configuring a new team, however, we usually find major differences in the strategy used. In this case, the odds are that we need to conduct a wider search to create a pool of candidates large enough and rich enough for our needs. This is because we must find the combination of individuals who work well together. Although many individuals might perform equally well, the team functions well only if the mix of new hires is right. The best strategy is to start with individuals who have the key KSAOs and then find out who among the recruiting pool best fits with or complements these key individuals. Alternatively, we might locate those who have the skills that are relatively rare and recruit successfully here before seeking complementary teammates.

Because compensation systems often differ at the team level (see Chapter Six), they affect where and who you want to recruit. We may not want to recruit applicants who thrive on and are used to traditional, individualistic incentive plans.

Recruiting may be a matter of scheduling and availability. Committees and ad hoc groups are often staffed with volunteers. Though an individual with the right skills may be willing to work on the team, perhaps other assignments preclude being able to participate. Therefore, staffing may boil down to availability in addition to, or perhaps even instead of, specific skills no matter how high the level. This might be particularly true under time pressures.

We do see occasions of few differences between team and individual recruiting processes. This might occur in the brown-field scenario, where teams must be staffed with existing employees. To illustrate, at a unionized manufacturing plant in Michigan, an organization moving to a team-based manufacturing system recruits just as it does for individual positions. The new position on the team is posted internally with a job description and requirements. Candidates contact the personnel department to indicate interest.[9]

As noted, the availability of suitable candidates is a critical issue to consider when staffing teams. Some research suggests that the selection ratio is large for team staffing,[10] but it seems to depend on the context, including such issues as the type of team and the level of member skill required by the team. For example, recruiting for production teams may reveal a favorable selection ratio, while applicants for computer software new-product teams are few. In general, the unemployment rate has a major impact on this ratio as well.

One last point worth stressing is that the people who do the recruiting may differ in the two cases. For staffing most individual positions, HR usually does most of the recruiting. For team-based positions, the team leader or even workers on the team may share recruitment obligations with HR.

Recruiting team members builds on many assumptions that are contingent upon the team type. However, Exhibit 3.2 illustrates the relative emphasis placed on each recruitment strategy for our six types of teams. Note that in some cases several components are emphasized. For example, a management team in an organization requiring a lot of change might wish to recruit externally. However, if things are going well the organization may wish to have someone like those already identified and with specific organizational knowledge. Thus it would recruit internally.

Exhibit 3.2. Relative Emphasis of Recruiting Strategies by Team Type.

Team type	How to recruit			Who does the recruiting?				Candidates	
	Informal network	Massive recruiting effort	Placement firm	Human resources	Team leader	Unit manager	Team members	Internal	External
Management	X		X	X		X	X	X	X
Project	X			X	X	X	X	X	X
Production		X		X		X	X	X	X
Service		X		X	X	X	X	X	X
Action and performing		X		X	X	X	X	X	X
Parallel	X				X	X	X	X	

Screening and Assessment: Picking the Right People

Staffing specialists attempt to ensure a balance of fairness, technical adequacy, and feasibility of the processes that they design, develop, and implement for selection.[11] In any staffing situation, multiple stakeholders exist (such as the union, management, and candidates for the job); they often hold competing views regarding the three factors requiring balance. In developing and implementing assessment procedures, managers must be sensitive to these viewpoints. In fact, to this end, some writers suggest that the stakeholders themselves be involved in selection system design.[12] Doing so, they are more likely to have their needs met while still maintaining fairness and technical adequacy.

Scientific personnel selection may involve using any of a number of approaches or tools to assess applicants. Each tool has certain strengths and weaknesses. In using these tools singly or in combination, the HR professional or manager is seeking to observe or stimulate an applicant's behavior in a manner that lends itself to drawing some conclusions (inferences) regarding the level of job-relevant traits or qualities that they might have.

The tools used for personnel selection are likely to depend on the type of team that has been staffed. For example, informal processes such as a nomination or recommendation by a trusted manager (or a reference from an outsider) are often used for ad hoc committees. More formal techniques, such as carefully developed and implemented assessment centers, validated biodata forms, and situational or experience-based interviews, might be used for staffing a set of production teams. Additionally, who is involved in the assessment and selection process varies depending on the team type. For example, earlier research[13] has suggested that team members are often involved in the selection process, though this is more likely to be true for teams that are self-managed.

Each technique for assessment is built on an underlying logic. If the manager is to be responsible for assessment, he or she must come to understand the conditions under which a given technique can and should be used for accurate inference about applicants. Specifically, it is the person in charge of selection who conducts linkage analysis.

Linkage analysis involves relating the key traits uncovered by team and position analyses to the kinds of past experience and accomplishment or current performance that is likely to produce or reveal the traits. In the most sophisticated version of linkage analysis, extensive development work goes into obtaining research evidence of such a relationship.[14] Those responsible for actually reviewing applicants, then, are trained on just how to use or interpret work history summaries or responses to an interview to form conclusions about the suitability of a given applicant (see Figure 3.2). Like a chain, the success of the whole endeavor is only likely if each link is well formed.

If the focus is on using past behavior or accomplishments, techniques and tools such as work history questionnaire, resume analysis, nominations, references, and many versions of the selection interview have as their premise that an applicant's past behavior or accomplishments are useful indicators of capabilities and potential. In the context of staffing for team positions, careful analysis of the candidate's background, with emphasis on drawing conclusions concerning the KSAOs needed for the assignment can go a long way toward identifying those who are most likely to succeed.[15]

If the focus is on contemporary demonstration of capability, instead of relying on what someone has done in the past, other techniques are used that call for assessing suitability for team assignment by asking the candidate to demonstrate capabilities at the time of applying for a position on the team. Under this scenario, the staffing specialist selects, designs, or develops a worklike situation in which an applicant is to be assessed. In most cases, this implies constructing a simulation of the team

Figure 3.2. Linkage Work Is Necessary Work.

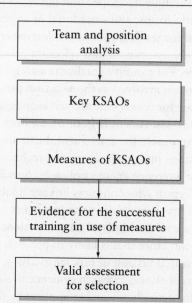

task and asking the applicant to explain or perform as if on the job.[16] This may be done with more than one applicant at a time. Variations of this approach are the work sample technique, structured interview, written or oral trade test, and assessment center methods.

The logic of this approach to assessment is that the applicant who has the appropriate set of skills can, if requested, demonstrate them in lifelike situations. Organizational staff, suitably trained for the purpose, then observe, take notes on what occurs, and make inferences regarding the candidate's suitability. In addition to the implication of staff training, the quality of these inferences is strongly influenced by the appropriateness of the simulation itself. It must capture important job demands; this is why it is always a good idea to use a professional to implement this approach.

Another version of contemporary demonstration has the applicant actually work with regular employees for a certain period of time during which the candidate is assessed. For example, finalists for jobs in a manufacturing company are paid for a day's work as a temporary employee. Everyone involved knows that this is a test of suitability (in this case a test lasting eight hours!).[17] After the episode is concluded, coworkers and the shift foreman are systematically surveyed for their observations and reactions, which are factored into the final decision. This strategy also helps decrease turnover by providing an applicant with an accurate assessment of what it will be like doing the job.[18] Upon realizing this, those who can do the job but are not temperamentally suited might withdraw from consideration.

From this last example, it can be seen that common organizational staffing practices such as using temporary workers, student coop or intern arrangements with colleges, and cross-training and job rotation might all be adapted to the need for good assessment. These techniques actually require more time than a traditional interview or assessment center, to observe someone and really get to know the person's capabilities. Of course, there are also liabilities to stretching things out too long.

If the focus in the staffing context is on assessing potential, it may be that the exact duties to be performed are not yet clear (as in setting up a task force or study group). Or there may not be any applicants with the exact background called for (and who thus may not have the ready skills). Under these circumstances, the staffing specialist must rely on inference regarding potential, which is usually based on assessment of traits or qualities that might be considered building blocks. Many of the traits or qualities thought to be applicable to most jobs fall into this category. To illustrate, applicants who have higher levels of "cognitive ability," are "cooperative," and have "good work habits" are more likely to succeed in a teamwork environment than those who do not, all else being equal. All of these qualities seem to be relevant to teamwork, yet they can describe someone who has not yet had much actual team experience.

Assessment of building-block traits is often done using paper and pencil or computer-administered tests. Stevens and Campion have developed a test used successfully to screen applicants for team positions.[19] The items reflect both team-relevant knowledge and ability to reason, the latter also useful in most team settings.

Assessing the ability of candidates is often done as a sequential process. Thus references or evidence of accomplishment of the initial pool is reviewed first. Those who seem more suitable are then invited in for testing. Those who test well are asked to schedule an interview. Although this can be done in one day, it is more common to take several days or even weeks.

Each assessment episode is likely to provide additional information and insights regarding the applicant's true capabilities and style. On the other hand, as can be seen from this example, there are costs as well. For instance, each assessment hurdle must be carefully considered, viewed as needed, and developed before it can be put in place. Moreover, administering or managing assessments demands the time of both the HR person (or managers involved) *and* the applicant. Finally, information from multiple sources must still be summarized and integrated meaningfully. This involves considering such things as the validity and reliability of the "hurdle" and, given the particular attributes covered, the relative weight to be given to scores obtained from each assessment. Only hurdles that are really necessary and useful should be retained and weighted.

In principle, it is possible for a given trait or quality to be assessed using many of the assessment techniques mentioned. To assess an applicant regarding a team-relevant attribute such as "conscientiousness," we use referees or work history, a work sample, an interview, or a test designed to get at this quality. All are possibilities. It is likely that certain qualities (for example, cognitive ability) are best inferred from information gathered using a particular approach (perhaps a paper-and-pencil test). Some attributes are hard to assess; they may be poorly defined (what does it mean to be a team player?). Similarly, the quality may not reveal itself under normal assessment circumstances (a person's ethical philosophy can rarely be tested). Also, there may be no established measure for the concept. With this in mind, we offer Exhibit 3.3 to illustrate how particular techniques might be differentially useful for assessment, depending on the KSAO of interest.

Exhibit 3.3. Examples of Sources of Data for Assessment.

KSAO	Referees	Interview	Paper and pencil test	Work history	Assessment center
Cognitive ability			X		
Conscientiousness		X		X	X
Written communication skills				X	X
Interpositional knowledge		X		X	X
Interpersonal competence				X	X
Team orientation	X	X	X	X	X
Conflict management skills	X			X	X
Presentation skills	X	X		X	X
Organizational knowledge		X		X	X

Under special circumstances, the HR specialist or manager first wants to verify that the trait or quality is indeed "real" and important. Then, in all likelihood, he or she contracts for some original scale or instrument development work to be done by an industrial/organizational psychologist.

A caveat: systematic and scientific personnel selection does not guarantee that only the right kind of people are hired for a team assignment. It can only improve the odds of this occurring. But to do so, certain conditions must be in effect, several of which have already been touched upon. For example, it is imperative to have a clear idea of just what traits or qualities are needed even before recruiting starts. Similarly, it is prudent to try to create as large a pool of potential candidates for the position as possible, to increase the likelihood that someone with the right mix of skills and abilities is included and available for discovery. It also seems well advised to take multiple assessments, perhaps over some reasonable period of time (as with the multiple hurdle model) to ensure that you obtain insights regarding an applicant's more typical behavior. But most important, it is critical that whatever measures are used for assessment have some (not necessarily perfect) validity. Whatever assessment device is used, professional standards require use of some validation strategy. It is critical that the individual charged with team staffing use a validation approach, as required by the "Uniform Guidelines on Employee Selection Procedures."[20]

A final consideration is that staffing for different team types calls for appropriate approaches. Exhibit 3.4 describes helpful tools, depending on the type of team and the staffing challenges implied.

Selection Decision and Hiring

Based on the results of assessment, a decision is made for each candidate. Even at this phase, the decision process depends on the type of team as well as the team's needs. If team members are involved in actual assessment of candidates, their input is likely to be considered in the selection decision. However, sometimes the final decision is made by one individual. For example, a chief executive officer may consider team members' opinions but have the final say in who should become a top management team member. Similarly, a unit manager might have the authority to staff a project team, albeit with input from a team leader.

HR is typically involved in most hiring processes. A member from this department contacts the successful applicant and discusses compensation and benefits issues in closing the deal. Again, this varies by team. For ad hoc teams using existing employees, less-formal processes are followed.

Exhibit 3.4. Assessment Tools Emphasized for Different Types of Teams.

Team type	Past performance	Referee	Interview	Assessment center	Paper and pencil test
Management	X	X	X		
Project	X	X		X	X
Production			X	X	X
Service	X		X	X	X
Action and performing	X		X	X	X
Parallel		X			

Team members are generally "hired" or chosen by the team leader or other team members.

Orientation and Initial Training

The effectiveness of teams is affected by the assumption that new hires must be ready, willing, and able to perform at the time they are brought on board. That is, the staffing problem is to recruit, screen, and select fully capable individuals. Alternatively, the organization may have in place a variety of mechanisms designed to orient and train individuals in the skills and abilities needed to work well in teams. In this case, the team staffing problem is to locate and hire people with potential (that is, with appropriate work values and aptitudes). Supervisors' training and performance management efforts then bring out this potential. In most organizations, the goal is probably somewhere in between.

The staffing process is built around training practices and must complement them. In particular, it must emphasize KSAOs unlikely to develop in training or on the job. Staffing must take account of whether newly hired people have access to training, as well as the likely effectiveness of the training for individuals and for whole teams. An adequate team staffing process can fail to meet its objectives if other team support is not in place.

Special Considerations

The role of the team leader is a critical consideration. The designers of the team must decide how much authority the leader is given. Additionally, they must decide whether the staffing needs should be built around the leader's strengths and weaknesses. Diversity of gender, race, background, and ideas is necessary for the team to produce a credible work product.

Political and practical issues are important as well. Individuals are often on teams because they reflect certain political realities. At other times, they are members because of their functional expertise. Thus, a team member represents a constituency in teamwork as well as himself or herself. For example, a union leader may be chosen as a member of a labor relations committee because of the union representational role.

THE CASE OF THE GREEN-FIELD SCENARIO

Typically, a green-field situation implies that an organization is in a position to build a business, product line, or facility from scratch. It may simply replicate a design used before (as in a franchise), but most of the time management takes advantage of an opportunity and chooses to innovate with regard to physical space, technology, work policies, or practices.

Team staffing and start-ups of this sort are linked in several ways. For the most part, in today's world a start-up project's planning and implementation are often done by teams (indeed, in the case of a new manufacturing facility, many sets of teams). Sometimes these are called task forces or project teams. Moreover, many new operations being put in place are designed and built around team-based management thinking. That is, the products to be manufactured, stored, or delivered, or the services to be provided, are made so by people working in teams. In any start-up, these have to be designed with due regard to the business practices used. More to the point, they have to be staffed eventually with appropriate personnel. Finally, the transition to the new facility or practice itself presents challenges. It can involve organizational transformation, which has to be managed, and typically calls for teams created for the purpose.

Some teams are temporary (a task force) while others last longer (a new production team). Some are staffed by current employees; others are staffed by temporary employees or new hires. Some are one of a kind (the Olympic basketball dream team), while others are among many with the same general role (account management teams). Some are expected to relate closely to other teams, and others operate with relative independence. Some are cross-functional, others more or less homogeneous. Finally, teams vary in the number of hierarchical levels they include. Each of these differences poses unique needs for staffing.

A special feature of a pure start-up is the potential for a staffing specialist to attempt to bring together the best combination of people to accomplish the team's goal. Starting from scratch implies that one is unconstrained by existing commitments to people. Although this gives a lot of flexibility, it also presents a challenge. Very little research exists regarding how best to build a team. But as pointed out earlier, there are some logical strategies. One often starts with trying to recruit, select, and hire whoever has the most task-critical skills. The assumption is that resources expended in the search here are well spent. Alternatively, one might start by doing the same for people whose skills are very much in demand. In both instances, one then backfills with other types of team talent needed.

In some cases (as in certain committees, projects, and task forces), staffing takes on additional, political considerations. Thus the quality of the people brought on first (or those who decline first) fulfills what might be called a "signaling" function. That is, getting someone good to serve on or lead a team is interpreted by others (especially those who are also being recruited) as a sign that the team's mission is important or that the team is likely to succeed. Both considerations affect the quality of the pool of individuals, some of whom will be selected. The message here is clear: staffing a start-up under these circumstances involves recruiting the most respected individuals.

BEST PRACTICES

Our work in the area of team staffing suggests that the process is often done unsystematically. Despite the fact that team staffing is contingent upon so many issues—such as the type of team, the staffing situation, and the organizational culture—there are still ways to increase the quality of the process. Here are some critical issues that those responsible for team staffing should pay attention to:

- *Use a staffing process that takes account of the type of team.* Different kinds of teams have varying needs for staffing.

- *Understand the team's role in the organization, the team's division of labor, and the function of the position.* This helps staffing specialists determine the KSAOs necessary to be an effective team member, as well as the requirements necessary for the team as a whole to be effective.

- *Conduct teamwork analysis to identify critical KSAOs.* If the job includes not only individual position requirements but also team task management, team process management, and team boundary management activities, it is not sufficient to conduct a job analysis. Rather, it is necessary to analyze the entire team to determine the necessary KSAOs for the job.

- *Pay attention to political issues.* As with traditional staffing, political issues can play a large role in team staffing. A person may be justifiably selected for a team by virtue of representing a certain political role or constituency. Awareness of this type of issue and how it plays out in the team's functioning is important.

- *Choose the most effective and efficient selection tools.* Staffing specialists should conduct linkage analyses to determine just which tools and strategies are best to assess those KSAOs deemed important to the position and the team. One must consider the logic and logistics of selection techniques as well.

- *Determine the type of validation strategy to use.* Be it content, criterion, or construct validation, ensure that you conduct the appropriate type of validation so that you have support for the selection decisions that you make.

- *Consider who is to do the assessment.* Given the culture and climate of the organization, determine which organizational members can best select new team members, if trained in the use of the tools.

- *Carefully assemble and integrate information.* Candidates are usually assessed through multiple methods, by several people, over a period of time. This means that a great deal of information is generated. It is good practice to create a database to capture and summarize the information as an aid to decision making.

- *There is some safety in numbers.* Those responsible for offers should all work from the same information base. All other things equal, those candidates for whom there is a positive consensus across evaluators and decision makers should be made offers first. On the other hand, some effort should be extended to review candidates for whom there is mixed but strong support.

- *Include human resources.* HR representatives should, in most cases, play an active role in all of the steps involved in team staffing. After all, they are the professionals in this area.

- *Manage the staffing process after the first selection decisions.* Because of the dynamic nature of organizations and teams, team staffing needs are likely to continue after selection. Create and update selection processes likely to be used in the future. Choose a process manager to ensure that systems are in place and that quality is upheld.

- *Staffing is only a start.* Good selection decisions are necessary but not sufficient for an effective team. Training, leadership, organizational culture, and other factors are also important, as other chapters of this book discuss.

PART TWO

LEADING, TRAINING, MEASURING, AND REWARDING TEAMS

4

THE ROLES OF LEADERS
IN HIGH-PERFORMANCE TEAMS

Stephen J. Zaccaro, Michelle A. Marks

EFFECTIVE TEAMS REQUIRE effective leadership. Despite its self-evidence, many have ignored this simple statement. Indeed, the current vogue of self-managing teams might appear to obviate the need for team leadership, by distributing the functions of the role to team members. However, "even the most autonomous, independent, or otherwise self-reliant work teams need some direction, support, and/or linkage to their organization's larger supra-system."[1] A recent book on team leadership makes the same point: "It was a short time ago when many practitioners believed teams and leadership were mutually exclusive. We believed somehow that teams which were empowered, autonomous, high-performing, self-managing, or otherwise set apart from traditional supervisor/subordinate relationships were also devoid of leadership, not unlike a ship without a rudder. . . . If leadership is missing, the team's direction becomes unclear."[2]

This chapter is about leadership roles. As organizations have become more dynamic and team-based over the last few years, these roles are changing. To be effective, leaders now need to use a greater variety of influence strategies, such as consensus building, persuasion, and sense making. The ambiguity that has always confronted top management is beginning to affect middle-level and even lower-level leaders as well. Indeed, increasing use of self-managing teams raises significant questions about the purpose of their position in organizations.

Leadership roles exist in all groups, even self-managing teams. Team leaders have responsibilities significantly different from those of other members, and successful accomplishment is critical for team success. Broadly defined, a leader role is a formalized position of authority in which the incumbent is responsible for

- Linking the team to its external constituencies, stakeholders, and larger external environment
- Establishing strategic and operational directions for team action based on these linkages
- Facilitating team operations to accomplish these directions

These universal leadership roles appear to exist for leaders in all types of organizational teams and at all levels. However, in the spirit of this book, we maintain that leadership is very much contextual—how these leadership functions are accomplished varies by the type of team and by the position of the leader within the organization. For example, first-line supervisors typically lead small-scale organizational units. A major focus of their leadership is to direct and coordinate the activities of individual team members. Their midlevel counterparts lead units composed of multiple teams; thus interteam coordination becomes a major aspect of their responsibilities. At the top of the organization, executives have the responsibility for providing the vision and strategic directions for the organization as a whole. To help their organizations succeed, they need to create a climate that lights a fire, not *under* their followers but *within* them. They also need to extend to organizational units the resources they need to be effective.

Most organizations have at least a minimum hierarchical structure. They can also be viewed as linked networks of teams. Thus organizational effectiveness requires that leaders align their teams with other teams at the same level, and with teams at levels above and below them. This alignment centers on the strategic direction established by organizational executives. It also involves coordinating team activities and resources with those assigned to other teams. Creating and maintaining this alignment is perhaps one of the most crucial aspects of the leader's role.

This chapter has five purposes. The first is to identify and describe several key leadership functions that are critical for team and organizational effectiveness. Our emphasis is on three basic leadership functions: managing the team's external linkages, providing the direction for team action, managing the internal dynamics of the team. Our second purpose is to describe how these basic roles change for leaders at different organizational levels. The third is to consider leader roles in the six different types of teams defined by Sundstrom in the first chapter. (To review, they are management, project, production, service, action or performing, and parallel teams; refer to the first chapter for descriptions of the team types.) Our fourth purpose is to describe the organizational support mechanisms needed for individuals to succeed as leaders. Finally, we describe some best practices for leader roles in team-based organizations.

The five purposes aside, the chapter is divided into five sections. In the first, we begin our description of leader roles with a case study of a team-based organization that illustrates the nature and importance of leader roles at different organizational levels. Section two examines central leadership functions, while section three describes how these functions vary by organizational level and by the type of organizational team. Section four considers the organizational support required for successful leadership. The final section summarizes the best practices that are indicated throughout the chapter.

CASE STUDY OF LEADERSHIP ROLES: THE BOEING 777 PROJECT

The importance of leadership is most apparent in times of change in an organization. Effective leaders, particularly those at the top of the organization, recognize the necessity for change and develop the policies, structures, and climate to facilitate change. Other leaders, typically those at lower organizational levels, accept and implement the new policies and structure. They also contribute to elaboration of the culture parameters established by organizational executives. It is partly through these processes that leaders add value to teams and organizations.

This value is apparent in the activities of the top leaders who were responsible for the Boeing 777 project. It represented a cultural shift for the Boeing Corporation, in terms of how managers and employees relate to one another and how airplanes are designed and made. The vision behind this project was developed by Frank Shrontz, the CEO and chairman. He envisioned a manufacturing process that was (1) customer friendly, (2) technologically advanced, (3) functionally interdisciplinary, and (4) more efficient in terms of product delivery. These goals became the basis for a new way of operating that Shrontz urged his company to adopt.[3]

Top executives establish a vision for change, one that would align the organization more effectively with a rapidly changing environment. For

Boeing in the late 1980s, military defense spending was responsible for up to 50 percent of its business. Thus, the end of the cold war, with its attendant decrease in military spending, along with the worst downturn in the history of the airline manufacturing industry created a critical need for Boeing to change some of its ways in order to remain successful. Accordingly, Shrontz sought to reposition Boeing in its commercial and military businesses by developing new product lines, and to open new avenues of business for potential Boeing products.[4] His vision provided both a new direction for the company and a new manufacturing philosophy that was to guide the company's internal operations. This vision become the basis for Shrontz's interactions with his top managers as he facilitated the emergence of a consensus regarding how the operational culture of Boeing should change.

The operational implementation of this vision and philosophy was accomplished by many Boeing managers, but particularly Philip Conduit, who at various times during the developmental phase of the 777 jet was general manager of the Boeing 777 division, executive vice president of the Boeing commercial airplane group, and president of the corporation. Another important contributor was Alan Mulally, who was vice president of engineering for the 777 division and, after Conduit moved up, general manager for the division. Both men have been described by their colleagues and employees as people-oriented and having the ability to integrate different functional perspectives. Accordingly, they shared in the philosophy and values espoused by Shrontz.

Conduit was operationally responsible for developing the new manufacturing process of the Boeing 777 project. His approach incorporated three key elements: a computer-based "design-build" process, input from the customer/client (that is, the major airlines) early in the design stage, and a cross-functional, team-based organization.[5] The new design process allowed engineers to develop sophisticated computer models of the developing airplane instead of paper or mock-up versions, thereby cutting design time significantly. Permitting the airlines (customers) to have input early in the design stage allowed major savings in money and time during the development period. Finally, cross-functional teams were used to facilitate more effective communication among people of different functional specialties, such as engineers, production managers, finance people, marketing specialists, and suppliers. This approach led to a reduction of more than 50 percent in engineering and design problems.[6] Furthermore, the leadership of these teams varied with the stages, from engineers early in the design stage to manufacturing specialists in the production stage.[7]

Note that these operational and structural changes followed from the visionary direction established by Shrontz; they were technologically advanced, customer friendly, and functionally interdisciplinary. Conduit's implementation illustrated the role of leaders who report to the CEO: to parlay visionary principles into operational plans and to give direction to lower organizational levels.

Mulally and other operational managers were responsible for developing in detail the team-based approach for the Boeing 777 project. They created a three-level hierarchy of cross-functional design-build teams.[8] The top level was a team of the five or six executive managers from each discipline involved in the project. This team met once a week, received reports from managers at the second layer, and coordinated the design-and-development process. Thus, they established the direction and operational parameters for the entire project.

The second tier was composed of teams of twenty-five to thirty-two people, who communicated with the top management group and met to resolve major problems such as scheduling delays and conflicts with suppliers. They also developed operational plans for the more than two hundred work teams that formed the bottom layer of this organization. These work teams each had five to fifteen workers, also from various disciplines, who were responsible for different parts of the plane.[9]

Several aspects of this structure are particularly noteworthy. First, all of the teams are cross-disciplinary in composition—from the top management team to each of the functional work teams at the lowest level. Second, teams develop norms for decision making that preclude a strong *intra*disciplinary focus. As indicated by one team member, "We have a no-messenger rule. Team members must make decisions on the spot. They can't run back to their functions for permission."[10] Such a norm creates important support for the kind of cross-functional environment envisioned by Shrontz and Conduit.

A third aspect is the two-way perspective of managers in the middle group.[11] They are responsible for providing information to the top management group and representing their constituencies. At the same time, they have to represent the policies and operational strategies of this top group to the two-hundred-some work teams. They also need to resolve problems that cross the activities of various teams and provide direction for these teams.

The value of this structure was in facilitating communication and information upward and downward in the organization, and across different functional specialty groups. This promoted a degree of *vertical alignment* that was necessary for organizational success. However, a problem emerged among the work teams at the bottom level. Each one concentrated on designing and building specific parts of the new plane. Thus, Boeing found that some teams were creating design elements that conflicted with those developed by other teams. To solve this problem, they formed five integration teams, who were tasked with facilitating information flow among the various cross-functional design teams and resolving team conflicts. In one example, where two work teams placed different oxygen and air flow systems in the same place on the plane, an integration team helped the two teams come up with a solution that combined both systems.[12] Although the three-tier management system and the cross-functional teams created a successful vertical alignment, the function of the integration teams was to create horizontal alignment, in which the goals and activities of the various organizational units were oriented in the same direction.

This case study illustrates the several leadership roles we describe in this chapter. Most if not all of the leaders in this organization were responsible for accomplishing, to a greater or smaller degree, three basic functions:

1. Understanding the requirements and demands of the teams' and organization's external stakeholders, that is, acting as the liaison to these stakeholders

2. Developing the direction and operational strategies for the organization and its teams

3. Managing and coordinating the operational activities of the various organizational units and members

How these functions were completed changed at various organizational levels. Shrontz developed a vision for the company that emerged from his understanding of changes in the larger environment and his anticipation of future changes in customer and client demands. His direction setting reflected a long time frame that transcended any individual project within the Boeing Corporation. His operational management and coordination consisted of urging and building consensus on the cultural and organizational climate changes he felt were necessary for Boeing to succeed. He also was responsible for selecting the top managers (such as Conduit) who were to put into operation his strategic vision.

Conduit and his managerial team developed the specific organizational structure and employee empowerment philosophy for the Boeing 777 project in a manner that reflected Shrontz's principles. Managers at the various levels were responsible for developing these plans further and translating them into monthly and daily activities. Also, each team leader was responsible for linking his or her team with teams and leaders at higher (and in the case of upper and middle managers, lower) levels, and with teams and units at the same level. Thus leaders at every level engaged in linking activities, direction setting, and operational coordination.

The success of this team-based organizational structure is self-evident for Boeing. Design problems were cut significantly during the development stage.[13] A year after being introduced into the market, the Boeing 777 was operating at a 97.7 percent reliability rate (measured as on-time departures), which was described as the best yet for a new Boeing jet.[14] As of fall 1997, more than three hundred 777 jets had been ordered from major airlines worldwide.

This success was driven by many factors; however, the effective leadership of Frank Shrontz, Phil Conduit, Alan Mulally, and other team leaders at all organizational levels contributed significantly to the effort. In the remainder of this chapter, we describe in more detail the three leadership roles outlined in this case study. We begin with a model of leadership, linking leader roles to team effectiveness

LEADERSHIP ROLES

The leader roles we describe in this chapter are grounded in a functional approach to leadership.

Functional Leadership

There are few conceptual models of how leadership processes lead to team effectiveness.[15] But one perspective of leadership, the functional leadership approach, specifically addresses in broad terms the leader's relationship to the team.[16] The central assertion of the functional approach to leadership is that the leader's job is to do, or arrange to get done, whatever is needed for the group to function. "If a leader manages, by whatever means, to ensure that all functions critical to both task accomplishment and group maintenance are adequately taken care of, then the leader has done his or her job well."[17]

This perspective defines leadership as *social problem solving*, where leaders are responsible for (1) diagnosing any problems that could potentially impede group and organizational goal attainment, (2) generating and planning appropriate solutions, and (3) implementing solutions within typically complex social domains.[18] Three important leader roles follow from this definition. The first is *team liaison.* Because most team problems originate from their environment, diagnosis requires that leaders be attuned to developments and events outside the team.[19] Indeed, vigilance, environmental scanning, and forecasting are the leadership functions linking the team to its external environment.[20] Further, the team leader is responsible for interpreting tasks assigned to the team. In the army, for example, company commanders and platoon leaders are typically required to translate their superiors' intent into collective action. Although this translation is likely to involve multiple leadership activities, a primary one is acquisition of information regarding the team's mission and the resources required to complete it.

The second leader role suggested by the functional perspective of team leadership is *team direction setter.* Team action occurs with a purpose. It is typically up to the leader to establish the purpose. The nature of this direction can be as broad as a "vision" or as narrow as a task assignment. It can short-, medium-, or long-term in focus. Regardless of its scope, the direction established by the leader provides the raison d'être for the group's internal dynamics. Further, an effective leader establishes a direction for the group that keeps it aligned with its operating environment. Here is where the leader's role of liaison is critical. The leader needs to develop an understanding of the team's external context thorough enough that the direction he or she establishes for the team is consistent with the performance expectations of the team's stakeholders.

The third role is *team operational coordinator.* To facilitate team effectiveness, team leaders often require that appropriate member contributions be identified, and they often establish how best to combine them.[21] They are required, during collective action, to establish, coordinate, and monitor the correct timing, sequence, and level of individual actions. They are required to review and interpret accurately these actions and their consequences. They make changes in team action patterns that no longer fit environmental demands. Finally, team effectiveness requires that leaders establish and maintain the appropriate psychological climate in the team. All of these requirements concern internal maintenance of team dynamics, so that the team can continue to respond effectively to its constituencies and stakeholders.

These activities can be distributed to other team members, as they often are in self-managing teams. However, before this can happen, team leaders need to enable the team to accomplish these activities on its own. They do this by staffing the team with individuals who already possess leadership skills, or they develop these skills in existing team members. Further, they establish the conditions under which the team disburses leadership. This means they form the norms, standards, goals, and rules that guide how team members work together in accomplishing leadership functions. Thus, even in fully self-leading or self-managing teams, the basis for team effectiveness is established a priori by formal leaders.

The activities in these three fundamental leadership roles are intertwined. The leader's understanding of the team's operating environment forms the basis for the direction established for the team; this direction in turn determines the most appropriate internal structure and combination of member contributions within the team. As the team performs effectively, it alters its operating environment by changing the expectations of its constituencies and enhancing its overall position within the organization. Finally, effective leaders often proactively follow their own vision for the team. This means that they attempt to influence the team's operating environment to provide more support and resources for their team. For example, middle organizational managers establish goals and priorities for their departments and lobby top executives to support the direction they wish to establish. If successful, these managers change the operating context for their team, making it a more supportive one.

Leader as Team Liaison

The leader's liaison role within the team or organization consists of three sets of activities: networking, sense making, and representing. Networking concerns establishment of information sources within and outside the team; (in top management teams, these sources necessarily exist outside of the organization). Developing these information sources is a critical task for team leaders. From these sources, team leaders gain the information they need to frame the direction to be established for the team. They also need information contacts to determine how well the team is meeting the expectations of its external constituencies.

Where do team leaders develop information contacts? First, because they need to be aware of how, where, and when to acquire team resources, suppliers have an important place in their information network. Note that the word *suppliers* refers to sources of both material and personnel resources. Second, team leaders need to know about the disposition of team products. Accordingly, customers, clients, and related constituencies are nurtured as sources of information. Third, team leaders cultivate contacts among their peers within and outside the organization. The information provided by these sources helps the leader determine the effectiveness of the team relative to other organizational units. Finally, the effective leader needs to network within the industry and within his or her profession. Information from these sources can portend longer-term environmental changes to which the team needs to respond if it is to be effective.

Acquiring information is not enough. Team leadership requires making sense of this information in a manner that is helpful to other team members. Sense making provides a "frame of reference" for team action.[22] This is a causal map of the team's operating environment that denotes the forces, events, and dynamics influencing the external performance expectations for the team. A well-developed frame of reference helps team members understand what they must accomplish as a team, as well as why they must accomplish it. It gives meaning to their collective activities. Thus, an essential team leadership task is to develop a coherent understanding of information acquired through the established networks.

Team representation occurs in two directions. First, team leaders represent the performance expectations of external constituencies to the other team members. In teams at lower organizational levels, such as production and service teams, leaders serve as the central conduit from upper management and the team's customers. At the top of the organization, team executives convey the expectations of constituencies outside the organization, such as stockholders, regulatory agencies, and financial institutions.

Second, team leaders represent their teams to external constituencies. The goal of this representation is twofold: to safeguard the interests of the team in the organization as a whole, and to shape the operating environment in a manner that maximizes support for the team. Thus, successful team leadership is likely to produce greater ease in resource acquisition, and more enthusiastic clamor for team products.

Why is the team leader's liaison role important for team effectiveness? When team leaders form networks with leaders of other organizational units and represent the requirements of these units to their team, they promote interunit coordination for their team. They also facilitate alignment of the team with its operating environment. Information networks also provide the grist for group information processing. Teams develop plans for collective action based on the information they acquire about performance expectations and task parameters. An essential aspect of team cognitive processes is forming accurate individual and team "mental models," or structured knowledge about the team, its responsibilities, and its operating environment. The frame of reference developed through leader sense making becomes encoded in these models and provides meaning for subsequent team planning and actions.

Leadership and Team Direction Setting

A major purpose of a leader's liaison and external linking activities is to develop the appropriate direction for team action. Trends and forces in the team's environment dictate several possible courses for the team or organization. The team's stakeholders in turn convey a bevy of expectations that are often contradictory. A central role of the team leader is to discern from all of this the most appropriate direction for the team, given its resources and capabilities.

This is not to say that the leader's direction setting is entirely reactive. Many strong leaders have a vision for their team and organization and are skilled enough to manage their operating environment to implement the vision. Visions are statements of preference about what a leader believes his or her team or organization *should* be. Accordingly, these statements reflect the primary value orientation of the visionary. They also influence how team leaders interact with constituencies in their team's operating environment and the choices they make about competing expectations from these team stakeholders.

To be useful, a leader's vision needs to be translated into long-term strategies; shorter-term operational strategies; and then goals, plans, and tasks. Otherwise, it remains amorphous and withers away. Generally, in an organization top executives and top management teams establish a vision and a long-term strategy. Managers and team leaders at the next operational levels are then responsible for translating this strategy into operational strategies for various organizational units. Lower-level unit leaders in turn form team goals and task assignments from these operational strategies.

This vertical translation suggests two important distinctions about the direction setting of leaders at different levels: (1) direction setting proceeds from more ambiguous information at higher organizational levels and (2) direction setting reflects a longer time frame at higher organizational levels. The quality of team direction is how well it aligns the team with the trends and expectations in a changing environment. Leaders of a top management team, who are typically trying to develop a strategic direction for the organization as a whole, need to respond to more stakeholders, more performance expectations, and more environmental trends than leaders of production and service teams do. For this reason, the information networks of top management team leaders need to be more widespread and diverse than those of leaders at lower organizational levels. Typically, the broad direction and operating strategies have already been established for leaders of teams at these levels by upper management. Their task remains to explain the operational strategies to their fellow team members and translate them into operational goals and plans.

For most organizational team leaders, direction setting takes the form of setting task goals for their teams. Good team goals have certain characteristics:[23]

- They are difficult.
- They are specific.
- They are linked to team resources and capabilities.
- They are measurable.
- They are the basis for team feedback and rewards.
- They generate commitment.
- They are flexible and adaptive.
- They are coordinated vertically with other organizational goals.
- They are coordinated horizontally with other team and unit goals.

Difficult and specific goals are more likely to lead to higher performance than easy or vague goals.[24] Difficult goals push team members to work harder. Specific goals facilitate task planning and development of performance strategies. Thus, team leaders need to establish goals for their team that fit within the operational strategy the organization has established for their team but that reflect the maximum potential of team capabilities.

However, team goals cannot exceed team resources. Leaders who establish goals and tasks that cannot be accomplished, given the limits of the potential skills, knowledge, expertise, and material resources possessed by the team, obviously risk failure and team demoralization. Thus, when setting goals, leaders need to carefully consider the individual and collective capabilities of the team. If the requisite capabilities are not already present, then team leaders need to link team goals with strategies for developing these capabilities.

Team goals need to be measurable so they can serve as parameters of team success and the bases for feedback to individual team members. The specificity of a goal forms the basis for measuring progress toward the goal. For example, if a team leader sets a goal of increasing the team's production of a new product line by 20 percent, then he or she also has to establish the means of measuring team success, that is, attainment of a 20 percent production increase.

For team goals to engender team performance, members need to commit to them. To accomplish this, leaders must link team goal attainment to personal goal attainment. They can do this by establishing team goals that consider the collective aspirations of team members. Or they can associate member self-concepts to team and organizational outcomes. This association can occur by (1) increasing the intrinsic value of team members' work-related efforts such that work becomes a more salient component of their self-concept; (2) empowering subordinates such that their self-esteem or self-worth, and by extension their self-efficacy, is enhanced; (3) increasing the intrinsic value of goal accomplishment by clarifying the meaning of subordinate effort and associating daily efforts to an overall mission or vision; and (4) enhancing subordinates' faith in a better future.[25] Although these aspects of team leadership fall more readily into the category of operational management, the contents and structure of the team goals established by the leader play an important role in developing team member commitment to team goals.

A mistake made by many team leaders is to establish team direction, with corresponding goals, and then refuse to adapt when change is warranted by environmental circumstances. The purpose of establishing team direction is to facilitate alignment between the team and its environment. This alignment, not the specific direction or goal, is the critical barometer of team effectiveness. Thus, leaders need to be ready to modify team goals when they are no longer adaptive. This can be disconcerting to team members, but leaders can assist team adaptation by explaining the rationale for change (this harkens to the leader's role as team liaison and sense maker). Further, one role of upper-level and middle-level organizational leaders is to provide the information that alerts their direct report team leaders to the need to change direction.

Because organizational teams are units in a larger system, their leaders need to work together to ensure coherence and integration of team goals and directions.[26] Obviously, there needs to be vertical integration, where goals established for teams at one level are congruent with the operating strategies established at higher levels. Likewise, the operating strategies developed for whole divisions within the organization must be linked to the long-term strategy and vision developed by the top management team.

Horizontal goal integration is just as important. Organizations cannot work well if different units are pulling in opposing directions. Thus team leaders at various organizational levels need to align the goals of their team with those of other units at the same operating level.

Thus far, we have provided a number of prescriptions for the leader's direction-setting role. Why are these prescriptions necessary for the team to be effective? Direction setting by the leader influences team effectiveness by focusing the energy and activities of team members so that they are consistent with the performance expectations of team stakeholders. Establishing the purpose of action provides it with meaning. Team members are more motivated to work hard if their actions have meaning for the organization. For this reason, leaders need to link the directions they set for their teams with the rationale for these directions within the larger organizational context.

Direction setting also has important cognitive influences. First, establishing goals leads to activation of member expertise and to cuing of established task plans and strategies. If the performance situation facing the team is a novel or complex one, where existing team strategies are inadequate, then team goals—especially hard, specific ones—motivate the cognitive work necessary to develop new task strategies.[27] When team members develop a plan and implement it, goals serve as a mechanism of control. They are the basis for feedback about how the group is progressing; further, they motivate change if the team is perceived to be off track. That is, goals prompt individual and team processes (cognitive and behavioral) to reduce discrepancies between where the group is and where it ought to be.

We have already noted the importance of direction setting for team coordination. Goals and strategies serve to organize the activities of multiple organizational units and members. They define the common purpose for collective action. Of course, such integration cannot occur without a great deal of intervention by the organizational leaders who are implementing organizational directions. Nonetheless, establishing these directions is what drives the processes of vertical and horizontal coordination.

Leadership and Team Operational Management

In treatments of team leadership, operational management is often given the most coverage. However, this aspect of team leadership cannot proceed effectively without external linking and direction setting. Linking activities bring the information that team leaders and members need to use in planning. Also, as we have noted, the direction established by leaders responsible for the team focuses planning and is the basis for determining whether the team is successful.

Operational management refers to the leader's management and organization of the team's internal structure, task assignments, workflow, and system monitoring. Once team direction is translated into goals and strategies, team leaders need to (1) identify task needs and requirements, (2) develop and evaluate possible solutions, and (3) select the most appropriate solution and plan its implementation using available team resources. Team leadership also involves effective communication of solution plans to team members. This communication needs to convey specific information:

- The actions required for solution implementation
- How these actions need to be coordinated
- What situation constitutes task or mission accomplishment

Two other aspects of operational coordination are, first, selecting and managing team members in accordance with the overall purpose of the team within the organizational structure, and, second, coordinating the material resources needed to complete team tasks.[28] The first activity involves obtaining, developing, and motivating team members. Team leaders cannot establish anew the knowledge, skills, and attitudes necessary in team members to complete a task each time it is assigned. Instead, good team leaders lay the groundwork for effective teamwork in the future by nurturing and developing team members. Whenever teams then need to address task assignments, members more readily respond to and implement the plans and performance strategies developed by team leaders.

Team operational management also requires that team leaders procure adequate material resources and use them effectively for team action. Lack of such resources cripples team efforts, regardless of the motivation of team members and the quality of a leader's solutions and performance strategies.[29]

These leader performance functions emphasize primarily the leader's response to team problems, which include generating possible solutions, planning the most appropriate performance strategy, and coordinating team members in implementing the plan. These functions represent how effective leaders respond when facilitating team goal attainment, particularly in complex and dynamic environments.[30]

The influence of this role on team effectiveness is almost self-evident. Nonetheless, the leader's ability to influence team effectiveness depends very much on how he or she accomplishes these managerial functions. For example, a central responsibility of team leaders is to motivate and energize their fellow members to work hard on behalf of the team.[31] One fundamental approach is to raise the team's "collective efficacy," the team members' belief that, collectively, they can succeed in the face of most challenges they are likely to face.[32] If team members believe their team is capable of achieving its goals, that is, being successful, they are more likely to choose to engage the task.[33] Strong team efficacy beliefs emerge in part from (1) a history of successful achievement, (2) observation of modeled behaviors that lead to successful performance, and (3) persuasion and social influence processes.[34] Effective leaders use one or more of these strategies to build task confidence in the teams.[35] They model appropriate task strategies, allowing newly developing teams (or new team members) to acquire collective task competencies. They also model teamwork, or how team members should work together. By their actions, such leaders establish the acceptable interaction patterns in the team. If they model and promote idea exchange, constructive criticism, and mutual support, the team is likely to feel more efficacious with respect to its assigned tasks.

Team efficacy also emerges from leaders who exhort their members to work hard and do well. This is related to the empowerment processes of transformational and inspirational leaders.[36] By their actions,[37] such leaders fuse each member's personal goals with the team or organizational mission. Team members identify at a personal level with the purpose and goals of the collective as a whole and are therefore more committed to their accomplishment.[38] Thus, transformational leadership is fundamentally directed at aligning the motive states of individual members with the purpose of the team as a whole.[39] Team leaders who continuously link the member's personal goals and team goals, and persuade their team that it can successfully meet the goals, enhance the efficacy of their team as a whole and the state of empowerment within the team.

There are stages in leadership influence on development and maintenance of successful team coordination processes.[40] First, leaders need to facilitate identification and combination of the contributions from team members that are most likely to lead to task success. This means developing their own awareness, as well as that of the collective, of what resources are available to the team. This identification is followed by leader planning of how to effectively combine and integrate these resources.

The second step is for leaders to offer training, instruction, and opportunities for team members to learn the roles and tasks that need to be integrated into effective teamwork. The focus is not so much on learning individual roles but rather on developing the interaction patterns necessary for team success. Finally, the team leader needs to facilitate development of mechanisms that regulate and standardize these patterns. Ideally, once these are established, they are reinforced by the team members themselves as they monitor their joint actions.

These steps produce regulated coordination patterns in the team. However, they do not necessarily foster team adaptation, a key element in team effectiveness; indeed, they may cause the team to become more rigid in its responses within a dynamic environment, particularly if these patterns were successful in earlier tasks. If team complexity increases to the point that established interaction patterns are not sufficient, the team leader needs to reconsider team resources, recombine them into more viable coordination patterns, and reorient team regulation mechanisms.[41] Also, to promote team adaption, team leaders need to foster displays of flexibility and creativity among team members, albeit within the confines of team task requirements and environmental conditions.

Effective team coordination, decision making, and performance means that team members must have an accurate shared understanding of their operating environment and how, as a team, they need to respond. A major responsibility of the leader is to facilitate this collective understanding. Shared mental models of expected team and member actions serve as key mechanisms by which leaders structure and regulate team performance. Leaders develop in the members an understanding of the team's tasks within the organization's overall strategy, the action steps necessary to complete their tasks, and the role requirements for each member in collective performance. In essence, team leaders convey their own understanding and mental model of the problem situation as derived from their external linking activities. Thus, leadership processes and the quality of a team leader's mental models become key determinants of subsequent team mental models. Further, team mental models mediate the influence of leadership on team coordination and team performance.

This argument suggests a process of leader-team performance that begins with development of a leader's mental representation of a problem situation. This mental model reflects not only the components of the problem confronting the team but also the environmental and organizational contingencies that define the larger context of team action. Here, the leader develops a model of what the team problem is and what solutions are possible in this context, given particular environmental and organizational constraints and resources. This *problem model* then drives the development of a team interaction model that encodes how the team ought to respond to the problem situation. The leader forms this second mental model from his or her own understanding of team capabilities and the resources of individual team members in the context of the problem at hand.[42]

The next step in this process of leader-team performance is to communicate the leader's mental model of team action to the members. This step is a critical one for leaders because if they develop a perfect plan for team problem solving but cannot communicate the model or plan effectively to the team, then the team response is inadequate. If this communication is successful, team members form and share an accurate model of expected behaviors and role requirements in accordance with their assigned mission and the problem they need to confront.[43]

Another influence of leadership on team cognitive processes is to facilitate the information processing activities engaged by the team as it accomplishes its task. Indeed, the leader often "takes over" several of these processes (problem construction, definition of solution alternatives, and implementation planning), especially early in the team's development. However, this does not obviate involvement of other team members in these responsibilities. Indeed, in constructing team problems, deriving solutions, and planning their implementation, team leaders draw heavily on the functional expertise and diversity within the team. In effect, they coordinate the contribution and combination of team knowledge and information resources; where gaps occur, they make interpretations and decisions that move the team along.[44]

One of the most critical influences of leadership on the cognitive processes underlying team effectiveness is to encourage collective "metacognitive" thinking in the team, especially after major task engagements.[45] Metacognition refers to reflection upon the cognitive processes used in problem solving; in essence it represents "knowledge and cognition about cognitive phenomena."[46] Sternberg and his colleagues also define metacognitive processes as executive functions that control application and operation of cognitive abilities and skills.[47]

To achieve a high level of expertise that promotes adaptation in a dynamic operating environment, team members need to set aside time to consider, individually and collectively, the consequences of their strategies, how they considered and arrived at a team solution, and how they worked together to implement selected solutions. This is a difficult process to initiate and complete successfully. Once teams have succeeded at a task, members may not see the need for reflecting upon collective information processing and interaction patterns; likewise, if they fail, they are more likely to engage in such reflection—but it may be focused on "fixing blame," with negative consequences for subsequent team cohesion and efficacy. The team leader needs to manage this process so that it occurs when necessary and is a constructive exercise that strengthens the team.

CONTEXTUAL INFLUENCES ON LEADERSHIP

We have defined three basic leadership roles in teams. We have argued that these roles are universal in that all organizational team leaders are required to engage in these roles to some degree. However, there are many influences on how team leaders complete these roles. In this section, we talk about two of these, *organizational level* and *type of work team*.

Organizational Level

Table 4.1 describes how leader roles differ at three organizational levels.

EXTERNAL LINKAGE AND LIAISON. For executive leaders at the top of the organization, liaison and linking activities occur with diverse stakeholders outside of the organization as a whole. In these linkages, they represent the entire organization. Their task is to understand the organization's operating environment, which is likely to be complex and ambiguous. Thus, more than their counterparts at lower organizational levels, these leaders need to establish larger information and social networks. They also must spend more time with these sources, seeking to understand the broad operating environment. Therefore top managers are typically more externally focused than managers at lower levels.[48]

A number of researchers who have made extensive observations of organizational leaders note that executives spend a proportionally larger amount of their time engaged in liaison activities than lower-level managers do, and that the focus of this linking is decidedly more external (to the organization).[49] Indeed, when Conduit was recently elected Boeing's new chairman, replacing Shrontz, he was described as having to maintain more contacts with U.S. governmental officials and foreign leaders and be less involved in company operations than before.[50]

The linking and liaison activities of midlevel managers reflect a two-way perspective,[51] where they provide the link between top organizational management and the work teams at lower levels. This linkage has several functions: (1) to provide upper management with information about company operations that are critical to their strategic decision making, (2) represent top management's perspective to lower-level work units, and (3) represent the perspective of work units to upper management. These functions are necessary for successful vertical alignment within organizations.

Middle managers typically coordinate multiple work units. Thus, more than is the case for managers at other levels, they need to work

Table 4.1. Differences in Leader Roles
by Organizational Levels.

Leader's level	Roles	Role expectations
Top level	External linkage and liaison	Links with diverse external stakeholders
		Represent organization as a whole
		More ambiguous environment; requires broad information net
		Need to devote more time to sense making
		Develop organizationwide frame of reference
	Direction setting	Long time perspective to develop vision and broad strategy
		Span of direction setting includes multiple large organizational units
	Operational coordination	Develop consensus
		Establish new policies and structures
		Select top operational managers
Middle level	External linkage and liaison	Two-way perspective; creating vertical alignment
		Focus also on horizontal alignment
		Less ambiguous environment; information sources increasingly inside organization
		Translate frame of reference developed by top executives
	Direction setting	Medium-term perspective; establish operational strategies and goals
	Operational coordination	Indirect supervision
		Interteam coordination
		Elaborate new policies and structures
Lower level	External linkage and liaison	Upward perspective; facilitating vertical alignment
		Focus also on horizontal alignment
		Information sources almost entirely inside organization
		Highly structured operating environment; translate strategies developed by middle managers

Table 4.1. Differences in Leader Roles
by Organizational Levels, cont'd.

Leader's level	Roles	Role expectations
Lower level	Direction setting	Short-term perspective
		Establish work team and small-unit goals and tasks
	Operational coordination	Direct supervision
		Single-unit coordination
		Implement established policies and structures

with other middle managers to create an effective horizontal alignment. Also, unlike upper-level executives, the information network of middle managers is likely to be more internal to the organization, with the goal of facilitating horizontal and vertical alignment. External linkages are likely to be with suppliers and middle managers from customer organizations. Whereas top executives use their external linkages to gain better understanding of the organization's operating environment, middle managers link with external stakeholders to resolve operational issues and problems.

Leaders of teams that operate at lower levels of the organization interact with other units on the same organizational level, with suppliers who sell resources directly to the production units, and with their immediate supervisors. They also need to coordinate closely with the other organizational units with whom they are aligned in organizational action. The major liaison activity for team leaders at this level, however, is to translate the frame of reference and strategies developed at upper and middle organizational levels into daily and monthly work plans for their units.

DIRECTION SETTING. At the top of the organization, leader direction making may take the form of a vision, defined as a desired image of the organization within its environment at some specified future point in time. This vision then becomes the basis for strategic planning by organizational executives and for leader direction setting at lower organizational levels. Thus at middle organizational levels leaders translate organizational (or system-level) visions into subsystem goals and strategies. Likewise, at the lowest levels of organizational leadership, managers convert strategies developed by their superiors into relatively short-term goals and tasks for their units.

Top management team leaders are required to set directions reflecting a long time frame. For example, John Kotter noted from his interviews and observations of top executives that they operated within time frames spanning from five to twenty years.[52] In recent interviews, both Shrontz and Conduit, in their successive roles as Boeing CEO, described likely changes and major competitors for Boeing from a twenty-year time frame.[53] Also, some of their strategic plans (supersonic transport, work on the space station, satellites, and space travel) were clearly grounded in the year 2005 and beyond.[54]

As top executives reach agreement on long-term strategies for the organization, a key focus of middle-level team managers is to translate these strategies into shorter-term (one-to-five-year) operational strategies. Team leaders at the middle and lower levels of the organization then translate these operating strategies into still-shorter-term (immediate to one-year) tasks and goals. Thus, in the Boeing 777 project, successive general managers Conduit and Mulally put into place a manufacturing process that reflected Shrontz's vision and produced the first 777 jets in roughly a five-year time frame. The leaders of the various work teams developed the short-term goals and plans for the parts of the plane assigned to their respective teams.

OPERATIONAL COORDINATION AND MANAGEMENT. Operational management involves implementing vision or strategies within the organization. At the top level, this entails both structural or policy changes as well as changes in the climate of the organization. At lower levels, internal management involves allocating and distributing resources in line with formulated directions. It also includes empowering organizational personnel and enhancing collective motivation. At each of the levels, decisions are made that reflect different time perspectives, with shorter time frames operative at lower levels. For example, top executives implement structural and climatic changes that are expected to endure over a long period of time. At lower levels, the expected time frame of resource and tasking decisions is shorter.

At the level of work teams, leadership involves direct supervision of single organizational units in which leaders define short-term unit tasks and goals within the context of objectives established at higher levels. Problems confronting the leader are fairly concrete and reflect a short time frame. They typically concern resolution of immediate conflicts, crises, and emergencies that can impede production.[55]

At the middle-management level, leadership becomes increasingly more indirect; leaders manage multiple units or subsystems of the organization, each with its own supervisor. With their multiple components, problems at this level are more complex but still fairly well defined. The time horizon for these problems is longer than for lower-level managers. One of the central roles of middle managers is to translate the even longer-term perspectives, strategies, and objectives established at top organizational levels into concrete, short-term objectives for first-line managers. They also need to allocate organizational resources among functional units in line with organizational objectives. The major task for managers at this level is to coordinate multiple organizational units.

At top levels, operational management takes the form of three executive functions. The first is to urge and develop a consensus around the executive's visionary principles and long-term strategic plans. The second is to select the division chief operating officers and other operational managers who are primarily responsible for implementing these plans. The third is to acquire and distribute to various organizational divisions the resources necessary for strategic plans to be accomplished. Executive interactions with subordinates are to be more persuasive and collegial than authoritarian. Collegial interactions are more likely to engender enthusiastic support and employee empowerment than are autocratic interactions.

Type of Team

The nature of leadership roles varies according to the type of team being led. In the first chapter of this book, Sundstrom defined six team types: management, project, production, service, action and performing, and parallel teams. To review, each team type varies in terms of (1) its typical level of authority within the organization, (2) the permanence of its existence, (3) the temporal urgency of its interdependence with other units, and (4) its degree of specialization. We would add that the types of groups are likely to differ in terms of the functional diversity across team members and the level of the organization at which they are most likely to operate. Accordingly, the nature of leadership and how leaders accomplish their roles of liaison person, direction setter, and operational manager vary according to the type of group they lead.

MANAGEMENT TEAMS. Top management teams have high group authority, permanent status, variable external linkages, and high functional diversity. Operational management extends indirectly to the entire organization. Most members of management teams lead other teams. A primary focus of leadership in management teams is coordination of multiple organizational units.

The permanence of management teams means that their planning time frames are likely to extend further into the future. Also, the greater functional diversity in management teams allows team leaders to distribute environmental scanning activities to other team members. Each team member, having a different area specialization, is likely to contribute information sources to the leader's network that would otherwise not be available. Thus, leaders of management groups generally develop larger social and information networks than do managers of teams with less diversity.

Greater functional diversity in top management teams also gives the leader more capacity for making sense of the team's or organization's operating environment.[56] Such teams can bring a range of perspectives to interpretation of environmental information, and perhaps produce a more accurate frame of reference for the organization as a whole. For this to happen, team leaders must soften lines of authority and develop team norms that facilitate constructive cognitive conflict while avoiding affective conflict. An appropriate team climate that supports exchange of interpretation means that team members are more likely to contribute to meaning making, as regards patterns in the team's operating environment. A nonsupportive climate results in team members' adopting the frame of reference developed by the team leader, even if it is an inaccurate one.

PROJECT TEAMS. As with top management teams, project teams are likely to have greater functional diversity. Thus they also afford the leader greater networking, environmental scanning, and sense-making capabilities. However, they typically have temporary status, moderate to low group authority, and low external linkages. The temporary status of the team means that it is generally given directions that are short-term in focus (although their work may have long-term implications). The work of project teams typically focuses on accomplishing specific tasks that require a variety of specialized contributions. Functional leadership responsibilities in such teams may be rotated according to the expertise needed at a particular stage in the team's work. However, the formal leader (for example, the chairperson) of the project team needs to focus on coordinating the handoff of these responsibilities when appropriate.

PRODUCTION AND SERVICE TEAMS. Production and service teams have moderate to low group authority, permanent status (although service teams can be temporary), time-urgent linkages, and low functional diversity. Leaders are concerned primarily with team management and supervision. Operating environments are fairly predictable, having been structured by higher-ranking managers. Also, team directions are established by the leader's superiors; the major responsibility of the team leader, then, is to translate team goals into operational plans.

The time-urgent external linkages of production and service teams in terms of working with other organizational units influence the leader's time frame of action. Leaders in high-linkage teams are likely to be more reactive and have a shorter time frame for action than leaders of teams having linkages of low time urgency. Leaders of high-linkage teams need to shape their teams to be able to adapt quickly to environmental and task contingencies. This means that members are trained in collective quick-response strategies (and in service teams given greater responsibility for environmental scanning and decision making). Leaders of such teams must spend considerable time in horizontal and vertical alignment activities, so that their team's rapid responses do not interfere with the actions of other organizational units.

ACTION AND PERFORMING TEAMS. Action teams have moderate authority, temporary or permanent status, highly time-urgent external linkages, and typically moderate levels of diversity. They tend to operate at low and middle levels of the organization. Such teams are typically composed of highly skilled individuals whose combined capabilities are crucial for collective success (performance is highly interdependent, with examples being surgery teams, rapid-response teams, and sports teams). Performance events are likely to be very discrete, often calling for urgent and specialized responses. Leaders of such teams, more than other types of organizational teams, need to be especially attuned to performance conditions in the operating environment so that the team is aware of the parameters required in its responses. Thus, team leaders spend an inordinate amount of time defining action requirements for a particular performance event, and structuring team responses accordingly (as with a coach preparing the team for a game against a particular opponent).

The operational management responsibilities of action team leaders depend heavily upon whether the team has temporary or permanent status. If the team is a permanent one, then members are likely to understand each other better and have a good sense of how each of them will act in a typical performance event. The role of the leader, here, is to make sure that typical team performance patterns are adapted to the unique requirements of a particular situation. Many of the other operational responsibilities are likely to be adopted by other team members. For example, sport teams that have been together for a while may not need much guidance from the leader on how to work together; any such leadership can come from team captains. Instead, team coaches are likely to focus on how to best combine member capabilities so as to address an upcoming opponent.

If the action team is temporary, then members come together for specific performance events (airplane crews, surgical teams). Even though they may have worked with one or more of their fellow members in previous performance episodes, they are generally unfamiliar with the team constituted as a whole. Instead, members trust that each person is skilled and knowledgeable enough (from highly specialized training) that they can respond as a team to performance requirements. Leaders of such teams have two primary operational responsibilities: to help ameliorate any coordination problems early in the team's tenure, and to be aware of any performance contingencies that are not reflected in prior member training or fairly unique in the team members' experience. Thus, a leader of a plane crew or a surgical team intervenes rather forcefully if an emergency situation arises that requires unusual response from the team. In other situations, team members operate according to routine and well-trained patterns and require little intervention from team leaders.

PARALLEL TEAMS. Such teams operate on a limited, often temporary, and independent basis within the organization. They have low to moderate authority, low external linkages, and moderate levels of functional diversity. Such teams have a specific mandate and disband when the mandate is completed (examples being committees charged with ad hoc rule making, contract awards, or personnel selection). Leaders of such teams are more likely to serve as administrative coordinators and chairpersons than as supervisors with strong authority. Their operational responsibilities are likely to consist of coordinating assignment of task responsibilities and integrating member contributions into a final team product. Their major liaison responsibilities typically consist of clarifying the mandate from those organizational constituencies responsible for establishing the team. They also need to discern the permissible parameters of team products. Thus for example, leaders of personnel selection teams learn from relevant organizational stakeholders what kinds of qualities or characteristics they need in potential candidates.

SUMMARY. The nature of the work team informs leadership activities. The higher the team's authority, the more its leader is responsible for setting the direction of both the team and organization (as with top management teams). Thus they require environmental scanning to determine the best direction for their constituencies. If the team is highly diverse in terms of functional specialization (for example, top management teams), then the leader has more resources for environmental scanning and interpretation; however, more energy must be focused on team coordination and resolving the almost inevitable conflicts. The temporal status of the group determines the time frame of the team's direction setting, with temporary teams having a shorter time frame. Finally, the external linkages of the team determine how much time the team leader should devote to vertical and horizontal integration.

These points mean that the conduct of leadership varies significantly with the type of team, as articulated in Chapter One. However, the fundamental roles of team leaders described in our chapter remain the same. For all teams, leaders need to engage in liaison, direction setting, and operational management activities. Leaders of various types of teams differ only in how much relative emphasis to place on each role and how each is to be accomplished.

ORGANIZATIONAL SUPPORT FOR LEADERSHIP ROLES

A variety of organizational support mechanisms contribute significantly to leaders' being able to accomplish the roles we have described in this chapter. First, leader responsibilities must be clearly defined at all levels of the organization. Leaders should have a clear understanding of what they are to accomplish with their subordinates and the nature of their reporting relationships to their superiors. This kind of understanding is engendered by leaders at top executive levels and cascades down through various organizational levels and work units. It requires a high level of communication directed at role clarity and articulation of team responsibilities, particularly in relation to the roles and responsibilities of other team leaders.

Second, top leaders have to establish a climate that promotes employee participation in company decision making. This is the process of developing empowerment. The sharing process can be difficult for team leaders who perceive that they are "losing power." However, if empowerment is valued from the top of the organization, then team leaders at all levels become comfortable in this process. (A particularly dysfunctional situation is one where team leaders are told to share decision making with their subordinates but are not given similar opportunities with their own superiors.) This organizationwide empowerment climate was a major aspect of the Boeing 777 project, with employees at all levels expected to be partners in the project.

A third support mechanism is the selection system used to identify the leaders having the right knowledge, skills, abilities, and work orientation to lead different types and at different organization levels. Conduit, who was selected by Shrontz to run the Boeing 777 project, was described by his subordinates, peers, and colleagues as being approachable and a good communicator, with an ability to get individuals of different perspectives to work well together. He was an engineer with a strong technical background. He also allowed a great deal of subordinate participation in his decision making. These qualities were critical for management of the innovative Boeing 777 design-build manufacturing teams.[57] Upon promotion to CEO, the press commented that Conduit had a global view, the ability to see the big picture and envision the future ten to fifteen years hence,[58] qualities necessary for success at the top level. Placing the right leaders in top positions promotes leader effectiveness at lower organizational levels.

This is, of course, more easily written than done. Successful leader selection is often based on effective leader development and assessment systems that have operated throughout a leader's time in an organization. Organizations need to establish an assessment and feedback system that helps leaders identify their strengths and weaknesses early in their careers. This system should incorporate a 360-degree process, where leaders are receiving feedback and performance evaluations not only from their superiors but from their peers and subordinates as well. This kind of feedback system is likely to be more effective in promoting change and improvement in multiple performance areas than are more traditional evaluation systems.

Organizations also need to establish a system and climate of supportive coaching and mentoring. Leaders model the behaviors of their superiors, particularly early in their careers. If their superiors are not supportive and do not model appropriate leadership functions, they themselves are likely to mirror the same behaviors with their subordinates. However, by mentoring and coaching young leaders, appropriate role behaviors emerge more readily. Further, young leaders learn that such support is expected for their subordinates.

Leader development programs need to focus on developing the more complex cognitive and social competencies required for leadership positions at higher organizational levels. A consistent theme in the literature on managerial and executive development is that such skills develop from training and work experiences that push the leader to the limit of current skills and competencies. When these comfortable patterns of thinking and behaving no longer suffice in completing required work assignments, the individuals likely to succeed at higher levels of organizational leadership are those who can develop new and functional frames of reference and behavior patterns.[59]

A central focus of managerial development, then, should be to provide challenging work assignments to potential executive leaders that push them to construct new approaches to leadership in a more complex operating environment. These stretch assignments can be grouped into five categories[60]:

1. Transitions: the manager moves to a new position or is assigned new functional responsibilities.

2. Creating change: the manager is given responsibility for decisions that could entail changes in current organizational policies or components.

3. High level of responsibility: the manager is assigned tasks and projects having significant consequences for the organization. These tasks demand resolution of complex problems that entail more boundary spanning than do tasks with less responsibility.

4. Nonauthority relationships: the manager must cultivate new forms of social influence that are likely to be more operative at the executive ranks.

5. Obstacles: the manager learns how to cope successfully with the difficulties engendered by circumstances posing obstacles.

Successful leader development programs that support the emergence of effective leader roles in the organizations should have some or all of these characteristics.

Finally, organizational support for effective leadership often means that dysfunctional leaders have to be terminated or limited in their scope of influence. Even though this is quite self-evident, many organizations are reluctant to recognize and remove ineffective leaders. However, the continued influence of such leaders inhibits and interferes with other leaders' effectively accomplishing their own responsibilities. Sometimes the most important support that an organization can provide for effective leadership is to remove those leaders who are ineffective and either unwilling or unable to develop better ways of operating.

SUMMARY AND BEST PRACTICES

In this chapter, we have outlined three major roles associated with effective organizational leadership: team liaison, direction setter, and operational coordinator. These roles are essential performance requirements for leaders at all organizational levels, but how they are enacted varies with the leader's place in an organizational hierarchy and how many layers exist in it. Further, the roles are inextricably bound up in effective leadership. As the team leader scans the team's operating environment and acts as a liaison, the appropriate direction for team action should come into focus. This focus, in turn, becomes the basis for specifying team goals and plans. Finally, the leader's management of team and organizational operations should be grounded in these goals.

If the leader fails to enact one of these roles, other roles are rendered deficient. Team direction cannot be set without an accurate understanding of its responsibilities and challenges from the operating environment. Even so, a clear direction grounded in accurate interpretation of environmental dynamics is not helpful if leaders do not follow with effective operational management of the team such that team goals are met. Finally, the leader cannot interpret the team's operating environment and develop a direction without having a thorough understanding of his or her team and its capabilities. Thus, an effective leader can successfully enact all of these roles, even in complex organizational environments.

Specifying these roles leads to some best practices for effective leadership. There is a significant amount of research on managerial activities linked to leader effectiveness and organizational performance.[61] We conclude this chapter with a delineation of specific activities, grouped under the three specified leadership roles, that constitute some best practices associated with organizational leadership.

Team Liaison

As team liaison, the leader's major responsibility is to be acutely attuned to the team's operating environment and make sense of acquired information. Accordingly, leaders should

- Develop information networks with all relevant constituencies and stakeholders
- Use networks, particularly when the team's operating environment becomes uncertain or team actions are potentially risky
- Interpret and clarify for team members information acquired from the environment
- Anticipate and address external obstacles to successful team action
- Coordinate team goals and activities with goals and actions of other teams

Team Direction Setter

As team direction setter, the leader helps the team establish its purpose and goals:

- Establish clear, difficult, specific goals[62] congruent with the time frame and work requirements
- Explain how achieving team goals helps the team succeed in its environment
- Translate long-term goals into short-term goals; translate goals into operational plans

Team Operational Coordinator

The leader's operational management of the team requires developing team members, motivating collective action, and coordinating members' contributions:

- Develop the knowledge, skills, and capabilities of subordinates in line with task requirements
- Create a sense of strong self and collective efficacy in team members
- Emphasize coaching instead of supervising
- Foster team empowerment and self-management as much as possible
- Give performance feedback in the context of individual and team goals
- Offer opportunities for postperformance reviews and reflection

TRAINING FOR TEAM EFFECTIVENESS

Michael J. Stevens, Michael E. Yarish

AN INFORMATIVE NATIONAL survey of managers identified training as a key factor in the success of work teams, and inadequate training the greatest hindrance to effective team performance.[1] Training is especially important as organizations make the transition from a traditional, hierarchical style of management to one based on empowered teams. It is risky to assume current employees will have the necessary knowledge and skills; it is prudent to provide training designed to support effective work teams.

Many successful, team-based organizations dedicate substantial resources to team training. For example, Motorola delivered more than one hundred thousand training hours and budgeted $120 million for education in one year. At the Corning company, team members spend 5 percent of their work time in training, at a cost of 3 percent of the payroll.[2] In 1990 alone, by one estimate, industrial corporations spent as much as $40 billion on all training programs.[3] Managers may wonder whether their training dollars are spent wisely. Unfortunately, team training is all too often treated as a fad, designed without properly assessing how and where it is needed, and inadequately evaluated.

This chapter describes how training can be properly designed, delivered, and evaluated to support work teams. We have four purposes:

1. To present a case example of an organization that successfully used training in making the transition to a team-based structure

2. To describe the training process as applied to team-based organizations, including needs assessment, design and delivery, and evaluation of training

3. To outline the unique training needs of different types of teams

4. To summarize the current best practices for training in team-based organizations

The chapter has four sections, one for each of these purposes.

CASE EXAMPLE: PHELPS DODGE COPPER REFINERY AND ROD MILL, EL PASO

The Phelps Dodge Corporation is among the world's largest and most productive manufacturers of copper and copper-related products. It employs more than fifteen thousand people around the world and operates mines and manufacturing facilities in twenty-seven countries. In 1996, the corporation had one of its most successful years ever, despite a drop in world copper prices of 25–30 percent during the year. Dividends were up 11 percent, stock value reached an all-time high, copper production grew by more than 50 percent relative to the previous three years (without a commensurate increase in capital expenditures), and its rate of recordable accidents was about one-fifth that of the industry norm. Although corporate performance in the metals industry is clearly a function of numerous economic and financial variables, in a January 1997 company newsletter, the vice president and general manager of mining operations described the role of teamwork this way: "Teamwork is the key to making our organizations more efficient. By working together in teams, we brainstorm, solve problems, and implement good ideas that help us make copper more safely, more easily, more efficiently, and less expensively." This vice president closed by stating that "Teamwork is the best way to tap all the mental power available to us to take full advantage of our people resources."[4] Although the gains of the parent company are certainly impressive, we limit our discussion here to the experience of just one of its operations, a large copper refinery and rod mill in El Paso, Texas, with approximately 750 employees.

The Phelps Dodge copper refinery in El Paso began operation in 1929, while the rod mill was built adjacent to it in 1969. Over the years, the refinery has experienced the long and traditionally adversarial history of unionization typical of the industry. In 1985, however, a decertification election successfully removed the union from the refinery's operations and opened the way for a more cooperative relationship between management and employees.[5] In November 1991, the plant manager began a new generation of improvements in participative management with the formation of work teams across all the 500 hourly and 250 exempt employees at the refinery. The change was motivated primarily by the plant manager's personal conviction that cooperative involvement of all employees would be the key to spurring the El Paso refinery to greater levels of safety,[6] production, quality, and profitability through cost containment.

The objective was to take naturally existing work units and organize them into cohesive teams that would eventually assume responsibility for improving operations in their areas of the refinery. Initially, the teams would continue to report to an assigned supervisor or member of management, referred to as the "coach." The coach was to operate in the role of facilitator for the team and was also to assume overall accountability for team performance, but eventually the teams were expected to move toward self-management. In making the transition to the new teams, training was the only viable support system available as an option to management. Relying on the staffing function was not possible since the workforce was very stable (average company tenure was 16.1 years) and turnover was rare except for occasional retirements. Changes in the reward system were not seen as feasible at the time. Retaining the current structure was preferred, given technology, workflows, and current levels of capitalization. Opportunities for systematic work redesign were limited. That left training.

Though much of the intensive groundwork was done early on, the entire process of implementing the teams across the plant, including both line and office support staff, spanned just over four years. When the last team officially graduated from the forty-hour in-house training program, the refinery operation was completely organized into fifty-eight teams with three to seventeen members each.

Team Implementation

When the team concept was introduced, its implementation called for five specific steps (described next). Because plant management did not include anyone with an adequate level of expertise needed to guide the process, they wisely turned to outside expertise for help.

STEP ONE: STRATEGIC PLANNING. An initial strategy session involved the top managers and key middle managers. As the concept of managing via empowered teams was introduced, core values and beliefs were explored, questions were addressed, and unanimity of support was sought and obtained. This strategic planning process reviewed the overall implications and demands of making such a profound change in how the plant manages its people and systems, makes decisions, allocates work duties and assignments, and so on. A steering committee was appointed from this top team and charged with developing an operational plan for introducing the program and its concept to the entire plant. Eventually, it was decided that the introduction should be made by the plant's top managers in a series of short, consecutive meetings staggered to reach all the refinery employees working the various shifts of the 'round-the-clock operation. This would be followed by bulletin board announcements and a letter mailed to the residence of each employee.

STEP TWO: STEERING TEAM OVERSIGHT. The next step involved setting up a permanent steering team charged with oversight and coordination of the implementation process. Managers were appointed from key functional areas of the plant: production, finance, engineering, quality, human resources, and administrative support. They met periodically to set specific goals, identify required activities, and develop realistic completion dates. An onsite facilitator from the external consulting firm was also appointed at this time to identify (via needs analysis) and eventually oversee delivery of the training that would be required.

STEP THREE: MANAGER AND SUPERVISOR TRAINING. The third step began almost immediately: training all plant management and supervisory personnel in the team concept. One of the crucial challenges in a transition to a team-based organization involves reshaping the roles of managers and supervisors. They must learn to function without relying on the trappings or "perks" of formal authority, and instead lead through empowerment. During the early stages of implementation, the teams reported to supervisors or managers who were supposed to be operating as team coaches or facilitators. In this sense, the teams were not truly self-directed but would have a degree of traditional managerial oversight. The supervisory training was designed to get managers to move away from a directive style of management toward a facilitative one. Training included such topics as introduction to the philosophy of participative management, what it means to be an empowering leader, and coaching for commitment rather than compliance. Benefits of this new role for managers were emphasized. Training consisted of twenty hours of classroom instruction conducted in five one-half-day sessions.

STEP FOUR: IDENTIFICATION OF PILOT ACTION TEAMS. The fourth step consisted of identifying and organizing a select number of pilot "action teams" from among the refinery's hourly and nonexempt employees to set the pace for the rest of the plant. Pilot teams consisted of naturally occurring work units and were initially selected based upon the criteria of (1) consistent, adequate demand for the team's product or service, (2) natural workflow among team members, (3) easily measured output or results, and (4) naturally positive relationships among team members. After some spirited discussion, two teams were eventually identified to begin the extensive training and preparation that would be required.

STEP FIVE: PHASED TRAINING FOR TEAMS. The next step involved further communication with all employees in the plant. Pilot teams were identified in announcements on bulletin boards and the plant newsletter, and a kickoff event was held. Pilot teams were the first to receive the forty hours of classroom training; other teams followed in staggered phases through the plant.

On the basis of a training needs assessment, the knowledge, skills, and abilities (or KSAs) needed by team members were identified. From this, training topics were selected:

- Introduction to the team concept
- Managing group dynamics
- Conducting effective team meetings
- Total quality training
- Goal setting for teams
- Team problem solving
- Managing individual team members' differences (that is, personality profiling)
- Team building
- Interpersonal communication skills
- Constructive conflict resolution
- Collaborative decision making
- Diversity

The first two pilot teams graduated from the training program in January 1992, followed by seventeen more teams that year and an additional seventeen teams in 1993. Eleven teams completed the training in 1994, four finished in 1995, and the remaining seven teams graduated by the fall of 1996. In all, it took nearly four years before the last of the refinery's fifty-eight teams completed the required training. Although the company had originally turned to outside experts for help with implementing the transition to teams, it quickly became apparent that the magnitude and expense of the operation was so significant that they eventually hired the external consultant as a full-time employee to serve as director of the plant's own in-house training and development department. In addition, three refinery supervisors entered the training department as full-time trainers for the teams.

The Next Generation of Teams

After the training was complete, Phelps Dodge–El Paso started making plans to move to fully self-managed teams. Up to that point, all fifty-eight teams reported to a supervisor or member of management. However, some of the more effective teams evolved quite naturally to the point of requiring little supervision. Instead of letting this evolution continue informally, the plant's management team explicitly adopted the objective of moving to fully self-managed teams. A new vision statement articulated the commitment to provide training and other required resources, and to make the policy changes necessary to expand the concept to the remaining two hundred rod mill employees by the end of the decade.

A steering committee was appointed under the direction of the plant's department heads and instructed to develop a set of criteria for formally certifying a team as being self-managed. Eventually, criteria were selected that focused on whether or not the teams demonstrated the maturity or ability to adequately set and meet team goals consistent with company policy and procedure, cooperate with other teams and functional areas within the plant, excel in meeting performance targets (in the areas of safety, quality, production, cost control, and environmental compliance), and demonstrate stability as a team. The steering committee eventually expressed these criteria as a more specific set of guidelines within which the self-managed action teams would be free to operate (see Table 5.1). The forty hours of team training were the basis for ensuring that teams could meet the performance expectations in Table 5.1. Training therefore played an integral part in developing fully self-managed teams.

Table 5.1. Guidelines for Conduct and Regulation of Self-Managed Teams at the Phelps Dodge–El Paso Copper Refinery and Rod Mill.

Teams may	Teams may not	Teams need approval to
Make or change work schedules	Do anything illegal or unethical	Make outside purchases with company funds
Schedule vacations	Violate company policies or rules	Change pay rates
Cover emergency overtime	Discipline employees	Change standard operating procedures
Make job assignments		Change production requirements
Write work orders		
Train and qualify employees		
Review employee performance		
Counsel employees		
Meet and make agreements with other teams		
Stop production in its work area when necessary		
Control overtime		
Achieve team goals in safety, quality, production, and cost		

Source: Phelps Dodge training material; used with permission.

THE TRAINING PROCESS

The Phelps Dodge–El Paso example provides an excellent illustration of how one company went about leveraging its training and development function to support movement to teams. The case shows the three integrated stages of a well-developed training function: (1) training needs assessment, (2) training program design and implementation, and (3) training evaluation. The next three sections of this chapter discuss these three stages and explore in detail how the training and development function can be effectively aligned to assist organizations in making a successful transition to teams.

Training Needs Assessment

When conducting a training needs assessment, managers must recognize that ideally this is a process designed to systematically uncover training needs based on a thorough analysis of (1) the task requirements, (2) the individual employee, and (3) the organization. Ultimately, the training objectives, the design of the program itself, and the criteria for evaluating the training program's success all stem from the findings of the needs assessment. Properly done, the needs assessment uncovers the essential job-related KSAs or other attributes that an individual needs to be an effective contributor in the team environment (either as a working member of the teams or as a member of management overseeing the teams). More often than not, a needs assessment for team training is less than systematic and may be based on simple gut impressions of managers or outside experts as to the required training. However, systematic analysis greatly increases the likelihood that the eventual design and content of the team training program is neither deficient (does not fail to include important training) nor contaminated (does not include unnecessary or unwanted training) in any important aspects and thus is more likely to achieve its intended objectives as efficiently and effectively as possible.

Although much of the specific detail uncovered in a team training needs assessment is unique to a given work situation in a given organization, a few guidelines are useful in a variety of settings. As a helpful way of structuring this discussion on needs assessment, we review training needs as they relate first to assessing task requirements (which includes assessment of taskwork, teamwork, managerial, and intact team training needs), second to assessing the individual employee's training needs, and finally to the organization and its context for the training system.

ASSESSMENT OF TASK REQUIREMENTS. In a traditional nonteam environment, assessment of task requirements for training typically involves systematic review of only the technical performance requirements of the position (sometimes called "taskwork"). In a team environment, however, assessment of task requirements for training invariably looks at more than just the taskwork demands of the position. To be sure, evaluation of taskwork is an essential component in assessing the training needs for teams, but with teams we typically go beyond just the position's technical or operational taskwork demands and examine such components as teamwork-related training needs, managerial and supervisory training needs, and intact team training needs. Each of these elements is discussed in turn next.

Task-related training needs

In production and service work, team members may be expected to gain proficiency at multiple tasks, and to rotate among the jobs done by their teams. Job rotation often requires cross-training and can yield well-established benefits to employee motivation[7] as well as flexibility in staffing. Cross-training also gives employees a broader, systemwide perspective of their jobs and increased capacity for innovative problem solving.

From this integrative perspective, the creative value can be seen in the Phelps Dodge refinery example. Prior to implementation of teamwork, employees who worked in the furnace area had relatively narrow job descriptions and titles such as ladler, tapper, bricklayer, water tender, inspector, control room operator, and so on. However, as a team all employees in the furnace area are now expected (and given incentive) to become cross-trained in as many of these different jobs as possible. Once this happens, employees are then in a position to see and appreciate connections that would go unnoticed from within the "chimneys" of a narrow task-focused job. With an enlarged perspective of the work they do, team members are now in a position to recognize connections that were either viewed as inconsequential before or simply unnoticed. This insight then serves to fuel the creative and innovative problem solving that drives an organization toward genuine continuous improvement and creative breakthroughs. Occasionally, these insights lead to innovations that result in cost savings or improvements worth millions of dollars. More often than not, however, the results are of a less heroic nature, such as when a few thousand dollars are saved because a team figures out how to modify a furnace so that it can use an ordinary spark plug rather than an expensive specialized one, or when labor and overtime costs are reduced as staffing flexibility and process streamlining are used to increase productivity. Though mundane, such minor daily advances carry a tremendous cumulative weight when aggregated over time and across enough teams.

Despite these benefits, cross-training and job rotation are not appropriate for all work teams. For one thing, it can be prohibitively expensive; cross-training increases not only direct training costs but also the costs associated with the slowdown that occurs as team members must work their way up a new learning curve.[8] In addition, cross-training and job rotation are all but impossible for some types of teams (surgical teams, highly specialized military or flight crews, and so on). But when an organization places a strategic premium on the benefits derived through continuous improvement and creative problem solving, a more systematic approach to cross-training and job rotation must be viewed as a critical element in realigning training and development for teams. This need to consider the benefits of cross-training, relative to its costs in a particular situation, merely serves to reinforce the importance of a thorough and comprehensive needs assessment that clearly uncovers the appropriateness of a team training program before it is designed and implemented.

Teamwork-related training needs

Assessing teamwork training needs involves systematic review of the KSAs needed to function effectively as a member of a given team. Previous research has identified two essential categories of teamwork-related KSAs relevant for training and development.[9] The first consists of *interpersonal* KSAs. In team settings, the demands placed on individual members to interact effectively with each other on a personal level are profoundly enlarged, compared to what occurs in a more traditional or autocratic work setting. Team success usually requires (among other things) individual members who can communicate and collaborate effectively, build rapport with one another, manage conflict constructively, encourage productive team discussions, and so on. Table 5.2 lists the interpersonal knowledge and skills required for teamwork.

The second category of essential teamwork-related KSAs consists of those capabilities associated with *self-management* of the team and its members. Certainly, teams vary widely in the degree to which they are empowered to be self-managing, ranging anywhere from fully autonomous to still being directed by a team leader who is a supervisor or member of management. The degree to which teams are self-managing, however, implies almost by definition that many of its essential managerial or supervisory functions are performed collectively by the members of the team. If this is the case, team success also requires (among

Table 5.2. Essential Knowledge, Skills,
and Abilities Relevant to Teamwork Training.

INTERPERSONAL KSAS

Conflict resolution	Ability to foster useful conflict, while minimizing dysfunctional conflict
	Ability to match the conflict management strategy to the nature of the conflict
	Ability to use integrative (win-win) strategies rather than distributive (win-lose) strategies to resolve conflict
Collaborative problem solving	Ability to use the right level of participation for a problem
	Ability to minimize barriers to team problem solving
Communication	Ability to employ open networks of communication
	Ability to communicate openly and supportively
	Ability to use active listening and probing techniques
	Ability to pay attention to nonverbal messages
	Ability to appropriately use everyday socialization (e.g., small talk) to enhance interpersonal relations among team members

SELF-MANAGEMENT KSAS

Goal setting and performance management	Ability to set specific, challenging, and accepted team goals
	Ability to monitor, evaluate, and provide feedback on performance
Planning and task coordination	Ability to coordinate and synchronize tasks, activities, and information
	Ability to establish fair and balanced roles and workloads among team members
Operations management	Ability to run effective and efficient team meetings
	Ability to make operational contributions or improvements

Source: Adapted from Stevens and Campion (1994); used with permission.

other things) individual team members who can help it perform such basic managerial activities as effectively setting goals, planning or coordinating tasks, monitoring individual and team performance, meeting appropriate cost or operational targets, and so on. Although a number of these dimensions are highly task dependent (as with operational targets), much of the remainder involves generic managerial practices and is likely to be relevant to most types of self-directed teams. A detailed summary of these self-management KSAs relevant for teamwork training is also provided in Table 5.2.

For employees in a traditionally autocratic organization, these interpersonal and self-management KSAs are less important. At best, some basic level may be required, such as minimal communication skills that enable an employee simply to understand the scope and content of the directions given by a supervisor, or conflict resolution skills that go no farther than basic familiarity with the company's grievance procedure. The needs assessment stage of aligning the training and development function for teams must therefore analyze the degree to which it is appropriate for instructional programs to include elements that stress development and mastery of these essential interpersonal and self-management competencies. This was clearly the case with the Phelps Dodge–El Paso team training curriculum, where as much as two-thirds of the training content revolved around most of the elements identified in Table 5.2.

The degree to which these teamwork-related KSAs vary from team to team also points to the importance of conducting an appropriate needs assessment before designing and delivering the training program. For example, it was noted above that teams may be deliberately designed with varying levels of self-management (a project management team might be fully autonomous, while a military tank crew would be led in a highly autocratic fashion), making self-management KSAs an issue of either more or less importance for team training, depending on the circumstances. In such cases, the components of a teamwork-related training program must be adapted to the particular requirements of the work done by the team. This helps ensure that training resources are not misdirected.

Managers' and supervisors' training needs

As the transition to self-directed teams occurs, a fundamental shift must also take place with regard to the basic management or supervisory style expressed throughout the organization. In addition to the changing role and task demands for the employees, the comparable demands facing managers and supervisors also change. Rather than functioning in the traditional, autocratic role of directing employees, managers and supervisors must now function as team coaches and facilitators. Further, they must view one of the essential functions of their role as being to ensure that required resources are made available for the teams they oversee, and that disruptive obstacles or barriers are removed. Also, managers and supervisors must function as linking pins to coordinate between the teams and other parts of the organization.

At Phelps Dodge–El Paso, the group of employees perhaps most challenged by the change to teamwork was the supervisors. Much of their challenge revolved around the fact that the new teamwork system was asking them to give up the very authority and control that had historically served to define their place and function within the company. Now they were being asked to relinquish much of that control to the employees on the plant floor, whom they had previously directed. Additionally, the supervisors were also challenged by the inherent difficulties faced whenever someone must unlearn old skill sets and acquire new ones. However, most supervisors at the plant were eventually able to make the transition to a more facilitative style of team leadership, but it first required relinquishing many of their old assumptions, values, and beliefs related to a highly directive supervisory approach and replacing them with new ones consistent with an empowerment philosophy. This was accomplished primarily through the twenty hours of classroom instruction (wherein supervisors were introduced to the philosophy of participative management, explored what it means to be an empowering leader, and practiced how to coach others for commitment), but a needs assessment was first conducted to identify the desired content for the supervisory training program.

Intact team training needs

To function effectively, teams require not only members and managers who possess the requisite skills and abilities (the task-related, interpersonal, self-management, and facilitator/coaching KSAs) but also the appropriate dynamics and processes operating within them at the group level (team cohesion and morale, positive work norms, workload equity, proper team role structure, presence of an open and trusting team climate, etc.) that permit teams to function effectively as a collective unit. With self-directed teams—that is, teams collectively responsible for managing their own internal processes, dynamics, and operations—the training needs assessment should examine the degree to which these internal group processes are critical to team success, and whether or not their mastery should be developed into a team training program.

Although there is a lack of systematic research addressing the question of whether or not it makes sense to train intact teams for their group processes and internal dynamics, experience seems to suggest that training whole teams makes sense for those with long-term assignments, relatively low turnover, and high within-team coordination requirements. This was clearly the case with the teams in the Phelps Dodge example. On the other hand, high turnover of team members and short-lived team assignments tend to eliminate the benefits of intact team training.

Managers should also be sensitive to the types of KSAs being emphasized in the training, because it may be possible to provide a fair amount of learning through instructional techniques outside the specific teams and team members involved. For example, generic conflict management and consensus decision making can be taught in practice training sessions with artificial classroom groups. Part of the implication of this strategy for training needs assessment is that not only must team members learn the characteristics required for effective team functioning (that is, they must acquire a common working model that can serve as a guide in becoming an effectively functioning team); they must also develop a level of comfort with, or mastery of, the actual behaviors that are required to put into place those processes and dynamics needed for team effectiveness. Such issues should be uncovered in the team training needs assessment.

TRAINING NEEDS ASSESSMENT OF THE INDIVIDUAL EMPLOYEE. After assessing task requirements for teams and coaches, the training needs analysis focuses on the needs of the individual employee. This assessment helps identify who within the organization has the requisite KSAs and who does not. It ensures that employees selected for training are the ones who will benefit most from it.

Individuals can vary greatly in their mastery of teamwork skills. For example, the mental health professionals of a state human services agency who form a project task force may already have the interpersonal skills needed to be effective team members but may be lacking in effective meeting or other self-management skills. This suggests a training program emphasizing self-direction rather than interpersonal skills development for this group of employees. Similarly, individual members of a corporate board of directors may have the needed meeting management skills but lack key interpersonal skills. This suggests a training program that is the opposite of the one provided for the mental health professionals.

Managers should be aware that there are a number of different techniques available for appraising the training needs of individual team members and coaches, to determine their training needs. For example, one relatively straightforward approach is simply to collect evaluations or ratings on the individual's current level of proficiency on the knowledge, skill, or ability in question, much as would be done in a traditional performance appraisal rating. As appropriate, these ratings could be provided by such sources as the team leader or some other member of management, coworkers or peers, subordinates, customers (both internal and external), and the individuals themselves. The advantage of gathering these assessment evaluations from multiple sources is that each one typically sees the individual's performance and proficiency from a different perspective and can therefore provide unique or additional insights into the person's relative strengths and weaknesses. However, such ratings are also subject to all of the limitations facing organizations in the use of performance appraisal systems generally (individual bias, perceptual limitations, differing agendas, etc.), so results must be collected and interpreted with caution.

Along with the assessment evaluations or ratings, two additional techniques are available to conduct individual employee training needs assessment: paper-and-pencil evaluations and behavioral simulations. Behavioral simulations are very similar to the traditional assessment center technique in terms of using simulated role-play exercises and trained raters to evaluate the individual's behavior in the role-play. Behavioral simulations are certainly more expensive and time consuming, both in terms of their development and administration, but they are typically rich sources of assessment data based on actual observed behaviors. On the other hand, paper-and-pencil evaluation or testing is much more efficient in terms of its usage and scoring. In addition, there are a wealth of commercial assessment test instruments readily available that have an extensive research record and have proven to be quite valid for many uses (for example, general cognitive ability tests are especially effective at predicting success of training in traditional, academic-style environments). There are also newly emerging paper-and-pencil instruments developed specifically to measure the degree to which individuals possess both the personality traits[10] as well as the skills and abilities for teamwork.[11]

In summary, we can do an individual's training needs assessment by using paper-and-pencil assessments, behavioral simulations, some sort of ratings or evaluations, or possibly a combination of these techniques. Keep in mind, however, that the ultimate objective is to gather critical information as to whether or not the individual has the capability to function effectively in the team environment (either as a manager or a team member). Once this determination is made, individuals can be assigned to a particular training course or program so as to derive the greatest possible value for both the organization and the individual.

NEEDS ASSESSMENT FOR THE ORGANIZATION. Compared to task assessment and individual assessment, organization needs assessment for team training is relatively underdeveloped, in terms of its technical and conceptual foundations. Nonetheless, the organization assessment is still important since its objective is to help us understand how the training system fits into the context or environment of the entire organization. It also helps us identify components or systems within the organization that either facilitate or inhibit effective transfer of training. That is, the organization needs assessment may be viewed as a systemwide review of those factors that potentially have a significant impact on the degree to which a team training program produces the desired changes in behavior back in the job setting.

Unfortunately, "transfer of training" problems are all too common.[12] The training manager must seek to identify barriers to transferring teamwork skills from the classroom. One way to avoid the question of transfer is to use on-the-job training techniques that rely on the supervisor as coach.

Another way to avoid these barriers is to use organization climate surveys to identify potential problem areas. For instance, if a climate survey shows that only a small fraction of employees positively endorse the item "My supervisor listens to my ideas and concerns," then it makes sense to devote a larger portion of the supervisor training curriculum to learning exercises designed to help participants develop better listening skills.

The Phelps Dodge–El Paso case also illustrates how resource constraints serve as an organizational barrier to effective training. In this particular example, managers determined that the scope of the required training was so demanding that it would easily outpace the company's internal capabilities for delivery, and the cost to contract for external training would be prohibitively expensive. Consequently, they found it necessary to set up and staff their own in-house training and development department before they could satisfy the demand for team training.

SHAPING CULTURE AND VALUES THROUGH TRAINING. Although the training needs assessment is intended to analyze the degree to which the current organization and its systems support the transfer of team training back to the job, a valuable question concerns use of training to help create an organization climate or culture conducive to teams. Experience has shown that it can. For example, skilled facilitators can be used to guide top leadership teams through a process of self-discovery in strategic retreats designed to help articulate the key underlying values that guide the organization. A mission or vision statement is often the tangible product of this endeavor. Moving from autocracy to teams inevitably demands organizationwide culture change, which in turn calls for articulating and reshaping basic values, beliefs, and assumptions (see Chapter Two). The organization must start at the top with such a change, or it will inevitably fail.

Strategic leadership retreats are nothing new to organization development facilitators. They have been around for a while but traditionally have focused more on identifying corporate strategies and business directions and less on shaping the organization's culture, values, and beliefs. To fully support the transition to teamwork, training and development professionals are in a unique position to facilitate these strategic efforts so as to help top leadership establish an organizational climate or context that manifests the openness, trust, empowered decision making, flattened hierarchies, team-oriented rewards, and other elements required to support teamwork.

Top-down change of climate and values was clearly evident in the Phelps Dodge–El Paso movement to teams. Though it did not begin with strategic retreats facilitated by the training and development function, nevertheless it did begin at the top, with a plant manager who had enough personal conviction, commitment, and leadership presence to drive the change himself. Eventually, he was able to get the rest of his top management team on board, and through the use of strategic planning sessions he was also able to involve the rest of the plant managers to help shape and guide the change process. Whether this process starts with a facilitated change session or not, the critical lesson from this case is that the change started at the top. This is much like what happens at many other organizations making the successful transition to teams. Sometimes this top-down change in climate and culture occurs because of the spontaneous initiative of an insightful leader, as at Phelps Dodge. But if it does not, skilled facilitators can step in and help the top leadership team make the necessary changes.

In summary, by the time the organization completes the needs assessment in stage one of the team training process, it should have clearly identified the specific training needed, who needs it, and the conditions in which it is to occur. Phelps Dodge–El Paso illustrates how this can be done. In their training needs analysis, managers concluded that all 750 employees would need team member training on such topics as managing team meetings, total quality management, team problem solving, interpersonal communication skills, constructive conflict resolution, and others (recall the earlier list under the heading "Phased Training for Teams"). They also determined that they needed to maintain their current efforts at providing systematic training in process control, quality control, and cost awareness to those teams and team members who needed it. In addition, approximately seventy-five managers and supervisors needed more advanced training on topics related to leading in a team environment (for details, see the earlier list under the heading "Managers' and Supervisors' Training Needs"). Their organization needs analysis also revealed the fact that the scope and logistics of this training effort would be so demanding that they would have to deliver it in-house over a phased-in period of several years to reach everyone effectively. Finally, the needs analysis also found that their internal resources to deliver the required training were inadequate, so they would have to set up and staff their own internal training and development operation first.

Unfortunately, the reality in most organizations is that training needs assessment data are limited at best, frequently involving little more than subjective assumptions made by managers or external consultants. In some cases, it simply reflects an outside expert's perfunctory "assessment" that the organization's training needs match nicely with the expert's training products or services! In any case, even if systematic needs assessment data are not available or cannot be obtained, managers should strive to evaluate their needs as systematically as time and resources allow. Once the training needs have been identified and prioritized, the design-and-implementation stage of team training follows naturally and appropriately.

Training Design and Implementation

Armed with the results from the needs assessment, managers can turn next to the design-and-implementation stage of training targeted to specific needs. This stage focuses on (1) determining specific training objectives, (2) choosing the trainer or outside vendor, (3) developing the curriculum or lesson plan, (4) matching the training program methods and techniques to the curriculum, and (5) actual delivery of the training program itself. We now discuss each in turn.

DETERMINING SPECIFIC TRAINING OBJECTIVES. Although broader training needs are typically identified in the initial needs assessment stage (for instance, the need for teamwork-related KSAs, such as those presented in Table 5.2), more specific program objectives should be articulated to guide design and implementation of a specific training curriculum. For example, although a broad training objective might require that team members be able to help improve quality and lower product defect rates, a more specific curriculum objective might include such things as knowing how to adjust settings on a plastic injection molding machine if they are out of specification, or scoring above 85 percent on an examination covering the particular company's statistical quality control process. To be helpful, such objectives should be as specific, clear, and measurable as possible.

CHOOSING THE TRAINER. Trainers can be external vendors or in-house providers. Each choice has advantages and drawbacks. At least five factors influence the decision to use external trainers. The first is availability of expertise; are there content and process experts on staff, or must we turn to outsider vendors to get it? Second, although fixed costs are higher for staffing and running in-house training, does the scope of its usage allow for the averaging of those costs over time and across a large number of trainees? Third, do we have enough time to develop the needed training programs in-house, or do we need to buy them off-the-shelf right away? Fourth is the potential need to protect proprietary information; do we need to deliver training programs that include proprietary information that must be kept within the company? Finally, there are other miscellaneous considerations; for example, would credibility be enhanced if training were delivered by supervisors or other subject matter experts from within the company, or can outside experts bring a fresh perspective? Once these issues have been addressed, the next step involves actual development of the team training curriculum or lesson plan.

DEVELOPING THE CURRICULUM. At this stage of the process, the specific training objectives are translated into an executable training session or lesson plan. This is where the actual content, timing, and sequencing of training activities are determined. The survey conducted in 1990 by Wellins and his colleagues[13] shows that companies with self-directed teams conduct a wide variety of training on many different topics. Many of the major topics potentially useful for the content of team training follow naturally from the areas targeted in training needs assessment. Exhibit 5.1 presents a summary list of topics frequently found in team training programs. Although the team training topics identified in the exhibit are primarily related to the interpersonal and self-management aspects of team work, they are by no means the only topics common to much team training. That is, job-specific technical or taskwork-related training (such as instruction covering use of equipment and machinery, teaching use of quality or work-flow process management tools, etc.) is a very important topic for production and service teams, especially if they have a cross-training component even though they are not listed in Exhibit 5.1. In addition, proficiency in using facilitation skills and leading others through empowerment are common topics for managerial team training even though they are not presented in the exhibit.

Managers should keep in mind that much of this training content is not appropriate for all teams. For example, team training in a manufacturing environment is likely to include substantial exposure to operational and quality tools, such as flowcharting and statistical process control; however, this same content would not be valuable for the typical project team. Illustrations like this simply reinforce the importance of conducting a valid needs assessment early on, to target program content and design for maximum impact and efficiency.

MATCHING THE INSTRUCTIONAL APPROACH TO THE CURRICULUM. Delivery of team training often involves six approaches: (1) videotapes, (2) traditional classroom lectures, (3) on-the-job activities, (4) role-plays and experiential simulations, (5) self-assessment instruments, and (6) computer-assisted instruction.

Videotape is perhaps the most commonly used technique in industry.[14] A main advantage of videotapes is that they can display events or model behaviors and skills with greater ease and with more consistent standardization than many other methods. This is valuable when the behavior or skill of interest cannot readily be presented in the traditional training environment. Some team training classes have used feature-length films to provide rich examples for analysis and discussion (the movie *12 Angry Men* is a very effective primer on group dynamics, while *The Bridge on the River Kwai* illustrates the impact of social and interpersonal relations). In addition, the availability of topics covered in off-the-shelf videotapes is quite extensive. Videotaping can also be a cost-effective means of standardizing the instructional component of self-study coursework, but the downside is that the initial cost can be quite expensive for customized productions. Videotapes have also been criticized because they tend to encourage passive learning, are unresponsive, and provide only one-way communication when it comes to student interaction.

Traditional classroom lectures involve oral presentation of material by someone who typically is a subject matter expert on the topic. Like

Exhibit 5.1. Typical Interpersonal and Self-Management Team Training Topics and Instructional Methods.

TEAM TRAINING TOPICS	INSTRUCTIONAL METHODS					
	Videotapes	Traditional classroom	On-the-job activities	Role-plays and simulations	Self-assessment instruments	Computer-assisted learning
Conflict management	X	X	X	XXX	XX	X
Listening and communication	X	X	X	XXX	XX	X
Collaborative problem solving	X	X	XX	XX	XX	XX
Meeting management	X	X	XXX	XX	X	
Goal setting		XX	XX	XX	X	
Selecting new team members		XX		XX		
Performance measurement	X	XX	X	XX		X
Feedback skills	X	X	XXX	XX	X	
Team roles		XX	XXX	XX	X	
Team development and morale	X	XX	XX	X	X	
Team norms and ground rules		XX	XXX	X	X	
Workload equalization		XX	X	X	X	
Individual differences		XX	X	XX	XXX	X

Note: the number of Xs in each cell indicates the degree to which the instructional method is suited for delivering the team training topic; the more Xs, the better suited the method.

videos, lectures are also a commonly used training technique, primarily because they provide a relatively low cost means for reaching large numbers of trainees in a short time span. In addition, if acquisition of knowledge learning is the main objective, lectures are an especially well-suited training method. When used along with appropriate support materials (handouts, workbooks, visual aids, etc.), the lecture method readily facilitates transfer of concepts, theories, and factual information for teams, as would typically be the case if the learning is about quality control tools or statistical process analysis techniques. Nevertheless, this method has been widely criticized because of its one-way communication aspect, the tendency once again to create passive learners, and inability to simultaneously target trainees who are at different levels of readiness or experience.

On-the-job training occurs when the trainee is introduced to the duties and requirements of the position while at the actual job site. Although this particular method greatly facilitates more immediate transfer of training, on-the-job training is all too frequently used as a casual strategy where the trainee is simply introduced to the job by a coworker who has been asked to "show the newcomer the ropes." However, when used in this ad hoc manner as a substitute for an appropriately designed team training program, the success of on-the-job training varies widely, based on numerous factors beyond the control of the training function (such as the experience of the coworker and his or her mentoring abilities, the motivation and learning ability of the trainee, etc.). But when properly designed and implemented, on-the-job training can be a very successful approach because it emphasizes use of proper modeling, immediate practice and feedback, and performance within the context and relevance of the actual job. For example, teams can often learn such concepts of collaboration and task coordination skills better when doing their task with on-the-spot coaching, rather than having to apply skills from the training room to their work; with coached working sessions, transfer of training becomes a nonissue because the training doesn't have to transfer. On the other hand, on-the-job training and practice can be problematic when faced with such considerations as cost (limited capital machinery for practice, potential for scrap rates that would be unacceptably high) or safety (learning cockpit procedures while in actual flight versus in a flight simulator). In such instances, it makes sense to move to on-the-job training only after trainees have demonstrated an adequate level of skill or proficiency in the classroom or other more controlled setting.

In *role-playing and experiential simulations,* trainees practice applying new behaviors and skills in a psychologically safe and controlled setting by acting out parts in contrived situations or case scenarios. These scenarios are typically simple in nature, but they can sometimes be quite elaborate or rich in detail. When combined with classroom lectures, modeling or demonstration of the ideal behavior, and on-the-spot feedback and critique, role-playing and simulations can be a highly effective way of initiating lasting changes in behavior. They are especially well-suited for helping shape attitude changes, or for improving skills and behaviors related to interpersonal effectiveness. An especially powerful—but also potentially intimidating—variation is the *self-confrontation* technique, which involves videotaping the role-play session. With this approach, the trainee reviews the videotape of his or her performance in the role-play while a trained evaluator provides in-depth feedback on successful and unsuccessful aspects of the performance. This feedback and evaluative critique is usually the key to the success of any role-play or simulation exercise, whether the session is videotaped or not. In addition, the success of role-plays and simulations also depends on both the participant's willingness to adopt the roles and respond within context as well as the skills of the training facilitator to help coach the individual through the exercises so that they provide a meaningful learning experience.

Self-assessment instruments include personality measures (for example, the Myers-Briggs Type Indicator,[15] the California Psychological Inventory,[16] the 16PF,[17] etc.) as well as other inventories of skills and personal resources (the Teamwork-KSA Test[18]), and preferences or values (the Measure of Styles of Handling Interpersonal Conflict[19] or the Listening Self-Inventory[20]). These assessment measures are typically used to enhance trainee awareness of their own personal strengths and areas for potential development, but they can also be used to help trainees develop greater appreciation for the individual differences that can exist among team members. Rather than simply being used as ends in themselves, however, self-assessments and inventories in team training are generally used as a starting point for subsequent team building or personal-development activities.

Numerous off-the-shelf self-assessment inventories are widely available at minimal cost, and those developed by reputable researchers who follow rigorous professional standards can typically be treated as sound instruments that provide favorable measurement properties (such as being both reliable and valid measures). Caution must be used to ensure that the results from these instruments fit within the organization's strategy and objectives. In addition, the quality of the results often reflects the honesty and motivation of the trainees in responding to the assessment items. Therefore, care must be taken to ensure that the purposes and intended uses of the results are communicated up front, openly and accurately, to the trainees (that is, whether or not results will be kept in company records or personnel files, if they will be used to make staffing assignments or whether they are for developmental purposes only, etc.). As a final caution concerning use of self-assessment inventories, we occasionally find that widespread use of a specific assessment technique within a company leads to emergence of a "common language" within teams (for example, team members become known by their personality "type"). Although this can certainly facilitate communication and lead to common understanding among team members, we caution against overreliance on any one specific assessment and its underlying theoretical perspective; not only can this create myopia within the organization and its teams but human behavior is typically far too complex a phenomenon to be reduced to simplified labels or categories.

Computer-assisted instruction (or CAI) is a recent innovation in instructional approaches. The real advantage of CAI is that it has the potential to provide instruction that is *interactive* with the trainee—that is, the potential to branch the training content and depth to meet the student's individual training progress based upon his or her responses. However, a current criticism with many CAI programs is that few are truly interactive; instead they are little more than high-tech variations of the more traditional video presentations or lectures.[21] Though it has tremendous potential, CAI does not automatically improve the quality of team training. Its success depends on the degree to which training needs and instructional design are properly matched—as with any other instructional technique.

CAI has been shown to be effective for training that involves sequencing and procedural learning, as well as for efficiently satisfying heavy training demands. For some kinds of team learning, computerized simulations can also be much cheaper and safer (clearly so with aircraft cockpit flight crews) than on-the-job or classroom training approaches. CAI has also been praised for its ability to individualize the pace, content, and sequencing of the training, and to patiently correct errors while reinforcing accuracy. Though initial development can be expensive, hardware costs are constantly decreasing. Additional concerns that have been noted about CAI include the degree to which the process can become mechanical or monotonous to use, the limited scope of human interaction, the reality that programming is time consuming, restrictions that are tied to commercial software, and the real tendency toward information overload.

In summary, no one technique is best suited for all team training situations. Managers must be cautious about adopting a particular training methodology simply because it is widely used or easy to implement. Managers should also be cautious about heavy reliance on a single technique or method. Rather, a comprehensive team training program invariably uses a mix. It may begin with self-assessments to develop baselines and raise self-awareness, followed by lectures to teach the principles behind a desired skill or behavior, coupled with videotaped presentation of the behavior being modeled the correct way, after which role-plays are used to allow practice and reinforcement, subsequently followed up with on-the-job assistance provided at the work site by an experienced coworker or mentor. Each approach should be considered for its different strengths and weaknesses and should be matched to the objectives of the particular lesson plan, the nature of the skill sets to be acquired, the availability of supporting resources, and trainee acceptance and preferences. Exhibit 5.1 provides a summary of the degree to which various instructional methods are suited for delivering the different team training program topics.

DELIVERING THE TRAINING PROGRAM. The final step in designing and implementing team training involves sorting through the specific logistics required for actual delivery. At this stage, care must be given to such matters as preparing materials, coordinating schedules for those involved, procuring facilities and equipment, disseminating and communicating the program information and schedules, and finally delivering the program itself.

Evaluation of Training

Training program evaluation consists of "the systematic collection of descriptive and judgmental information necessary to make effective training decisions related to the selection, adoption, value, and modification of various instructional activities."[22] Although there is some controversy about criteria for evaluating team training effectiveness, experts agree that at a minimum evaluation requires collecting reliable data in such a way as to support valid conclusions about a training program's impact. This presupposes accurate and reliable team performance data. Systematic training evaluation is challenging, since it frequently requires expertise in research design and measurement methodology that goes beyond the capabilities of the managers and staff in most organizations. This means that outside expertise usually must be brought in, often at considerable expense. Consequently, this last stage of the training and development process may be the most neglected. However, systematic evaluation is necessary to determine the true financial value of training and to improve its design and delivery.

The management at Phelps Dodge–El Paso discovered the value of such systematic evaluation when it examined the impact of its team training program shortly after the last action team had completed its forty hours of training. Plant managers could readily see that some of the fifty-eight teams were clearly more effective than others. If possible, they wanted to determine exactly how and why this was the case. Their hope was that if they could identify what the more effective teams were doing differently, then the information could be used to improve the performance of the less-effective teams, as well as serve to guide design and delivery of the next round of team training. With this in mind, the plant brought in outside expertise to help collect and analyze data that compared measures of team effectiveness (relative team performance on safety, cost, quality, production, etc.) to three different predictor variables: ratings of (1) individual team member contributions, (2) internal team processes and dynamics, and (3) organizational support and culture. After the results were tabulated, the findings clearly showed that teams with better-skilled members, more effective internal processes, and greater organizational support were significantly more likely to be among the plant's top producing teams (statistical correlations between team performance and the predictor factors ranged from $r = .52$ to .76). This information not only gave encouraging support to the belief that the company's training dollars had been well spent but it also pointed to specific and actionable steps that could be taken to target team training efforts so as to improve the performance of the less-effective teams in the plant.

TRAINING FOR DIFFERENT TYPES OF TEAMS

The effectiveness of each type of team described throughout this book is greatly affected by the training-and-development function. The training requirements and emphasis for each are somewhat different, as we discuss in this section.

Production Teams

Production teams are the type described most predominantly throughout the Phelps Dodge example. The training requirements for members of production teams are typically exhaustive. They require training to acquire and master interpersonal and self-management KSAs, and production teams typically also require a significant degree of technical skills cross-training in the functional areas of the work done by the teams. In addition, self-directed production teams need extensive training on the basic fundamentals of production and operations management (work flowcharting, process analysis, total quality principles and measurement, etc.), safety, and cost or profit awareness to the degree that these issues are relevant to the specific work of the team. It should also be noted that production teams typically are staffed with the expectation that people are assigned to work for a prolonged—perhaps even indefinite—period of time as team members. Consequently, the value of training intact teams is typically much greater for production teams with this extended expectation of team member longevity.

Service Teams

Most of the issues, as well as the content, of service team training closely parallel those of production teams. That is, self-directed service teams also need significant training to support the interpersonal and self-management aspects of their teamwork. In addition, they will require cross-training for those work elements related to delivering their service. To the degree that service team members interact directly with customers, one can also reasonably expect that a fair amount of customer service training is advisable. Finally, as with production teams, if people are assigned to service teams with an expectation of extended or indefinite membership, then they also derive much greater value from instructional efforts that emphasize training intact teams.

Management Teams

Compared to the other types of teams, top management teams require a special focus in the training they receive. Specifically, this chapter has discussed the importance of using facilitated strategic planning sessions with top management teams to shape the tone and cultural context for the overall transition to teams. Remember that a successful transition from autocracy to empowered teams requires a fundamental change in an organization's climate and culture (that is, its core values and beliefs). This change *must* start with the *top* management team and then cascade its way down through the ranks. Executive teams also have the responsibility to develop the overall strategic plan for the change effort, and they must ensure that this strategic change effort allocates adequate budgets, personnel, and other resources to support the effort.

In addition to the training-and-facilitation work required with top management teams, middle managers and lower-level supervisors also require significant training and development to learn how to operate effectively in an empowered environment. For most managers, the shift to self-directed teams demands that they discard most or all of the techniques and assumptions that made them successful in an autocratic organization; they must be replaced with the ability to coach and facilitate (they need to know how to train and mentor others, how to lead through empowerment, and how to create and maintain open work environments characterized by high levels of trust and involvement). In the Phelps Dodge example, the managers and supervisors were the employees who faced probably the biggest challenge in making the transition to teams. Training and individual development cannot be neglected for managers and supervisors.

Project Teams

Because the nature of project work is typically of short duration (although this is certainly not always the case), the value of training a specific collection of intact team members may be quickly outlived as individuals turn over and are replaced. Thus, a more worthwhile approach for training and development with project teams is to focus on developing competencies among individual team members that are transportable from one team assignment to the next. Such transportable competencies include the interpersonal and self-management KSAs, but they also embrace the ability to effectively manage a team's internal processes and dynamics in a generic sense (for example, how to move quickly through the stages of team formation and development, how to hold effective team meetings, how to establish and maintain productive team norms and ground rules, and so on). Although individuals can certainly be trained in their intact groups, they could also be in artificial groups created just for the specific training course. The strategy, however, is to emphasize training for the individual team member, rather than for the team as a whole, because this helps ensure that effective team processes are manageable regardless of the individual team assignments or project teams involved.

Action Teams

Whereas project teams want to use training that focuses on individuals acquiring skills and abilities, action teams want to focus on training that involves the entire intact team. Because action team performance is highly dependent on the coordinated and well-timed interactions of its team members, integrated task performance is the main focus of action team training sessions. The actual content of this task performance training is determined by the team's specific type of work (firefighting, musical performance, aircraft operation, etc.). Though much of this task-specific action team training may involve little more than repetitive drilling or practice sessions, it can also be some of the most complicated and demanding in terms of using high-tech simulations and exercises. At the same time, it can also be some of the least complicated in terms of interpersonal and self-management demands. For example, the interpersonal communication skills required of team members in a typical military crew are quite minimal and would not extend much beyond simply being able to understand and execute instructions from another team member. On the other hand, a musical jazz group is typically very receptive and open to the creative innovations of its members, while experience suggests that military leaders tend to be rather averse to collaborative problem-solving efforts among subordinates! Thus, the content and scope of training needs for action teams depend in large measure on the specific performance objectives and task requirements of each team.

Parallel Teams

Since the primary objectives of parallel teams involve coordination of parallel work efforts, training on some self-management skills may be of greatest value for parallel team members. In addition, since the coordination efforts between parallel team members frequently involve a fair amount of interaction and communication between team members, it is advisable to employ training on key interpersonal communication skills as well. Managers should recognize that although the work of parallel teams is significant, successful performance of its oversight function typically requires relatively minimal emphasis on these trainable interpersonal and self-management teamwork skills in comparison to other types of teams.

BEST PRACTICES FOR TEAM TRAINING

This chapter suggests several practices for supporting work team effectiveness:

- The top management team must start with a long-term vision for the organization. A vision was critical to the success at Phelps Dodge–El Paso, where the plant manager championed the vision, shaped the culture, and implemented the strategic plan to make it happen.

- The role of training is indispensable for transitioning from an autocratic brown-field site to empowered teams. If an organization is unable or unwilling to commit the resources needed for team training, success may well prove very elusive. For most organizations, the cost and scope of the required team training require an unprecedented level of commitment.

- The scope of skills and abilities that individuals must acquire is impressive and includes such things as greater breadth of task-work KSAs via cross-training and job rotation, an array of critical interpersonal and self-management KSAs, familiarity with effective team processes and dynamics, and a facilitative or empowering leadership style for supervisors and managers.

- Results should not be expected right away. Managers should be prepared to provide sustained training over a period of several years for true culture change. Viewed this way, team training is not a product that is delivered but a process that needs to be continuously refined as an organization's experience with teams evolves.

- Begin by carefully designing the training for supervisors and future team leaders, and deliver their training in advance of that for team members themselves. If possible, involve the supervisors in delivering the training to the new team members.

- For production, service, and action teams with low turnover, train as intact teams. For teams with high turnover or time-limited assignments (project or parallel teams), training should focus on individuals' acquisition of skills.

- As the organization starts moving to teams, begin by training a few highly motivated, high-performing pilot teams that are most likely to succeed. As they begin to experience success and are able to learn from their experience, then begin phasing in the training to other teams.

- Take account of the motivations and concerns of managers and supervisors, which differ from those of front-line employees. Managers and supervisors have to unlearn an old style, learn a new one, and recognize the importance of changing. Employees must acquire new skills and learn to meet the obligations of empowerment. Many managers view this situation with apprehension, while many employees view it with excitement and anticipation.

CONCLUSIONS

You *can* teach an old dog new tricks! Phelps Dodge–El Paso and other companies have shown that the brown-field transition from autocracy to empowered teams can be done without downsizing or large-scale replacement of employees. In five years, the El Paso refinery made a transition to teams with a retention rate over 90 percent because the training-and-development function enabled both line and management employees to function effectively in their new roles.

At the beginning of this chapter, we mentioned a national survey of managers that identified training as a key factor in the success of self-directed teams, and inadequate training as the greatest hindrance.[23] The scope and magnitude of training required for a transition to teams can be unprecedented in a workforce unaccustomed to them. A manager might ask, "Is it worth the effort and cost to retrain our current workforce? Why not just start over from scratch?" In fact, the term *greenfield site* has emerged to describe this basic approach, since it is often believed to be easier to plow under a "green field" in order to build and staff a new facility from scratch, rather than transition a long-standing operation and its people (or "brown-field site") to a team approach. Certainly, there are times when the strategy of hiring for teams from scratch makes a lot of sense, as when a new facility is being opened or expanded, or if the existing culture and attitudes are too entrenched to change. However, the reaction simply to replace employees who don't have the required skill sets is a short-term solution that has tremendous costs of its own. These costs are especially pronounced whenever employee commitment and involvement are critical to success, or when the people in the organization have a wealth of knowledge, experience, and history about the company, its clients, the operations and processes, and so on, that would be difficult—perhaps even impossible—to replace with new hires (often because of steep learning curves or other challenges and constraints). Thus, when a brown-field strategy is selected as the one to pursue, a key to a successful transition to teams is extended use of the training and development function. In this sense, training truly "represents a positive hope."[24]

6

MEASUREMENT AND FEEDBACK SYSTEMS FOR TEAMS

Steve Jones, Richard G. Moffett III

AN EFFECTIVE MEASUREMENT SYSTEM gives work teams the same kind of business data once used only to manage entire organizations. A measurement system lets a team see itself as a business and establishes accountability. With a measurement system, a team has direction and focus for its energies. Without the feedback from a measurement system, the members cannot experience the reason for being a team: to improve their portion of the organization's performance.

Those organizations that successfully implement teams use measurement and feedback systems that allow teams to track their progress and solve problems. These systems integrate with TQM structures. Companies such as Xerox and Weyerhaeuser have measurement systems developed at the team level that their teams understand and use to make improvements. At Xerox, each team member "owns" one of the team's measures. The member leads improvement efforts on "his or her" measure, enlisting the aid of the team and support personnel. Since improvement in team measures are the basis for performance appraisals, subsequent raises, and team pride, fierce ownership develops around the team measures. Ownership leads to high performance.

This chapter addresses four key issues in designing measurement systems for teams:

1. Alignment: linkage between team measurement and business strategy

2. Customers' needs: involving customers in the measurement effort

3. Buyin from participating in development of the measurement systems

4. Feedback that allows problem solving and continuous improvement

In addition, we discuss five approaches to measuring team performance to clarify the trade-offs in choosing one method over another.

This chapter focuses on systems for team performance measurement and means for providing feedback to teams. A *team performance measurement and feedback system* is defined as a family of measures that track how well the team is accomplishing its strategy. *Feedback* refers to regular and ongoing data received from the team's measurement system to promote problem solving and continuous improvement. With teams, performance measurement and feedback are so linked that we consider them together as a system.

OBJECTIVES OF TEAM MEASUREMENT AND FEEDBACK SYSTEMS

The primary objective of team performance measurement and feedback is to improve organizational performance by providing teams with the information they need to track their performance at the team level and solve problems. A secondary objective, not to be underestimated, is to build team pride and ownership of what they do as a group. An effective measurement system maximizes both of these objectives since they build on each other. To maximize these objectives, several conditions need to be met. First, the team must have the right measures, that is, measures that meet customer needs, align with business strategy, and afford the team some control. Second, the team must understand the measures and have ownership to the extent that they will fight if someone tries to take those measures away from them. Third, management has to believe in the measures. Fourth, the measures must be actively used for problem solving by the team. Fifth, management needs to support the team's improvement efforts.

If this sounds simple and straightforward, one wonders why everyone is not doing it well. The problem is that a team performance measurement and feedback system requires support itself to meet the five conditions. Failure to meet any one of them can drastically reduce the effectiveness of the measurement and feedback system. While we present ideas on how to develop a team performance measurement system, we identify critical supports and, later, discuss support features of the feedback process. We begin by examining a real-world case study of a team performance measurement and feedback system.

CASE EXAMPLE: "ELECTRIC COMPONENTS CO."

"Electric Components Co." (not the company's real name) manufactures circuit breakers and electrical components used in construction of new buildings and facilities. The product line is marketed globally; the keys to the company's business strategy are low cost and responsiveness in terms of turnaround on customer orders. One plant is transitioning to teams from a traditional command-and-control management style. Although it has been moving to teams for the past several years, Electric Components only recently implemented a team performance measurement system throughout the plant. Each team has its own measurement system; they vary considerably from team to team but share the four common measures of productivity, quality, cycle time, and on-time delivery. These measures are passed down from the corporate level to all the teams that assemble products. Those teams such as maintenance that do not assemble products have different measures reflecting what they in fact do.

To establish ownership, teams customize their measurement system in four ways. First, they can add a measure of their choosing that reflects the team strategy. Second, within limits they can determine the weighted importance of the measures to reflect their thinking about strategy. Third, within limits they can set their own performance standards for each measure. Fourth, in some cases they can influence how a measure is calculated so that it comes more under their control. For instance, on-time delivery for an assembly team can be calculated as being on time to the shipping department rather than to the external customer.

The assembly team developed a measurement system using the four required measures plus a measure of their own, called assembly start:

1. Quality (DPUs, or defects per unit): each assembled unit has hundreds of possible defects. This measure is the total number of defects for the month divided by the number of units assembled during the month.

2. Productivity (book dollars/labor hours): the catalogue value of units assembled in a month divided by labor hours for the month. Overtime and indirect labor hours are counted.

3. Cycle time: average number of days spent assembling each unit.

4. On time: percentage of assembled units delivered to the shipping department on schedule. Assembled units must pass quality control before going to shipping.

5. Assembly start: percentage of jobs that have all necessary materials ready when assembly is scheduled to begin. This includes engineering drawings, raw materials, and subassemblies.

The assembly team uses this measurement system to track and improve its performance. Members meet weekly to go over the numbers, looking at how the team is doing on each measure. They use supporting data, such as the type and frequency of defects, for problem solving and to develop their improvement plan. They develop action plans and assign responsibilities to team members to pursue those plans and report back at each meeting. (We look next at how this team developed its measurement system and at the support it needs to be maximally effective.)

In this chapter, we present different approaches to measuring team performance, with examples from each. The measurement approach used for the assembly team is called ProMES (Productivity Measurement and Enhancement System) for Teams. It is based on work by Pritchard[1] and modified by Jones and associates specifically for work teams.[2] Developed in the early 1980s, ProMES is a family-of-measures approach that identifies multiple measures and combines them into a composite index. Although the family-of-measures approach is a requirement for a good team measurement system common to all measurement approaches, the composite index is an option and is identified as such.

ProMES for Teams has three objectives: (1) to choose the right measures by closely linking the team's measurement system to the needs of the customer and the organization's business strategy, (2) to involve the team in developing the measurement system so its members have ownership, and (3) to make the system easily modifiable to accommodate changes.

The ProMES for Teams approach follows six steps. First, the team develops a clear understanding of the business strategy and customer needs. Training on these topics is often required so that team members have a complete understanding of the issues. In fact, the process of developing the measurement system is an opportunity to further clarify customer needs and business strategy. The teams need to understand the strategy at the level of cause and effect. For instance, if the organization's goal is to reduce costs by 40 percent and increase the customer retention rate by 10 percent, the teams need to fully understand what actions cause these outcomes to occur. Also, the role that teams play in this strategy should become clear. This procedure develops the proper context for the team to develop the team performance measurement. An important part of the context is that the teams view the measurement system as a means of forming and executing their strategy, rather than as a control mechanism.

In the case of the assembly team, the business strategy is to be the low-cost supplier that is most responsive in delivery time for an order. This gets the company the initial business with a customer, on which future orders depend. The assembly team's goal to support the company's business strategy is twofold: to hold down costs and reduce cycle time. If we look closely at their measurement system, we discern the team strategy. Members give their first measure, quality (as quantified by defects per unit), the largest importance weight, 35 percent. This measure is the most important because it drives productivity, on-time delivery, and cycle time. Defects result in more labor, longer assembly times, and delayed deliveries because of incurred rework. The measure they chose for themselves, assembly start, also reflects their team strategy. If they get everything they need to assemble the units when the job is scheduled to begin, then productivity, on-time delivery, and cycle time improve.

Second, the team determines the dimensions of its performance. The dimensions are important areas (sometimes called key result areas) in which the team must do well to be effective. Dimensions provide a map of the work domain. Typical dimensions are productivity, cost control, quality, customer service, training, teamwork, sales, growth, etc. The final set of dimensions is a blend of the important areas of team performance as viewed by the team, management, and customers. The dimensions for the assembly team are quality, productivity, cycle time, on-time shipments, and assembly start. These five dimensions are determined by inputs from customers, management, and team members. The team could have added safety and training as two additional dimensions, but these five were thought to be the most important. We want a measurement system that is streamlined, since the team has to collect and report this data continually.

Third (an optional step), the dimensions are weighted for importance. For example, if the organization's values say that quality is job one, then the dimension of quality, or its most important driver, should have the greatest weight. To determine the weights, each team member divides

100 points among the dimensions. The point assignments are averaged across team membership for each dimension. Management reviews the weights and may set limits within which they can vary. Customers have an impact on the weighting by virtue of the importance they place on certain areas of team performance (for example, quality or delivery time). The dimension weights for an assembly team might be

Quality = 35 percent

Productivity = 10 percent

On-time shipments = 25 percent

Cycle time = 15 percent

Assembly start = 15 percent

Fourth, one or more measures are determined for each dimension. As previously described, ideas for these measures originate with the members of the organization and the customers. The team selects items from a "menu" of possible measures provided for them by management or a steering committee. Ideally, most of the measures the team needs are already collected by the organization. The team might have to make adjustments to the preexisting measures to isolate the portion over which they have control. Alternatively, they might brainstorm a list of possible measures and then select the most appropriate ones using a set of criteria for good measures.

Fifth (also optional), if there is only one measure per dimension, the dimension weight becomes the importance weight for the sole measure within that dimension. For the example of the assembly team, the importance weights of the measures are the same as those for the dimensions. In a case where there is more than one measure per dimension, the team assigns importance weights for each measure by dividing 100 points across the measures within each dimension. As for the dimension weights, each team member assigns weights, and they are then averaged and reviewed by management. Finally, the measure weights are multiplied by the dimension weights. For example, in one chemical processing team, the quality dimension had three measures: press utilization, batches reblended, and batches doctored. The measure weights were 75, 20, and 5, respectively. These figures were multiplied by the quality dimension weight (.50) to get the final set of measure weights ($75 \times .50 = 37.5$; $20 \times .50 = 10$; $5 \times .50 = 2.5$) for the quality dimension.

Sixth (again optional), once the final importance weights have been established, the measures can be integrated into a composite index. To create the composite, the team determines the performance standards for each measure. In consultation with management, members determine the best possible case, the worst possible case, and the minimally acceptable level for each measure. The best case may be the goal, a benchmark, or merely a judgment agreed on by the team and management. The worst case is usually determined by historical data. The minimally acceptable level is defined as whatever point identifies that a problem may be appearing, such as a lower control limit in statistical process control. These judgments are displayed graphically in relation to the importance weights for the measure. This graphic display is called a *contingency*,[3] and it represents performance standards. The contingency is the relationship between performance on a particular measure and the effectiveness of the team. The contingency translates the "raw" score of the measure into an effectiveness score. Since each measure is weighted for importance, the team can only be as effective on the measure as that measure is important. The contingency for the productivity measure of the assembly team is given in Figure 6.1. Note that the vertical axis reflects the importance weight of the measure (the weight for productivity was 10 percent). The horizontal axis reflects possible values of the measure. The sloping line is the relationship between the measure and team effectiveness; it is determined by the judgments about best case, worst case, and minimally acceptable levels. For instance, the team is maximally effective when it produces $350 book dollars per labor hour, and minimally acceptable when it drops to $275 book dollars per hour. The worst-case scenario for productivity is to fall to $200 book dollars per hour. If the team produced $300 book dollars per hour for a month, it would receive an effectiveness score of 5.

Finally, all measures have contingencies, so that they can each be translated into a common denominator and summed into a composite, called the group performance index (GPI).

Feedback Report

Following development of the measurement system, data are collected and entered into spreadsheets to produce a feedback report, such as that for the assembly team shown in Table 6.1, which has three columns of numbers. The data column contains the numbers for how the team performed on each measure for the month. The effectiveness column contains the effectiveness scores obtained from the contingencies, which are programmed into the spreadsheet. (The GPI, 22.50 in this case, is the composite score across all five measures.) The third column presents the goal for each

Figure 6.1. Example of a Contingency.

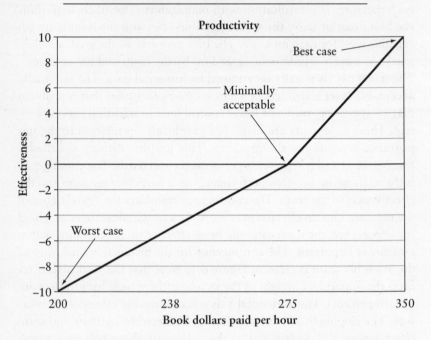

measure. The team members know that the score of 22.50 is good, but they have room to improve. A GPI of 0 would indicate they are just meeting the level of minimally acceptable performance; a GPI of 100 would mean their performance is the best it can be on all measures.

In addition to the feedback chart in Table 6.1, the team report includes graphs of all the measures over time. Software has recently become available that teams can use to create their own spreadsheets and graphs.[4] In addition to the feedback report, teams have backup data to give them more detail, such as type of defects, which jobs were not set up when scheduled, what items were missing, etc. This detailed information stimulates problem solving and action planning. The measurement system tracks the impact of the improvement efforts.

DEVELOPING TEAM MEASUREMENT SYSTEMS

Modern team measurement systems draw on influences from cost accountancy, productivity measurement, quality, and attitude measurement. It is not uncommon to find teams with measures of cost control,

Table 6.1. Assembly Team Performance.

Assembly team performance	Data	Effectiveness	Goal
Quality (35 percent): DPUs	.40	-17.5	.15
Productivity (10 percent): book dollars paid per labor hour	$350	10.00	$350
Cycle time (15 percent): average cycle time in days	12.5	15.00	10
On-time delivery (24 percent): jobs finished on schedule	89 percent	7.50	95 percent
Assembly start (15 percent): jobs set up when scheduled	75 percent	7.50	85 percent
Group performance index (GPI)		22.50	

productivity, quality, safety, and training, as well as survey-based measures of customer satisfaction and teamwork. In the past, such measures were typically the province of management and specialized departments such as accounting, engineering, quality control, marketing, and human resources. Today's high-performance teams collect data on a family of measures, understand them, and solve problems at the level where the work is being done. Although this reallocation of information empowers teams, it raises the critical issue of alignment.

Alignment of Work Teams with Organizational Strategy

A clear "line of sight" between the team's strategy and the organization's strategy is crucial. The team's measurement system captures its strategy as it aligns with the organization's strategy. This is not to say that all of the organization's goals should cascade mindlessly down to the team level; teams should look for ways to connect their strategy and therefore their metrics to the larger business strategy. To achieve this alignment, the executive team needs to articulate the business strategy well and communicate it meaningfully for teams. Team members should be able to demonstrate in-depth understanding of the business strategy; in other words, they need business literacy.

Many companies do an excellent job of communicating their business strategy. For instance, Xerox has developed a "Vision 2000" document that explains the vision and the competitive pressures out of which the business strategy is forged. From this effort, teams can clearly understand why the strategy is necessary and align themselves with it. For instance, to transition to digital products, certain teams need to upgrade their technical skills. To operate in an open systems environment, some teams develop and maintain products that interface seamlessly with competitors' products. What a team does to accomplish its portion of the strategy can be captured by a measure, which becomes a key part of the measurement system.

A logjam in a river presents a good model of team cause-and-effect strategy. Moving the right log causes all the others to move with the current. Through group discussions, the assembly team at Electronic Components determined that reducing defects would cut cycle time, improve productivity through less overtime, and improve on-time delivery to the customer. They also knew that the key to achieving their goals was the timing with which they got all the parts, materials, and engineering drawings to assemble the product. If everything was ready for them to start a job on time, then their cycle times were reduced, delivery times were met, and productivity was high. Once this "log" was moved, their other measures improved.

Frequently, we find that organizational strategies are too complex, that there are too many goals, or that the goals change constantly. At Victoria's Secret, they understand how this obscures the team's line of sight and have reduced their corporate strategy from more than three hundred pages to a single page.

From our perspective, alignment of company strategy, team strategy, and team performance measurement is the most critical factor in team implementation. A recent market survey on reasons for team failure found that the top three concerned goals and team accountability.[5]

Customer Needs

Inherent in understanding business strategy is understanding customer needs. It is not uncommon to find a disconnect between teams and their customers that results in measures being internally driven, rather than customer-driven. To avoid this myopia, we encourage teams to engage in dialogue with their customers prior to and during development of team metrics. Some teams invite their customers to attend meetings at which performance measures are developed. Direct understanding of the customer's needs often stimulates ideas for critical measures that the team might otherwise overlook. Through customer interviews, a manufacturing team at Duracell decided to use a measure of how quickly their product ran through their customer's machines. The team found that the greater the consistency of their product, the faster their customer's machines could run. The team would not have "discovered" this measure without asking what was important to the customer. It is significant that this measure (customer processing speed) became the most important measure for the manufacturing team.

Buyin

Team performance measurement is a participative endeavor for two reasons. First, team members must take ownership of their measures to maximize their performance on them. A good test of ownership is to see if members would defend those measures against the threat of losing them. Second, the purpose of having the measurement system is for the teams to solve problems, and problem solving requires participation. Therefore, we want teams to participate in developing their own measurement systems. We also expect measurement systems to differ from one team to another.

How much team participation is required in developing measurement systems? The answer is unknown at this time. Certainly, participation requires time, most of which is spent in meetings. This is expensive time for organizations, and it must be balanced against business pressures. We do know that teams do not have to participate in every decision that is made in measurement system development. There are a number of choice points in the development, such as goals, strategies, selection of measures, calculation of measures, importance weighting, and performance standards. We believe that teams should participate in at least some of these decisions to establish ownership.

Participation comes in many forms. Even relatively minor adjustments to the measurement system can result in significant buyin by the teams. In many organizations, measures that support the strategy cascade down from the larger organization to the teams. In a given facility, all teams may have some common measures that must be included in their measurement systems. Often, though, teams can make adjustments in the actual calculation of the measure. For instance, in calculating cycle time, a team may adjust the start date to reflect when they actually received the job rather than when the job was scheduled. One team might give quality a 5 percent greater importance weight than another team. A second team might set slightly different performance standards.

Probably the most critical area for participation is determining team strategy and goals. By allowing, and even encouraging, variations on the measurement theme, organizations extend opportunities for participation and later reap the benefits of buyin by the teams. The greater the participation, the less the measurement system is perceived as a mechanism of command and control.

Another means of getting buyin is through a steering committee, with representatives from the key constituent groups in the organization. The steering committee offers guidance for developing the team measures and for other decisions involved in team implementation. Some steering committees develop a menu of performance measures that the team then chooses from. Since managers are on the steering committee, it presents an opportunity for management participation.

We often forget that managers need buyin just as teams do. In the rush to empower teams, managers often feel disconnected from key decisions. Management typically suggests team measures, importance weights, and performance standards and reviews all team measurement systems. A healthy dialogue between management and teams prevents incorporation of measures that people do not believe in.

Team Performance Feedback and Team Dynamics

The information from a team measurement system produces important feedback about how the team is performing and serves as a tool to improve team productivity. Like a tool, however, its usefulness lies in how it is used. Consequently, performance feedback has a positive or negative impact on team member motivation and problem-solving processes.

TEAM MEMBER MOTIVATION. In many situations, performance feedback indicates a gap between a team's goal and its performance. The gap serves as a stimulus or challenge that motivates the team to put out more effort, increasing the likelihood of higher team performance. For many teams, this appears to be a natural reaction. One team specialist reported that when a team in his manufacturing organization receives feedback about its performance, team members intuitively pick out the gaps in performance and begin trying to plan how to bridge them. The gap between the team's goal (or expectation) and its actual performance can interact with its competitive spirit to motivate the team to increase performance.

However, some teams become demotivated if they receive negative performance feedback. If the culture of the organization punishes poor performance, teams learn that negative performance feedback signals impending punishment. Robert Pritchard and his colleagues described a situation in which they implemented a team measurement and feedback system in an organization where one of the managers tended to focus only on the few areas of negative feedback, ignoring the positive feedback for a number of other areas.[6] They found that the manager's behavior caused the team to view the feedback meetings as punishing rather than reinforcing. If a manager continues to concentrate exclusively on negative feedback, even though the team has made some progress, team members may develop an attitude of "Why bother? Nothing we do seems to make a difference in solving this problem" and stop performing. Also, constant negative feedback damages group cohesion and often leads team members to blame other members for being the cause of the negative feedback.

Another problem experienced by some teams is that constant negative feedback surfaces unresolved issues, such as goal incompatibility, and causes loss of motivation. For example, a team in a knowledge-based organization decided upon an ambitious collective goal that required a great deal of effort on the part of all team members. However, team members had individual goals, some of which were incompatible with the overall team goal. As long as the team was receiving positive feedback, the goal incompatibility remained hidden from view. But when the team began to get negative performance feedback and members had to extend increased effort and make priorities in their work to achieve the team goal, some members retreated to their individual goals. This resulted in conflict within the team. This situation is more likely to occur if the team goal has not been clearly stated or the organizational culture and reward system is based on individual performance.

PROBLEM-SOLVING EFFECTIVENESS. Performance feedback can also serve as basic data for a team to determine which problems it should solve and whether its strategy in solving a problem is successful. Suppose an equipment maintenance team gets composite feedback from its multidimensional performance feedback system indicating its overall performance has dropped. The team then starts its problem-solving process. First, the members examine the five performance dimensions of their measurement system and identify poor performance as limited to the length of time for repair and service of company trucks. Second, they analyze team records and processes to describe the conditions causing the poor performance. Third, the team uses the performance dimension in question to clarify the specific outcome to be achieved once the problem is solved. Fourth, the team generates alternative solutions and chooses the one most likely to solve the problem. Fifth, the team develops an action plan for implementing the preferred solution. Sixth, the team implements the solution, and the resulting performance feedback is used to determine whether or not this is the appropriate strategy. In this example, performance feedback serves as data that reveal a problem exists, and it serves as data to evaluate the adequacy of the implemented solution.

Using performance feedback to solve problems can derail if the team interprets the feedback not as data for problem solving but as an indication of failure. This view of performance feedback can cause or bring to the surface team dynamics that inhibit performance. These dynamics may result in team members' blaming forces outside the team, blaming individual team members (scapegoating), finding fault with the measurement system, or merely giving up. To avoid these negative consequences, a team must develop a culture that supports constructive use of performance feedback.

Creating a Team Culture for Using Performance Feedback

Certain factors help teams respond positively to performance feedback: (1) aligning the goals of individuals in the team and the collective team goal, (2) framing team performance feedback as a source of motivation and of data for solving problems, and (3) using a process that promotes improvement rather than evaluation.

ALIGNING INDIVIDUAL GOALS WITH TEAM GOALS. It is critical for a team to have common purposes displayed in clearly understood goals shared by all team members. When individual members' goals align with team goals, a synergy results that motivates team members to high levels of performance.[7] Clearly, the best way to achieve this is through the initial efforts a team puts forth in working together in honest collaboration to establish its purpose and goals and to develop its measurement system.

Sometimes, however, management assigns teams a purpose or goals to which members may not be committed. At other times, team members may think they understand the goals of the team when actually there is no shared understanding of them among all members. If a team experiences incompatibilities between individual and team goals, members can perceive the team as stuck. Katzenbach and Smith suggest that when this occurs the team revisit the basics; that is, the team needs to review its purpose and what the measurable goals are.[8] According to those authors, the team could "benefit from going back to ground zero and spending the time to uncover all hidden assumptions and differences in opinion that, when assessed by the full team, might provide the foundation for clarifying the team's mission and how to accomplish it."[9] The key is first to clarify the team goal and then align each individual's goals to it.

One service team, which had previously received its company's award for excellence, found that after some personnel changes and a few years of rebuilding its performance was mediocre to average. Team members did some soul-searching and found that they were operating as individuals rather than a team. They decided that they wanted to be the best team in their region. To help accomplish this, they jointly reestablished performance goals and specified and committed to team processes, roles, and responsibilities. According to their measurement system, the team then showed significant improvement over the previous year's performance.

It takes considerable skill to constructively facilitate a meeting in which team members confront themselves and each other about possible goal incompatibilities. If team members do not possess the necessary skills to facilitate this process, then a manager or outside facilitator could be used in assisting the team.

FRAMING TEAM PERFORMANCE FEEDBACK. We have seen that some teams view negative performance feedback as an indicator of failure or embarrassment,[10] but many others are able to use it as a source of motivation and data for solving problems. One way in which a team can develop more positive norms about processing performance feedback is through the statements made by managers, team leaders, or team members.[11] For example, a manager or team leader can explicitly state that at feedback meetings all blame finding and focusing exclusively on negative performance feedback are to be avoided.[12] Then, during the feedback meetings, the manager or team leader models the appropriate behavior and reinforces this behavior in all of the team members. This framing process should start at the first performance feedback meeting and continue to be reinforced in all subsequent meetings.

Additionally, the norms for framing performance feedback constructively can be developed into rules that the team uses to monitor its behavior on this issue. For example, a team may agree to use certain rules. First, positive performance feedback will be discussed and celebrated by all team members. Second, when discussing negative performance feedback, team members will not blame or attack individuals as causes of the poor team performance. Third, negative performance feedback will be used as data for performance improvement and not as an indication of failure. To monitor how well the team is following these norms, items relating to these norms can be included on a team effectiveness survey. An alternative to the survey approach is to have one of the team members volunteer to monitor the performance feedback session and indicate if any team member is violating the team rules. If none of the team members has the expertise to perform this role, an outside facilitator can be brought in.

Another way to help a team constructively frame performance feedback is to increase the team's confidence in its ability to make improvements. This is achieved by having the team go for small successes.[13] One team specialist has found that if a team cannot develop a new goal, a team leader or manager can replace the performance problem with activities that the team sees as valuable to do and that are likely to be successful. According to the specialist, the activities do not have to be directly linked to a performance measure; the key is to have the team regain confidence in its ability to make improvements.[14] Regardless of the tactic, it is important that the team achieve success and develop some confidence before it takes on a more difficult problem or goal.

Examples of Performance Feedback Review Sessions

Here are examples of procedures used in performance feedback review sessions. The first and second examples (for production and service teams) contain specific procedures used in actual organizations. The third outlines generic procedures used to strategically combine goal setting and performance feedback review.

PRODUCTION TEAM. Some organizations incorporate performance feedback reviews into regularly scheduled team meetings. One manufacturing company uses the following agenda for its regular production team meetings, scheduled for sixty minutes:

1. Objectives of meeting (3–5 percent of meeting time): review of the two or three objectives to be accomplished
2. Performance feedback review (10–15 percent): review of key team performance measures
3. Action item follow-up (6–9 percent): review of previous meeting's action items
4. Problem solving (30–50 percent): identification and diagnosis of problems, generation of solutions, and selection of solutions with the goal of improving performance
5. General information sharing (10–15 percent): announcements and general news

6. Other questions and issues (5–10 percent): issues unrelated to step four

7. Summary and review (5–8 percent): team leader's verbal review of decisions made; meeting objectives accomplished; action plans; and time, date, and place for next meeting

The times are rough estimates and vary based on the content and complexity of a meeting. Top teams of business units in this organization use similar steps, but with their meetings lasting three to four hours.

During the problem-solving phase of the meeting, team members use an established problem-solving process developed for a previous quality initiative implemented in the company. Team members pinpoint the problem or current situation; review the data, including quantitative and qualitative information; identify the root causes of the problem using various quality tools such as flow diagrams, histograms, and run charts; identify potential solutions; and develop action plans for implementing and evaluating the selected solutions. According to a team specialist in this manufacturing company, the key to success in this problem-solving phase is to concentrate on performance or process improvement and to avoid engaging in finding a person to blame for the poor performance.

SERVICE TEAM. A service team in a large company known for its team excellence uses a similar approach. The team has specific performance measures that encompass the important factors of its work, such as customer satisfaction, machine reliability (for instance, amount of time a service technician works on a machine), and parts (for example, cost of parts for a machine per output of that machine). The team meets every two weeks, for no longer than two hours, to discuss team performance and other important issues such as upcoming personnel absences. Prior to a meeting, the team member who is responsible for a certain area collects all the performance data for presentation to the team. Here is an agenda typical of these meetings:

1. Personnel issues: upcoming absences and how the work will be covered, changes in job duties, etc.

2. Problem accounts: technical problems associated with any machines the team services

3. Performance feedback: team member sharing of information from his or her area of responsibility

4. Other issues: such items as how decisions are being made within the team, communication problems, conflict among team members, etc.

When solving problems during the meeting, team members use a process that is based on the typical steps used in quality programs. This problem-solving process is very similar to the one used by the manufacturing team described earlier, but each service team member is responsible for one of the performance areas and facilitates the problem solving for that area. Data about the problem are shared with the team in the form of trendlines, bar graphs, and other presentation approaches common to quality programs. If the problem can be solved quickly, the team does so on the spot. If the problem is more complex, a separate meeting is scheduled. Again, the key to the process is to use the performance feedback as data to solve problems and to evaluate solutions to problems.

STRATEGIC APPROACH. A generic approach for providing feedback to teams, called team improvement review,[15] is designed to decrease the evaluative nature of such reviews and focus more on performance improvement. It calls for combining business planning (goal setting) and performance feedback in one meeting. The team reviews past performance feedback and makes plans for the future. The approach uses four thought-provoking questions:

1. What have our accomplishments and problems been? (past performance)
2. What should our goals be? (future)
3. What must we improve to meet our goals? (developmental needs)
4. What support do we need from others to succeed? (support needs)[16]

This approach does away with the usual performance-appraisal idea of assigning numbers or descriptive categories (such as "meets minimally acceptable level") to individuals. When numbers or categories are assigned, it seems to move the performance feedback into being evaluative rather than used as problem-solving data. As W. Edwards Deming says, individual performance appraisal "nourishes short-term performance, annihilates long-term planning, demolishes teamwork, [and] nourishes rivalry and politics."[17] By linking the review of the team's performance measurement feedback to business planning, the connection between the measurement system and the organization's strategy is reinforced, and team feedback now indicates how well the strategy is working rather than how well individuals are performing. This shifts the focus from individual evaluation to a systems-improvement process and avoids some of the potentially adverse effects of feedback.

MEASUREMENT SYSTEMS AND TYPE OF TEAM

Although our six types of teams do not require different methods for measuring their performance, we have chosen to present five measurement methods for these types. They are the measurement methods most widely presented at conferences and in the literature. ProMES for Teams was presented earlier with the assembly team. The other methods are team scorecard, objectives matrix, Zigon, and balanced scorecard.

Team Scorecard for a Production Team

The team scorecard, by Schilling and Valera,[18] adapts well to production teams. It addresses the question of how we translate the business strategy into measurable outcomes for our team. Typically, a team's scorecard contains five to ten measures. Current performance on each measure is compared against a year-to-date average, prior year's average, short-term target, long-term target, and minimum and maximum values. An example scorecard as shown in Exhibit 6.1.

As the exhibit reveals, the team readily understands how it is doing on strategic measures as they compare to targets and sees how it is performing for the year. This production team has six different measures, which have as a unifying feature the gaps between present performance and the long-term and short-term targets. The gaps between the targets and current performance present opportunities for improvements. The team targets the most important gap for improvement, while continuing to maintain its performance on the other measures. In addition to this information, the team "zooms in" and gets greater detail for problem identification, such as the type of complaints, which customers had complaints, and downtime for different machines.

Notice that the measures do not have importance weights and that there are two measures each for customer complaints and downtime. In effect, this says that customer complaints and downtime are twice as important as productivity (feet per minute) or housekeeping.

Objectives Matrix for a Service Team

Riggs and Felix,[19] of the Oregon Productivity Center, introduced the objectives matrix, also known as OMax or the Oregon Matrix. The procedures of the objectives matrix have been widely used to integrate a family of measures into a composite score. The Felix and Riggs procedure is still in use but has been updated by Heninger.[20] Using the objectives matrix,

Exhibit 6.1. Sample Team Performance Scorecard for a Machine Corrugator Team.

Performance measure	Current performance	YTD average	Prior year average	Short-term target	Long-term target
Linear feet per minute	539	548	543	534	600
Housekeeping	76	76	79	80	95
Number of customer complaints	1	3.3	3.3	2	1
Cost of customer complaints	260	1096	1096	550	130
Downtime frequency per day	23	24	26.4	25	22
Downtime minutes per day	98.6	118	117	104	95

Exhibit 6.2. Sample Objectives Matrix for a Financial Services Team.

PRODUCTIVITY CRITERIA	Baseline 0%	10%	20%	30%	40%	50%	60%	70%	80%	90%	Goal 100%	Score	Weight	Value
Loans serviced / Department hours	30	39	48	57	66	75	84	93	102	111	120	66	15	6
Late computer reports / 22 days	90	81	72	63	54	45	36	27	18	9	0	0	5	5
Manual coupons / Payments received	4	7	10	13	16	19	22	25	28	32	36	25	10	7
Policy errors / # of new policies	29.0	22.0	16.0	11.0	7.0	4.0	2.0	1.0	0.75	0.50	0.25	2	20	12
# of inquires / Loans serviced	0.90	0.80	0.72	0.64	0.56	0.48	0.40	0.32	0.24	0.16	0.09	.64	15	5
Investor complaints / Commercial loans	8.7	7.9	7.1	6.3	5.5	4.7	3.9	3.1	2.3	1.5	0.8	4.7	30	15
Hours missed / Department hours	11.0	10.2	9.9	8.8	7.7	6.6	5.5	4.4	3.3	2.2	1.2	.33	5	4

teams weight each of their measures for importance so that the weights total to 100. The team also sets a percentage of milestones or goal level for each measure, such that the baseline (where the team is now) performance level receives 0 percent and performance at the long-range goal level receives 100 percent. This procedure produces a composite score that can reach 100 but is more commonly in the low-to-middle teens. The objectives matrix can be attached to any system that uses a family-of-measures approach. Exhibit 6.2 presents an example for a financial services team.[21]

Measures for an Action Team

Jack Zigon, of the Zigon Performance Group, has developed an approach to team performance measurement that addresses a variety of situations and is particularly well suited to situations where team performance is difficult to measure.[22] Zigon emphasizes a variable approach to measurement using different methods depending on the team's line of sight with the organization's outcomes. One method, the team customer diagram, is used for teams when customer satisfaction is the primary product. Another method, the team accomplishment pyramid, identifies expected results at the organizational level and breaks them down into team results. A third method examines how team accomplishments support organizational strategy, such as cost savings to improve profits. A fourth method, the work process flow, is brought to bear in situations where a team supports a work process. From these methods, team accomplishments are determined and weighted for importance on a 100 percent scale. Following this step, measures are determined and performance standards (such as sales 10 percent higher than last year) are defined for each measure. Team performance is tracked on each measure relative to the standards.

An additional feature of Zigon's methodology is development of measures of individual accomplishments that are not covered by the team measures. Accomplishments may be measured with a quantitative variable (such as sales in dollars) or accomplishments may be measured through a judgment (as in a performance appraisal). A complete feedback report contains performance on each of the measures and may offer a separate performance report for each team member. Combined with the individual feedback report feature, the team report seems particularly well suited to teams that have large components of individual accomplishment. Historically, these teams (sales teams, R&D teams, and teams of scientists) have proven difficult to measure. It should be clear that a combined team and individual measurement system is more labor-intensive. For a team of eight people, nine sets of data are to be collected and nine separate feedback reports required.

As an example for an action team, part of a Zigon system for an oil exploration team is presented in Table 6.2. In addition, an individual measurement system for one member of the team, such as a geologist, could be nested within the team's system. Also note that the measures are linked to accomplishments that themselves are given importance weights. This linkage provides a line of sight between the team measures and the strategic business plan. For example, the most important weight (40 percent) goes to regional business results, indicating the strategic value of these results and their corresponding measures. Targets are also set for each measure so that the team can see that its level of performance supports the business plan.[23]

Balanced Scorecard for a Management Team

The balanced scorecard, introduced by Kaplan and Norton,[24] builds on a cause-and-effect concept. It supplements financially driven measures at the corporate level with measures addressing (1) customer interests, (2) internal business processes, and (3) innovation and learning. The balanced scorecard links the results (financial measures) with the strategy that causes those results (the three other measurement areas).

Typical financial measures are profit, return on investment, and sales; the customer area might be measured by customer satisfaction. Examples of internal business processes are productivity, scrap, rework, and cycle time, and innovation and learning can be captured by measures such as morale and employee suggestions for improvement. If we accept that employee morale has an impact on customer satisfaction; that employee suggestions affect productivity, scrap, rework, and cycle time; and that customer satisfaction, productivity, scrap, rework, and cycle time in turn have an impact on the financial measures, we can see the causal linkages.

The balanced scorecard illustrates two important principles of measurement: balanced perspectives and causal linkages to business strategy. A healthy balance between multiple perspectives is necessary for an organization to thrive. Shareholders have a financial perspective, customers have a quality-and-service perspective, supervisors have an internal-business perspective, and innovation and learning provide the renewable resources to keep the plant or corporate engine running. Since the management team's strategy encompasses these multiple perspectives, the measurement system should as well. In addition, strategy implies some notion of cause and effect, and the measurement system needs to capture the notion so

Table 6.2. Sample Zigon Measurement Report
for an Oil Exploration Team.

Accomplishments/Weights	Performance Standards
Regional business results (40 percent): deliveries, controlled costs, development opportunities, acquisition opportunities, exploration opportunities, good corporate citizen and partner	1. $2.5M to $3.2M net operating income 2. 1.1M to 1.6M total yearly cubic feet of gas 3. 3M to 3.5M total yearly barrels of oil 4. $50K to $75K lease operating expense 5. Cash flow increases at 3.5 percent to 4.5 percent per year 6. Reserve additions are greater than 10 percent 7. No citations from government agencies 8. No dissatisfied royalty owners 9. No fines
Investment opportunities (25 percent)	1. 15 to 25 new investment opportunities per year which meet corporate hurdle rates for drill wells, acquisitions, work overs/recompletions, facility modifications, and explorations 2. Continuous reduction in average project study cycle time
Oil ready for shipment (25 percent)	1. Production deliveries meet agreed-upon business plan 2. Lease operating costs meet agreed-upon business plan 3. No fines or shut-ins due to regulatory and environmental problems
Completed capital projects (10 percent)	1. Actual volume meets forecast 2. Cost per barrel of reserves meets corporate hurdle rate 3. Cash flow meets forecast (adjusted for price)

Source: Zigon Performance Measures; used with permission.

that the resulting feedback reveals to the management team how well the strategy is working.

Parallel and Project Teams

Organizations often do not require any measures for parallel and project teams if their work is short-term. Alternately, their accomplishment may be captured by single measures, such as dollars saved, or percentage of project milestones met. However, percentage of milestones met may fail to be useful if milestones are a best guess rather than known performance standards. Another problem with outcome measures, such as percentage of milestones met and dollars saved, is that the information they provide comes too late to lead to team improvement efforts. An alternative approach is to use process measures in addition to outcome measures.[25]

Parallel and project teams typically work on projects that span, or are outside of, traditional departments. These projects have internal or external customers. The key to developing process and outcome measures for these two types of teams comes from three perspectives: the customer's perspective in terms of meeting requirements, management's perspective, and the team's point of view in terms of capabilities. The customer's perspective tells a team how much value is added by their project if it is done a certain way; these are process measures such as estimates of quality improvement, time savings, and forecasts of the value of the completed project to customers. Management's perspective focuses on project status and costs; these are the traditional outcome measures such as milestones completed to plan and costs to plan. Measures from the team's perspective focus on capabilities; they are process measures such as the team's satisfaction with resources supporting the project, observations or survey of team decision-making processes, and assessment of availability of expertise to complete tasks.

A family of measures developed from these three perspectives gives project and parallel teams the information they need to make adjustments. It also presents management with the information needed to stay informed about project status.

Issues Raised by Different Measurement Methods

There are several key issues in the decision as to which measurement approach to adopt.

NUMBER OF MEASURES. It is not just a best practice but rather a common practice today for teams to employ a family of measures. How many should they have? The best answer is "a vital few," on the order of four to eight for monthly feedback. Most organizations have more data than teams can profitably use, so it becomes a matter of reducing the number of measures from the possible total to avoid choking the team with a measurement bureaucracy. There should be enough measures to capture the strategy, which requires some capacity for cause and effect, thus increasing the number of measures beyond that required simply to capture output. The number of measures also depends on the frequency of feedback. The assembly team with the ProMES example, which contains just five measures, receives monthly feedback. The example for the oil exploration team, which has twenty-three measures, is appropriate for quarterly or yearly feedback. We expect most production teams to require the least number of measures, service teams to require slightly more, and action teams and management teams to require the most.

INTEGRATION INTO A COMPOSITE. Two of the methods for team measurement (objectives matrix and ProMES) integrate the measures for a team into a single composite score. When tracked across time, the composite provides a picture that tells the team how it is doing overall and whether it is improving or declining. Thus, it promotes big-picture thinking and understanding the relationship among the measures. The composite tells the team if its strategy is working. This is particularly important since using a team measurement system to give feedback on strategy distinguishes the measurement system from a traditional command-and-control system.

Developing the composite requires the three steps of creating a common denominator, establishing importance weights, and setting performance standards. This extra work is probably not justified if the team is only concerned about improving isolated measures. For instance, if a team has a mandate to improve productivity, it could instead focus on improving that measure and put less attention on its other measures, so long as the other measures continue to remain at their previous levels.

ADDING INCENTIVES. Most teams want to be paid for their performance. A team's bonus is easier to calculate with a composite score. The assembly team feedback in Table 6.1 is an example of shaping team incentive. The amount of incentive was determined by the total of the incentive points; they were the same as the GPI, unless the effectiveness score was negative, in which case the team received zero incentive points. In the table, the assembly team received a GPI of 22.5, but they also had an effectiveness score of -17.5 on their quality measure. So they added 17.5 to remove the negative score, which gave them 40 incentive points. To calculate the dollar value of their incentive, they multiplied the amount of money in the bonus pool ($250 in this case) times the incentive points taken as a percentage. Their bonus was therefore $250 × .40 = $100 per team member.

Of course, something has to fund the team incentive. In this case an 8 percent increase in plantwide productivity yielded the funding mechanism. If the plant did not make the 8 percent improvement, there were no funds available for the bonus pool. This funding mechanism gave an additional measure for each team—plant productivity—that captured interteam cooperation.

INTERTEAM COOPERATION. A measurement approach should begin with a big-picture approach. In developing team performance measures, it is possible to focus so tightly on the team that the bigger picture of cooperation between teams gets lost. If teams need to cooperate to accomplish the business strategy, yet the team measurement systems contain no measures that address interteam cooperation, then the stage is set for suboptimization.

There are a number of means for addressing this issue. In multishift operations, the different shifts within the same department may share several measures, such as productivity, that are particularly sensitive to cooperation between shifts. In the assembly team example, productivity was measured across all shifts in the same department. In order to respond to customer needs, cooperation is often required across departments. Measures at the business-unit level such as productivity or customer return rates can be added to the measurement systems for teams whose cooperation is needed. Another approach is to use internal surveys to assess how well one team or department supports another. In the plant that houses the assembly team, the wire prep team uses an internal customer satisfaction survey to assess how well its efforts support other teams.

PURPOSE. The whole purpose of the measurement system is to drive performance improvement. Regardless of the method used for developing team performance measures, the system is only as good as its use. It is far better to have a low-tech, informal measurement system that is used as a basis for problem solving and continuous improvement than it is to have an elaborate, sophisticated measurement system that just re-ports the numbers but is not used by the team. The potential power of the team to focus on their measures, identify improvement strategies, set priorities, solve problems, and follow through is immense. The mea-surement system should tap that power through feedback.

BEST PRACTICES FOR TEAM MEASUREMENT AND FEEDBACK

1. Use the measurement system to capture the business strategy:

    The measurement system for a management team captures the corporate or business unit strategy.

    The measurement system for other types of teams captures their strategy as it supports the overall business strategy.

    A measurement system that is just cascaded down to a team without capturing its strategy and thinking becomes a form of command and control.

2. Bring in the customer's perspective:

    Involve the customer to keep the team's measures from serving only its own internal needs.

    Involve the customer in the measurement process by using some measures as defined by the customer.

    Add the customer's perspective to help the team see itself as a business.

3. Use team participation:

    Teams have the most buyin if they share in the decision making about their measurement system.

    Some teams go through business literacy training before engag-ing in measurement development; this allows them to more fully participate in discussions about business strategy and about why certain measures are critical.

4. Use constructive management review:

    Managers ensure that the measurement systems for different team are on target.

    Managers are in the best position to see that the measurement systems encourage teams to cooperate where necessary.

5. Align individual goals with team goals:

> With new teams, initiate honest and open collaboration to establish the common purpose and goals of the team.
>
> With older teams that become stuck, clarify the team's goal and align each individual's goals to it; do not hesitate to use outside facilitators if needed.

6. Use the roles of team leader and coach to facilitate feedback meetings:

> The best coaches and team leaders understand how their actions in team meetings empower their teams or have the opposite effect.
>
> The best coaches and team leaders understand their role as developing skills in their teams. That is, they prepare their teams to become successful in their problem solving; this includes guiding the team toward problems it can solve, supporting the team with the resources it needs to solve problems and make improvements, and encouraging the team to practice critical problem-solving skills before those skills are severely tested.
>
> The best coaches and team leaders ask good questions rather than impose all the answers and decisions on their teams.

7. Frame team performance feedback as a source of motivation and as data for solving problems:

> Avoid focusing exclusively on negative performance feedback.
>
> Establish team norms that promote a positive view of performance feedback by accentuating manager or team leader statements and behavior, or by using team rules.
>
> Increase team confidence by going for small successes.

8. Employ a process to promote use of performance feedback in improving team performance rather than evaluating individual performance:

> Establish problem-solving processes and incorporate team performance feedback as data to identify and solve problems, and to evaluate implemented solutions.
>
> Avoid using individual performance appraisal techniques in which evaluative numbers are assigned to team members.
>
> Link reviews of the team's performance measurement feedback to business planning; focus on how well the strategy is working rather than on how well individuals are performing.

9. Consider providing incentives for team performance (see Chapter Seven):

Although offering team incentives is tricky, in the long run they are usually needed to maintain motivation and focus.

Care should be taken in designing an incentive system so that it rewards interteam cooperation where appropriate.

Incentives should be added last, after all other parts of the team intervention have been established.

Adding incentives underscores the importance of tying team measurement systems to business strategy.

Management may need incentives to support teams, such as determining part of each manager's bonus by how well his or her teams are doing.

CONCLUSION AND FUTURE TRENDS

We have covered a number of issues that determine how well a measurement system helps a team with the improvements the company needs. We hope we have sufficiently made the point that a team performance measurement system is much more than a technology. Rather, it is a dynamic and interactive tool that is only as good as its design and use. How the tool is designed and used speaks volumes about the organization's culture. For instance, an organization that doesn't walk the talk about empowerment tends not to sufficiently involve teams in decisions about measurement development; coaches tend to make the decisions in team problem-solving sessions; and upper management is not sufficiently supportive of the teams as they attempt to execute the action plans. Alternately, truly customer-focused organizations involve the customer creatively in developing team measures and find ways to share the teams' feedback from the measures with customers. A team can also share its action plans with its customers as a means of "closing the loop."

In the future, we expect to see improvements in team performance measurement and feedback systems:

- Automation: currently most measurement systems for teams require some manual data input and may lag behind real-time events by a week or more. Greater automation replaces much manual input and approaches real-time feedback for most team measures.

- Strategy: team measurement systems become more clearly tied to business strategy, so that each team can see how well its own strategy is working and supporting the company strategy.

- Team cooperation: the measurement systems of different teams within a business unit become more integrated so that necessary team cooperation is reflected in the measurement systems.

- Customers: the boundary between customers and teams continues to dissolve with regard to measurement and feedback, as it has in other ways.

- Business savvy: effective team measurement systems engage teams in greater understanding of the nature of business.

- Business partners: high performance teams act more like business partners than employees by monitoring and improving their performance measures.

7

CREATING EFFECTIVE
PAY SYSTEMS FOR TEAMS

Edward E. Lawler III

REWARDS ARE AN IMPORTANT element in any formal organization. To be effective, organizations must answer the fundamental question of why individuals should commit their time, effort, and ideas to it. It is a major challenge to create an alignment between how an organization rewards its members and the strategic agenda of the business that accomplishes this end. There are many approaches to rewarding individuals for their performance and for their membership in organizations, as well as a variety of ways to organize and manage complex organizations. In this chapter, the focus is on specifying the correct mix of rewards for organizations that adopt teams.

The traditional approach to designing work organizations calls for hierarchical decision making, simple repetitive jobs at the lowest level, and rewards based on carefully defined and measured individual jobs and job performance. This "control approach" is losing market share, so to speak, to involvement or high-performance approaches to management.[1] The advantages of the involvement approach are said to be better organizational performance, including higher-quality products and services, greater speed, less absenteeism, less turnover, better decision making, better problem solving, and lower overhead costs—in short, greater organizational effectiveness.[2]

Employee-involvement approaches to organization design generally argue that three features of an organization should be moved to lower organization levels:

1. *Information* about the performance of the organization
2. *Knowledge* that enables employees to understand and contribute to organizational performance
3. *Power* to make decisions that influence organizational direction and performance

Some approaches to involvement also consider how pay systems should be changed as part of a move to a more involvement-oriented management approach. They generally favor rewards based on group or organizational performance but do not describe in detail how pay should be designed to fit particular involvement practices. Others simply suggest paying everyone "fairly" so as to avoid the dysfunctional effects of paying for performance.

Teams have emerged as a widely used vehicle for facilitating the movement of power, information, and knowledge to lower levels of an organization. As mentioned in Chapter One, survey data indicate that most U.S. corporations currently use one or more of the major types of teams.[3] As was also mentioned, they do not take a single approach to teams; they use a variety of teams having different designs and purposes. All types of teams, however, share at least one common attribute: to be effective, they require a supportive reward system.[4] Not surprisingly, traditional pay systems that emphasize individual jobs and performance are not adequate to the team task.

CASE EXAMPLE: TEAM-BASED REWARDS AT SOLECTRON

Solectron Corporation provides an interesting example of an organization that found it needed to change its reward system in order to support the creation of self-directed production work teams. Solectron is a very successful Silicon Valley high-tech company with more than fourteen thousand employees worldwide. A contract manufacturer of circuit boards, the company also packages software. It is well known for high-quality products and rapid growth. Solectron is one of the few high-technology firms to win the Baldrige Award (in 1991); it grew from $265 million of revenue in that year to $2.8 billion in 1996. In 1997, it became the first company to win the Baldrige Award twice.

In the early 1990s, management decided that Solectron needed to improve its performance because of growing competition and a shrinking competitive advantage. This led to creation of a variety of teams. The most common form was self-directed production teams, charged with responsibility for an entire part of the production process.[5] In their California manufacturing operations, 240 teams were created.

When Solectron began its movement to teams, a companywide variable-pay plan was already in place. Begun in 1985, the plan involved discretionary bonuses that focused more on effort than on performance and had no ability to focus on team performance. It did not support the right team behaviors, and as a result a participative design process was begun to create a team-based pay plan. The new plan was installed in 1995.[6]

The team-based bonus system is funded by a measure of location profit and return on assets. It provides a quarterly bonus payment to the members of all teams. The company set the maximum bonus that individuals could earn at a conservative 5 percent of their base pay. The amount the members of individual teams receive is based on the quality of their team's output and productivity against a team standard. The individual team members share equally in the dollar payout amounts. Temporary employees participate in the plan, as do nonexempt employees who are not on teams. Nonteam members are expected to set individual goals.

The goals of individual teams are based on a negotiation process with the team manager that leads to setting goals specific to each team. This is required because of the various products that are produced in the teams. One of the most unusual features of the Solectron variable-pay plan is that it was participatively developed, to heighten commitment to the plan on the part of team members as well as managers. There was also an effort to be sure that the development process fit the overall management style of the organization. An extensive communications and training program was used to introduce the plan. Since its introduction, an extensive meeting and communications programs has been used to develop an in-depth understanding of the plan.

The results of the pay plan implementation have been positive. Quality and productivity have improved.[7] In addition, overall satisfaction with the pay system has risen significantly because individuals feel that they have more control over how much they are paid. The pay plan has also encouraged individuals to learn more about the organization's financial and overall performance. A key element of the plan is public posting of team goals. This tends to stimulate teams to reach their goals and leads to peer and manager recognition for performance.

Interestingly, the group that most obstructed successful installation of the variable-pay plan was the managers. Believing it caused them to lose power, they raised a number of concerns that slowed the implementation process. The organization repeatedly stressed to the managers that the changes were needed to meet competition, and that it was critical to Solectron's long-term success that the plan be installed—and be successful. The results seem to justify installation of the plan. Among other things, the defect rate has gone down substantially, saving the organization $18 million in the first nine months the plan was in place.[8]

Installing the team variable-pay plan did not address all the pay issues that the move to teams raised. As teams developed, more and more questions were raised about the merit-pay system and the determinants of base pay. Team members questioned the validity of this whole approach to pay as they began operating in teams. Job descriptions have become more difficult to maintain, and as a result the organization is increasingly giving consideration to installing a skill-based pay system to replace their traditional system of job-based merit salary increase.

Overall, the movement to a team-based pay plan at Solectron seems to have improved the fit between the pay system and the organization design and management style. This occurred because it shifted what was measured, and how teams were rewarded. It is also due in part to the involvement that occurred in designing the plan, and to the extensive communication and training process that was associated with its implementation. Most likely, though, it is not a completed change effort. The fit between its team-based organization design and its individual job-based pay system is poor. As a result, Solectron probably will continue to further redesign its pay system.

REWARD SYSTEM OBJECTIVES

As is illustrated by the Solectron example, for teams to be optimally effective a reward system must recognize the kinds of behavior and skills that are needed. The challenge is to create a fit between the characteristics of the reward system and those of the team. Because teams differ, no reward system design is universally effective. The key is to design a system that fits the characteristics of the team and the organizational context in which it operates. This is not a simple task. It requires an approach that chooses among the major pay system design options, based on the outcomes they will produce when applied to a particular type of team in a specific environment.

Our consideration of the design choices looks at the outcomes that pay can affect and then considers two major design decisions: how to determine base pay and how to pay for performance.

Reward systems in general, and pay systems in particular, affect individual and organizational behavior in important areas.[9] The research on reward systems suggests that they influence a company's strategy implementation and overall effectiveness in six ways:

1. *Attracting and retaining employees.* Studies on job choice, career choice, and employee turnover clearly show that the types and level of rewards an organization offers influence the kinds of employees it attracts and retains. Overall, companies that offer the highest-level rewards tend to attract and retain the largest number of people. However, different rewards appeal to different people. For example, high levels of risk compensation attract entrepreneurial personalities, while extensive and security-oriented benefits generally attract those who like to avoid risk. Individual incentive plans attract people who want to operate on their own and control their own fate, while collective rewards are more likely to attract individuals who favor shared responsibility and collective action.

2. *Motivating performance.* Reward systems motivate performance if certain conditions exist. What are the conditions? Employees must perceive that the organization ties important—and timely—rewards to effective performance. They also need to feel that they can influence the type of performance that drives pay. People have mental maps of what the world is like, and they use these maps to choose behaviors leading to outcomes that satisfy their needs. Employees are inherently neither motivated nor unmotivated to perform effectively; their motivation depends on the situation, how they perceive it, and what rewards they need and value.

In general, an individual is most motivated to behave in a certain way when he or she believes that such behavior leads to attractive outcomes. This is often referred to as a line of sight. They also need to believe that they can behave in ways that produce reward, and that it is possible to perform at the desired level. These conditions have clear implications for pay systems: to be motivational, the systems must create a clear and achievable line of sight between a person's behavior and the receipt of amounts of pay that are important to them.

3. *Motivating skill and knowledge development.* Just as pay systems can motivate performance, they can encourage employees to learn and develop new skills. The same motivational principles apply, so individuals focus on learning the skills a company rewards. Some organizations have implemented skill-based pay, a relatively new compensation approach, to capitalize on this very point. With skill-based pay, they can strategically target the types of learning they want employees to acquire and thus improve employees' ability to perform in strategically important ways. By contrast, many job-based systems tie increased pay and perquisites to higher-level jobs, thereby encouraging individuals to learn those skills that they feel lead to promotion.

4. *Shaping corporate culture.* Along with other organizational features, reward systems help define culture. A company's approach to developing, administering, and managing reward systems influences many facets of an organization's culture. For example, reward systems influence the degree to which employees view a company as having a culture that is human-resource oriented, entrepreneurial, innovative, competence-based, team-based, entitlement-based, participative, and so on.

Reward systems shape culture precisely because they have such a strong effect on employees' skills, motivation, satisfaction, and sense of what is important to the organization. The behaviors they promote become the dominant patterns in the organization and influence employees' perceptions and beliefs about what the company stands for, believes in, and values.

5. *Reinforcing and defining structure.* Pay systems reinforce and define an organization's structure. Yet quite often this is not considered in designing pay systems. Thus their impact on structure is unintentional. But that doesn't mean the impact is minimal. Pay systems primarily affect the level of integration and differentiation in an organization. People tend to unite if they are rewarded in the same way and divide if treated differently. In the case of a group, pay systems cause the individuals in it to either pull together or compete with one another. They also cause teams to compete or cooperate, depending on whether the teams vie for rewards or share equally in a reward pool that is influenced by the performance of multiple teams. In addition, pay systems contribute to defining a company's status hierarchy and strongly influence its decision-making structures and processes.

6. *Determining pay costs.* Reward systems often represent a significant cost; pay alone makes up more than one-half of many companies' operating costs. Therefore, system designers must focus on how high these costs should be and how they vary with the organization's ability to pay. For example, a reasonable outcome of a well-designed pay system

might be an increase in costs if the company has money to spend and a decrease in costs if it does not. Another objective might be to have lower overall reward-system costs than do competitors.

Because reward systems affect so many critical features of an organization, they are a crucial determinant of strategy implementation and organizational effectiveness. For a strategy to be successfully implemented, the reward system must align with it in at least two respects. First, it needs to reward those behaviors the strategy calls for. Second, it has to support development of those organizational capabilities and core competencies that are necessary for execution of the strategy.

Design Options

In designing an organization's reward system, dozens of decisions are made. All of them are important, but two have a particularly large impact on the effectiveness of teams.[10] The first involves whether the pay system is based on a job-description approach or a skills-or-competency approach. This feature is a critical determinant of the capabilities of individuals, teams, and the total organization. The second is how the organization chooses to pay for performance, if at all. This feature is, of course, a crucial determinant of whether and how individuals are motivated to perform effectively. It also has an important effect on the structure and culture of the organization. We focus on these design decisions in the remainder of this chapter.

PAYING THE JOB OR THE PERSON. For decades, organizations have based their financial reward systems on the types of jobs people do. Most organizations take the approach of evaluating the job, not the person, in order to set pay levels. This approach assumes that job worth can be determined and that the person doing the job is worth only as much to the organization as the job itself. Job evaluation programs and salary surveys are used to determine what other organizations pay for the same or similar work. Pay grades are created (often as many as forty!), and jobs are placed in one of the grades based on the results of the job evaluation. This approach has several advantages: it assures an organization that its compensation costs are not dramatically out of line with those of competitors, and it gives a somewhat objective basis for pay rates.

PAYING FOR SKILLS. The major alternative to job-based pay is to pay individuals for the skills or competencies they possess. Rather than reward people for scaling the corporate hierarchy or "growing" their jobs, the company rewards them for increasing what they can do. This approach generates very different corporate cultures and employee skill-development patterns. Skill-based pay can help create a culture of concern for personal growth and development and a highly talented workforce. In factories that use this system, it typically means many people perform multiple tasks, which results in a highly knowledgeable and flexible labor force.

One of the first skill-based pay plans in the United States was installed in a General Foods plant in Topeka, Kansas, more than three decades ago.[11] The plant used skill-based pay from its inception, encouraging individuals to learn all of the tasks that their team was asked to perform. As individuals were certified to have learned a skill, anywhere from twenty-five to fifty cents was added to their hourly pay rate. Over time, most individuals reached the top pay rate; in effect, they almost doubled their pay from their entry wage rate. Skill certification was handled by a peer appraisal process, except in a few cases where technical experts were brought in to certify more complex skills.

The approach used in this plant is very similar to those in many manufacturing locations today. It is used most commonly in process technology operations such as chemical plants, oil refineries, and other situations where highly interdependent team behavior is needed. This pay-per-skill-learned approach is not common in union situations, where skill-based pay is used. There two, three, or four pay rates are established and over time individuals progress from an entry wage to a fully skilled wage (often level two), while some continue progressing to an expert level. This progression is based on their learning certain identified packages of skills; in that respect, it is quite similar to the pay-per-skill-learned approach. But instead of pricing individual skills, it simply bundles them together, sometimes giving individuals choices about which sets of skills they learn so as to complete a package allowing them to be "promoted" to the next higher pay rate. This approach is somewhat simpler to administer than the pay-per-skill approach since it involves fewer pay rates.

An alternative to traditional job-based pay plans that is used in some team situations is to establish a small number of very flexible, generic job descriptions. This approach reduces some of the dysfunctional features of a traditional job-based system but does not give individuals incentive to learn a specific mix of skills that in fact contribute to team effectiveness.

In most cases, skill-based pay tends to produce somewhat higher pay levels for individuals, but these costs usually are offset by greater workforce flexibility and performance.[12] Flexibility often leads to lower staffing levels and less absenteeism and turnover, both of which may drop as employees appreciate the opportunity to use and be paid for a wide range of skills. On the other hand, skill-based pay can be a challenge to administer. To date, for example, there are no well-developed systems for determining the worth of individual skills in the marketplace.

In general, skill-based pay seems to fit well in companies that want a flexible, relatively permanent workforce oriented toward learning, growth, and development. Many new team-based plants use this approach, as do plants that are moving toward high-involvement management methods. In addition, more companies are applying skill-based (often called competency-based) pay to knowledge workers, managers, and service employees where the strategy calls for high-performance teams or one-stop service and a high level of customer focus and satisfaction. Examples here are American Express, Frito-Lay, and the Aid Association for Lutherans.

FIT WITH TEAMS. Table 7.1 summarizes what has been said so far about job-based versus skill-based pay. The characteristics associated with skill-based pay seem to be a much better fit for most types of teams than are those associated with job-based pay. A key requirement for effective operation of any kind of team is learning on the part of team members. They need to learn about how to operate as team members. They often need to develop new technical knowledge about the organization and its work processes and methods as well. This is particularly true when the team is self-managing and when the individual team members have to work in a highly interdependent mode. Properly administered skill-based or competency-based pay is a powerful tool for encouraging individuals to learn what is necessary to make teams effective.

A key issue in many types of teams is management of lateral processes. This is often best facilitated by having individuals on teams learn multiple steps in production and service processes (so that they can communicate with individuals who are positioned before and after them in the process) and participate in lateral process management activities. Paying for skills also creates the possibility of varying individuals' pay by the amount of skill and knowledge they contribute to a team. Highly skilled individuals can be paid more; this is an important retention device, particularly in environments where knowledge and skill are important keys to team effectiveness and competitive advantage.

Type of Team

There is some variation among the skill needs according to type of team. Thus the importance of using skill-based pay (as well as determining what kind of skill-based pay is needed) varies somewhat with the type of team.

Table 7.1. Impact of Job-Based and Skill-Based Pay.

	Job-based	*Skill- or knowledge-based*
Attraction	Provides good market data	Attracts learning-oriented and high-skill individuals
Motivation	No impact on performance	Little impact on performance
Skill development	Learn job-related and upward-mobility skills	Motivate needed skill development
Culture	Bureaucratic, hierarchical	Learning, self-managing
Structure	Hierarchical, individual jobs, differentiation	Horizontal, team-based
Cost	Good control over individuals' pay rates	Higher individual pay

PARALLEL TEAMS. Parallel problem-solving teams (for example, quality circles and suggestion teams) are often the ones with the least need for skill-based pay. They rely on individuals' contributing their ideas to various problem-solving activities. Since the team activity is not a full-time commitment for people, investing heavily in learning additional skills may not be worthwhile. A few additional skills may be needed to aid with problem solving and group process, but these are often learned by individuals without their having to be paid for them. Skill-based pay that encourages cross-training, such as the pay-per-skill approach, is sometimes a significant aid because it gives individuals better overall understanding of the work process. It can also improve people's ability to solve problems, diagnose, and innovate in work system design. The question remains, however, whether it is worth investing in cross-training simply so that people can participate for short periods of time in parallel teams.

PRODUCTION AND SERVICE TEAMS. The situation with respect to the advantages of skill-based pay is quite different with self-managing production and service teams. Here, individuals typically spend all their time in a single team, and there is a great need for learning and development. Depending upon the kind of production or service process individuals are in, this learning may simply involve cross-training so that individuals understand the entire work process and better coordinate their work. Alternatively, it may involve developing particular kinds of management and technical expertise so that supervisors and staff support are not needed. This latter type of skill-based pay is particularly important if the team is doing complex knowledge work and it is impossible for any one individual to learn all the knowledge necessary to address the kind of issues that come up as the team does its work. This is often true in management, project, and action teams. A typical approach in this case is to identify a few individuals as in-depth experts in various areas, and to reward them with extra pay for their expertise. In the absence of a skill-based pay system, there is often no way to reward this kind of depth. Many organizations have for years recognized this fact by putting in technical ladders, which reward individuals for becoming more and more expert in a particular topic. Bell Labs had one of the best-known systems. It relied on maturity curves and promotion to provide a career track for their scientists, from new graduates to Nobel Prize winners. Typically, though, these technical ladders do not reward breadth of skills; thus there is nothing to encourage an individual to develop team skills and understand other parts of the work process. They also have been used only with technical employees.

PROJECT TEAMS. In a project team, skill and knowledge-based pay is a particularly good fit. A key success factor in knowledge work teams is the presence of some individuals who know multiple functions. In job-based pay systems, it is usually difficult to get individuals to learn multiple functions because there is no reward; indeed, there may be a disincentive for learning a second function such as marketing or engineering. When complex project work is involved, it is often impossible to have a person who has a good knowledge base in all of the functions that are required for a successful project. It is, however, both possible and important to develop a number of individuals who have mastery outside of the single function. Multifunctional expertise is critical in enabling the project team to integrate its work and make good trade-offs among the demands of the different disciplines in developing a new product or service.[13]

To encourage lateral career moves, an organization often has to do more than simply have a pay-per-skill approach. Lateral career tracks must be developed so that individuals are significantly rewarded for making cross-functional moves that do not necessarily involve obtaining a higher level of responsibility or a higher pay grade. In the absence of such a structure, individuals run the risk of actually losing money by making a lateral move. This comes about because they do not move into a higher pay grade and are in an area where they are not expert; thus they are likely to lose out on merit-pay increases or bonuses based upon performance. They learn a new function, but they are at a disadvantage when competing for pay increases since other individuals in the area are already experts in the function.

If a project team requires complex knowledge work, depth expertise in one or more areas may be critical to success. Knowledge-based pay, which rewards people for developing ever-deeper levels of expertise, as in a technical ladder, is a very helpful tool. It not only rewards people for developing important knowledge; it helps retain technical experts in the organization by paying them more than they would be paid in traditional job-based structures. The typical approach here involves defining multiple levels of technical expertise in disciplines such as engineering, accounting, finance, and human resources. Each level has a set of skill descriptors attached; as individuals demonstrate that they have mastered the skill set at a new level, they are given a promotion and pay increase, recognizing their additional skills and knowledge.

CONCLUSION. Given the positive fit between skill-based and knowledge-based pay and teams, it is not surprising that the research evidence on using this approach shows that it is most frequently used in team environments.[14] This is particularly true with respect to production and service teams. They make more use of skill-based or knowledge-based pay than any other kind of team structure. A good guess is that the combination of skill-based pay and teams started in the 1950s in Scandinavia and continued in the 1960s in the United States with the creation of the first team-based manufacturing plants. Today this may be the predominant pay practice among production and service teams. There is less knowledge available on how extensively skill-based pay is used in conjunction with project teams, and other kinds of teams. Project teams in particular seem to stimulate its adoption along with abandonment of job-based systems.

As more and more organizations move toward being team-based overall, the pressure to change to skill-based and knowledge-based pay is likely to grow. This very much underscores the point made earlier in this book, that in team-based organizations individuals do not so much have jobs as they have temporary task assignments. Given this situation, it is unrealistic to base someone's pay on his or her job. It makes more sense to pay the person based on the value added to the organization, that is, based on skills and knowledge. This also encourages learning skills and knowledge that help the employee add more value to the organization.

Table 7.2 summarizes what has been said about the applicability of skill-based and knowledge-based pay for teams. As can be seen, slightly different forms of pay-for-skills fit each type. Thus, the challenge is to design skill-based and knowledge-based pay systems that fit whatever type of team is the focal point of the design process.

Table 7.2. Teams and Skill-Based Pay.

Type of team	Pay
Parallel	Encourages cross-training and team skills
Production and service	Motivates cross-training, self-management skills, and some depth skills; retains most skilled team members
Project	Motivates development of depth expertise and cross-functional knowledge
Management	Motivates development of depth expertise and cross-functional knowledge and career tracks

Performance-Based Pay

The most important strategic decisions a company must make about its reward system are whether and how pay is to be based on performance. Although paying for performance is the most common approach in the United States, it is not the only approach that can be or is used. One alternative is seniority-based pay, frequently used by government agencies in the United States and in other parts of the world. Many Japanese companies base pay on seniority, although they often give bonuses tied to corporate performance.

Most U.S.-based businesses say they reward individual performance through a merit system. But creating an effective merit-pay system is more easily said than done.[15] In fact, some observers have concluded that many organizations would be better off if they did not try to relate pay to performance and relied instead on other factors to motivate performance.[16] The main reason: companies find it difficult to specify the type of performance they desire and to determine whether or not employees demonstrate it. A second reason is the fear that pay for performance will reduce intrinsic motivation. Despite the attention this fear receives, research evidence does not support the view that it is a serious problem.[17]

Organizations face a lot of choices in how they relate pay to performance. They must determine what kinds of rewards to give (the possibilities include stock, cash, and a variety of other options); how often to give them (ranging from time periods of a few minutes to many years); and whether performance is measured at the individual, group, or organizational level. Finally, they must determine what kinds of performance are rewarded. For example, managers might be rewarded for sales increases, productivity volumes, cost-reduction ideas, demonstration of ability to develop subordinates, and so on. Teams can be rewarded for quality and productivity, as is the case in Solectron, but they can also be rewarded for safety, cost reductions, and helping other teams.

Rewarding some behaviors and not others has a major effect on performance, so a company must pay close attention to its strategic plan in deciding what to reward. Once it develops a strategic plan, it can define key performance objectives and design reward systems to motivate the appropriate performance. In the process, designers of pay systems should consider issues such as short-term versus long-term performance, risk taking versus risk avoidance, individual performance versus team performance, team performance versus total corporate performance, cash versus stock, and maximizing return on investment versus sales growth. An organization can only make effective decisions about an issue such as whether to use stock options and what to reward after it carefully considers what supports the desired behaviors.

Three general points about relating pay to performance bear mentioning here. First, bonus plans generally do a better job of motivating employees than do pay raises and salary increase plans.[18] The reason is simple: with bonus pay, an individual's pay can vary substantially from time period to time period, while a raise usually becomes an annuity and as a result does little to relate current pay levels to current performance.

Second, objective performance measures are better motivators than subjective measures. In general, employees assign higher credibility to objective measures, such as sales volume or units produced.[19] Thus, they often accept the validity of these measures even if they do not accept the validity of a boss's rating. Thus, an organization that ties rewards to objective measures typically creates a much more credible link between pay and performance than does one that bases pay on subjective, nonverifiable measures such as a supervisor's rating.

Third, group and organizational plans generally work best in creating integration and teamwork.[20] Under these plans, it is usually to everyone's advantage if each person works effectively because they all share in the financial results of higher performance. If people feel they can benefit from another's actions, they are likely to support and encourage good performance by others.[21] This is not true under individual plans, which tend to produce differentiation and competition. On the other hand, group and organizational bonus plans separate individual behavior from rewards and as a result have a more difficult time establishing a clear line of sight from individual performance to the reward.

Table 7.3 elaborates on the consequences of three diverse pay-for-performance approaches. As can be seen, they have quite different impacts. In reviewing the right combinations for various kinds of teams, we look separately at parallel, work, and project teams.

Parallel Teams

Because parallel teams do not represent a fundamental change in the structure of an organization, they have the fewest implications for the reward system. Some argue that no pay-for-performance system changes are required to support their operation. However, there is evidence that rewards can and should be used—to motivate effective problem solving.

Advocates of participative management have suggested for a long time that the Scanlon plan and other gainsharing plans that share cost savings with all employees fit extremely well with the use of problem-solving teams.[22] There is a history of more than forty years of combining suggestion groups with the type of cost-saving bonuses that are part of the Scanlon plan, and the research shows positive results. Virtually every review of these plans argues that it improves the economic performance of an organization.[23] It works particularly well if combined with open financial-information systems and participative decision making. The major motivational weakness of gainsharing plans is that the line of sight between a suggestion and the size of a bonus is weak. A group can make a major breakthrough and receive only a small bonus because the savings are shared among all employees in an organization.

Profit sharing, stock-option, and stock-ownership plans that cover all employees also can be somewhat supportive of problem-solving groups. They distribute financial rewards bearing some relation to the effectiveness of the problem-solving groups and to the implementation of their ideas. Their major weakness, of course, is again line of sight; thus in many instances (as in large organizations) they do not have a significant impact on the effectiveness of the problem-solving groups.

Donnelly Mirrors is a good example of a company that has worked hard for decades to relate its problem-solving activity to the size of bonuses.[24] Through extensive education and communication programs, the company has done a good job of informing the workforce both about the economics of the business and about the financial impact of the suggestions the workforce develops through problem-solving meetings.

Donnelly is not an isolated example. A number of other Scanlon companies, such as Dana Corporation and Herman Miller, have used the

Table 7.3. Impact of Pay for Performance.

	Individual merit	Team incentives	Organization plans
Attraction	Good for high performers	Good if team does well	Good if organization performs well
Motivation	Good line-of-sight	Moderate line-of-sight	Weak line-of-sight
Skill development	Encourages learning skills that lead to rewarded performance	Encourages team skills	Encourages learning about business
Culture	Performance-oriented, job-focused	Team-focused	Business involvement
Structure	Individual accountability	Team integration	Organizationwide integration
Cost	High if significant merit awards given	High if significant rewards given	Possible self-funding from profit improvements

same approach. It is hard to determine exactly how good a line of sight they have developed, but there is little doubt that the logic of bonuses for everyone based on improvement suggestions is well accepted and generally seems to be meaningful.

The alternative to gainsharing and profit sharing is to give bonuses, stock, or other valued rewards to teams for their suggestions. A number of organizations have used this approach, which in most respects is simply a group version of the classic individual-suggestion-program approach. An estimated savings amount is calculated, and individuals who contribute to the idea are given a percentage of the estimated savings. It closely ties the development of the idea to the financial bonus. This involves a number of risks, however. Often, the estimated savings are not realized. Thus individuals are rewarded even if the company does not gain. Further, individuals may feel they are not rewarded fairly because they get only a percentage of the savings. There are almost always issues of who should be included among the recipients of the bonus. Finally, most useful suggestions have to be accepted and implemented by many people. The classic suggestion program does not reward people for accepting and further developing the suggestion. Thus, they may not have the motivation that is needed to produce gains. Quite the opposite, of course, is true with gainsharing plans where no one gains unless an idea is successfully implemented.

What clearly is incompatible with parallel suggestion teams is use of suggestion systems that reward individuals. They are in direct conflict with the idea of having teams develop ideas. They reward the wrong kind of behavior and compete directly with group-suggestion and problem-solving approaches. In cases where they are used, individuals have been known to claim ownership of ideas developed as part of the group problem-solving process. Also, with such a system in place individuals are much less willing to share their ideas and thoughts in a group setting than they are where only collective rewards for groups developing a suggestion are offered.

A number of organizations use recognition approaches to reward teams for their successes. Unfortunately, there is virtually no research evidence to indicate how effective recognition rewards are in this application. The variety of recognition vehicles used is enormous. Some companies emphasize appearances before senior executives, while others give symbols that involve significant outlays of money (such as vacations and televisions). Although little research has been done on recognition programs, an educated guess is that they can be powerful if they are used astutely.

The key is to give recognition when groups accomplish something significant and to deliver a reward that is valued by the group.

Determining what is valued by a group can be a challenge. For example, there may be disagreement among groups or even within a group as to the value of a trip to a ball game or a chance to present an idea to the CEO. With the exception of the issue of how much recognition rewards are valued, most of the other considerations with recognition programs are the same as those involved in giving financial rewards for producing an idea.

Xerox Corporation provides a good example of a company that has used recognition extensively to reward quality improvement teams. They run a very high quality companywide TV broadcast that features the improvement ideas of carefully selected teams. There is no question that this is a powerful reward, and that teams compete quite hard for the honor of being on the telecast and receiving the attention and recognition the exposure brings. It helps that the CEO of Xerox hosts the program and is knowledgeable about the suggestions that have come out of the individual groups.

Production and Service Teams

Perhaps the most common way to reward the members of work teams today is to appraise their individual performance. Instead of rewarding the team as a whole, organizations simply add a dimension to the performance appraisal of individuals that focuses on how good a team member the person is. This usually counts toward their overall appraisal and determines the amount of their pay increase or bonus. In essence, this approach continues the historical individual-pay-for-performance practices of most organizations but adapts it slightly to a team-based environment. In some ways, it creates a conflict in direction that can be self-canceling with respect to effective team behavior. It asks individuals to compete for a given amount of money but changes the basis of the competition from individual performance to performance as a team member. In other words, individuals end up competing with other team members for who is the most helpful, cooperative, and best team member. This, of course, fails to change the performance focus from the individual to the team and does nothing to focus individuals on how effectively the team is performing. Thus, it makes sense to use this only where work teams are loosely interdependent and need a minimum of highly interdependent behavior to be effective.

There are three ways of directly rewarding performance at the team level. First, rewards can be tied to team performance through use of a merit-pay system that bases salary increases or bonuses on a team performance appraisal. Second, special awards can be given to teams in recognition of outstanding performance. Third, a gainsharing or profit-sharing plan can be used, structured so that it pays all teams the same bonus or, as is the case in Solectron, pays bonuses that are funded by the overall plan but adjusted to reflect the performance of particular teams.

The most powerful way to motivate team performance is to establish objectives and metrics for successful team performance and then link rewards to team success.[25] Merit pay in the form of salary increases or bonuses can be distributed equally to team members based upon the results of a team performance appraisal. For team performance pay to work, there must be clear and explicit objectives, accepted measures, and good feedback about team performance.[26] Team performance appraisals are opportunities for teams to conduct self-appraisals and obtain customer evaluations. These data can be used to assist managers in determining team ratings.

Frequently, managers are uncomfortable with giving a reward of the same size to all team members, so they differentially reward individual performance. This is potentially counterproductive. Bestowing differing rewards to individual team members can undermine cooperation and collective effort. Further, if there is high interdependence among team members, it may not be possible to measure individual performance accurately; as a result, the rewards end up not based on valid measures of performance.

If the work of team members is not highly interdependent, then it may make sense to combine team and individual merit pay.[27] A bonus pool can be created based on team performance, with the amount divided among members based on the kind of measures of individual performance that are considered in Chapter Five. For this not to be divisive, it is critical that the manager solicit input from team members about the relative contributions of individual members. A mature work team may be able to use a peer evaluation system to differentiate individual rewards based on individual contributions to the team's performance. It is possible to have teams do appraisals of individuals in which they divide up a pool of money that originally was generated by the effectiveness of the team. This, in effect, rewards individuals for being cooperative in producing the bonus pool while still recognizing individual performance. It is more effective if team members assess team performance before they assess individual performance, because team performance sets the framework for appraising individual performance.

The experience of Motorola highlights a major problem with team-based rewards. For years, Motorola had team-based incentive plans in many of its manufacturing facilities. The bonuses were often quite large and were targeted to meeting specific performance objectives. In many cases, they did motivate the teams to perform well as teams, but they did a poor job of recognizing the interdependencies that existed among the teams. Since Motorola tends to have large manufacturing facilities doing relatively complex work, their teams often need to cooperate with each other to produce a product, and they share a number of key services such as maintenance and technical support. Because of the team incentive plans, a considerable amount of conflict developed among the teams over who got first access to help and support, and there was tremendous focus on the inequities that were perceived to exist whenever some teams got large bonuses and others did not. Ultimately, Motorola decided to abandon their team-based incentive plans because they failed to produce a general environment of cooperation in the workplace, and they caused too many parts of the organization to optimize their performance at the cost of that of the overall organization. The learning from Motorola is clear: strong team incentive plans should be used only where teams operate relatively autonomously with respect to their production and service needs.

The second way of linking pay to team performance is through the use of special award or recognition programs. In contrast to appraisals with their goals and formula-driven approaches, these reward exceptional performance after it has occurred. To be effective, special awards should be used only to recognize truly special team achievements. Because work teams perform ongoing and repeated work to produce products or services, performance that meets the requirements of customers should happen regularly, but extraordinary performance is likely to be rare. Therefore, special rewards are best used to supplement and not substitute for other team pay-for-performance systems. Special awards can be motivating and enhance team cohesiveness. There is a certain pride that comes from being associated with a successful team, and public recognition solidifies it.

Gainsharing, profit-sharing, and stock plans are the third major approach to granting rewards for team performance. Gainsharing requires that the work unit covered by it be relatively autonomous and responsible for a measurable output, as was mentioned earlier. These plans typically give the same amount of reward to all teams in a particular work unit or location. They suffer from poor line of sight but can be effective and may be the best choice if the work of teams is highly interdependent.[28] Of all these plans, gainsharing clearly provides the best line of sight and has been widely used to support and reward production teams in Weyerhaeuser, Monsanto, 3M, and a host of other corporations that use production teams in factories whose process technologies create interdependent work. If the work is not interdependent, then each team can be rewarded from a common bonus pool for its performance.

In choosing among the approaches to rewarding teams, it is important to remember that—as the Motorola example highlights—rewarding a work team for separate performance is not always appropriate. The critical issue here is the degree of integration and differentiation. If the team is not highly autonomous, then providing rewards at the team level may be counterproductive. If there are critical interdependencies between a team and other parts of the organization that need to be accounted for, rewarding a team for its own performance may push differentiation too far. For example, work teams in manufacturing plants often work separate shifts, and what happens during one shift affects other shifts. In addition, the interdependencies with staff groups may be important. If a work team develops its way of doing things and members become close, they may become myopic in their understanding of the needs of the broader organization, and suboptimization can result. Using a gainsharing or profit-sharing plan that rewards team members based on the performance of the larger organizational unit can serve to integrate the team into the rest of the organization and act as an offset to the strong cohesiveness that tends to develop in a work team.

In general, an organization composed of work teams needs to make sure its pay-for-performance systems motivate the right kind of team performance. Often, this is best done through a mix of team-level and organizational-level pay-for-performance systems.[29] The more that work teams stand alone as performing units, the more rewards should be focused at the team level. The greater the interdependencies between work teams and functional groups, and among different work teams, the more pay-for-performance systems should operate at the organizational level.

In very individualistic countries, such as the United States, there continues to be a strong demand for individual pay for performance.[30] Thus how assessment of individuals is handled in a team environment is quite important. The evidence clearly suggests that assessment of individual performance should be handled in the context of the work team.[31] If teams are rewarded collectively, they are motivated to handle the problems associated with someone who is not contributing his or her fair share to the team's performance. In many cases, they also recognize and reward the best performers, since it is in everyone's best interest to have good performers on the team.

By formally recognizing individual performance, the reward system reduces the pressure on the team to appraise and deal with poor performers. Indeed, in situations where the performance appraisal is a forced distribution rating system, it creates the undesirable situation wherein it is in the best interests of individuals to have some poor performers on their teams. They are much more likely to encourage and support performance improvement on the part of poor performers when there is a collective pay situation in which poor performers hurt everyone's opportunity to earn a bonus.

Not everyone accepts the idea of only having team or collective pay for performance and no individual pay for performance. This brings us back to the point made at the beginning of the chapter on attraction and selection. In a team-based environment, individuals who desire rewards for individual performance should not be put on many kinds of teams.

Project and Management Teams

Project teams present a particularly interesting challenge for reward systems. They often require a reward system that is specifically designed to support them. Traditional pay-for-performance systems focus on individuals and tend to measure and reward performance on an annual schedule. Both of these practices are inconsistent with motivating project teams. The obvious first choice for motivating a project team is a reward system that establishes metrics for successful group performance and sets rewards that are tied to the accomplishments of the group. It also is desirable to have the rewards distributed at the time the team completes its project. Thus, one popular and effective approach to rewarding project teams is to give spot bonus awards to them when they complete their projects.

Rewarding a project team's performance may be difficult if, as is often true, the membership of the team changes during projects. It may not make sense to reward everyone equally when some individuals are there for 10 percent of the team's activities, while others are there for 100 percent. Unequal rewards are a possibility, but it can be difficult to determine how large they should be because the amount of time spent may not be a good measure of someone's contribution to a project.

One example of a kind of pay bonus plan that can be created for project teams is provided by a high-tech company that does new-product design by creating cross-functional dedicated teams charged with developing a product. At the beginning of the design process, they are given a number of milestone targets to meet, and the members are told to dedicate their efforts to the development process until the new product is ready for manufacturing. In the case of this technology company, specific bonus amounts are tied to reaching the key milestones in the product development process. Equal dollar amounts are given to all members of the product development team when the goals are met. The bonuses can add an additional 20–30 percent to the employees' annual pay, so the incentive is significant. Because the design process often lasts for more than a year, the incentive is more than just a transitory one. The incentive plan, however, ends before the product is actually in the marketplace; thus the employees are not rewarded based upon the ultimate success of the product.

An alternative or complement to rewarding project group performance at the end of each project is to rely on a gainsharing, profit-sharing, or stock-ownership system that covers a total organizational unit. This may be a preferred alternative to rewarding individual teams when, in fact, the teams' activities have a major impact on the effectiveness of the unit and it is difficult to measure the effectiveness of the team. It may be preferable as well if project teams are in existence for short periods of time and, as a result, timely measurement and rewarding of the performance of individual teams is difficult. It clearly makes the most sense when organizations want their project team employees to have a long-term, organizationwide focus.

Sometimes it is necessary and desirable to focus on individual performance in a project-team environment. The best approach to doing this is to measure the contributions of individuals to the team's effectiveness at the completion of each project. Individual ratings can be modified by the success of the overall project. In many cases, peer ratings, as well as customer satisfaction ratings, are called for. Peer ratings are particularly critical because in most project teams peers are in the best position to assess the contribution of team members. Over the course of a year, individuals may accumulate a number of ratings that reflect their contributions to each project on which they worked. Performance-pay treatment then becomes a "simple" derivative of how effectively they performed on each of the projects on which they participated. Alternatively, spot bonuses can be paid at the end of each project.

Many of the same issues that arise when project teams are paid for performance also arise when management teams are paid for their performance. A major difference exists however, because management teams are usually permanent teams, and thus spot bonuses and one-time awards are less relevant. Sometimes they are also not as highly interdependent as project teams, and this means that a greater possibility exists for rewarding individual performance. Like project teams and production teams, they can either be rewarded as stand-alone entities based on performance appraisals or measures of team performance, or they can be rewarded based on organizationwide gainsharing, profit-sharing, or stock-based plans. The choice among these is essentially one of the degree to which line of sight and motivation are important versus the degree to which integration of the total work unit matters.

Pay-for-performance plans that focus on an individual team's performance tend to separate the team from the rest of the organization. In the case of management teams, this may be a critical problem because it gives the management team a different reward orientation than that of the teams or individuals who report to them. Of course, if the management team supervises relatively unrelated operations or business units, then it may make sense to measure and reward the management team separately. On the other hand, if the success of a unit they supervise depends upon a high level of integration among the members of the management team and the people who report to them, then rewarding the management team or the managers separately simply does not make sense. Instead, they should be included in either a corporationwide or a business-unitwide plan that treats them the same as it treats the reporting teams or individuals.

Unfortunately, there is no automatically right approach to rewarding management teams for performance. What clearly is right is to consider the degree to which the team itself should be integrated, and how integrated the team has to be with other parts of the organization. Once this is determined, the need for integration should be used to determine the degree to which the team is rewarded separately or as part of an integrated unit that might include the part of the organization reporting to the team, or in fact the total organization.

Summary: Paying for Performance

Table 7.4 summarizes what has been said in this chapter about the fit between rewards for performance and three different types of teams. It clearly makes the point that one size does not fit all. The key to all the approaches shown is measurement of performance and interdependence. Valid measures of performance need to be available, and the reward system must reinforce the key interdependencies among individuals and among teams; otherwise, the reward system rewards the wrong kind of performance and does more damage than good.

Table 7.4. Teams and Pay for Performance.

Type of team	Pay for performance
Parallel	Gainsharing or other business unit plan to reward savings; possible recognition rewards for teams
Production and service	Team bonus or business unit bonus if teams are interdependent; possible individual if based on peer input
Project	Possible one-time or more frequent bonuses, based on project appraisal; also, profit-sharing and stock plans
Management	Possible team bonuses; also, profit-sharing and stock-based plans

CONCLUSIONS: REWARDING TEAMS

Traditional approaches to pay simply do not fit a team-based environment. This is hardly surprising, given that the pay systems in most organizations were designed to support and reward individual behavior. As long as they remain in this mode, they are at best neutral and in most cases counterproductive to creating effective teams. Unfortunately, there is no easy answer to the question of which kinds of reward system practices fit best in a team-based environment. It all depends upon the kind of team, and the technology and strategy of the organization. Two general approaches to pay do seem to potentially fit best with teams. The first is an emphasis on paying the individual instead of the job, and the second is a pay-for-performance approach that focuses on collective performance more than individual performance. Taken together, these two generic approaches encourage individuals to learn the right skills to make teams effective, and they motivate the right type of performance focus on the part of individual teams and organizations.

PART THREE

INFRASTRUCTURE FOR TEAM EFFECTIVENESS

8

INFORMATION TECHNOLOGY AND HIGH-PERFORMANCE TEAMS

Creating Value Through Knowledge

Tora K. Bikson, Susan G. Cohen, Don Mankin

IF TEAMWORK IS THE KEY to effective organizations, information is the key to effective teams. Information is not only necessary but increasingly *is* the work. Information is the raw material to be manipulated and transformed, the basis for the process by which these actions occur. Information is exchanged by team members as they analyze and deliberate. Ultimately, it is the result of the process: the solutions, decisions, new information, and knowledge they generate.

All work is becoming more knowledge-based, not only work such as market research and engineering design but even production and assembly. Team members need tools to help them gain access to information, manage and analyze it, share it among themselves, and communicate it to others. These tools come in the form of new information and communication technologies that enable teams to function effectively within the rich digital material that, from the executive suite to the shop floor, now constitutes the very essence of modern work.

In this chapter, we examine how digital information and communication media help make teams more effective. We begin by suggesting that as work becomes more team-based and knowledge-oriented, the technologies for supporting work evolve in the same directions. We then present the main point and organizing theme of this chapter: knowledge is the modern organization's most important strategic resource, and the basis for new and improved products, services, and work processes. To remain competitive, organizations must find new ways to create, transform, and use knowledge. Teams supported by new information and communications technology are the primary means for accomplishing this goal.

The chapter discusses information resources that the different kinds of teams need to engage effectively in this knowledge-embedding process. We focus on a case study of a project team from the dynamic, knowledge-intensive, emerging "new media" industry. The concepts and insights from the case can be extended to action, production, service, management, and parallel teams as well. Although we primarily address the differences among types of teams, they have important features in common, and we discuss these in the final section.

CONVERGENCE OF TEAMS AND INFORMATION TECHNOLOGY

Today's teams must be able to share information quickly, make decisions locally, take action, and communicate laterally inside and outside the organization. Requirements for timely communication, cooperation, and coordination—combined with the competitive necessity for knowledge-based products, services, and processes—have created the need to use information technology in new ways.

In the past two decades, information technology has evolved from stand-alone systems for individuals to networked systems used by teams for connection and collaboration. Distributed networking capabilities, advances in open systems, telecommunications, multimedia capacity, and shared digital environments have created opportunities for users from the same or different locations to work together. Computers and communication technologies continue to improve in performance while decreasing in price. As a result, networked electronic tools are now in widespread use. Open systems enable integration across organizations as well as between parts of organizations. Very fast telecommunication networks can now transmit interactive multimedia applications—voice, video, and data—in real time. Mobile communications, cellular telephone technology, and wireless connectivity enable people to work together from almost any location. Shared digital environments allow groups of people to share experiences and respond to common events from miles apart, for example in finding oil reserves or rescuing people from an earthquake.[1] Technological advances have helped transform computer-based interactions into social ones, enabling collaborative and team-based work.

These advances have stimulated the development of a class of computer-based applications and systems commonly called "groupware." These technologies, such as Lotus Notes, support groups doing collaborative work (see Chapter Five). The growing interest in media that enable communication, cooperation, and coordination reflects the evolution of technology to support changes in the nature of work. It reflects especially the continuing effort to develop tools for helping teams create value-added products and services.

Knowledge-Embedding Processes in Teams

That knowledge is important for high-level professional, managerial, and high-tech teams is obvious. Its importance is less obvious for teams with purposes more modest and commonplace. Increasingly, teams of all kinds and levels are expected to embed their knowledge in their work processes, the products they produce, and the services they provide. The formal technical and scientific knowledge of industrial scientists and engineers is not the only source of new ideas, innovations, and improvements. Managers are beginning to recognize the business value of the day-to-day innovations that come from experienced workers sharing their tacit knowledge about task processes. Production workers, for example, implement modest shop floor modifications of production machinery that can have major impact on costs and quality. Computer users "tinkering" with new technologies reinvent their work and their tools to better match their needs, occasionally creating new products and services in the process.[2]

The widespread use of teams and technical advances that support social computing enhance the knowledge-embedding process. Teams bring together the specialized expertise of their members to create new knowledge or new applications of existing knowledge. Networked technology provides tools to gain access to information, analyze it, shape and manage it, and share it with others.[3] Together, teams and information technology enable knowledge to be collaboratively created and deployed to achieve competitive advantage (Figure 8.1).

The knowledge that is created can be embedded in product designs, provided in customer services, used as a basis for process improvements, or leveraged into new business opportunities. IBM offers "business solutions": not just computer hardware and software, but redesigned business

Figure 8.1. Collaboration to Create Added Value.

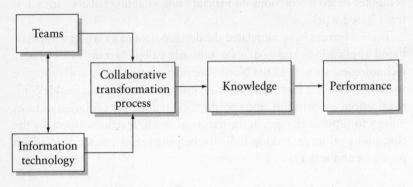

processes, training, and consulting on getting the most out of new technologies. IBM sales teams, comprising members with technical skills to provide expert consulting and the sales skills to close deals, work with their customers in a mutual exploration of their business missions, critical processes, and needs. They increase both their own and their customers' knowledge as they work. The solution emerges from the collaborative effort between consultants and customers. Another example can be found in the shop floor improvement teams that regularly examine production data, use analytical tools such as statistical process control, and brainstorm new ways to improve their performance.

Some companies are beginning to recognize the strategic importance of this team-based, knowledge-embedding process. They are developing mechanisms to help elicit and capture the knowledge created by teams, using the outcomes to develop new products and services or even new lines of business that fill a market niche. This is the business model for Digital Evolution, the company that provides the case discussed in this chapter.

Knowledge-Based Project Team: Case Example

"In a small, fast-paced company, you have to have dynamic collegial management. Old project management specs and time lines don't really work. You have to have people who are aggressive about completing a project and who really want to be on the team and make it happen. I was looking for people I could work with under very trying circumstances: high stress, crummy locations, long hours—people you can argue with at two in the morning over cold pizza, . . . still realizing that you both have the same goal."

These are the words of a project leader at Digital Evolution, a Los Angeles software company, in response to our question about the keys to successful team staffing and management. The firm's business mission is to develop innovative digital communications products and resources in several vertical markets, including entertainment, health, education and training, and varied retail sectors. The project team that serves as a focus here is engaged in producing a multimedia automobile dealership management system for a major automaker, as part of the client's larger "showroom of the future" strategy. (Other team projects have involved development of an interactive system to help customers choose health plans and an online multimedia history of contemporary rock music.) This case yields valuable insights about today's teams and the team-technology relationships that characterize contemporary knowledge-based work groups of all kinds.

Organizational Context

We first encountered the project team at Digital Evolution's high-tech, high-touch headquarters. The team had just completed a successful prototype for the car dealership management system (CDMS) and was developing a real working version for use in future pilot trials. With about twenty-two members, this is currently the largest project team in the eighty-person business. The company itself has grown in size at a rate of about 8 percent per month and more than doubled its revenues annually since its inception.

Just over four years old, the company was founded by its current president and CEO to fill what he perceives as a new business niche. He describes Digital Evolution this way:

> We are network-centric, platform-independent, and . . . oriented toward knowledge-based value creation. At the core, we have to be innovators, not [just] appliers. . . .
>
> New digital communications media are advancing technologically at breakneck speed. In this business, if you analyze an issue and say 'Here are the problems and here are the available tools,' you're destined to fail. To be effective, you have to be able to say 'Here are the problems; let's create what we need to solve them'. . . .
>
> Value creation comes from the ability to gain knowledge from our clients and to apply that knowledge, . . . along with our core competencies, to create products that fulfill a special industry or sector need.

According to Digital Evolution's president, few companies today are positioned to compete in this niche. Although many companies can generate Websites, CD-ROMs, or other multimedia products for their customers, they typically lack the expertise in back-end programming and big system architectures necessary to integrate such products with a client's existing applications and databases. In addition, many companies that sell proprietary technologies and customization services to meet clients' digital communication needs are not platform-independent and may not be able to choose the best solution path for the customer. Finally, many system integrators building solutions that are largely prespecified by clients are not usually skilled in front-end interface design, especially with multimedia technologies. Rarely do any of the provider businesses consciously set out to create new knowledge-based value in the resulting deliverable.

In contrast, Digital Evolution thinks of itself as a "practical digital think tank." According to its CEO, "We don't learn first and then implement what we know. We have to learn while implementing." Given the rapid rate of change in network technologies, clients' task demands and potential ways of addressing them are both continuously evolving. Thus Digital Evolution project staff say they live in "Web weeks"—for instance, the president notes, "What Microsoft posts on the Web today we have to take into account in our development work tomorrow."

In fact, it is partly for this reason that Digital Evolution feels it literally cannot afford to accept a project from which it cannot learn. Delivering innovative services to clients is regarded as an excellent vehicle for "developing intellectual assets." Therefore, Digital Evolution takes on just two types of activities: (1) work-for-hire that involves creative problem solving or intrinsic value for future work, and (2) joint ventures that can produce new knowledge-based products or tools that are potentially modifiable to serve similar needs among other clients and that therefore have significant market potential.

Project teams are staffed with people who have the competencies needed for continuous learning and creation of new value-added multimedia digital communications resources. From the president's perspective, the first requirement is that they be smart and enthusiastic ("This is 99 percent of it," he says). The mix of professional employees is about two-thirds technical specialists (systems architecture, database design, programming languages) and one-third artists (fine arts, graphic arts, music, animation). They report to a technology director and an art director respectively. The relatively flat management structure also includes individuals responsible for internal R&D, business development, marketing, internal administration (for example, human resources), and business and financial affairs.

Any project has, at a minimum, a project manager and its own technical and art directors. The number and specialties of team members vary depending on the project, and the team may rely on clients' experts or external consultants to complement its own members' skills (see Figure 8.2).

Generally, employees work on only one project at a time; their involvement may be limited to particular phases of the effort, after which they move to another project. Because their generic skills are useful across projects regardless of subject area, teams are highly fluid.

The Project Team at Work

When we next encountered the CDMS project team, the pilot version of the system had just been accepted by the client and the specifications frozen. Subsequent effort would involve production of a working version of the pilot system: a CDMS functionally integrated with the client's existing applications and ready for real-time use in field trials with a subset of twelve dealerships.

For this stage of work, CDMS team members relocated to the customer's headquarters in a city about an hour's drive from Digital Evolution, exchanging jeans and T-shirts for slacks, dress shirts, and ties. The uniformly furnished building with its corporate decor presented a

Figure 8.2. A Typical Project Team.

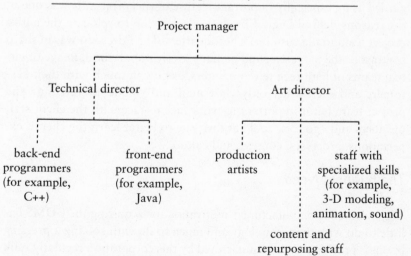

sharp contrast to the casual art-filled surroundings of our earlier meet-ings. In the words of the project leader: "We've definitely come to school here. . . . One lesson we've learned is that, when dealing with a client, perception is reality. We have to meet the client's dress code expectations as well as behavioral expectations. The project manager for [the cus-tomer] is a good source of clues. . . . We've also learned about how to formalize some of the customer-team interaction processes, especially the process of status reporting. We're willing to learn. We are immers-ing ourselves in their processes intimately, and then adapting to them."

The center of team activity at the project site is a lab-like room jammed with linked workstations and housed within the customer's in-formation systems (IS) department. Front-end programmers are exercis-ing all the system functions that a dealership end user might conceivably invoke, while back-end programmers are determining that those actions or action sequences in fact operate with internal consistency and inter-operate reliably with appropriate data generated from the client's main-frame-based applications. After each function is fully tested and revised by the CDMS team, it is transferred over the network from the lab to the client's IS department for further testing by their staff. Unlike other projects where there is a distinct geographical or organizational separa-tion between customer and supplier, this transfer is effected relatively in-formally. The discrete and formalized steps usually involved in such projects—handing off defined deliverables at prespecified points in time or official milestones—are replaced by ongoing, day-to-day interactions between the project team and the customer.

The opportunity for close, in-person interactions with clients was re-garded as an especially important feature of this project. It was one of the reasons behind Digital Evolution's decision to relocate the entire project team to the customer's headquarters. Their decision was in sharp contrast to the pervasive, and perhaps overly popularized, image of vir-tual teams of high-tech telecommuters keeping in touch with their cus-tomers and each other only via e-mail and videoconferencing. The project team felt it important to work face-to-face with the client staff members and "go to school" at their site to better learn the client's ex-pectations, processes, context, and culture.

The Business Need

The automobile manufacturer's motivation for acquiring the CDMS has little to do with the technology and much to do with solving a pressing business problem. Cars manufactured by this corporation regularly rank very high on all assessments of quality and performance but with equal regularity rank near the bottom when it comes to buyer satisfaction with sales and financial services.

Conceived as an application to support dealership practice, the CDMS employs a graphical user interface to "step through the entire process from the first sales stages to the end of the financing procedures," as one project team member described it. Along the way, the system gives sales staff immediate access to up-to-date inventory information, helps sellers and buyers engage in what-if trade-offs among the options offered, tracks and displays resulting choices, and eventually will permit a seamless transition from sales to finance.

According to the project leader, initially the CDMS "works kind of like an interactive glossy multimedia brochure" in the showroom. For example, sellers can quickly show potential buyers still and moving images of cars in their range of interest. Once the buyer chooses a model for more detailed examination, the application brings up a set of options (a "package") plus other special alternatives. Clicks on the color palette then allow the buyer to view the selected model with the preferred exterior and interior colors. Likewise, alternative wheel options can be tried out on the model, or a sunroof, or a particular sound system, and so on until a desirable configuration has been reached.

At that point, the seller can bring up a summary of the selections and their cumulative cost. Or the buyer may wish to revisit some earlier choices in view of those made later. In any case, once the buyer has reached a decision, the CDMS determines whether a car configured just as the buyer wants is available in stock there or at another dealership in the vicinity. If not, the CDMS may be used to engage in a "fuzzy" search to find out whether the desired model—configured with a close family resemblance to the chosen options—can be found nearby. Or the buyer may prefer to have the car special-ordered exactly as configured in the selection process.

Whatever the buyer decides, the relevant information is retained and transferred to the finance module of the CDMS for use by financial services staff. They invoke their part of the application without having to repeat questions or reenter data related to the prior selection process. Instead, the finance representative begins where the sales staff left off, reviewing different approaches to paying for the car along with their associated costs and benefits, and gathering the information required by the credit application. In the end, the CDMS prints a record of the sales and financing agreement that, when signed, officially documents the transaction.

The Knowledge Value Added

From Digital Evolution's perspective, this application is designed to be leveraged. Among other value-added capabilities Digital Evolution envisions for the CDMS, CDMS-generated data can be used by the manufacturer to learn about buyer preferences. At present, like most automobile manufacturers, this corporation routinely receives sales data but has no way of knowing how well sales reflect buyers' first choices. CDMS data may also be integrated with ordering and shipping systems when buyers go for cars not in stock.

The CDMS interoperates with an online, independently maintained *Consumer Reports* database that contains evaluations of cars from all major manufacturers. Potential buyers may use the system to examine dynamically generated data about the manufacturer's car and similar models of cars from different manufacturers. This enables comparison shopping without leaving the showroom—a considerable advantage for a manufacturer whose products consistently rank high on quality and performance dimensions.

The CDMS remembers buyers and prospective buyers. For the former, it can be used to produce follow-up inquiries, tune-up reminders, or current news of interest to owners of a particular type of vehicle. Or, when prospective buyers who do not reach a decision the first time around return to the showroom, the CDMS can be used to refresh their memory (and the seller's) about the models and configurations under consideration.

Dealerships with a technologically sophisticated clientele may readily make the "brochure" module of the CDMS directly available on computers in their showrooms or on Websites to those who prefer shopping electronically on their own. In fact, dealerships could easily put the entire credit application on line as well, so that all of a buyer's prepurchase choices and other data entered from home would be in the system when the buyer arrived at the dealership.

Combining the team's expertise with the client's knowledge of dealership needs and existing databases enabled the CDMS project team to create substantial additional value in the product. The team learned conceptual and technological lessons that could be applied to the development of systems for supporting sales and financial services for almost any class of durable consumer product.

Team Composition and Performance

The CDMS team is still structured as depicted in Figure 8.2, although its size changed over time. In the early months of the project, about eight team members put together an initial "proof of concept" system for demonstration purposes. Moving closer to a functioning pilot system required expanding the team.

Although some of the needed programmers could be recruited from existing Digital Evolution staff, Java programmers were new hires. (Previously, Java programming "was not one of the core competencies here," according to a team programmer we interviewed.) Graphic designers, fine artists, and production artists were needed as well. The designers and fine artists take on layout and content design, while production artists work to optimize their use of multimedia resources (for instance, by making them as little demanding of memory as possible). The CDMS today relies on about one hundred thousand lines of code and a huge store of multimedia digital objects (called "assets" by Digital Evolution professionals).

Having good art and making it work within the technology continues to be one of the hardest challenges for this interdisciplinary team. But as the project leader notes, creative resolution of these tensions remains a source of growth and strength: "Art will push the technology, and vice versa. A good example is our 'text refresh' tool. . . . The artists wanted to be able to scroll the text on a screen, wrap it around the image, and so on, without any of the image objects moving—whether they were outside the text or within a text box. The technical staff explained why this couldn't be done in the system, but the artists insisted on it. So eventually the techies figured out how to build it. This is how the art stretches the technology—we take on approaches we wouldn't otherwise have contemplated."

Besides shared goal commitments and respect for each other's skills, other project team members identified two additional dimensions of constructive disputes: not personalizing arguments ("We don't attribute negative motivation to the one who disagrees") and not forcing solutions ("We can leave things at an impasse for a while until we come to a compromise"). Thus, although there are "lots of inherent places for friction" in the project, according to its leader, "we're more productive because of it." For instance, the friction-engendered text refresh tool just mentioned by the project leader will be valuable to Digital Evolution for many future multimedia projects; its utility goes well beyond CDMS-like systems.

Technology to Support Project Team Performance

Even though CDMS team members are acutely aware of how the technology they are developing should support and enhance dealership performance, the information and communication technology they themselves use in their work has become so internalized as to be nearly transparent. Of the many questions we asked, it seemed hardest for the team members to answer those that targeted their own technological support.

For example, members take it for granted that they always have access to one another and other Digital Evolution professionals, as well as to external consultants and customer liaisons, by e-mail regardless of location. That is what makes it possible for project teams like this one to work full-time at customer sites and yet feel fully connected to their home base. They also take for granted using the Web to stay updated on technical events in the broader environment that may affect their development plans or future prospects.

Besides generic communication facilities for close or distant interaction, the team makes use of standard development tools in its work. The Developer's Studio suite, for instance, includes "source safe," a programming management system that permits all project staff to read everything in the CDMS and to share components—but it also has check-in, check-out services so that two programmers cannot simultaneously revise the same piece of code. Additionally the project relies on a spreadsheet-based bug-tracking tool as well as a standard flowcharting tool for graphic representation over time of both the interrelated subtasks and the team members responsible for them.

However, the two most significant technologies supporting the team's work were developed by Digital Evolution professionals themselves. One is an online procedure for status self-monitoring and contact reporting. The very ease of informal horizontal interaction with members of the client company made it necessary to institute some formalized interaction processes, especially as the CDMS project grew in size and complexity.

In response to this need, Digital Evolution devised a daily reporting procedure. It documents tasks completed each day by the project team, meetings with client representatives, work orders (official descriptions of CDMS work or revisions approved by the client), and change requests (any new work or revisions to the CDMS proposed by the client that require additional budget). These reports are circulated to client representatives and the project team. "We used to just talk to them," the president said; "now we write down everything they say to us and feed it back to them to verify it." The procedure has proved very useful for team self-management and in particular for preventing communication-based project breakdowns.

The other critical team support technology is the asset management system. As explained earlier, the CDMS project has developed a huge store of digital multimedia objects. Such objects are evoked by the CDMS as users interact with its varied "showroom" functions. As CDMS components are written or revised, programmers need to be able to find various assets, reuse them, create more of them, and the like.

The asset management system addresses this need. By virtue of naming conventions and other descriptors, it is possible to locate each image in the system and determine exactly where it is used in the CDMS. So, for instance, when the manufacturer introduces its new product line, all the 1998 model cars in the CDMS will be changed to 1999 models with relative ease. Since it was created by the team itself, both artistic and technical professionals understand how to use the system. Because it so effectively facilitates shared use of multimedia information resources, the system is expected to become a standard team-support technology at Digital Evolution. It is important to note that the need for this system was not foreseen early on at Digital Evolution, but it soon became apparent with the CDMS project, their biggest and most complex project to date. Since the asset management system enables Digital Evolution to leverage the assets created by one project to serve subsequent needs of the same or other projects, the senior managers now view the system as essential to the future success of the company.

BEST PRACTICES FOR DIFFERENT TYPES OF TEAMS

This project team illustrates several best practices for teams that perform knowledge work and use information and communication technologies to facilitate effective collaboration. As a project team, it illustrates practices that particularly fit cross-functional groups assembled to complete a task within a defined period of time. In the section that follows, we use the Digital Evolution case as the basis for identifying best team-technology practices for project teams. Then we briefly discuss the five other types of teams—action, production, service, management, and parallel teams—emphasizing information technology support for team performance. But first, a caveat is in order.

We use the term *best practices* loosely. Because of the scarcity of organizational research on information technology support for different types of teams, no clear scientific evidence exists to support identification of best practices. Thanks to the rapidly changing nature of computer and communication technologies, we cannot even describe practices as being *well accepted* in organizations. In a world in which significant change occurs in Web weeks, practices must continuously evolve and improve.

Project Teams

Table 8.1 summarizes best practices for project teams based on Digital Evolution's CDMS team. All of these practices depend on new, networked information technology. Some of them apply to all teams (such as respecting others' skills and not personalizing arguments), but the cross-functional nature of project teams makes them especially important. The wide cultural chasms often found in technology-focused project teams, like the ones at Digital Evolution (as between artists and computer scientists) pose even further challenges to their effectiveness. Therefore, translating such universal homilies as "respecting each other's skills" into implemented work practices can make the difference between successful and unsuccessful projects.[4]

Because the competitive environment forces project teams to develop innovative products and services, learning and innovation processes are key. Digital Evolution models how an organization chooses projects based on learning potential; it assumes that learning occurs in the process of delivering products and services and views learning from projects as a means to develop intellectual assets. Finally, learning must occur rapidly to keep pace with changes in technology and the competitive environment.

The processes of coordination and cooperation occur across functional and disciplinary boundaries within project teams, as well as with groups external to the project team such as project sponsors, the constituencies represented by individual project team members, and other stakeholders. Project team members must be able to work with others of different backgrounds, work experiences, knowledge bases, and skills. We use the term *laterality* to describe this ability to relate to others quite different from oneself.[5] The assistant CDMS project manager told us that he has both an artistic and technical background and is able to act as a bridge and interpreter between the artists and technologists. Team members emphasized the respect and appreciation they have for each other's knowledge and skills. They also talked about the creative resolution of conflicts between artists and technologists that results in new team capabilities. Decision making is iterative and participative, and project management does not prematurely force solutions. Although these processes of cooperation and coordination are critical for all types of teams, they are particularly critical for project teams that need to harness expertise from different perspectives to develop innovative solutions.

A customer orientation helps a project team develop products and services that meet customer requirements. Although it may not make sense

Table 8.1. Project Team Best Practices for the Digital Evolution Case.

Key categories	Best practices
Learning and innovation	Accept projects based on learning potential
	Learn while implementing
	High-velocity learning ("Web weeks")
Coordination and collaboration	Laterality
	• Can act as a bridge and interpreter between different functional areas
	• Respect for each other's distinct skills
	• Creative resolution of tensions among participants from different functional areas
	Not personalizing arguments
	Iterative processes (not forcing solutions prematurely)
Customer orientation	Relocation of project team to customer's site
	Commitment to achieving customer priorities
	Willingness to adapt to customer expectations (for example, dress code and behaviors)
	Formalizing customer-team interactions through regular status reporting
	Clear linkage of technical personnel across organizations
Information technology to support team performance	E-mail access to each other, external consultants, and customer liaisons
	Access and capability to use the Web
	Early prototyping
	Use of standard development tools, for example, Developer's Studio suite, bug-tracking tool, flowcharting tool
	Creation of customized information technology tools for project
	Online procedure for status self-monitoring and contact reporting
	Asset management system for digital multimedia objects
Output	Knowledge value adds capabilities to product and services being created
	Value creation model to expand business

for all teams to co-locate with their customers during a project as the team from Digital Evolution did, it kept the team focused on the customer's needs and taught them "tacit" lessons about the work context. Committing strongly to achieving the customer's priorities, communicating the team's progress, and linking technical personnel across organizations help ensure that the products and services being developed are those that customers will use. But commitment requires more than just good intentions and slogans. Whether through co-location or other means, project teams need explicitly to implement activities and linkages that maintain an ongoing focus on their customers.

Digital Evolution's use of technology to support project team performance is quite sophisticated. The project team takes for granted technological supports that many companies and project teams still lack. All project team members use e-mail. They are connected to one another, to other Digital Evolution employees located at company headquarters and elsewhere, to customer liaisons, and to anyone else outside the company that might be a useful source of expertise. They have access and the capability to derive whatever information they need from the Web. They are aware of the importance of early prototyping, and they developed an initial prototype of their product for the customer prior to beginning the pilot system development work. They use standard project management and software development tools such as flowcharting and bug-tracking software. Perhaps most important, they created customized tools that have ramifications well beyond this one project. For example, the asset management system for digital multimedia objects will be used for other projects and other clients. It ensures that the intellectual assets created for one project can be applied to other projects.

Finally, the product being developed for their automotive client embeds value-added capabilities that not only address this automotive company's business need but can be used to develop systems for supporting the sales and financial services of almost any consumer durable.

Action Teams

The information needs of action teams reflect the intense, dynamic, high-stakes, time-critical, and externally driven nature of their work. Teams must respond, often with little notice, to challenging and rapidly changing events and conditions generated for example by formidable adversaries, unfavorable environments, and watchful stakeholders. They must be able to work together effectively from the moment the engagement begins.

New electronic media increasingly support the challenging work of action teams. Firefighting teams in the U.S. Forest Service, for example, rely on a range of advanced technologies to support their communication, cooperation, and coordination needs during periods of action as well as between such engagements.[6] The mission for these firefighting teams is expressed in terms of fire protection program objectives issued by the Forest Service's headquarters in Washington, D.C., and made available online to all national forests and ranger districts. The Washington headquarters also oversees the National Fire Management Analysis system, which provides an array of tools for understanding and decision making related to fire protection. For example, it is the basis for an annual modeling exercise conducted by each national forest, with input from its ranger district, to plan for the coming fire season while using its own fire history as background. Results are aggregated from all forests by the Washington office, where the system is used to examine alternative fire-suppression strategies from a cost-benefit standpoint and make fire protection policy recommendations.

Other information technologies are used to track equipment, supplies, and personnel so that teams and materials can be rapidly deployed when a fire breaks out. The same technologies are used to track and deploy resources during a fire. In the past, radios and telephones were used by dispatching offices to pass along requests for equipment, materials, or personnel until they arrived at units that could help meet those needs. Now, an automated resource order system (AROS)—a networked, agencywide system—uses intelligent forms that "know" where to go to get the needed resources and to automatically activate the request-filling process.

The actual work of fighting a fire is assisted by a simulation program called BEHAVE, which models fire behavior. First an infrared aerial photo of a fire is superimposed on a digitized map of the forest and its surroundings; this allows the fire management team leader to know where the hottest spots are and to locate roads, firebreaks, camping areas, nearby residences, and so on. The resulting electronic fire map can also be linked to other forest data collected or maintained on line— about timber, ground fuels, moisture content, current wind direction and velocity, and the like. The fire officer can then simulate different fire-suppression strategies and observe their results to guide the firefighting team.

In some regions, "kits" of portable computers loaded with the appropriate software and data are taken to a fire site—sometimes by parachute—to provide access to a communications network and continuously updated data. This way, the firefighting team stays in contact with broader organizational resources. When necessary, the network can also be used to request and coordinate support from other federal, state, or local agencies in the vicinity.

The National Fire Management Analysis system also provides a vehicle for organizational learning between engagements, up and down the hierarchy as well as over time. Information collected by lower-level units is transmitted upward to inform policy; the top-level unit aggregates the information across sources to develop planning models, analyze fire-suppression strategies, and make the results available throughout the agency for local units to use. These models and findings are subsequently combined with local knowledge and data to support unit-by-unit fire protection plans and fire behavior models.

The Forest Service example demonstrates how computer-based tools can be used to support action teams of all kinds, whether their mission is to fight fires, contain oil spills, or deal with police emergencies. What all action teams have in common is intense, time-critical activity during engagements, and less intense periods between engagements when they prepare for the next time that events and circumstances require them to take action.

During engagements, action teams need systems that can rapidly deliver task-critical information about fast-changing, situation-driven events in real time. They also need locally customized decision-making support to help explore options and strategies and to coordinate deployment and redeployment of human and material resources. Finally, they need timely communications with others: their own organizational unit; other relevant units of the organization; and external experts or organizations, depending on the nature of the team's engagements. These links, activated as needed, mean that additional resources and other support are always within reach. They also help ensure that action teams stay attuned to the policies that should inform and guide their performance.

Between engagements, time is less critical and actions are not driven by immediate events. Therefore, the action team's needs shift from information support for real-time action to planning and preparation for the next event. Interestingly, the general resources are similar but now the purpose and particular features differ: information to help plan and develop strategies for future events, management systems to ensure that resources are available when the immediate need arrives, and communication systems to promote enterprisewide goal sharing and continuous organizational learning from prior engagements.

Action teams have different domains and purposes, but they all address immediate challenges posed by difficult events and conditions.

Their effectiveness probably depends as much on planning and preparation as on execution. What is true for the Forest Service firefighting teams is true for all action teams: as much attention needs to be paid to information resources to support the planning and learning as for the action itself.

Production Teams

The distinguishing feature of production teams is that they continuously generate tangible outputs.[7] They need information and tools that help them coordinate activities, track work in progress, communicate with those immediately upstream and downstream from them in the production process, monitor performance, and collaborate to solve problems.[8]

For example, production teams at Encore Computers assemble midsize computers for simulations such as those used in pilot training. Encore is a low-volume manufacturer that builds systems to order, so throughput is not an important issue but quality is. In the early 1990s, Encore undertook a major effort to make each production team concentrate on continuous quality improvement. They also developed an extensive database on all aspects of the plant's operations, including daily quality reports. All of this information is available on computers located throughout the facility, and production team members are trained to access the information.

Production team members use the defect data reporting system (DDRS) to audit defects. All team members audit the work on their direct "supplier" and are responsible for the work they pass on to their "customer." Whenever team members detect a defect, including procedural errors and ones of their own doing, they write it up on a form and enter it in the system themselves. On Monday, every team gets a report (their choice of either hard copy or e-mail) of the defects supposedly attributable to them. By midnight Wednesday morning, they either "own it" or pass it on to the person or unit they think is responsible. The teams figure out what to do about the problem (with support from managers, technical staff, and plantwide quality committees). In the first year of the system's operation, the teams identified $200,000 worth of defects they had resolved via this system. Everyone in the plant now uses the system, and production team members and staff groups are less likely to blame each other for production problems.

This example illustrates several best practices. The information system is used to provide critical performance data, which in turn are used by teams to solve problems and make improvements. These data are provided regularly, enabling the team to monitor its quality constantly. The focus on quality fits its product; if the teams worked instead on mass assembly of computers, then productivity data would probably be the focus. The information system also connects production teams to technical staff groups in the plant, which expedites problem solution. Everyone in the plant has been trained to use the DDRS system and has access to it. The system enables team members to make better-informed decisions about their work, and it helps to empower them. Production team members are also connected to others in the company (both inside and outside the plant) through e-mail, and the Encore culture supports open communication. The information and communication technology used by the production teams helps them develop knowledge about how to improve their product and processes over time. Finally, although it is not explicit in the example presented here, Encore's production teams also have access to information about production schedules, task requirements, and work in progress.

Encore's production teams are by no means unique. The very nature of production demands information about customer requirements, production tasks, availability of materials and supplies, overall processes, and outcomes. Whether they are producing computers, pet food, or wood products, all production teams require information about various aspects of the production process. In recent years, comprehensive, integrated ERP (enterprise resource planning) systems for coordinating and tracking production from order to delivery have become a multibillion-dollar business. Traditionally, these systems focused primarily on make-to-stock and repetitive manufacturing. But some of the newer systems are designed to address manufacturers' desires for tailorable products and mass customization. They include features that support make-to-order, engineer-to-order, and project-based manufacturing. In the hands of well-designed production teams, these new, more flexible systems can be a powerful tool for generating and applying knowledge for continuous improvement of manufacturing processes and their outputs.

Service Teams

In contrast with products, services are intangible and simultaneously produced and consumed. Service team members may not have to be co-located, but they may need to perform service at customers' sites (as with telephone repair crews). The value of service is time-dependent and perishable, and service quality depends on many factors.[9] Some services are provided in brief encounters with customers (retail sales), while others entail long-term relationships (management consulting).[10] These characteristics have implications for the design of information technology and communication tools to support service team work.

Mobile communications can connect service team members who are geographically dispersed and often on the move. For example, field service teams at one gas and electric utility company communicate with one another and customer service representatives via two-way radiophones. Their mobile data terminal system indicates the location of reported gas leaks.[11] Mobile communications provide more flexibility than e-mail; they enable people to communicate from any location.

Service team members can use information tools to create shared understanding of the services they are providing to customers. An electronic whiteboard or shared database can be used to represent the information that is presented to customers. In essence, a shared artifact is created, thereby enabling more effective collaboration among them. By making information explicit, the intangibility and variability of the service provided by team members is reduced. For example, a commercial bank decided to use an application implemented in Lotus Notes as the mechanism for document management in the lending process. In the bank, portfolio managers were responsible for generating new business leads, negotiating lending deals, and maintaining borrower relationships. Account executives analyzed potential deals for their creditworthiness and were supported by credit analysts. Service teams composed of portfolio managers, account executives, and credit analysts worked together to get loans approved.

Before implementation of the Lotus Notes application, problems such as lengthy delays in paper exchange, lack of version control, and difficulty in accessing loan documents in preparation were common. Afterward, portfolio managers, account executives, and credit analysts shared credit documents stored in a common database. Team members could open, print, or even edit any document, any time, in any banking office. Close-to-real-time coauthoring and approvals eliminated costly delays and increased service responsiveness. The documents from one loan could be used as templates for others, and a client's loan history could easily be assessed.

The shared database increased service team members' understanding of the criteria for approving loans. Judgments of the degree of tolerable business risk and creditworthiness became more consistent and explicit. The document management system supported immediate transactions as well as development of long-term relationships with clients. Employees could learn about the loan approval process by electronically accessing loan documents.

A key function of information technology for service teams is to connect them with customers. Service teams need feedback from customers on the quality of their services. An information system can be designed to listen to customers (both internal and external) and to provide data that can be used in making improvements.[12] The commercial bank is considering tracking client satisfaction with its new commercial loan approval process and using its information system to assess service quality.

Both examples illustrate information technology best practices for service teams with varying purposes and functions. These practices include systems for anytime-anyplace (ATAP; see Chapter Nine) communication among members, real-time data acquisition and analysis, shared artifacts to support collaboration, direct connection with customers, and collection of service quality data that can be used for feedback, learning, and improvement.

Management Teams

Little research exists on information technology support for management teams. In fact, management team members are often the least accepting of new information technology and may lack the capacity to take advantage of its potential.[13] Therefore this section is speculative, making inferences about practices that have future promise, based on the tasks that management teams perform and limited observations of their tools in use.

Senior management teams link internal operations with external factors and direct and redirect strategy to respond to changing competitive conditions. They ensure corporate coherence, in which diverse parts of the organization work together to meet competitive challenges across product lines and markets, and product families share common features. Coherence leverages core competencies across business units and functions, allowing quick, effective response to environmental jolts.[14]

An example of how information and communication tools help achieve this coherence is found in the oil and gas company we studied that formed a high-level management team to lead implementation of a successful future growth strategy. Business success, in the view of the division president, requires teamwork to manage core business fundamentals and strategies, and nimbleness to capitalize on new business opportunities. The company created cross-functional management teams to span key business processes, with the executives on the top team serving as contact points for these management teams. The contact role is separate from a supervisory role, and the contact executives support teams from functions different from those they lead. This design requires the management team members to work together closely. E-mail has helped them to a certain extent, but to achieve true coherence they need information and communications tools that can integrate real-time information on the internal operations and performance of the organization with information on changing conditions in the external environment.[15]

Another key role for senior management teams concerns effective management, distribution, and use of information. This role is illustrated by the senior management team for the International Atomic Energy Agency (IAEA), a United Nations organization charged with promoting peaceful uses of atomic energy and preventing its proliferation in weaponry. The team is constituted like the top-level oil and gas company management team described above; e-mail is in widespread use at all levels of the organization. A 1997 policy manual notes that "information management, like financial and personnel management, is a managerial responsibility. It is of critical importance to Agency efficiency and effectiveness, and consequently should also be well managed, based on best practices."[16] This directive means that managers must plan for and guide use of the technological resources required for creating and distributing the information needed by the programs they oversee.

Such a role also surfaces in a description of managerial competencies. Another IAEA manual notes that managers must "ensure that the team is kept well informed on all relevant issues," using computers as a "management tool to obtain and distribute information" and to promote its free and open flow "inside and outside the Agency," as appropriate.[17] As a corollary, managers are expected to understand the capabilities of computers and the applications in use. In some organizations, use of communication and information technologies is an option for senior management teams, but in the IAEA it has become a necessity at the highest job levels, and its institutionalization in official policy manuals sends a strong signal to the rest of the organization that competent and productive use of these tools is closely linked to effective mission performance.

A final point to note is the capability of computers and networks to link senior management to professionals and peers in other organizations. The cultivation of "loose ties" has been shown to engender new insights and to bring high-level managers in contact with perspectives and alternatives that they would not be likely to encounter in day-to-day communications within their organizations.[18] But this kind of extramural interaction in the past has been difficult for managers to arrange, since their days are typically filled up with scheduled and unscheduled meetings and other interactions.

Electronic mail connections with those in other organizations enables managers to develop and sustain loose ties,[19] operating in much the same way as casual in-person interactions. In contrast to the IAEA policy, many organizations have not encouraged or supported collegial interactions beyond their own boundaries. However, the emergence of online connections at operational levels of organizations with customers and suppliers has stimulated development of broader interorganizational network use. In the future, more senior management teams can expect to experience the benefits of e-mail-based connections with their counterparts in other organizations.

These examples by no means exhaust the ways in which management teams can make effective use of new networked media. Executive teams could use tools for gathering information from multiple external sources and for aggregating these data quickly to construct high-level views of results and trends. Management teams could also use analytical tools to generate alternative scenarios so that they can test the implications of varied options and assess whether their strategic initiatives are resulting in increased market share or profitability.[20] Although we are not aware of any management teams that are presently using such applications, typically referred to as "data mining" or "knowledge management" tools, their potential impact on effectiveness of management teams is significant. Management teams would be well advised to explore these and other applications and generally to promote use of information and communication tools to enhance collaboration, learning, and knowledge creation for themselves and throughout their organizations.

Parallel Teams

The need of parallel teams for information resources is perhaps less salient than for any other team type. Their work is typically less intense, involving regular but not necessarily frequent meetings, and is usually secondary to the members' primary job responsibilities. Parallel teams usually lack authority to implement the results of their work. Despite these limitations, when given appropriate authority, resources, and charter, parallel teams can be highly effective. A new team in Digital Evolution demonstrates how a well-designed parallel team can contribute to an organization's functions. It also illustrates a modest role for technology in their performance.

Digital Evolution is organized around project teams that create added value by building on innovations developed in earlier projects. Innovations with significant and broad applicability could be the core of joint ventures that create substantial returns for the company and its customers.

We asked the CEO and president how the company captures reusable insights and builds upon innovations that arise in independent projects of varied size, nature, and duration. Because this is a high-tech company, it might be assumed that technology would be the answer—a data warehouse, a document repository, groupware for collaboration. To be sure, technology plays a part. But the solution turns more importantly on a parallel team whose task it is to recognize the knowledge-based innovations that projects engender in the course of their work and think about ways to capitalize on them.

Until recently, this function had been accomplished informally, the CEO explained. Project leaders typically meet about once a month to share problems, solutions, new technologies, or techniques; this is a natural incubator for innovation. There was also a small group of people who tried to keep up with what was going on across the projects, make connections between project ideas, think of ways to leverage them, and so on. Now the company has constituted an internal innovation team to perform these activities more formally.

According to the CEO, this parallel team has two main missions. One is to recognize and refine innovative ideas embedded in ongoing projects. Digital Evolution's staff continually build innovative technologies or techniques in response to project-specific needs. The innovation team is charged with stepping back and considering how these efforts could have much broader utility and value, internally (as with the asset management system) or externally. The team's second mission, the CEO continued, is to figure out "what we should be playing with," adding that "after all, innovation comes from play."

The internal innovation team at Digital Evolution is illustrative of positive parallel team practices in a number of ways. First, the company explicitly recognizes the key roles that innovation and organizational learning play in its primary business processes; the functions performed by the innovation team are therefore central rather than peripheral. It is equally important, perhaps, that for many members this parallel team's tasks are self-motivating and intrinsically rewarding; employees enjoy learning from one another, and mastery of new software tools is seen more as a right than a responsibility. Third, the team does not have to wait and wonder about whether the results of its transformative knowledge-sharing deliberations will ever reach those who are empowered to act on recommendations, since the decision makers themselves are also on the team.

Two practices represented by the establishment of this parallel team are especially noteworthy. One is the reliance on humans to handle the functions of organizational memory and learning. Many large and small organizations are making investments in groupware, document management software, and database management systems to capture organizational memory and learning. Digital Evolution, too, realizes that such technologies are critical for retention and reuse of the information objects it develops (as with the asset management system) and for purposes of recordkeeping (such as the contracting reporting system). In the fast-paced world of today's networked organizations, capture, retention, and documentation of what has been created and shared in electronic media is a daunting task, one that merits considerable attention. But by itself it is not sufficient to accomplish what humans do in the name of memory and learning: transfer knowledge to new situations, make inferential leaps or synergistic connections, or reinvent today's tools to serve tomorrow's needs. That is the job of the innovation team at Digital Evolution. Perhaps, as they grow larger and more formal, technology support will become increasingly necessary, but for now technology is an adjunct, not the core of this congenial, highly social, and apparently very effective practice.

The other practice to underscore is explicit assignment of responsibility for recognizing, articulating, and considering the future value of innovations that spring from day-to-day practice. Research literature on organizational innovation confirms the view that most innovations come from individuals who generate them in the course of trying to solve a problem in their daily work. Because their focus is on the work itself, such individuals are happy to have handled the challenge successfully and go on to their next task. Even when such innovations could be broadly useful to the organization, however, they are rarely recognized at an institutional level, publicized, or made available for redeployment. The parallel innovation team at Digital Evolution is intended to address this shortfall in ways that informal, collegial, lateral relationships can not. In the process, it may also overcome another problem that project-based organizations may experience: ensuring that the value-added contributions of projects outlive the projects themselves.

Although the two practices just described are based on an innovation team in a leading-edge high-tech business, it is easy to see how their lessons can be applied to parallel teams with quite different charters. Perhaps the most important lesson from this example, one relevant to all team types and not just parallel teams, is that technology is most effective when augmenting human capabilities, not replacing them.

BEST INFORMATION PRACTICES FOR ALL TEAMS

The nature of a team, the domain of its tasks, and the environment in which it works all influence the kinds of information resources required to support effective performance. Table 8.1 summarizes these resources for project teams; Table 8.2 summarizes them for the other types of teams discussed in this chapter.

Commonalities that cut across all team types are evident in the tables. The details and domains may vary with type of team and even with different teams of the same type, but some needs for information and communication resources apply to most teams:

- Internal communications. Almost all teams need systems, technology-based or not, for communication and coordination among team members.

- External communications. Teams need systems for external communications, for example with customers, suppliers, other teams, stakeholders, and technical experts.

- Task information, applications, and analytical tools. Teams require information directly relevant to their specific tasks, and software tools that enable them to extract new knowledge from this information, such as databases, simulations, analysis tools, and decision-making tools.

- Performance feedback. Information on performance is critical for all teams (Chapter Six).

CONCLUSION

The context within which teams function can be designed to encourage, support, and facilitate team performance, regardless of the type of team. Engendering an organizational context that nurtures knowledge-based teams, however, involves much more than assessing their needs for information and acquiring the technologies to deliver it. Rather, these new interactive tools must become part of how teams work, enabling them

Table 8.2. Information Technology Best Practices Supporting Five Types of Teams.

Type of team	Best practices
Action teams (between engagements)	Simulations for modeling and planning for engagements
	Resource management systems for tracking equipment, etc.
	Communications for organizational learning
Action teams (during engagements)	Simulations of engagements
	Resource management systems for rapid deployment of resources
	Communications among team members, other teams, etc.
Production teams	Critical performance data on quantity and quality of production
	Connections with customers, suppliers, technical staff
	Information on orders, production schedules, work in progress, etc.
Service teams	Communication among geographically dispersed members
	Shared databases and other artifacts (for example, information on work orders, progress)
	Communication with customers (for example, feedback on quality of service and responsiveness)
Management teams	Information on internal operations and performance
	Information on changing external conditions, markets, competitors, etc.
	Communications with professionals and peers in other organizations
	Systems for aggregating data from multiple sources into high-level views
	Analytical tools for generating alternative scenarios
Parallel teams	Systems for capturing, retaining, and documenting what the team creates and shares
	Social mechanisms (for example, meetings, shared assumptions to avoid overreliance on technology)

to integrate their diverse expertise and incorporate it into the tasks at hand. The organization must provide the context—the climate, the policies, and the incentives—for this transformative process to occur.

Frequent, open communication—in which individuals are not afraid to express their real views even if they disagree with others—is critical to knowledge work. Confronting and resolving differences constructively is, in fact, one of the chief ways that interdisciplinary teams succeed in doing what cannot be done by individuals working independently.[21] Project teams at Digital Evolution express and reconcile divergent approaches by e-mail, in-person meetings, and late-night arguments, and they feel free to leave disagreements unresolved until solutions emerge. The culture accepts and expects interactions of this kind. In other organizational contexts, concerns about voicing honest disagreement (especially disagreement with the views of high-ranking others when important outcomes are at stake) have led to adoption of decision support systems with the capability for anonymous commenting and evaluation.[22] Either avenue is more productive for teams than being unable to allow dissenting ideas to surface.

Further, organizations must find a way to reward team performance as well as individual performance. A number of organizations have introduced groupware technologies with the aim of making accessible to others information resources developed or used by any given individual. Without a culture that values and rewards intellectual teamwork, organizations should expect to get only the most superficial benefits, if any, from investments in such groupware.[23]

Much the same holds true for organizational support for innovation and learning. Innovation, for instance, inherently involves risk taking; not all new ideas prove to be workable, and even the solutions ultimately found to be viable are likely to undergo significant change between inception and actualization. Only in organizational cultures that tolerate ambiguity and permit risk taking can team innovation thrive.[24] In one organization we studied, for example, attempted innovations are regarded as failures not if they do not work but only if the organization fails to learn from such trial-and-error experimentation.

Many organizations also appear to believe that learning from experiences, whether positive or negative, is simply a matter of capturing them, documenting them, and making them accessible in a shared electronic repository. To be sure, knowledge capture is a start, but it is only a start. Creative transformation and reapplication of knowledge in new situations over time is a dynamic process that most often springs from a community of practice as its members engage with one another and with the tasks and tools at hand in an effort to reach shared goals.[25] These "improvisations" do not arise as planned functions of automated systems; rather, they reflect the malleability of interactive media as teams adapt or reinvent them to meet new challenges. As they explore and test the capabilities and limits of their new technologies, try new things, and share their knowledge with others, the technology becomes second nature. User and tool merge, work tasks and interactions flow, and new levels of effectiveness and creativity are attained.

How, then, can organizations develop or acquire communication and information technologies that are sufficiently transparent and modifiable to support creative value-adding knowledge work? One possibility is that these problems will disappear in the future as workplaces are increasingly inhabited by new cohorts of workers who have grown up with these technologies and for whom they feel natural. This is surely part of the answer, reflected for instance in Digital Evolution professionals' taking their networked multimedia tools for granted. On the other hand, the pace of technological advance is so rapid that none of the tools in use today are ones that they grew up using. New technologies will continue to stretch the capabilities of ever-more-sophisticated generations of users.

Another possibility is that interfaces to communication and information technologies will soon be so vastly improved that even those who are not computer professionals will experience these media as natural and transparent, interposing no obstacles between them and knowledge work. This, too, is part of the answer. But even though it is clear that contemporary interfaces and high-level languages have put the full power of networked computer systems within the grasp of nontechnical professionals, we are still far from having systems whose functions are intuitively obvious. When asked about this prospect for the future, one information scientist in an organization we studied said "I don't believe in miracles."

User experience and technical advance no doubt help produce more natural and effective interactions between computer-based tools and the people who use them. However, we believe that the real answer lies in the nature of the development and change processes themselves. That is, the processes for developing and implementing new ways of working, such as teamwork, and the new technologies for supporting them must be dynamic, participatory, and designed for learning. Best practices for guiding successful change processes can be built on these guidelines:

- Design and implementation processes should integrate user experience and technical expertise.

- These processes should involve all key stakeholders.
- Designs and plans should be dynamic and open to change.
- New technologies and ways of working should be implemented as experiments and be designed for learning.
- Users should be allowed, even encouraged, to explore the possibilities and limits of new tools and new forms of work.

The outcomes of dynamic, participatory change are systems that embed the joint knowledge of all of the stakeholders collaborating in the process. In effect, the practices listed in Tables 8.1 and 8.2 reflect such processes. How an organization gets there may be more important than the specific practices noted. These processes are essentially the same, regardless of team type. To support value-creating knowledge-based teams, the nature of the social and technological change processes themselves is ultimately more important than the types of technologies on which they are typically focused.[26]

COMMUNICATION TECHNOLOGIES FOR TRADITIONAL AND VIRTUAL TEAMS

Daniel Mittleman, Robert O. Briggs

ELECTRONIC COLLABORATION technologies allow people separated by time or distance to quickly and easily share information, generate ideas, make decisions, and store their work for later retrieval. These tools free work teams from the physical limitations of time and place. In global organizations that communicate across continents and work around the clock, the new tools enable team members to communicate and collaborate across time, distance, and departmental and organization boundaries. Teams that do this are commonly called "virtual teams."

Virtual teams represent a growing phenomenon propelled by the explosion of computer networking. Ten years ago, practically no business or personal computer was connected to the Internet. In August 1998, it was estimated that a total of more than one hundred thirty million people were connected to the Internet around the world, with online participation growing at a rate of 30 percent per year.[1] As of October 1997, 59 percent of all U.S. companies and 38 percent of those in Europe have already implemented internal networks, or "intranets," for collaborative activities such as document sharing, e-mail, online chatting, and group scheduling.[2] These numbers are expected to grow to 77 percent in the United States and 75 percent in Europe by the end of 1998.

Among the many types of electronic collaboration tools, the most important and widely used are

- Audio communication systems such as speaker phones for audio teleconferencing
- Video communication systems such as room-to-room video teleconferencing (VTC) systems and desktop VTC systems
- Real-time data communication tools such as chat groups
- Different-time data communication tools such as e-mail and bulletin board software
- Electronic whiteboards, which allow people to mark up a drawing palette and then send the information over distance or store it in a computer
- Keypad voting systems, which look like TV remote controls and tally the votes of everyone in a meeting
- Group support systems (GSSs), which structure brainstorming, problem-solving, and decision-making tasks
- Group calendars and group project management software

It is not enough to simply apply these tools to traditional organizational processes. Collaborating with electronic tools requires teams to rethink how they interact and how they organize their work.

This chapter has four purposes:

1. To describe tools and technologies available today that teams can use to work virtually, or to collaborate over time or distance
2. To consider how technology support needs differ among six types of teams
3. To describe the mechanisms by which methods and tools help teams be productive
4. To describe best practices—and caveats—for team leaders and facilitators who use new communications technologies to support their teams

The chapter includes five sections, starting with the context in which collaboration technology is used and how these tools enhance teamwork. Next is a case study of a cross-organizational project that makes use of cutting-edge tools along with team processes that effectively support those tools. Section three examines technology support for four kinds of team interactions: (1) same-time, same-place meetings; (2) meetings at the same time from different places, such as videoconferences; (3) communication at different times through the same place, as in team rooms; and (4) communication at different times from different places, as in exchanges of e-mail. Section four considers how communication and information technology needs differ among six types of teams. The last section presents best practices for leaders and facilitators who use technology to help their teams collaborate over time and distance.

CASE EXAMPLE: "FIRSTGLOBAL" VIRTUAL MEETING

Many teams report that judicious use of collaborative technology lets them reduce project cycle times by an order of magnitude, or increase their output fivefold. To picture the potential of the collaborative technology and processes being used, imagine that an organization called "FirstGlobal Banking" has initiated a team product development project using managers located on four different continents. They use collaboration technologies to meet and work, without ever coming together in one physical location.

Initial Team Meeting

The initial team meeting takes place in FirstGlobal's virtual meeting facility (VMF). The VMF is a virtual round conference table made up of physical tables in the shape of pie slices sitting at company offices around the world. The VMF integrates audio, video, and data conferencing technologies to create the illusion of shared presence. Each pie-slice space uses full wall projections on the two side walls, with multichannel sound, to create the sensation of being present in all of the physical spaces at once. Computer workstations around the virtual table run GSS software to provide shared data connectivity.

Karen and Bob are assigned to participate on this fifteen-member team out of the Washington office. Lesley and Jill join in from Capetown, Roger and Helmut from Geneva, and Bruce and Mei from Hong Kong.

Karen arrived at the Washington VMF room early this morning, about fifteen minutes before the scheduled start time, and watched the local technicians start up the room technologies. When the room was ready, Karen was able to see each of her teammates as though all of them were in the same room.

Lesley, the team's chair, calls the meeting to order from Capetown: "Good afternoon. As we have not all worked together before," she says, "I think the first order of business shall be introductions." A schematic representation of the virtual conference room appears on the computer screen before each team member. Karen enters background information about herself onto an icon representing her position at the VMF table. From the organization's intranet database, she finds a bitmapped image of herself along with her resume and posts that information onto the icon, adding personal information—her interest in impressionist art—to provide a fuller picture of herself. Then she selects the virtual business cards of the other attendees from their icons and reroutes them to her own computer so that their contact information is added to her address book.

Lesley shows a meeting agenda on everyone's computer screen and suggests they begin the project with an exercise to make sure they share an understanding of their objectives and scope. Because this team has never worked together, Lesley thinks it important to establish shared goals and get a sense of one another before jumping straight into the project task. She knows that face-to-face verbal discussion is important for team building, so she asks everyone to talk verbally about their understanding of the project, while a discussion folder, labeled to show it remains anonymous, is opened for team members to add their thoughts on line. A healthy discussion ensues, both verbally and on the computer. Helmut notices that several spoken comments merit remembering, and he adds them to the online discussion folder.

The technology does not replace spoken discussion at this meeting; it merely supplements it when appropriate. The meeting still requires leadership; if anything, the leader's task is more difficult as she must now mediate not only the team members' interactions with each other but also interactions with the technology as well. Helmut's decision to take on the role of scribe is fairly typical; individuals learn to use collaborative tools as a shared scratch pad to keep ideas focused among themselves.

Following the initial discussion, Lesley asks Mei to lead an activity in which the group develops a detailed project plan using a GSS outlining tool. In this activity, everyone is able to add to the outline directly and see it grow on their own screens. In addition, each person is able to attach discussion comments to items on the outline. As the outline grows, so does the online discussion about issues related to each item. Karen actively participates in these discussions, placing anonymous comments into the database, but signing her name to a few of her comments when specific opinions are based on her experience and expertise.

Group support systems software differs from chat or discussion software in that, among other things, it adds structure and focus to the collaboration. Karen makes selective use of anonymity as there is sometimes merit to having an idea evaluated without knowing who contributed it, and sometimes knowing the author's rationale for submitting a suggestion.

Roger suggests a short break after an hour of this activity. Bruce decides that this break period is a good time to strike up a conversation with Karen. He e-phones Karen at her VMF station, and a personal videoconference is created. Bruce mentions his interest in art and asks about the current Renoir exhibit at the National Gallery in D.C. Karen says that the gallery has a Website for the exhibit and sends Bruce the Web address in an e-mail message while they are still chatting. Roger uses the break time to copy a PowerPoint slide from his computer back in his office, edit it, and paste it into the online project discussion to reinforce a point he wants to make.

When Bob steps out into the hallway in Geneva to get a cup of coffee, he notices Lesley through the virtual wall display next to the coffeepot. One entire wall is composed of a video screen showing the breakout area of the Capetown slice of the VMF; other walls show breakout areas from other cities. Lesley waves to Bob, so Bob walks down the hall and waves a greeting back to Lesley. As they stand next to one another sipping coffee, Lesley catches up on the latest gossip out of the Geneva office.

In traditional co-located meetings, much actual work—and much team building—occurs during unstructured break and meal times. By extending the collaboration technology into the break room, the VMF enables those unstructured interactions to occur almost as though the participants were physically together. Because Roger can access his own computer through the company intranet, he can bring a PowerPoint slide or other material from his office into the meeting no matter where he is physically that day.

After the break, Mei takes editing control and allows teammates to give her verbal instructions for rearranging the outline into a form on which they can come to consensus. She splits the team into subgroups, asking each to take one project task and write a detailed plan for executing it. Within an hour, each team is able to report back deliverables, due dates, and owners for their assigned subtasks. The full team then reviews and amends a few points and takes an online vote to accept the project plan. Finally, Lesley assigns action teams to begin work on the various initial tasks of the project. The action teams have forty-eight hours before their initial reports are due in the collaborative online database for everyone to review. In all, this initial meeting lasts just over three hours, significant work is accomplished, and the project is under way.

It is easy to hand off leadership to another team member, even if that person is on the other side of the world. Facilitation of meetings at the VMF takes several forms. Lesley uses a supportive style, asking participants to engage both verbally and on line; Mei acts more as a chauffeur, driving the technology herself as participants give her verbal instructions. Several styles are possible; each best fits a different form of activity and the different personalities of the meeting leaders.

Subteam Meeting

Karen and Mei each request to be on the subteam working on product promotion issues. Mei takes the lead immediately after the meeting ends by e-mailing Karen with a suggestion of how to proceed. It is late evening in Hong Kong, but Mei is willing to draft a preliminary report first thing in the morning for Karen to review the next day. By e-mail, Karen agrees and suggests that Roger might contribute, since he worked on a similar promotion design the previous year.

When Karen arrives at her office the next morning, not only is the preliminary draft already in the database but Mei has left an e-mail message suggesting Karen place a videocall to her right away. As Karen dials Mei using her desktop videoconferencing system, she finds that Mei and Roger are already speaking with one another. Mei has enlisted Roger to work on the action team and the two have been able to rework a copy of Roger's old promotion plan they found in the database to fit their needs on this project. Karen suggests they check their preliminary draft against comments made on line the previous day to make sure the draft meets the objectives of this team. Mei explains that they've already done that.

The three teammates then use a shared word processor to step through the preliminary draft to make final edits to it. After they complete the document, they placed it in the project folder so other action teams can read and comment on it.

Individual Work

Karen has a business trip to Chicago later that day. From her hotel room that evening, she decides to log on to her computer back home and use the GSS asynchronously to read the project reports coming in from other action teams. She sees that every action team has filed a report; she reads through and comments on them in the appropriate places. While doing this work, Karen receives an e-phone call from Bruce telling her about a new Website on impressionist art. Bruce is able to bring up the Website and share that window with Karen so they can both view it together.

Karen is on the airplane back to Washington the next day as the team briefly meets on line to review the initial subteam reports. She joins the meeting from her laptop on the plane using the AirFone and a modem. Though she doesn't have a videolink, she does receive audio that she can listen to using a headset and data that she can view on her screen.

The tools used by the full team in the VMF are integrated with tools used by individuals from their own homes and offices. In this sense, it doesn't really matter where a team member is physically; collaboration looks and feels largely the same. The team has access to a central information repository from any site. Further, through the company's intranet, each person always has access to his or her personal repository of information.

Subteam Virtual Meeting Work

Over the next three weeks, Karen, Mei, and Roger meet a dozen times from their own offices and homes, as well as in the VMF when they deem the full virtual environment important to productivity. They use collaborative project management software to plan their promotion schedule and shared views of project management tools to develop their program. Over this time, they get to meet each other's families by videolink when working from home. In fact, Mei's husband and Helmut's wife trade recipes and threaten to use the VMF to cook a meal together!

Interim Report Meeting

After three weeks of subteam work, Lesley decides it is time to call the full team back together for a progress check on the project. They meet again in the VMF. Karen, Mei and Roger are the first subteam to present. While Mei gives most of the verbal presentation, Karen manages the graphical presentation on the public datascreen using a shared pointer to draw the team's attention to Mei's talking points. Online discussion comment windows are open for team members to provide real-time reactions and commentary for later review. Roger tracks the written discussion, asking follow-up questions and fielding inquiries made to the presentation team. At one point during the presentation, Lesley asks for control of the pointer to note an inconsistency in the schedule. Bob downloads a graphic from the presentation to his own station, marks it up, and then returns it to the group later in the day during his own presentation.

After all of the subteams present and receive feedback, Lesley congratulates the group for their progress to date. New assignments are presented, some subteam assignments change, and the next stage of the project begins. . . .

The technology represented at the FirstGlobal VMF and used by its managers all exists or is in development at companies and universities. Many subsets of these technologies are currently in real-world use, as examples from several actual settings in this chapter show. What may not necessarily be clear but is a key to the success of the FirstGlobal example is that the technology alone does not provide collaboration solutions. Rather, it is a combination of the technology and supportive work processes.

Although the team at FirstGlobal is a project team, different configurations of collaboration technology can support all of the team types described in Chapter One of this book.

TEAM SUPPORT SYSTEMS

What sorts of tools make up the technology suite used by FirstGlobal? How do the team members know what kinds of tools to use in which situations? How do they know what processes to follow? This section of the chapter addresses these issues by categorizing collaborative technologies and their use into a matrix. Before discussing the tools and technologies in detail, it might help to develop a systematic view of how these tools fit together to support teams.

One way of thinking about a systematic organization of the tools is according to what they help the group do. This approach comes out of the academic research done in group support systems but applies to all collaborative technology. Two different research teams, one led by Jay Nunamaker at the University of Arizona and the other under Joseph Mc-Grath at the University of Illinois, have categorized how collaborative tools support teams in very similar ways, though using very different terminology. If we put together the work of both teams, we assemble a comprehensive picture of how tools and technology can help teams (Table 9.1).

The first way in which collaborative tools help teams is through support of gathering and presenting information. These tasks include finding, storing, processing, and retrieving information. Nunamaker calls

Table 9.1. Tools and Technology for Team Use.

Nunamaker's categories	Internal communication	External communication	Process deliberation	Task deliberation	Information access
McGrath and Hollingshead's categories	Process support		Process structure	Task structure	Task support
	Group internal communication support systems	Group external communication support systems	Group performance support systems		Group information support systems
Tools	Presentation support system	Presentation support system	Group calendar	Group support system	Group support system
	Audio conferencing	Audio conferencing	Workflow management system	Distributed GSS	Distributed GSS
	Video conferencing	Video conferencing	Project management system	Application sharing	Document management repositories
	Document conferencing projector	Document conferencing projector		Keypad voting system	Shared-knowledge repositories
	Desktop video conferencing	Presentation support		Workflow management systems	
	Electronic whiteboard			Conversational structuring system	
	Application sharing				
	Screen sharing				
	Distributed GSS				
	Real-time conferencing				
	E-mail				
	Non-real-time conferencing				
	Voice mail				

this task support.[3] McGrath and Hollingshead[4] call GSSs that do this "group information support systems." Nontechnical task support tools include file cabinets, blackboards, and paper handouts. Electronic and computerized forms of these include printers, electronic whiteboards, and collaborative document management repositories.

The second way collaborative tools support teams is by helping them communicate. Communication might be described as choosing words, behaviors, and images and presenting them through a medium to other team members. Nunamaker labels this issue as process support. In a traditional face-to-face meeting—and in a same-time, same-place GSS meeting—process support is usually given without using electronic technology. However, in a meeting where participants are distributed across space, such as a same-time, different-place meeting, it is impossible to provide process support without technology. In these meetings, we use telephone, videoconferencing, and shared whiteboards with telecursors (mouse pointers that show up on the far screen) to convey process support information. McGrath and Hollingshead describe two types of GSS that fall into this category as "group internal communication support systems" (GCSS) and "group external communication support systems" (GXSS).

The third way collaborative tools help teams is by assisting with the process of deliberation. Deliberation includes brainstorming, problem-solving, and decision-making activities. McGrath and Hollingshead call GSSs that do this "group performance support systems." Nunamaker has separated this construct into two categories, called task structure and process structure. Tools that provide task structure help us organize or model the actual information the team is creating. For example, if a team is evaluating three different sites on which to build a new factory against four criteria (cost, availability of labor, proximity to suppliers, and proximity to customers), they might choose to organize this information into a three-by-four matrix. Tools that produce and manage a matrix structuring of the information are task structuring tools. Other problems might best be structured as lists, trees, or networks. Affinity models and fishbone diagrams are examples of well-known models for structuring task information. GSS technologies can be used to maintain most of these structures.

Process structuring tools help a team organize its approach to a problem by prioritizing, ordering, or assigning out actions. Meeting agendas are probably the simplest and most common process structuring tool. GANTT and PERT charts are two more sophisticated, yet common, process structuring techniques. Project management software and group calendar software are two automated tools commonly used by teams.

We can organize the types of meetings for virtual teams in four categories of a groupware matrix:[5]

1. Same-time, same-place meetings (STSP)
2. Same-time, different-place meetings (STDP)
3. Different-time, same-place meetings (DTSP)
4. Different-time, different-place meetings (DTDP)

This suggests a fifth category—anytime, anyplace meetings (ATAP)—for seamless and continuous collaborative work. We might also use this fifth category to describe project-level work independent of when or where the team is meeting. The Appendix "Tools, Manufacturers, and URLs" gives trade names and URLs (uniform resource locators, more commonly known as Website and online addresses) of manufacturers that produce technologies well suited to each category of tool (listed in Table 9.1) for virtual meetings.

The next five sections of this chapter discuss the structures and tools that can be used to support each of these types of meetings. Because we refer to these five categories often, we use the initials to save space.

SAME-TIME, SAME-PLACE (STSP) INTERACTIONS. STSP meetings are the most common and most traditional of the four types. Virtual teams often find benefits from coming together face-to-face during specific stages of a work project, such as at the beginning when team members are just getting to know one another and sorting out their respective roles, or when the team passes a major milepost and is changing its focus to a new task. Face-to-face meetings are helpful in these cases because team members benefit from nonverbal communication interactions, such as smiles, nods, handshakes, and hugs. The immediate feedback team members receive from others contributes to group cohesion and trust. Even when computers and presentation technology are used in STSP meetings, team members can still see and hear each other in low-technology mode.

The STSP meeting room has changed some since computer and communication tools have been added to it, but it many ways it still resembles the old-fashioned meeting room. The U.S. Air Force Innovation Center (Figure 9.1), located in the Pentagon, is in many ways like a traditional meeting room, but it uses several forms of electronic and computer technologies to enhance virtual teamwork. The room contains two overhead projectors tied to display computers. Presenters can show videotapes, computer slide shows, or, potentially, even video teleconferencing (VTC) images through the projectors. On the wall in the corner is a whiteboard tied to a scanning device, enabling images placed on that whiteboard to be stored in group memory or faxed to work group members who were not physically present at the meeting. At each workstation is a networked personal computer (PC), allowing each team member to engage in structured and possibly anonymous interaction using GSS software. But both the conventional meeting room and the Air Force Innovation Center room are about the same size, the table is the same shape, and the focus in both cases is on the leader sitting at the table.

More than one thousand rooms now exist similar to this one in the Pentagon, with hundreds more being built each year by corporations, schools, and government agencies both in the United States and abroad. Many Fortune 500 companies have been using facilities such as this for several years now. Marriott Corporation has been using STSP groupware since 1991 and began measuring its effectiveness since the opening

Figure 9.1. United States Air Force Innovation Center.

day. The company reports that its center is booked over 85 percent of the time, doing tasks that take about one-tenth the time they took previously using traditional meeting tools and techniques. At this rate of usage, they estimate savings of over $1 million a year in person-hours alone.[6] Marriott's findings mirror those of IBM, which tested a GSS called TeamFocus with sixty-four teams across seven manufacturing plants over a two-year period to solve a variety of business problems. By using a mix of collaborative technologies and techniques, the company was able to reduce average project length by 92 percent and decrease project person-hours by 55 percent.[7]

Marriott uses its center for a variety of purposes, the most common of which is idea generation or brainstorming. They find that although their managers are all in the same room, they receive several benefits from brainstorming through a computer network rather than calling out ideas and having a leader or facilitator write them on a flipchart. For one, the GSS software allows everybody to enter comments at once. In a room with a dozen managers, each person can add an idea to the list at the moment the idea comes to mind. There is no need to wait for floor time. In fact, with twelve people in the room, there is twelve times as much floor time to go around! Second, the GSS allows managers to enter their ideas anonymously. Marriott—like most other companies that use GSS—finds anonymity to be among the most beneficial features. It promotes truthfulness, as there is no political risk to telling the truth anonymously. It promotes consideration of more creative and riskier ideas since there is no fear of social reprisal for saying the emperor has no clothes. And it promotes better decision making because the ideas presented are evaluated on their merit, not on the popularity or power of the contributor.

The World Bank has gone one step further than Marriott. Noel Jones, a senior management consultant at the World Bank, reported that they shipped sixteen laptop computers equipped with GSS to a Southern African nation with which the bank was preparing an assistance strategy.[8] Realizing the importance of consulting with clients, the bank's project team wanted to gather a large amount of information from people in the country.

Although there were concerns that participants might lack keyboarding skills or would prefer face-to-face dialogue, the decision was made to try the technology with the fallback that traditional discussion sessions would be held if stakeholders could not cope with the technology. Far from having difficulties with the GSS, almost all the participants welcomed the chance to share their ideas via computer. Based on an online evaluation at the end of each session, more than 97 percent of participants said they would recommend the technology to other groups. Results of the sessions seconded the enthusiasm of the participants: each group produced more than forty pages of text. The information gathered was perceived to be high in quality and went far beyond the initial expectations of the project team. The stakeholder groups were so fascinated by the GSS that, without exception, they requested that the project team leave it behind when they returned to headquarters.

GSS software usually includes tools for polling or voting. These tools are useful even if the team is not engaged in decision making. Polling tools can help focus discussion or surface difficult issues as well.[9]

SAME-TIME, DIFFERENT-PLACE (STDP) INTERACTIONS. With the recent growth of the Internet and intranet-connected computers, STDP distributed collaboration is becoming common. A distributed meeting is one in which participants are scattered among different places. A distributed meeting differs from the traditional STSP meeting along several dimensions. First and most obviously, the distributed meeting exists simultaneously in several physical locations. This dimension includes individuals participating alone as well as members of co-located subteams. Second, meeting participants communicate over multiple channels, which might include any combination of telephone, video, or text. Communication channels used in a distributed meeting need to be explicitly enabled. Each channel added may consume enormous bandwidth (that is, it might contain a lot of data) thereby adding expense and slowing down the meeting.

It is important to understand exactly which channels add value to the team's collaboration so that necessary channels are made available while unnecessary channels are avoided. For example, many companies have rushed to add videoconferencing technologies only to find that video images bring limited (though predictable) value to STDP meetings. Video is helpful during meeting initiation and transition stages—such as introducing participants and moving from speaker to speaker—but during the actual working stages of a meeting, video images are far less useful than audio and shared data images. Third, meeting participants at different locations may be subject to different external pressures. It may be morning for some participants, lunchtime for others, and late evening for still more. Participants may vary in language and culture. They may be distracted by different local problems, issues, and concerns. Fourth, although STSP meeting attendance (or lack thereof) is obvious and explicit, STDP participation is much more implicit. Participants may tune their telephone or computer to the meeting but, unbeknownst to other participants, focus their energies on other tasks at hand. Or they may attend multiple distributed meetings simultaneously, dividing their focus among them. Leading a different-place meeting so that all participants recognize the value and salience of their participation is a difficult task.

Two examples of STDP implementation are at Ford and Hewlett-Packard. Ford developed interest in STDP meetings as attendance at the annual Ford Systems Integration Center (FSIC) summit had dropped because of both travel expenses and the several days' time required for attendance. Team members who were vital to the meeting were unable to travel, and the process lagged. In 1996, FSIC began using multipoint audio, video, and data conferencing to create a virtual—rather than physical—summit.[10] A total of ten computers—four in Michigan, three in England, two in Germany, and one in New Jersey—connected to form a Microsoft NetMeeting data conference. A multipoint audio/videoconference was established in parallel. The audience could see and hear meeting presenters while their PowerPoint presentations were displayed on the data conference monitors. PowerPoint and other presentation packages allow for a presentation to be viewed on audience PCS as well as on a large projection screen. NetMeeting chat was used as a side channel to communicate conference status, issues, and problems, such as when they needed to adjust sound volume or video settings.

The FSIC invited participants to attend the summit in local conference rooms. Because travel restrictions were no longer a consideration, more than fifty team members now participated at each remote location during the two-week summit—a significant increase from the number of remote participants who previously attended. The presentation was projected on two separate screens to an audience of more than eighty people in the Michigan conference room. For Ford, STDP meetings made it possible for additional people to contribute to the work process.

At Hewlett-Packard, the number of participants did not increase, but their ability to offer feedback and suggestions did. HP implemented a customized meeting process with technology from three different vendors. They are automating the presentation process for R&D teams located in California, Colorado, Japan, Germany, and France with fifteen to twenty people per room participating. They use a PictureTel videoconferencing system along with Intel ProShare for application sharing, all displayed in frames on electronic whiteboards from Smart Technology. The presenter controls the slide show, which shows up on the whiteboard in each room. Distributed participants can provide verbal feedback, mark up the slides, and even alter the information, if appropriate, all in real time. Although a video channel is open through all of this, participants report that being able to view and mark up the information is the most important and most often used tool.[11]

Previously, staff at Hewlett-Packard used a combination of existing media to communicate in distributed meetings (audioconferencing with projection slides). Someone would place a conference call on a standard telephone, and a physical copy of the presentation slides would be faxed to everybody participating in the conference. The presenter would rely on verbal cues to let the participants know which slide was being talked about and where the presenter was on that slide. Though these technologies permitted STDP meetings, they were not very efficient. Visual presentation information was limited to what could be sent over a fax machine. Responses to the information could only come by telephone.

Additional lessons can be pulled from both of these cases. At Ford, they understood the need for a separate process information channel so that the main task discussion would not be interrupted by background requests. At HP, they understood the importance of crafting a custom technology solution even though it meant combining products from three different vendors to do so. They analyzed their particular needs and deployed tools to address them rather than relying on a single turnkey solution.

DIFFERENT-TIME, SAME-PLACE (DTSP) INTERACTIONS. The DTSP cell of the matrix is probably the most difficult to comprehend. Johansen suggests it might refer to a "team room" concept, where a work team exists across two or three shifts. It might include members who travel frequently or telecommute. Or it might encompass members who each have an office but come together in shared space to work on a given project. In this last sense, the team room is like a private clubhouse where the team establishes and contains its identity with visual symbols or markings on the walls. The team room differs from an organizational conference room—though in practice a conference room may be appropriated for the task—in that it belongs to the team and is not used by others during the course of the project. (Jean Wineman and Margaret Serrato talk more extensively about team spaces in Chapter Ten.)

The U.S. Navy's operations planning team (OPT) based in Hawaii uses DTSP collaboration technology to support high-pressure, round-the-clock, time-critical functions. The OPT at the U.S. Navy Pacific Command (CINCPAC) in Hawaii is a team of seven to nine analysts assigned to produce responses to potential crises seventy-two hours to two weeks out. This team works in conjunction with other planning teams following a structured hierarchy of processes and procedures. In 1994, the OPT required approximately ten days to step through a comprehensive planning exercise for a major long-term event. The planning process might have included several teams handing off information across two or three shifts, working out of a single secured room. That was considered normal and acceptable during the cold war, when the enemy was well known and fairly predictable.

In the post-cold-war world, the enemy may be smaller, faster, and less known. It was deemed that there is a need to significantly reduce the planning cycle. The leader of the CINCPAC OPT set an initial goal of reducing the planning cycle from ten days to four days by adopting GSS tools to support the process. He implemented a commercial GSS, developed an online planning template, and began constructing a repository of previously used crisis-response solutions that could be applied, as appropriate, to future situations. The GSS served as an ongoing data store across shifts, so that team members could hand off work and the process could continue around the clock. After a year of drill, the OPT succeeded in reducing its planning cycle to four days. Now they are reevaluating what they have learned and trying to bring it down to twenty-four hours.

DIFFERENT-TIME, DIFFERENT-PLACE (DTDP) INTERACTIONS. When virtual meetings last a long time, participants may contribute to the meeting asynchronously, checking in and out of the meeting independently of other participants' attendance. The meeting may contain a less-defined temporal beginning and end. The concept of a meeting lasting an hour to several hours fades and blends with the concept of the overall project. Participants enter and leave the virtual meeting space as the meeting carries on.

The DTDP concept refers to work team members' sharing the same virtual space on an intranet. In this manner, the team may be distributed physically but holds shared access to an online bulletin board, chat room, or database. Such is the case with Manhattan-based workers at a Morgan Stanley division who used to work until midnight cutting and pasting a one-hundred-page daily update of bond prices and interest rates from Tokyo, London, and New York, to be faxed to more than one hundred key traders and brokers worldwide. But the information often arrived in Tokyo long after the opening of trading. Delays inevitably shorted traders on information and cost the company money. Morgan Stanley addressed these problems by installing an intranet. Tokyo, Hong Kong, and London traders now access the central repository in New York when they arrive at work and receive the data on time. Even more offices around the world now update the documents continuously, so traders get the latest information.[12]

Chrysler is using a similar approach, but on an "extranet" and treating their suppliers as partners in the process. The result at Chrysler is a reduction in operating costs by more than a billion dollars a year. Chrysler is using Lotus Notes to support a DTDP collaborative process they call SCORE (for Supplier COst Reduction Effort), an incentive program to motivate suppliers to help the auto manufacturer reduce its costs. A supplier suggesting a cost-savings approach receives a portion of the cost savings achieved.[13] As of early 1997, 160 of about 900 production suppliers and thousands of nonproduction vendors were participating in SCORE on line. Submissions tripled since SCORE went on line in 1994, to an average of 165 per week. Chrysler has plans to give 340 additional suppliers access to the system. During the 1997 model year, Chrysler estimated that it realized over $1 billion in cost savings— fully 2 percent of overall operating costs for the corporation—thanks to suggestions from the project.

ANYTIME, ANYPLACE (ATAP) INTERACTIONS. When he developed the groupware matrix, Johansen predicted that eventually tools and techniques would emerge that lead to anytime, anyplace collaboration. Such tools and techniques are in fact beginning to appear. One example is at IBM.

Principals of the IBM Global Services Notes Practice have become virtual teleworkers, using computer and communication tools to increase their own productivity while decreasing IBM's expenses. The principal of U.S. Western Area 11 of the Global Services Notes Practice no longer has an office in an IBM building. Rather, he leads his consultant teams virtually through his cellular phone, pager, and laptop computer while constantly visiting ongoing projects and prospective new clients. These tools give him immediate access to incoming messages, the ability to send immediate outgoing messages, and the capability to share documents at any time from any place via a modem. Most of the projects he oversees maintain online project management databases, many of them in Lotus Notes. This principal has the ability to log on to most of these databases from his laptop, allowing him to keep abreast of team progress and to view exceptions from the norm. He routes his incoming voice messages through a central audio service, controlling features so that callers may ring through to him at whatever phone he has designated as his "hot" phone for the day, page him with a return phone number, or leave him voicemail. His voice mailbox can page him to let him know when a new voicemail message is added to the queue.

To further support his connectivity, he can "hotel" at any IBM office and make use of all of its local resources, including teleconferencing and high-speed data links. In addition, he has ISDN in his home office, which gives him fast access to the Internet for better data and videoconferencing from home.

These tools have produced a significant culture change within the IBM Notes National Consulting Practice. The Western Area 11 principal says that since IBM has implemented these technologies and taken traditional offices away, he now spends significantly more time being client-focused. As he no longer has an office of his own, he is at a client site almost every day, increasing his interactions and visibility. Moreover, he is better able to maintain a pulse on all of the projects he manages.

ATAP tools are not a category of their own; rather, they are tools from the four cells of the groupware matrix that contain seamless interfaces, enabling their use anytime, anyplace.

VARIATIONS TO SUPPORT TYPES OF TEAMS

Each type of business team described in this book uses electronic tools and technologies differently because of the unique nature of its group composition and objectives. The Appendix illustrates how each work group type differs in the way it is likely to be virtual.

Management Teams

Management teams, for example, can be organized over distance, as some organizations split their top management by geographic region. Ticketmaster, for example, runs its American operation out of Los Angeles but locates vice presidents at hubs of regional centers in such cities as New York, Chicago, and Orlando. However, the top management team collaborates daily. When a company's regional operations span continents, as with multinational corporations such as Exxon, executive communication not only crosses distance but time zones as well. According to its Website, as of 1996 Exxon had thirty-one major refining and marketing operations in seventeen countries on five continents.[14] By definition, management teams do not cross organization boundaries; they are the skeleton of that very structure. Top management teams in particular make heavier use of videoconferencing than other forms of groupware. Top management's use of collaboration technology, as with its use of executive support systems, tends toward tools that have a short learning curve, intuitive user interface, and a summary or condensation of information.

Project Teams

Project teams, on the other hand, often cross-cut organizational structures to team up people with appropriate skills and experiences. Since these people may be distributed by distance and time zone, project teams can display virtuality in all three dimensions. Price Waterhouse demonstrated this by teaming four executives from three states to pull data from executives around the world over four days and win a multimillion-dollar consulting bid.[15]

Owens-Corning Fiberglass is an example of a company that uses videoconferencing heavily among its project teams. It is organized globally by product line. Thus all plants operate to similar organizational goals and standards but each must also adhere to the laws, regulations, and environmental issues of its own locality. For example, when the Owens-Corning global packaging division worked to develop a global standard for packaging, the division assembled eight parallel distributed teams that met using videoconferencing. The teams reported that the videolinks provided a greater sense camaraderie and teamwork, the ability to include more people with diverse skills, and a reduction in product development cycle time.[16]

Project teams require shared access to a central repository no matter on which dimension they are virtually distributed. This shared repository enables team members to track the status of the project and to check out, modify, and check in shared materials as needed. Distributed databases, such as Lotus Notes, and distributed document management systems, such as Notes or BSCW, are excellent tools to support this need.

Production Teams

Production teams differ from the other types of work groups considered here in that they are less involved in knowledge work and more likely to be routine or process-oriented. As such, in many production settings individual team members do not have their own desktop computer assigned to them and are neither required nor expected to engage in text communication. Rather, production team members are very interested in automated tools that monitor and regulate the production activity. They want tools that report deviance from expected norms; they want to communicate with one another to solve process problems and share a repository of knowledge about the production process.

Production teams tend to be distributed not within the organizational structure but over time—such as shiftwork—and over distance when production is shared across multiple factories. The use of videoconferencing at 3M has enabled real-time coordination of production process at two physical locations thousands of miles apart: White City, Oregon, and Austin, Texas. Engineers in Oregon and Texas are required to communicate during productions runs of the visual systems division. Batches must adhere to preset standards, and significant shortfalls require that production at both plants cease until the problem is solved. In these situations, 3M is using videoconferencing to convene virtually. By supporting shared troubleshooting and enabling the solution to be implemented immediately at both plants, videoconferencing reduces the cost of lost production time. 3M reports that with videoconferencing, the White City plant cut production downtime substantially.[17]

Service Teams

Service teams can be distributed over both time and space and require information support from a central repository and ongoing process monitors. The network support function at Andersen Consulting provides an excellent example of these needs. Network support at Andersen is a worldwide, round-the-clock operation. As the Andersen consultants may require access to shared data or need to use collaborative technology to communicate at any time from any place, network operations must be continuously live. To accomplish this, they employ a "follow the sun" strategy, with technicians hubbed in the United States, Singapore, and France. These teams take regular turns dealing with network issues, service, and upgrades.

Previously, Andersen handed off live control of network support, employing a process of faxing information back and forth during a series of conference calls between teams of three people per location at the change of each eight-hour shift. Communication is critical as teams collaborate to share information or resolve problems left from the previous shift.[18] This process was time-consuming, produced communication confusion, and left the firm with no central repository of service information. To improve this DTDP collaboration process, Andersen installed LiveWorks LiveBoards[19] at each site to display the status of daily information. The LiveBoard functions as a virtual scoreboard, showing the status of each ongoing situation. In addition, the LiveBoard displays from a central repository so that consistency of information is maintained. Each shift updates information and hands off the work to the next shift on another continent.

Action Teams

Action teams may be distributed in any of the three dimensions, with the most likely one being distance. They require tools for immediate communication. Their technologies must be fast, easy to operate, and in many cases mobile. The tools coming into use with military action teams are a good example of this. During the summer of 1997 the U.S. Marine Corps conducted "Hunter Warrior" exercises with navy ships off the Pacific coast and marine units in the California desert. The marines fielded six-man infantry teams using off-the-shelf Apple Newton MessagePads equipped with global positioning system cards, laser rangefinders, and cellular phones. They wanted to see if small teams could win and survive against a traditional force by using long-range precision munitions instead of conventional, confrontational warfare.[20] The MessagePads allowed the teams to send and receive electronic messages, forward intelligence reports, request supplies, call in heavy firepower—even plan navigation. As the laser rangefinders give exact distance and azimuth to targets, the marines were able to compute precise coordinates to fire on the enemy. The exercise was a battlefield success, with the smaller units coordinating to knock out three hundred of five hundred targeted military vehicles of the larger conventional regiment.

However, this technology and related techniques drive large-scale culture changes that the Marine Corps may not be ready for.[21] As with all of the technologies discussed in this chapter, changes in organizational structure and power relationships might occur. In this example, marine commanders were asked to lead from the rear rather than the front—a reversal of centuries-old marine practice. The upshot of this change was not anticipated by exercise planners and is requiring additional consideration of the merit of the technology and process that brought battlefield success.

Parallel Teams

Parallel teams function virtually on all three dimensions of time, place, and structure. However, they function with much less time criticality. Parallel teams, coming together from different units and possibly different cultures, need to create a shared core for their interactions. This can take the form of a physical environment, a shared data repository, or a language or culture common to the team. Because the teams are starting anew, face-to-face meetings are helpful in establishing a shared vision and culture. Further, a collaborative information repository reinforces common language and work practices. Parallel quality circle teams at the Internal Revenue Service made use of collaboration technology recently in just these ways.

The IRS Manhattan office established several quality teams of three to twelve people from across functional areas to develop methods for problem solving and quality improvement. These teams met several hundred times over a fifteen-month period using a group support system to provide a shared language, enable anonymous and honest idea contribution, structure their interactions, and maintain their ideas in a shared repository. The quality teams reported a high level of satisfaction with the technology and a belief that it played a major role in the success of the teams.[22]

BEST PRACTICES IN LEADING OR FACILITATING VIRTUAL WORK TEAMS

In the business practice examples described earlier in this chapter, productivity gains are achieved by applying both electronic technologies and facilitative techniques concurrently to virtual work groups. From these business practice examples, several generic lessons can be extracted.

STSP Best Practices

- It is useful to begin measuring returns from group technology immediately after installation (as Marriott did), if not even sooner. If measures are taken prior to installation, those benchmarks make it possible to show gains or losses resulting from the technology. But watch out for the learning curve. It takes time for leaders and participants to learn to use the technology effectively.

- Taking a GSS on the road, as the World Bank does, introduces significant technological and logistic complexities. Before doing so, first become comfortable using it in a fixed and stable setting.

- The process of polling is not just for decision making. If you have keypad or GSS tools available, consider using them at the beginning of a discussion process to take a straw poll. This helps focus and frame the discussion.

STDP Best Practices

- Ford managers understood the need for a separate process information channel so that the main task discussion would not be interrupted by background requests. But remember that each additional process channel uses bandwidth and may contribute to slowing down the primary task channel.

- Hewlett-Packard managers understood the importance of crafting a custom technology solution even though it meant combining products from three vendors to do so. They analyzed their particular needs and deployed tools to address them, rather than relying on a single turnkey solution. But be careful that all of the vendors involved use compatible data communication standards.

- The action of moving from one process stage to another needs to be complete and explicit in STDP meetings.

DTSP Best Practices

- One way technology can save time and effort is by supporting reuse of information, as the U.S. Navy OPT is doing. A well-indexed central repository can provide an archive of best practices, previous solutions, or boilerplate information that gives a team a running start in solving future problems fast.

- Create a scoreboard. The facilitator or leader can create a computer frame of the project's status or agenda and mark up the frame with check marks and notes to focus participants exactly on the topic at hand.

DTDP Best Practices

- The real key to the success of Chrysler's project is that they designed the business process and then applied the technology to it. Don't build or purchase collaboration tools without first analyzing business processes and determining the problem that the tools are meant to solve.

- Distribute photos and short biographies. Some GSS software includes facilities to paste up pictures and biographies of meeting participants so that others can see their faces and learn about them. The pictures might include shots of the meeting space itself so that others can picture what people look like assembled in the meeting room.

ATAP Best Practices

- Understand that there is a learning curve involved with any new technology, and the initial productivity results may not be indicative of what can be expected in the future.

- Because leaders and facilitators need to learn to use the technology before they can be effective, do not introduce a new technology in a high-pressure or critical-path project. Start with something easy.

- GSS supports larger teams than are otherwise appropriate. Do not be afraid to add participants to GSS teams. More participants increase ideas and buy-in to the end product

CONCLUSION

This chapter has examined how electronic collaboration technologies allow virtual teams—people separated by time, distance, or organizational structure—to share information, generate ideas, and make decisions quickly, easily, and in a way that documents the work for storage and later retrieval. Tools that support virtual teams do so by providing communication channels, structuring deliberation, or affording access to external information.

For five types of interaction (same-time, same-place; same-time, different-place; different-time, same-place; different-time, different-place; and anytime, anyplace), virtual meeting tools are new and evolving. A rich variety of tools already exist, and a growing set of organizational best practices are evolving along with them.

10

FACILITY DESIGN FOR HIGH-PERFORMANCE TEAMS

Jean Wineman, Margaret Serrato

THE HIGH-PERFORMANCE work team requires high-performance workspace. The physical facility can be viewed as a tool for enabling work and ways of working. When designed appropriately, this resource plays a vital role in the success of work teams. Ignored, the workspace is counterproductive, requiring group members to expend extra effort to accomplish tasks or to adapt to inappropriate working conditions.

This chapter discusses the range of physical design factors that contribute to the creation of high-performance settings for work teams. As organizations restructure to less hierarchical, more team-based structures, the task of designing workspace has also changed. The focus is no longer on maximizing individual effectiveness (satisfaction and performance) but now extends beyond the individual to the effectiveness of the space in supporting group work and the goals of the organization as a whole. These topics are addressed:

- Current trends in workspace design
- Facility features that enhance group effectiveness (including design and layout of individual workstations, group working areas and support services, and the organizational context)
- Best practices for the design of supportive workspace for six types of work groups

CURRENT TRENDS IN FACILITY DESIGN

As organizational structures become less hierarchical, the character of work groups changes, from those instructed as to their tasks to those with more responsibility and independence in defining and structuring their work. Flattening of the organizational hierarchy and empowerment of the workforce has resulted in office spaces with fewer distinctions based on status. Individual workspaces have become increasingly more standardized and interchangeable. This allows an organization to reorganize and reassign spaces easily to accommodate turnover and change.

Work groups have also changed in composition. Greater proportions of women and minorities are joining the workforce. As organizations downsize and increase the "flexibility" (the ability to expand and contract as business fluctuates) of their workforce, temporary and part-time workers often replace full-time positions. The newly emerging working group is one that is diverse in character, including full-time and part-time employees as well as a range of specialized consultants. This growing diversity of the workforce is accompanied by concern that there be greater ergonomic adjustability of the furnishings and equipment (to a wider range of body sizes) and greater individual control of working conditions (environmental systems, personalization, and so forth).

Emphasis on working groups and collaboration leads to an increase in the proportion of space devoted to group-oriented activities. Individually assigned spaces shrink in size, often in an effort to create additional group space. Computer networks are introduced in an effort to enhance interoffice communication. Information technology support increases to allow multisite and multinational collaboration.

As alternative modes of work become more common (flexible working schedules, work from remote locations), new trends in facilities include "hoteling" workstations (shared by different workers at different times), technology support for home offices and telecommuting, and nonterritorial offices (with no individually assigned spaces).

Fewer permanent employees means a workforce with less commitment to a particular organization, and higher turnover. Attraction and retention of qualified workers becomes an increasingly important issue. Organizations focus on improving the quality of the workspace and providing attractive support facilities (day care facilities, health club facilities) to improve their competitive ability to recruit and retain the best workers.

It is difficult to quantify the extent to which an organization should invest in the physical facility. However, there is a growing body of research demonstrating the positive effects of improvements in the physical setting on productivity. Studies carried out in numerous companies, such as Aetna, Corning Glass, Levi-Strauss, and Lotus,[1] as well as large multicorporation studies[2] have shown dramatic improvements in productivity. Results of up to 15–20 percent improvements in productivity have been recorded when the physical setting of offices is improved.

It is clear that a minimal investment in improving the workspace can result in manifold savings in personnel costs over the life cycle of an organization. Typically, over a ten-year period, an office organization that constructs a new building spends about 5 percent of corporate costs on construction, furniture, and equipment and another 2 percent on maintenance and operations, while 93 percent of expenditures are devoted to employee wages and benefits. This is a 13 to 1 ratio of "people" costs to building costs. In the case of an organization that leases space, the ratio is about 5 to 1.[3] The leverage suggested by these ratios indicates that corporate investment in the facility has significant long-term value if it improves worker productivity or reduces worker absenteeism and turnover, and therefore reduces expenditures on salaries by even as little as a few percentage points.

CASE EXAMPLE: FACILITIES OF AN AUTOMOBILE PRODUCTION PLANT

Group space can no longer be thought of as a collection of individual workstations. The underlying premise of creating a working group is to bring individuals into contact with one another and to create a community of knowledge. In fact, the design of effective group space must break out of traditional conceptions of office planning and consider creation of space to enhance both the community of the group (interrelationships between the group members) and the organizational (global) level of community (the interrelationships between the group and other groups or individuals within the organization). A critical consideration at both the local and global levels is not only creation of spaces themselves but how those spaces link together to constitute the fabric of the organization and the blueprint of opportunities for encounter.

Along with this new conception of a more integrated whole is reconsideration of the use of time and space. Group work is a fluid process of movement, from individual activity to group activity and back again. Groups typically engage in a complex variety of tasks that compose a larger project. The group may be involved in more than one project, as well as having members who are engaged in more than one group. It is important to think of the organization today as highly "recombinatory."[4]

When we think of groups working, we tend to focus on decisions that are made by the group meeting as a whole. In fact, much of the work, and even the decision making, is accomplished individually or in small groups. In fact, it is not uncommon to find that the most productive ideas germinate from interactions a member of the group has with others outside the group.[5]

An illustration of the importance of communication for product success is the interest of the automobile industry in enhancing collaboration between managers, engineers, and production workers. In late 1989, the "trim and chassis" department of a Ford Motor Company production plant was reorganized in an effort to improve the quality and efficiency of production of the Ford Taurus and Mercury Sable. This reorganization brought together in one location all of the employees whose jobs related to production.

Before the move, all the engineers and engineering managers worked in the engineering department in the "front" administrative office building; industrial engineers and process engineers occupied two large bullpen areas, with the associated engineering managers in adjacent enclosed offices. The production line was in a separate building a few minutes' walk away. This building housed the production workers and the production supervisors.

Production management and engineering personnel moved into an office area in the center of the production floor. They had to walk through the production floor to reach the offices. Now engineers are on the production floor discussing with production workers how to improve processes. Opportunities for informal interaction with production staff are supplemented with structured meetings, such as weekly "employee involvement meetings." Outcomes of these interactions range from reorganizing equipment on the production line to suggestions for product improvements. To respond more effectively to customer concerns, teams of engineers and production employees have been organized to respond to such quality issues as "water leaks," "wind noise," and "squeak and rattle." Data on customer complaints and maintenance records are routinely monitored and response solutions developed collaboratively among design engineers, production process specialists, and line workers.

In this example, disciplines that might otherwise work in isolation are brought together in a process of collaboration to enhance product output. Communication is the key to success. If one aspect of a project is developed in isolation, it may engender redesign or result in downstream development that is marginally effective in attempting to accommodate an earlier solution. In collaborative teams, potential problems surface during development.

At the production plant, facility design has encouraged development of a community of "shared knowledge," workers in any one specialization are aware of and interacting with others in related specialties, managers are in contact with production workers, and production workers provide inputs to product design. The work process involves movement and (often unplanned) meetings with groups of differing compositions. The result is a boost in product quality and production efficiency.

FACILITY DESIGN FOR EFFECTIVE WORK TEAMS

This discussion of effective work settings for groups is subdivided into three sections. The first considers minimal requirements to support worker comfort, well-being, and accomplishment of work tasks. The next section, micro group layout, addresses aspects of designing group space, from individual workspaces to the kinds of spaces that support group interaction and performance. The final section, macro group layout, discusses how work group space interfaces with other features of the organizational context, group boundaries, and the design of organizational space to promote a shared community of knowledge.

Fulfilling Basic Needs

In discussing the design of workspace for groups, one must begin with provisions for basic worker comfort and satisfaction. Whether someone is working in individual or shared space, the workspace should provide an environment that enables accomplishment of work tasks with minimal expenditure of time, effort, and stress. Aspects of the work environment that influence worker comfort and satisfaction include furnishings (adequacy and arrangement of work surface, seating, filing, and storage), conditions of the ambient environment (heating, ventilation, air conditioning, and noise), lighting (adequate task and ambient levels), and electronic support (computer network, telephone, electrical, and so forth). There is substantial evidence that even for simple tasks, failures in workplace design adversely affect health, well-being, and job performance.[6]

At a minimum, the physical facility should reduce or eliminate negative health effects and environmental stressors. Employees are becoming increasingly aware of the possible health and comfort threats of indoor air pollution and inadequate working conditions. Employee advocates argue for better lighting and ergonomically responsive furnishings to reduce associated risks of eyestrain; fatigue; headaches; cumulative muscle and nerve problems in wrists, necks, and shoulders; and lower back pain. At best, the physical facility should support worker satisfaction and productivity. Several studies have suggested that introducing ergonomically designed systems furniture and improved office layout lead to productivity improvements. Investments in energy-efficient lighting systems and improved HVAC performance have been shown to reduce building operating expenses as well as increase worker performance by providing task-appropriate lighting and improved control over temperature and ventilation.[7]

Micro Group Layout

As groups are empowered to define and schedule how they work, the group workspace should provide the resources and flexibility to support these diverse activities. Spaces to facilitate the primary tasks of the work group are important, but equally as important is the design of space to support the other, less-formal activities of work. In fact, the long-term viability of the group is often as important as its immediate tasks. Workspace should reach beyond facilitation of work tasks to support the social and cultural well-being of the participants.

Through the life cycle of a group project, varying types of facility support are required, from group space to individual space, from structured space to informal space. Typically a group moves back and forth through these spaces. For example, at the outset of a project, brainstorming may take place in a larger group space, with little need for computer support (although a group could use a computer-mediated approach). Following this might be a series of individual or small-group meetings, returning to the large group, and so forth. These transitions from separation (individual or small group) to integration (large group) should be seamless, in other words accomplished easily and without disrupting the group process. The intensity of group activities varies over time as well, with deadlines often bringing a rush of activity that taxes the resources available to the maximum.[8]

CO-LOCATION AND PROXIMITY OF GROUP MEMBERS' WORKSPACES. Studies of the productivity of R&D teams suggest that communication is an important indicator of performance.[9] Workers talk (face-to-face) with others who are in close proximity. As early as the classic Hawthorne studies, initiated in 1924, research demonstrated that social relationships (social interaction, friendship formation, and informal group liaisons) are affected by physical proximity and accessibility of workstations. These results have been corroborated by numerous subsequent studies.[10] Beyond a distance of about thirty meters, workers are not likely to talk (directly) unless there is a particularly important matter.[11] Physical distance and physical barriers (such as doors, stairs, and changes in direction of corridors) act as deterrents.[12] If group members are distant from one another, they may be unable to coordinate activities.[13] Although similar proximity may be achieved through computer-based interface, at this time the best predictor of interaction continues to be physical closeness.

A question that is often raised with respect to communication is the concern for time "wasted" in social conversation. A manager might say, "Fine, I'm happy to encourage work-related communication. But how do I control social conversations?" The answer here is complex, and to some extent it depends on the organizational context. It is sometimes difficult to separate work-related interaction from casual social contact; one may lead to the other. In fact, it is recognized that individuals must develop a level of social relationship with coworkers that establishes the basis for exchange of ideas. This understanding has developed out of extensive research on open office planning.

Proponents of open office planning suggest that removal of barriers (walls, doors, hallways) enhances communication and work performance. Based on studies of the positive effects of proximity, this appears to be true. However, the bulk of research studies of open plan offices indicate the opposite.[14] A number of factors contribute to these findings. First, although the physical proximity and increased visual access provided in open offices should enhance communication, open plan offices generally lack the visual and auditory privacy that individuals need to develop stronger, more lasting relationships or that supervisors require to provide confidential feedback. Second, it may be that the conditions of open plan offices (increased noise level, visual distraction, and loss of privacy), although not affecting communication levels directly, contribute to reductions in work performance. Third, it is important to distinguish between proximity as physical distance between workers (physical density) and functional distance, or the number of workers that are easily accessible to a person (functional density). Most often, a move to open office planning is accompanied by an increase in physical density: more workers are accommodated in the same overall square footage. This increase in physical density allows a worker to be in closer proximity to other workers but also results in associated increases in noise level, visual distraction, and loss of privacy.

It is quite possible to decrease functional distance while keeping the number of persons per square foot constant. In one example, groups of three to five offices (enclosed on three sides by full-height partitions, with a glass wall and open doorway on the fourth side) were arranged around small work areas. This brought workers into closer functional proximity than their previous, more traditional arrangement of individual offices along a corridor; however, physical density remained about the same. In this example, friendship opportunities and work satisfaction increased.[15] It may be that some of the negative outcomes that have been associated with open planning are due to the effects of increased physical density and not the openness of the workspaces themselves. In any case, it is important to consider the nature of the tasks involved, and the extent to which these job requirements demand close visual and auditory contact. It may be that open planning, or a modified open plan, with small subgroupings of workspaces is appropriate for work teams, as in a newspaper office, where members of a team must stay abreast of rapidly changing information, or for members of a telemarketing team, where team viability is dependent upon the mutual support of, and opportunities for consultation with, other team members.

An essential component of group (team) effectiveness is "team viability," a term that refers to group members' satisfaction, participation, and willingness to continue working together over a certain period of time or longer. Viability might also include cohesion and ability to communicate and engage in problem solving effectively.[16] Proximity of workstations and informal gathering places, features that foster informal interaction, is considered an important ingredient in designing space to support the longevity of groups.[17]

Workspace arrangement and definition of physical boundaries affects patterns of interaction and leadership within the group.[18] For a group such as a management team, there may be a trade-off between keeping a manager and the work unit he or she coordinates proximate, and proximity among the managers themselves. If the relation to the work unit is paramount, informal interfacing among the members of the team should be encouraged in other ways, such as through careful planning of shared pathways and the location of other functional spaces and support services. This is discussed in more detail below.

An ophthalmic products company with central offices located in Atlanta reorganized one of its research divisions to address a particularly promising research challenge. The reorganization created a project team, combining personnel from several departments, into two subgroups, each addressing one aspect of the problem. Even with these two distinct subgroups, all workers were co-located in a partitioned office floor. Furthermore, individual workers from one subgroup were interspersed with individuals from the other. Co-location strongly supported informal interaction among the members of the larger group. An adjacent coffee bar offered informal meeting space, and a fully enclosed "project team room" provided a place to lay out project materials, store project resources, and hold group meetings.

SHARED GROUP WORKSPACE. For groups with reasonably long life spans—as with project teams, production groups, and service groups—shared group workspace supports development of a shared knowledge base. Even in groups with very specialized individual tasks, bringing some of those tasks out to a common group workspace raises awareness among all group members. "Common" space ranges from simple (a shared work table) to complex (the nonterritorial office, where no space is individually assigned). The functions supported may range from group meetings, publication layout, and product display to use of shared equipment, or combinations of all of these. A typical solution might provide small, individual home-based offices, group work areas, various small and large conference rooms, resource areas, and break areas.

Group workspaces that are assigned to project groups for the life of a project, or that house project-sensitive materials, should be located within a group area or adjacent to it to encourage easy, seamless access. Locating group workspace within the group area also provides a means of controlling access if control is needed. These spaces allow group members to lay out materials and equipment that are dedicated to their project(s) and do not have to be removed at the end of each day. Most often the group workspace is similar to a small conference area: a space to accommodate six to eight people, with room for resource materials, drawings, models, computer terminals, and support equipment.

This group workspace may be more or less enclosed, depending upon the nature of the tasks. If it is an open area, it should be supported by an adjacent enclosed conference room. This is also an opportunity to modulate the boundary between "public" clients and workers. A successful example is an office design for a local office of a state department of human services, where a ring of "systems furniture" workstations encloses a central, open conference area. Each workstation has a bay where public assistance clients sit facing the case worker across a desk surface. (This is seen as a safety advantage over having clients seated in the same cubicle with the case worker.) The central area, accessible only to the case workers, is a space for impromptu conferences; it allows workers to move freely from one another's space to lend support or seek consultation.

The advantage of developing group common space is primarily encouraging interface and shared knowledge within the group; however, shared space presents another opportunity. Often these activities by their nature demand less privacy and, unless they involve project-sensitive materials, are excellent opportunities to interface with the larger organizational context. More permeable boundaries surrounding shared group space enhance exchange of knowledge at the level of the organization as a whole. For certain group situations, it may be appropriate to have a combination of both a closed project "room" for private activity and public display or meeting areas that interface (through visual and permeable boundaries) with the larger organizational context.

How many organizations can afford all this extra space? One way to achieve a workable solution is to reduce individually assigned space so as to capture common space. As in the nonterritorial office that we discuss later, individual spaces no longer need to accommodate one or two guest chairs or a small table for meetings, and storage requirements can be reduced to what is needed for personal resources.[19]

An example of this trade-off occurred almost by default when the Florida A&M School of Architecture designed its new building. Faculty who had for years shared offices with one or two others were keen to have single-occupancy office space. They said, "Design us individual offices that are so small no one would ever think of suggesting they be shared." Working with state standards for faculty offices, the designers reduced the individual offices to just below minimum standard and allocated the additional square footage to create faculty common areas (thus allowing the total allocation to faculty to meet state standards).

INDIVIDUAL "HOME BASE" WORKSTATIONS. In most situations, no matter how effective the group facilities, workers need a home base, a place for privacy and reflection, a place to spread out their own work materials, a place that gives them identity within the larger organization. As the demands for group activity increase, it is even more important that there be places of retreat.[20]

The extent to which this individual workspace is enclosed also depends on job tasks and specialization. The most flexible system allows an individual the chance to modulate the degree of visual and acoustical privacy afforded by an individual office space. An example of this might be a folding or sliding panel that can be opened for increased contact, or closed to ensure privacy.[21]

ALTERNATIVES TO INDIVIDUALLY ASSIGNED SPACES. For corporations with a sizeable proportion of workers who frequently work outside the office or telecommute from remote locations, the concepts of hoteling and check-out workspaces allow the company to substantially reduce facilities costs by building or leasing less space. It is estimated that about 6.6 million Americans now perform their jobs at least partially from home offices or at locations outside the office, supported with mobile communications and computer-based systems connected electronically to the main corporate office,[22] and it has been suggested that as many as 66 million Americans will telecommute by the year 2000.[23] As a result, by adopting a hoteling system, large corporations radically reduce space requirements. IBM recently reduced the office space for its New Jersey sales and service staff by 75 percent. Ernst and Young, another prominent user of hoteling concepts, consolidated offices in the Chicago Sears Tower from twenty-one floors to seven floors.[24]

With a hoteling system, the corporate office maintains fewer individual offices than there are employees. These office locations are not pre-assigned to individual workers. Instead, workers call ahead to reserve a space or are assigned a temporary space as they arrive in the office (sometimes referred to as "moteling" or check-out). Each employee has his or her own movable storage cart or pedestal (affectionately known as the "puppy") containing personal files and other materials, which is rolled to any available office space. Electronic devices such as cordless telephones and laptop computers are an important ingredient in the success of such office systems.[25] If a space is reserved ahead, all of the work materials, phone, and computer can be in place and ready when the worker reaches the office. This also opens up easily assignable spaces for visitors from other sites, consultants, and other temporary employees.

In these situations, workstations are generic and interchangeable. This has the advantage of reducing potential status differences as symbolized by the workspace and its amenities. Unintended status differences among members of a work group may affect the interaction patterns of the group, the social influence of group members, and ultimately the mode of decision making.

The nonterritorial or free-address office is an example of office space devoted to the concept of shared space. In this work setting, a variety of activity areas are provided to accommodate different tasks; all of the activity spaces are available to everyone. Groups and individuals move from space to space as they work, depending upon the needs of the task. Thus "work" is a fluid process of movement in and out of spaces, from group activities to individual activities and back again over the course of the day. One advantage of this system is that it is very space-efficient. Space and often equipment resources are used as needed. It is a system that tends to self-management.

In this setting, each type of space can be tailored to its specific purpose. Instead of an individual office space functioning for individual work, small group meetings, and storage of reference materials, each use has its own space. The library and resource area is designed with low lighting levels and comfortable chairs. Open meeting areas are furnished with movable tables and chairs (for easy reconfiguration) and whiteboard or tackboard surfaces. In a true free-address office, no one has an assigned home base; these workspaces are allocated as individuals come to the office.

In 1994, Chiat/Day headquarters in Venice, California, underwent a radical transformation from traditional to alternative office space. The office had reorganized into multidisciplinary teams some time earlier, but the physical space did not support teaming work patterns. The teams had no team workspace; once they were assigned a project, all the members of the group retreated to their individual offices. Now, workers check out phones and PowerBooks as they arrive at the office and then sit wherever they please. Choices include project rooms, study carrels, the library, or the combined recreation room and cafeteria. The project rooms, or "strategic business units" as they are called, are small-to-medium-sized conference rooms with phones, computers, and VCRs, designed specifically to support teamwork.[26]

As a greater percentage of workers telecommute from remote locations, the group workspace becomes the point of interface for brief, intense working visits. Organizations experience a corresponding reduction overall in the demand for continuous single-occupancy workspaces. As this demand diminishes, more space is allocated to generic workstations that can support the task needs of a range of workers. These spaces are coupled with generic group spaces to support working visits with electronic linkages to remote locations.

MEETING SPACE AND CONFERENCE AREAS. Working groups of any type should have easily accessible space available for the group to meet face-to-face. The location of such spaces encourages collaboration across boundaries within the organization. Available, easily reserved, and well-equipped meeting spaces facilitate impromptu meetings. For this reason, these spaces should not be contained within the boundaries of a group space, where they may be viewed as "owned" by one group to the exclusion of others.

For groups, where many tasks are accomplished in meetings these events should be positive and productive experiences in which all members of the group have an opportunity to actively participate. In addition to accomplishing the specific tasks of the meeting, these group events function to build group cohesion and support the kind of social relationships that form the basis for exchange of ideas. The success of group meetings is affected by the size, furnishings, and environmental conditions of the meeting space. The furniture arrangement within a meeting space also affects the nature of interaction and participation among group members, which in turn determines the social influence of certain members of the group, and ultimately how decisions are made.[27] To build a committed and motivated project group, members must feel comfortable with one another. An arrangement that encourages social contact should maximize eye contact and minimize distance between group members; thus a round or square conference table functions better than a long, linear one, particularly for smaller groups.[28]

Choices should be available to accommodate groups of various sizes. As the number of group-based activities in organizations increases, the demand for available meeting spaces also rises. The traditional corporate office, with several ten-to-fifteen-person conference rooms, is no longer workable. Smaller team spaces are needed. These should support group work at three levels: a larger teaming room to hold up to ten people; small conference spaces where one or two people can escape for concentrated work; and medium-sized spaces that can accommodate three or four workers but might be used by one or two if other spaces are not available.

DISPLAY AREAS. The idea of shared group workspace suggests another opportunity to contribute to developing a shared community of knowledge: through "display." *Display* refers to presentation of work or the products of work (through planned displays, bulletin boards, and electronic information centers), but perhaps more important it also refers to unplanned demonstration of work in progress, through visual access to working groups.

Display is an opportunity to share ideas or work-in-process with other group members and with individuals in the larger organization. These opportunities allow an individual or group to develop understanding of the contributions of their own work and the work of others to overall production.

Macro Group Layout

Macro group layout concerns the relationships among spaces at the organization level and is an important ingredient of organizational community.

CONCENTRATED CIRCULATION PATTERNS. The layout of physical space affects patterns of circulation and interaction.[29] In any workplace, there are paths of circulation around major blocks of offices and support services, creating a circulation pattern for the workplace as a whole (the global system). The global spatial layout of offices and circulation paths influences how individuals or groups encounter other individuals or groups within the organization as a whole.[30] There are similar paths of circulation around individual workspaces or groups of workspaces, which create a local circulation pattern for the workplace (the local system). The local spatial layout influences encounters with one's closest neighbors. In planning group workspace, it is important to consider spatial layout on both the local and global levels, and how these two systems interface with one another.

Research has shown that concentrating major circulation paths and collection points, such as elevator lobbies and support services, increases interaction.[31] To enhance interaction within work groups and among work groups across the larger organization, it is recommended that circulation paths at the local level be concentrated (integrated) and well connected to a concentrated (integrated) global spatial layout.

INFORMAL GATHERING PLACES. Current design solutions for offices and laboratories recognize the importance of communication and provide space such as "break-out" areas, designated for less formal, often unscheduled, interaction. Research on effective project teams indicates that success depends as much on team members' interacting with others within the organization but outside the project team as on interaction among the team members themselves.[32] Peters and Waterman, in their book *In Search of Excellence,* suggest that many of the best ideas produced by teams find their germination in unscheduled "serendipitous" encounters with workers outside the team.[33] As described above, patterns of overall or global circulation in the building affect the communication patterns of workers by promoting chance encounters and aiding in accomplishment of intended contacts. These serendipitous encounters may be enhanced by locating support facilities so that they are shared by workers whose physical separation might otherwise inhibit communication.[34]

Social interaction is encouraged by locating semipublic gathering places such as coffee bars, break rooms, and copy or mail rooms near work areas. This is a well-accepted principle among architects and designers and has been suggested by researchers;[35] however, little research has directly addressed this question.[36] Although they should be easily accessible, the number of local break-out spaces should be minimized to concentrate rather than disperse individuals. Centralizing support services across groups that normally would not have reason to interact enhances informal exchange of information, experience, and planning strategies. Instead of locating common resources to minimize travel distance, they should be strategically located to enhance interface. Activity areas serving a broad segment of the organization, such as eating areas, conference areas, and display areas, should be strategically positioned along primary-use corridors, in locations that have high visibility. Spaces should be furnished to enhance exchange of ideas (that is, with tables, chairs, and whiteboards).

Opportunities for visual observation of work and work output (display) and for natural interface between workers provide information about group accomplishments to members of the larger organization, without disrupting group processes. Achieving this natural interface depends on two aspects of spatial layout. First, as described previously, it is important that shared group workspace be located along circulation paths that are integral to the overall circulation system of the organization, such that individuals within the organization naturally pass by. Second, the boundary between the group workspace and the circulation path should allow observation. Depending upon the job tasks, this boundary may be more or less permeable; if the group work is of a confidential nature, this interface is not appropriate or desirable.

As many organizations have done in recent years, FSC, a catalogue company selling educational materials to support science and art curricula in elementary and secondary schools, reorganized its workforce into catalogue-based project teams. Previously separated into departments by function (product testing, copywriting, layout, publishing, and so forth), the new organization created a team approach to producing each catalogue line, with team members representing each functional area. This new organization worked effectively for all the teams, but they tended to operate in isolation and that affected production. Employees and management alike were concerned that duplicate efforts went unnoticed, and that there was a general lack of "shared knowledge." This was particularly problematic since several of the catalogues shared products or product lines.

In the existing facility, an older building with several additions, catalogue teams were located far from one another and circulation was maze-like. Copywriters and layout and printing professionals voiced the need to discuss common difficulties and their solutions with their counterparts on the other teams. When a particular catalogue team discovered a new product or product line, it was difficult to share this knowledge. In fact, the catalogue teams wished to display new products for examination and comment by others before products were adopted for distribution.

There was a general feeling that the physical separation and isolation of these working groups was a strong contributing factor. Fortuitously, the opportunity arose to design and construct a new facility. As the organization embarked on the programmatic planning for this new building, it became a design priority to create common group workspace for each catalogue team, display space for new products and product lines, and (through spatial layout) community of shared knowledge throughout the organization.

GROUP BOUNDARY MODULATION. Boundaries serve to modulate relationships between the work group and the organization. Boundaries may be real, such as walls, partitions, and subdivisions created by furnishings, or they may be symbolic, such as changes in surface treatments, floor or ceiling heights, etc. These real or symbolic features may function to differentiate groups from one another; regulate passage of information, goods, or people; or serve as a point of exchange with others inside or outside the organization.[37] If the boundary becomes too loose and ill defined, the group may lose its identity and ability to function as a separate entity within the organization; if, on the other hand, the boundary is too closed, the group may suffer from isolation and separation from the activities of the organization or its customer base.[38]

Boundaries simultaneously separate and connect groups to other groups and to the parent organization. Although often considered in nonphysical terms as the lines of demarcation that surround a work group and separate it from other groups in the organization, it is the physical constitution of the boundary that leads to separation or integration of the group within the organizational context. Critical design considerations arise related to the clarity or distinctness of the boundary and its permeability (the ease with which group members can move and communicate across boundary lines).[39]

Within a boundary that is well defined, individuals identify themselves more easily as a group and are viewed as such by others. The boundary definition also delineates space as belonging to the group. A space, assigned to a group, even a temporary group, is essential.[40] Occupying a place enhances group identity and differentiates the group from others. This "territory" (defined by space and its boundaries) establishes the parameters for managing external relationships.

The group boundary regulates the extent to which the group is *integrated* within the larger organization. For a production team, this integration may be for coordination in terms of pace and timing of exchanges with other work units.[41] For groups that are not involved in production synchronization, interrelationships may be less time-dependent; however, integration within the larger organizational context remains important for communication.

The group boundary also functions to regulate the extent to which the group is separated or *differentiated* from the organizational context.[42] To the extent that the boundary is closed, informal interaction with individuals outside the boundary is discouraged. This differentiation may reflect a degree of specialization, independence, and autonomy from other work units. Separation may.also isolate activities from interference and contamination (as in the example of a surgical team).[43]

For groups able to work with some autonomy and without frequent interfacing with other groups, the physical separation of a defined boundary may promote independence and responsibility. A pertinent example is that of an insurance company group whose people worked in their own fully enclosed workspace. Over a period of time, the group developed its own modes of work, and productivity was high. When the group was moved to another location that lacked enclosure, other employees soon became aware of the group's informality and customary afternoon breaks. After hearing complaints about the informality and receiving requests for similar break privileges from other employees, the supervisor began to increase surveillance of the group and denied afternoon break privileges to all employees. As morale fell, the group's effectiveness suffered and work fell behind schedule. The group was eventually dissolved.[44]

Depending on the strength of the boundary (how closed or open it is), the group is likely to experience more or less control over distractions and interruptions (privacy). The extent of physical enclosure affects both perceptions of group cohesiveness and feelings of privacy.[45] To work effectively, groups need privacy to concentrate on tasks, but also the option to open up these boundaries, or move to less bounded space, to obtain input from others.

The suitability of the physical boundaries of group space is a function of job type, work tasks and duration, and corporate culture. The extent to which the group space boundary is defined depends on the frequency of required external interactions, standardization of the group's procedures and practices, external pacing of its work, and demands for ongoing synchronization with the parent organization and other groups.[46] Certain organizations, such as architectural firms and newspaper offices, have traditionally maintained a largely open layout because of the rapidly changing nature of the information that is being handled as well as the need to keep all members of the "team" current on new developments. With the support of information technology, and recognition of the importance of boundary control in promoting concentrated work, these traditional patterns of open planning are being replaced by layouts with increased boundary control.

Work group space should be designed as a system of bounded layers, extending from the individual worker to the global system of the organization as a whole. Balance is achieved through modulating boundary conditions within an overall integrating system.

Designers are often challenged with what may appear to be conflicting objectives concerning boundary management. An example arose during the planning for a new sciences facility at Winthrop University in Rock Hill, South Carolina. Each of the departments that were to be moved to the new building was vocal about the need to maintain its own departmental identity and contiguity. Their concerns were to be in close proximity to immediate colleagues and to provide a clear place identity for students. The administration, on the other hand, cognizant of the importance of interdepartmental collaboration, held the objective of creating a workplace that enhanced opportunities for cross-disciplinary exchange.

The proposed system of bounded layers allows an organization to achieve both relatively private individual workspaces and a larger community of knowledge through more accessible group spaces located along integrated global circulation paths. This layered system begins on the local level with the individual workstation and the enclosure surrounding that space (either more or less enclosed depending upon the requirements of privacy versus interface); moves to the group space as a whole with appropriate boundaries providing separation or integration with the larger organization; through the group common space(s), again with appropriate boundaries; and ends with integration of the global spatial system.

Critical design decisions concern modulation of boundaries at each of these levels of interface. The outcome of these decisions depends on careful analysis of the particular group and group tasks to determine the most supportive approach: Who is involved? What is the extent of group work? What is the scope and duration of this work? What are the needed resources and methods of work? How much separation or interface is appropriate?[47] Decisions based on individual groups and group needs must be balanced with overall flexibility.

FACILITY SUPPORT FOR SIX TYPES OF WORK TEAMS

For the six kinds of work teams described in this book, facility support varies, with some aspects becoming more critical to group performance than others. Exhibit 10.1 summarizes the facility support features that are either critical to supporting the work of the particular type or important to its success.

As described earlier in relation to management teams, other relationships may take precedence over the proximal location of individual workspaces. This would also be true of certain types of temporary groups, such as parallel groups, where the group convenes for scheduled conferences in what may be common or group-assigned (permanent or temporary) workspace. Both management teams and parallel teams are involved in tasks that require privacy and typically need little immediate external linkage. Therefore, the boundary surrounding the group workspace can be strong (full-height walls). For these groups, conditions that enhance informal interface among individual members (outside of scheduled meetings) depend on the design of the global spatial system (concentration of circulation and informal gathering places).

Production and Service Teams

Where whole-team specialization is low and interaction requirements among the individuals in the group are high, boundaries that separate individual workspaces should be low to allow easy communication. In today's fluid organizations, a free-address system provides the kind of task area appropriate for service groups with remote, visiting, often absent, or temporary members. An example is the 1,700 square foot space planned for the strategic services group of CRSS International (a Jacobs Engineering company), a service group of about ten people. The workspace is to be organized into a variety of task areas (see Figure 10.1). Centrally located is the group teaming area, an open space with individual work tables that can easily be arranged and rearranged depending on tasks. To one side are located two break-away settings. These fully enclosed spaces accommodate up to three people and are designated for concentrated individual or group work. A glass panel allows visual connection to the rest of the work area. A 400 square foot "strategy room" and resource (library) area provides a space for larger gatherings or informal reading. The space is semi-enclosed, with movable walls that can be opened to the teaming area or closed to create a private conference area.

Exhibit 10.1. Facility Features That Support Each of the Six Group Types.

Facility features	Group types					
	Management teams	Parallel groups	Production groups	Service groups	Action and performing teams	Project group
Co-location and proximity of workspaces			*	*	*	*
Shared group workspace	+	+		*	*	*
Individual home-base workstations	*	*	+	+	*	*
Meeting space and conference areas	*		+	+	+	+
Display areas		+	+	+	+	+
Concentrated circulation patterns	+	+	+	+	+	+
Informal gathering places	+	+	+	+	+	+
Group boundary modulation			*	*	*	*

* denotes critical feature; + denotes important feature

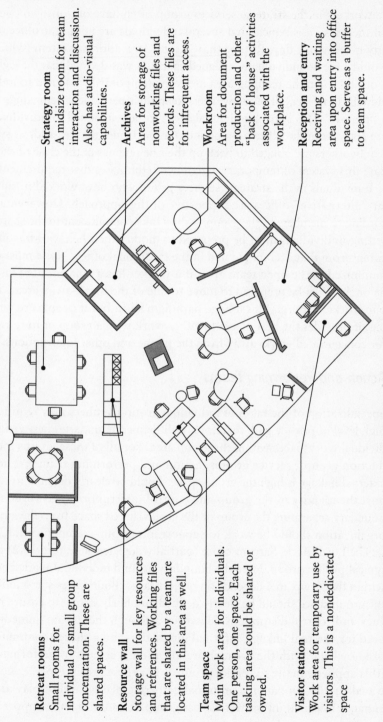

Figure 10.1. Design of Free-Address Space for a Strategic Services Group.

Strategy room
A midsize room for team interaction and discussion. Also has audio-visual capabilities.

Archives
Area for storage of nonworking files and records. These files are for infrequent access.

Workroom
Area for document production and other "back of house" activities associated with the workplace.

Reception and entry
Receiving and waiting area upon entry into office space. Serves as a buffer to team space.

Retreat rooms
Small rooms for individual or small group concentration. These are shared spaces.

Resource wall
Storage wall for key resources and references. Working files that are shared by a team are located in this area as well.

Team space
Main work area for individuals. One person, one space. Each tasking area could be shared or owned.

Visitor station
Work area for temporary use by visitors. This is a nondedicated space

Source: Adapted from CRSS International, Inc., Strategic Services Group, with permission.

Workers in the strategic services group often have out-of-town commitments, so it is typical that several individuals are not in the office on any given work day. Rather than a total free-address system (which would have no individually assigned space), it was decided that the eight work tables in the teaming area are to be temporarily assigned to individuals. However, all of the workers keep their permanent belongings in a "puppy." This allows individual areas to be reassigned if individuals are away from the office for a period of time. Under the free-address system, workers are obliged to pack up their belongings at the close of each day; this system of temporary assignment eliminates that requirement.

Individuals in the strategic services group who have worked in similar "alternative" offices are supportive of this approach. However, according to members of the group, it does take commitment to the shared setting. Individuals must be prepared to modify their behavior to some extent from that accommodated in the traditional office. Noise must be minimized in the open team area; if a worker has a concentrated task, he or she must be prepared to move to one of the break-away areas. As one worker reports, "It's a huge paradigm shift; but if people are willing, it provides the best places to either work with a group or to retreat for concentrated work, away from the phone and other interruptions."[48]

Action and Performing Teams

Specialization of the tasks of individual group members may require a high level of privacy and, therefore, well-defined boundaries between individual workspaces within the group area. For all of these groups (production groups, service groups, action and performing teams), where external linkage is high the group space should be clearly defined, to support the identity of the group and control interruptions; however, the boundary separating the group or the group shared space from the larger organization should be weak to support intragroup communication.

The Lord, Aeck, Sargent office (partially depicted in Figure 10.2) is a typical project group. Here the boundary around individual workspaces within the group area depends on project tasks. Boundaries surrounding the group space should be clearly defined and fairly strong to ensure privacy and control disruptions. However, although there is no immediate need for external linkage, informal interaction and a shared community of knowledge with the broader organization is critical to performance (this applies equally to service groups). For these group types, concentrated circulation patterns, informal gathering places, and display areas enhance informal interaction across group boundaries and support the development of a shared community of knowledge.

Figure 10.2. Example of a Team Workspace.

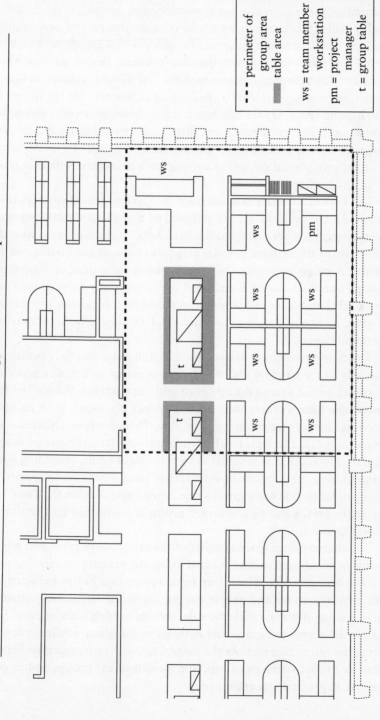

Legend:
- - - = perimeter of group area
█ = table area

ws = team member workstation
pm = project manager
t = group table

Lord, Aeck, Sargent is an architectural firm located in Atlanta. Architectural groups, like most other research-design groups, are composed of highly skilled professionals who have considerable control over creative projects with extended time spans. Research-design groups have high internal interaction requirements that imply diverse, flexible settings. Their need for direct external linkages with the rest of the organization is low. This type of group presents a challenging dichotomy for the design of work group space. On the one hand, the creative group process requires protection from interruptions and distractions from outside the group;[49] however, these requirements for privacy must be balanced with the value, for most professional groups, of serendipitous encounters with colleagues from other groups.[50]

The LAS office space is subdivided into four workstation bays (Figure 10.2). Group members are assigned to a workstation in a bay with other group members. The modularity of the layout combined with the similarity of the stations permits groups to expand and contract as required. A group may extend to include two or three bays, or contract to a single one. Each station is equipped with a computer terminal on a network. This means that employees can access their files from any station. A move from one station to another involves moving only personal effects and papers.

The four-person bays are enclosed by full-height walls, opening on one side to the window wall and on the opposite side with a generous doorway to the shared group space and the corridor. Within the bay space, the four workstations occupy corner positions, with an open bookcase for separation on the third side. This openness within the bay space supports the high level of interaction characteristic of design groups. However, it is modulated by full-height walls, providing some control over the amount of interaction (and noise) and supporting group identity. For work groups that extend across more than one bay space, interface among the larger group is supported by the shared group space.

The shared group space consists of the group work table and whiteboard or tackboard surface located along the primary circulation path for the organization. The group table serves as a buffer between the group workstations and people moving along the circulation corridor. In this sense, it plays a dialectic role, serving as both interface and barrier. It delineates the space that belongs to the group while serving to bring the group together. At the same time, it permits nonmembers to observe the activities, drawings, and models of the group, and to participate in professional exchange.

In addition to the group areas, there is a large conference area that can be fully closed down or opened up along one side onto the main circulation corridor, and an open library and resource area.

This system of bounded layers successfully supports the needs of the LAS office. At the level of the individual, relatively open groupings of workstations enhance interface. For the group, full-height partitions support the creative process by subdividing large groups and protecting these subunits from distraction and interruption. Modularity allows flexibility. The larger group is brought together around the shared group table. Group tables, located along the major circulation spine, have the role of display for the larger organization, to enhance exchange among groups and support development of a shared community of knowledge.

Key Contingencies

Workspace design solutions must support organizational goals and work in concert with corporate culture. In addition, the space should be designed to accommodate changes as these aspects of the organization change.

FLEXIBILITY. In any office, flexibility is an important design component to accommodate changes in work processes and organizational change, with minimal disturbance of work process and minimum cost. An example is the fixed-service spine, housing all hardwired services such as power, data, and voice lines. For work groups, membership frequently changes as a project moves through various stages of completion; new members may be added or others may move on to other tasks. Groups may be dissolved and reconfigured. All of these changes require a facility that can accommodate change seamlessly, without disruption of work processes. Highly bounded group areas, designed for specific group members, artificially restrain group size.

SUPPORTIVE CORPORATE CULTURE. The effectiveness of group workspace depends on whether the activity patterns supported by the designed space are consistent with organizational objectives and culture. For example, providing workspace to encourage exploration and creative group processes does not guarantee those outcomes unless informal meetings are encouraged and resources are provided for new ways of working and thinking. Just as important to planning and design is successful management (decisions about use of space, and equipment and furnishings) over time. Interactive hands-on planning processes empower the end users.

BEST PRACTICES: FACILITY DESIGN FOR WORK TEAMS

Reflecting the increasingly complex and changing business environment, many companies are rethinking their organizational structures. Traditionally hierarchical configurations, characterized by long-term, fixed-size, single-purpose groups, are shifting to more flexible, multitask groups with greater responsibility and independence. The concept of work is changing from one based on a fairly static relationship between a worker and his or her workspace to one that is group-based and dynamic. A typical day for an office worker may begin with checking into a small, individual home base workstation to pick up messages and review or receive assignments. During the day, this worker is engaged in a multiplicity of tasks, many of which involve interactions with groups of other workers. As the day progresses, the individual moves to various settings to attend meetings, work with small groups of other workers, access resources, and accomplish individual tasks.

The following is a summary of recommendations for designing workspace to support this new conception of work. For each recommendation, a notation is made as to whether it is based on established research data, and whether it is considered a well-accepted, emerging, or recommended design practice.

1. It is of primary concern that the workspace provide *basic worker comfort and well-being*. (This recommendation is based on research and is a well-accepted design practice.)

2. For groups with reasonably long life spans such as project teams, production groups, and service groups, *group members' workspaces* should be *co-located or within reasonable proximity* to support intergroup communication and collaboration. (Recommendation is based on research data; well-accepted.)

3. Particularly for these groups with long life spans, *shared group workspace* should be provided to support development of a shared knowledge base. This common space ranges from a simple shared work table to a nonterritorial office with no individually assigned space. (This is based on research data; an emerging practice.)

4. Although they may be reduced in size because of allocation of space to group-based activity areas, most individuals need a *home base workstation*. As the demands for group activity increase, it is even more important that workers have these opportunities for retreat. (This is based on research data; well-accepted.)

5. For corporations with a sizeable proportion of workers who frequently work outside the office or telecommute from remote locations, *alternatives to individually assigned spaces* may be appropriate. (This is an emerging practice.)

6. Working groups of any type should have available choices of easily reserved and well-equipped *meeting space and conference areas*. The location of such spaces encourages collaboration across boundaries within the organization. (This is well-accepted.)

7. *Display areas* contribute to development of a shared community of knowledge. Display may be the presentation of work or the products of work, or visual access to working groups. (Recommended.)

8. *Concentrated circulation patterns* at both the local (group) and global (organizational) levels enhance opportunities for interaction. (This is based on research data; recommended.)

9. *Informal gathering places* support opportunities for less formal, often unscheduled, interaction among the members of a group and across groups. (This is well-accepted.)

10. Successful workspace should provide private space for individual work (individual level) and appropriate settings for group activities (group level), within the context of a shared community of knowledge (organizational level). These opportunities can be achieved through a system of bounded layers. At each level of spatial differentiation, *boundary modulation* creates the desired level of separation or integration. (This is based on research data; recommended.)

CONCLUSIONS

Effective group workspace provides the materials, resources, and varied and flexible spaces to support both individual and group activities. However, the role of space goes beyond simply task support: the design of space actively structures the context of work as well as the interactions of workers within the group and the larger organizational setting. Layout of space and modulation of boundaries within space create opportunities for communication and ultimately the exchange of ideas that distinguishes outstanding performance.

Recent changes in patterns of work have resulted in a growing need for varying types of facility support, from individual space to group space, from structured space to informal space. In the future, we are likely to see these trends continuing for more diversity in the types of space available, alternative options for space use, and increasing technological support. The nature of the particular physical solution depends on the organizational context.

Effective group workspace is created when the design of the physical facility is part of a larger organizational plan. Changes in physical space should be those that support and enhance work patterns, organizational culture, and overall organizational goals. Above all, the primary motivation for change should not be to consolidate workers in less space or to reduce space costs. In the best case, this may be the fortuitous outcome of a business strategy aimed at enhancing interaction and responding to work processes.

If strategic planning suggests transformation from traditional to alternative office space, the change process should be carefully considered and managed. Not all employees are able to adapt to radical transformations such as the free-address office. As one employee commented in reference to the new Chiat/Day office, "Humans need to nest a little bit, no matter how progressive the atmosphere. So people would go to the same areas every day."[51] In response to a similar experience, CRSS's strategic services group opted for a modified free-address system, one where individuals would be temporarily assigned a workspace at one of the teaming area work tables. As new office options are explored, the best strategy may be a combination of more than one kind of space. An effective office may incorporate shared group spaces, free-address spaces, and hoteling space. The intent is for space to work (as a tool) in achieving organizational goals.

PART FOUR

BEST MANAGEMENT PRACTICES FOR HIGH-PERFORMANCE TEAMS

11

SUPPORTING WORK TEAM EFFECTIVENESS

Best Practices

Eric Sundstrom

EXCELLENCE IN supporting work teams is fast becoming a competitive necessity, as more businesses adopt team-based organizations. Your competitors are probably already realizing the well-documented benefits of teams, in productivity, service, safety, and cost efficiency.[1] However, it is no longer enough just to have teams. Staying competitive means doing better at supporting teams than others do. Fine examples of team support appear in companies that dominate their markets, such as Federal Express, Motorola, Saturn, Solectron, and Xerox.

The preceding chapters examine nine support systems that managers can use to create a context that promotes team effectiveness:

- A *team structure* that defines team responsibilities, scope, authority, resources, accountability, and reporting relationships in just enough detail (Chapter Two)
- A *staffing system* that assembles team members having the mix of knowledge, skills, abilities, and other attributes needed for the team's role in the organization (Chapter Three)
- *Leader roles* that align and coordinate the work of multiple teams while giving each team the direction and coaching its members need (Chapter Four)

- *Training* that gives members the necessary teamwork and team liaison skills (Chapter Five)
- *Measurement systems* that give teams specific, timely feedback on performance (Chapter Six)
- A *reward system* that gives adequate incentives for individual and team performance, plus incentives for cooperation among teams (Chapter Seven)
- *Information systems* with convenient, responsive datalinks among team members and with the team's external counterparts (Chapter Eight)
- *Communication technology* that supports internal and external team interactions and decisions, especially in *virtual teams* with geographically separated members (Chapter Nine)
- *Facilities* that allow appropriate face-to-face interaction within and among teams (Chapter Ten)

This concluding chapter reviews the management practices for establishing the conditions for team effectiveness. It has three purposes:

1. To summarize best management practices for applying the nine team support systems
2. To identify the support needs of different kinds of teams
3. To identify emerging issues for supporting effective teams in tomorrow's organizations

The first section revisits the best practices from the chapters and condenses them into checklists. Next is a discussion of the most important support systems for the six kinds of teams. The last section identifies trends in teams and their support and describes the challenges ahead.

SUMMARY OF BEST MANAGEMENT PRACTICES

Managers considering a team-based organization might ask, "Where do we start?" Depending on the situation, a case can be made for beginning with any of the support systems. But as outlined in Chapter Two, a critical first step is an explicit decision to organize work teams—for business reasons, not just because teams sound like a good idea. Organizations that adopt teams because competitors do, or because an executive was inspired by a seminar, or because of the allure of teams, all have trouble. Organizations that succeed with teams have definite business strategies; leaders can explain why teams represent the best vehicle for implementing those strategies.

With clear business reasons for adopting teams, executives plan for implementing a team-based structure consistent with the organization's culture, capabilities, and technology. Early steps include determining exactly what the teams will do and how they are to be organized. At the same time, it is best to evaluate the organization's existing support systems and their readiness to meet team needs. It may help to revamp some support systems before designing a team structure. One large manufacturer, for instance, started with its reward system, another with the measurement system. Some companies made—and paid for—the mistake of starting team-based organizations before laying the proper foundation.

Team support systems work best if the organization is guided by a business vision and strategic plan and if the culture is conducive to teamwork. Teams do well where executives introduce teams as part of a business initiative while promoting an organizational culture—or shared beliefs, habits, and values[2]—consistent with employee involvement and participation.[3]

It is no coincidence that the cases in this book concern companies in which managers worked interactively with employees at all levels and at practically every step of the transition to teams. At "MotorCo" (Chapter Two), for example, local leaders consulted employees on most important features of the team design. Employees saw their recommendations clearly reflected in the new team structure. At Digital Evolution (Chapter Eight), leaders designed a team structure for their business plan and created a culture of involvement by giving the project teams autonomy in both strategy and tactics, while maintaining accountability through an electronic reporting system.

Success of team support systems calls for a handful of executive practices to lay a proper foundation. After outlining them, the following section revisits the practices for team support systems suggested in prior chapters, summarizes them in checklists, and discusses how they can complement one another.

Foundation Practices by the Executive Team

Successful team-based organizations described in this book have active leadership from the top, often from an executive team consisting of the CEO and executives who report directly to the CEO. Whether at multiple sites, as with Boeing (Chapter Four), or a single site, as at Digital Evolution (Chapter Eight), the top team led and legitimized the transition to a team-based structure and created an organizational culture that nurtured employee involvement. An example is Xerox's transformation to a team-based organization in the 1980s, when the company had to match the efficiency of Japanese competitors or go out of business. The CEO and top leaders used a retreat to plan a restructuring of the organization and then actively led the implementation. Xerox leaders helped conduct training for managers who reported to them and a cascading series of training sessions that flowed down the management hierarchy. Throughout, the top team members actively communicated their plans, sought suggestions and success stories from employees at all levels of the organization, and updated the implementation plan in response to employees' ideas.[4] They established a clear direction for the future and instilled a culture of involvement.

Team-based organizations become isolated when executives fail to reinforce innovation. At the Topeka plant of General Foods in the 1970s, for instance, the plant steering team implemented a team-based manufacturing organization. Corporate leaders rejected the plant's approach, and Topeka's successful production system became an isolated experiment.[5]

Ideally, corporate executives facilitate the spread of successful innovations through the organization. In the MotorCo case, local change led by a local management team was mandated by a higher-ranking management group that reinforced the local innovation. Corporate leaders treated MotorCo as a pilot site, intending it to be the first phase of wider organizational change. It went more or less as planned, and the leaders soon initiated similar changes in other locations. MotorCo became a demonstration site, or beachhead, for learning in a wider transition to a team-based organization.[6]

An important form of support for work teams comes from having the CEO and top executives work as a team themselves. Executives can pool their talents to develop strategy and jointly manage the organization's subsystems, including team support systems. Success by team-based organizations with strong executive teams, as at Federal Express and Xerox, exemplifies the value of teamwork at the top.

Effective executive teams ideally develop and use strategic business plans.[7] An example is Harley-Davidson's response to the influx of inexpensive, reliable Japanese motorcycles into this country in the 1970s, which cut the business in half. Executives developed and implemented a joint plan for restructuring, demonstrating the kind of collaboration they expected of teams throughout their organization.[8]

Transition to a team-based organization, like other organizational change, requires that the executive team first establish and use measures of key results.[9] FedEx uses as a performance measure the number of packages per week delivered to incorrect addresses. This measure is collected for all units involved with delivery, aggregated or "rolled up" for reporting at each management level, and used with other companywide performance measures to guide decisions at all levels. Once the executive team has defined its key performance measures, measurement and feedback systems can support teams as described in Chapter Six. Without solid measures linked to the organization's key results, teams flounder.

The organization's culture derives mainly from its leaders.[10] Although individual leaders can aid employee involvement,[11] it takes a concerted effort by the whole executive team to create a culture in which teams thrive. Ideally, the executive team makes culture an explicit part of its strategic plan, writes appropriate management objectives, budgets for them, and formally measures progress toward them. Key practices include giving employees business information, notifying them in advance of planned changes, formally seeking and using their ideas in decisions about the organization, and rewarding employee involvement.[12] To help employees see the results of participation, executives publicly explain how policies have changed in response to their ideas, as with the companywide TV broadcasts at Federal Express.

Success in establishing teams calls for operating as a learning organization by making fast, systemwide changes in a dynamic environment.[13] At Harley-Davidson, when executives saw competitors adopting just-in-time inventory, they replaced their automated warehouse and overhead conveyors with simple pushcarts.[14]

Executive leaders act as gatekeepers for organizational learning; they either promote or stifle organizational learning (see Checklist 11.1). At General Foods in the 1970s, corporate executives thwarted organizational learning by refusing to recognize the team-based innovation at the Topeka plant.[15] The General Foods organization apparently did not adopt the new practices, but other companies soon did. To promote organizational learning, General Foods executives might have done three things: (1) reinforce innovative practices by recognizing and rewarding them, (2) communicate throughout the organization the value of the innovations, and (3) act to convert local successes into organizationwide practices.

Team support requires careful tailoring at the outset and active management to maintain the fit as teams evolve. Phelps Dodge (Chapter Five) illustrates how team training changed from externally provided class-room instruction to internally provided, intact-team coaching. The plant steering team actively managed the training and its evolution.

•

Best Practices Checklist 11.1: Foundation by Executive Leadership

☐ Executive team: lead from an explicit business vision and strategic business plan.

☐ Executive team: use results-oriented measurements to guide planning and decision making, and expect employees at all levels to do the same.

☐ Executives and executive team: actively solicit employee involvement in decisions at all levels.

☐ Executive team: for organizational learning, reinforce expanded application of successful, local innovations.

☐ Executives: make an explicit decision about using teams, based on business objectives.

☐ Executive team: review the support systems for teams, and actively manage them.

•

Best Practices for Team Structure

An effective work team needs a structure that defines its responsibilities, scope, resources, authority, and accountability (Chapter Two). So who designs a team's structure? A traditional answer is to start with the team manager. As illustrated in the MotorCo case, however, best management practices for designing a team structure call for an inclusive design process that gives those most directly involved in the work an active part in designing the team structure.

A second answer to the question "Who designs the team structure?" is the team members themselves. Within broad limits, most kinds of teams have substantial autonomy in defining specialized work roles, work processes, scheduling, and other details of their work.[16] Autonomy allows team members to apply their expertise. The team manager's job is to accurately determine how much responsibility the members are capable of taking, impose just enough structure, and give them support for working out the details. Even experienced managers have difficulty determining how much structure is just enough. When in doubt, it is better to give too much structure than too little.[17]

In transitions involving multiple teams, the task of designing the team structure often goes to a design team. Especially for production and service teams, companies report good results from using design teams composed of representatives from relevant parts of the organization.[18] A useful approach is the diagonal-slice[19] team, which cuts across the organization to include all levels and departments or regions having a stake in the team design. For example in a state human services department, a design team included a case worker, a first-line supervisor, managers at three levels, a member of the executive team, and three subject-matter experts. Members were chosen from nominees so that the team included a representative of every job in the system and every region of the state.

Designing the structure of a single team does not always warrant a formal design team, but it does call for collaboration among those with an interest in the team structure. As illustrated again in MotorCo, managers invite ideas from those who make up teams or deal with them. Designing one-of-a-kind project teams, as at Digital Evolution, might involve people outside the organization.

Once a team structure is ready to be proposed, the next step is to review other team support systems to make sure they constitute an adequate foundation for team effectiveness. Other systems can and should be configured in advance, especially staffing and reward systems.

Team launch starts with a chartering session: the manager meets the team to discuss its duties, scope, resources, authority, and accountability. Chartering promotes effectiveness in several ways: (1) team members learn exactly what they are expected to do, along with the resources they are given to do it; (2) members learn how their work supports the business strategy; (3) the chartering session allows the manager to present relevant business information that explains the team's resources and performance requirements; (4) the manager invites involvement by asking the team to propose changes in the charter; and (5) chartering marks the start of a goal-setting process that ideally leads to specific, difficult goals that are accepted by the team.[20] The manager explains the minimum results and asks the team to set its own goals beyond those.

In its first few weeks, a new team may benefit from having a team facilitator, a nonmember whose job is to help the team hold efficient meetings and develop smooth interactions among members themselves and with the team's counterparts. As discussed in Chapter Two, facilitators also help more experienced teams resolve conflicts or learn new tools for teamwork. Many organizations make part-time or full-time facilitators available to their teams,[21] and some assign the role of facilitator to a team member.

In long-lived work teams, such as production and service teams, best practice calls for phased increases in team responsibility. As illustrated at Phelps Dodge, it takes time for people new to teams to develop the skills for management tasks, such as participation in team members' performance appraisal, discipline, and decisions about pay.

Checklist 11.2 lists best practices concerning team structure. Some involve the executive team, and most involve team managers.

•

Best Practices Checklist 11.2: Team Structure

☐ Executive team: use inclusive team design processes (for example, diagonal-slice design team).

☐ Design team: evaluate existing support systems for teams, and propose needed changes.

☐ Team managers: define and refine the team structure, including team responsibilities, leader roles, reporting relationships, and measures of results for which teams are accountable.

☐ Team managers: charter each team to establish team duties, authority, resources, accountability, measures, and reporting—in just enough detail for the team.

☐ Team manager: arrange for a team facilitator to help inexperienced teams get started.

☐ Team managers: give teams phased increases in authority over time, with accompanying accountability for measurable results, in just enough detail.

•

Best Practices for Team Staffing

As outlined in Chapter Three, supporting work teams through staffing calls for assembling team members who bring the best possible mix of talents to the work. In other words, effective staffing means finding individuals with the knowledge, skills, abilities, and other attributes—the KSAOs—that satisfy each team's requirements. Usually this means finding members with five qualifications: (1) KSAOs required of everyone in the organization, such as conscientiousness and basic teamwork skills; (2) technical knowledge and skills needed for the team's work; (3) interpersonal skills needed to collaborate with teammates and counterparts; (4) ability to master new knowledge and skills as the team's work evolves; and (5) compatibility with teammates.

Finding team members with these qualities calls for analysis of the team's role in the organization, as well as individual roles in the team, to identify performance requirements of the individual-in-team. Requirements vary with the type of team. One skill needed in many teams is liaison with external counterparts (suppliers, customers, peers, and others). For example, Chapter Three notes that workers at Johnsonville Foods are expected to write letters to external customers. Another key skill is conflict management, especially in management teams.

Best practice for team staffing begins with clarifying the roles in the staffing sequence, including definition of requirements, recruitment, screening, assessment, hiring, and placement. Sometimes staffing proceeds quickly and informally, especially for parallel teams. More often, however, the importance of a staffing decision warrants a larger effort. A human resource manager might initiate a formal sequence, coordinate the staffing process, and exercise signature authority in the final decision. The "Software Inc." case in Chapter Three is an example. Especially in a team-based organization, however, many others besides the HR contact have active parts in the staffing sequence, including the team's manager, leader, members, and even customers.

Starting with defining the requirements for open positions, the team manager and leader might participate in deciding how the staffing steps are done, or in carrying out the steps, or both. Depending on the kind of team, members may take part in some steps, such as defining the requirements, helping to recruit, or conducting structured interviews. Ideally, the staffing roles of team manager, team leader, and team member are clarified at the start.

Today, most work teams require the capacity to learn new skills, so an important element of team staffing is to test for job-related general ability, or "cognitive ability." Research consistently finds it among the best predictors of individual learning capacity.[22] Other evidence demonstrates best performance by teams whose members have high cognitive ability.[23]

For the staffing process to yield prospective members with the needed KSAOs, multiple screening and assessment steps are usually required, including assessment of general teamwork skill. Besides a test of cognitive ability, for example, the initial staffing process for the Saturn plant included an assessment center exercise that required work on a cooperative group task, with ratings by observers. Among many resources available for screening and assessment outlined in Chapter Three, those likely to prove valid for selecting team members include demonstrations of task-related, technical skills during team interaction, as in assessment centers and work samples.

For compatibility among team members, it is wise to give team members substantial influence in staffing decisions, if not the final choice. For example, a unionized chemical processing plant in Kentucky uses a traditional assessment sequence with background screening, individual testing, and a work sample to select two or three final candidates who meet all KSA requirements. Then, before the physical exam and interview with the HR manager, candidates go to an employee panel interview. The panel consists of five employees who will soon work with the new team member. They ask a series of prepared questions and, based on the answers, make a recommendation about a job offer. The panel interview gives team members a part in the selection process and choice of future teammates.

Checklist 11.3 lists eight practices for supporting work team effectiveness through staffing. Though the practices refer to the staffing manager or team manager, they might involve people in other roles as well. Responsibilities for staffing in team-based organizations vary substantially, even within the same company, and often involve many people in any one decision.

Besides involving those with an interest in the outcome of staffing decisions, team staffing has to meet legal requirements that apply to all selection decisions. In most organizations, this means that an HR manager ensures that selection procedures have the needed job relevance and validity. Fortunately, assessment procedures commonly used to select team members have solid validity, especially structured interviews.[24]

•

Best Practices Checklist 11.3: Team Staffing

☐ Staffing manager: define and clarify key roles in the team staffing process, including responsibilities of HR staff, team manager, and leader; and joint duties.

☐ Team manager: identify requirements for new team member knowledge, skills, abilities, and other attributes (KSAOs) by analyzing the team's role in the organization and the individual's role in the team.

☐ Staffing manager: ensure use of a legally defensible staffing sequence that incorporates carefully chosen assessment tools with demonstrated job relevance and validity.

☐ Staffing manager: screen prospective team members for cognitive ability and teamwork skill.

☐ Staffing manager: assess prospective team members' technical skills in the context of team interaction, including assessments of interaction skills specific to the type of team.

☐ Team manager: involve as many people as possible in screening and assessing prospective team members, and work toward consensus at each step.

☐ Team manager: if possible, let the team leader or members participate in the final decision regarding a prospective new team member.

☐ Staffing manager: keep a staffing database, and use it to actively manage the staffing process and update staffing procedures.

•

Best Practices for Leaders' Roles

Success with teams depends on leaders' roles at all levels, starting with executives. The role of executive calls for cooperation in an executive team to establish the organization's vision, business strategy, structure, and culture.

As leaders of management teams, executive leaders have roles that carry responsibility for aligning their units' mandates and efforts with the organizational strategy, and for coordinating peer units. Each leader's role includes the expectation of representing his or her unit to the higher-ranking team—and the responsibility of ensuring alignment with the organization's strategy and with peer units. In other words, leaders' roles are the organization's linking pins, connecting adjacent levels in the management hierarchy and uniting each level with the next higher one.[25]

The linkage function or *external liaison* is central to leaders' roles in team-based organizations. Each leader's role encompasses the expectation of maintaining close communications with counterparts, including peer managers of other units, customers, suppliers, regulators, professional peers in other organizations, and others in a network of interested parties. Liaison is especially important in team-based organizations because of their decentralization and delegation of decisions. Self-managing teams need much information about counterparts inside and outside the organization, and the leader's role is a key interface with many counterparts.

External liaison represents a departure from traditional roles, which focus on vertical communication between supervisor and supervisee in the chain of command. Newer leader roles emphasize horizontal communication with peer leaders, customers, suppliers, and others. For most

leaders, it takes time and training to adjust. First-line supervisors in particular need assistance in making the transition to horizontal communication.[26]

Team leaders' roles call for maintaining balance among potentially
conflicting expectations: meeting management's mandate while ensuring
meaningful participation in setting team goals; facilitating timely performance of team duties while promoting harmony among members; providing direction while allowing members to make important decisions by
consensus; ensuring coordination of members' efforts while encouraging
innovation; carrying out team duties while creating opportunities for
members to develop new skills; and providing performance feedback
while building members' capacities for self-management. These forms of
balance are difficult to attain.

Checklist 11.4 summarizes nine practices for the leader's role involving external liaison, team coordination, and coaching. They apply to
managers—to whom several teams or team leaders report—and to each
team leader who works with a team in day-to-day operations.

Best Practices Checklist 11.4: Leaders' Roles

☐ Team manager: explicitly define and clarify the roles of team
leader and manager.

☐ Team leader: cooperate with peer leaders to align team duties
with the unit's mandate.

☐ Team leader: communicate with counterparts (manager, customers, suppliers, peer team leaders, others) about team performance and environment, and keep the team informed.

☐ Team leader: anticipate potential barriers to team success, and
address them in advance.

☐ Team leader: help the team set difficult, specific goals consistent
with the team's mandate, and with customers' current needs
and peer teams' goals.

☐ Team leader: help define, assign, and coordinate specialized
roles in the team.

☐ Team leader: help the team develop cooperative work plans to
achieve team goals in ways that give team members increasing
responsibility and opportunities to develop new skills.

☐ Team leader: Ensure that members receive feedback on individual contributions to the team.

☐ Team leader: advise team members on individual development,
and arrange needed training.

Best Practices for Team Training

Today's companies rely heavily on training for employee development in general, and for support of the transition to a team-based organization in particular. It is doubtful whether an organization can succeed in moving to a team-based structure without at least some training (Chapter Two). Teams at older, established sites may need a great deal of training, as described in Chapter Five. At Phelps Dodge–El Paso, the workers had forty hours of training. For executive teams, the lesson is clear: allocate resources for the necessary training—budget, personnel, space, and leaders' time—as part of the same business plan that calls for teams in the first place.

The Phelps Dodge case illustrates an assessment of training needs after the team structure is defined. At El Paso, an external consultant did the assessment, though many organizations give the task to a training manager. Structured interviews, questionnaires, or observation can identify the knowledge and skills needed by team leaders and team members. Commonly identified training needs in the past have included basic teamwork skills—such as meeting management, active listening, group decision making, conflict management, feedback, and problem-solving—and business knowledge and practices such as statistical process control.[27] Today's needs analysis also focuses on coordinator roles and external liaison.

Best management practices for delivery of training for teams calls for a "cascading" approach like the one Xerox used in its companywide transition to TQM. Training proceeded through the management hierarchy, starting with the executive, followed by their direct reports, then the top tier of middle managers, and so on. Each leader served as co-trainer for his or her direct reports. Cascading training allows leaders to master the skills needed for their roles before their teams start work, so they can actively facilitate their teams.[28] A few years after Xerox trained its leaders, an aluminum manufacturer in West Virginia used the opposite approach: contractors conducted team training for hundreds of unionized workers and then their supervisors—but not the managers. Unfamiliar with teams, the managers had no idea how to lead them. Workers saw little besides confusion and barely went through the motions of what they understood as "teams" (to them, just a four-letter word). Much of the training had been forgotten or discredited when shortly afterward the union went on strike for other—perhaps related—reasons and the plant closed.

A cascading approach complements another helpful practice: conducting training in phases. A New England telecommunications company, for example, conducts team training in regional offices at intervals of about nine months, starting with the managers and leaders at each office and then the service workers, with their leaders as facilitators. Each wave of training is revised in light of learning from the previous one. Managers send the curriculum in advance, so those at each office know what to expect when their turn comes.

Phased training allows team managers to invite team members who have already mastered the skills to serve as visiting experts and coaches in subsequent training. At a state department of human services, for example, some workers trained to work in service teams are invited to serve as cotrainers in the next training. The same organization holds best-practices conferences where workers from across the state present team innovations, successes, and lessons learned.

Best practice for conducting team training (Checklist 11.5) calls for a just-in-time approach, recognizing that new skills learned in any kind of training tend to fade and disappear unless quickly applied. As described in Chapter Five, this means short training sessions on skills just before they are needed. Meeting management skills, for instance, can be demonstrated and practiced in work meetings with real deliverables. Although classroom training of the kind used at Phelps Dodge has been a mainstay in the past, it is perhaps best replaced where possible with facilitated work sessions in which brief training modules accompany the work.

Team training today often calls for whole teams to practice and simulate their key tasks, especially in action teams such as cockpit crews and military units. For such teams, the range of simulation technologies and facilities continues to expand,[29] though it remains a challenge to define the specific competencies targeted by team training.[30]

●

Best Practices Checklist 11.5: Training for Teams

☐ Executive team: incorporate training into the organization's strategic business plan, and provide budget, personnel, space, and leaders' time for training to launch and sustain teams.

☐ Training manager: conduct a training needs assessment for leaders and team members for teamwork skills, coordinator role skills, and external liaison.

☐ Training manager: use a cascading approach; train executives first, then involve them in training their direct reports, and so on down the management hierarchy.

☐ Training manager: conduct training in phases; use learning from early phases to improve later training, and have participants in early phases be experts and cotrainers in later sessions.

☐ Training manager or team manager: give training to intact teams if they are long-lived and stable; otherwise train in team-like groups.

☐ Team manager or training manager: give team training just in time, in short modules during actual work sessions immediately before the knowledge or skill is applied.

☐ Team managers: after training, invite high-performing team members to attend best practices conferences with representatives of other teams.

☐ Team managers: conduct an evaluation of training that assesses use of knowledge and skills by teams and its relationship, if any, with team outcomes.

•

When classroom training is the most practical option, best practice is to train intact teams, especially long-lived ones with stable membership. Where teams are more fluid, classroom training can just as well use teamlike groups to practice the skills. If training individuals separately, however, it makes sense to prepare them to coach their teammates on the same skills.

A crucial management practice for training is results-oriented evaluation. Training has been evaluated by asking trainees to rate their experiences. So-called smile ratings, however, miss the crucial point of whether or not team members actually use the knowledge and skills learned in training to benefit their teams' work. Ideally, evaluation of training involves assessing the extent to which the skills are used and their connection with performance measures.

Best Practices for Team Measurement and Feedback Systems

As described in Chapter Six, successful team-based organizations use measurement systems to offer timely feedback on team performance. The best measurement systems incorporate critical elements of the organization's business strategy into specific team measures that amount to local versions of the organization's general performance measures. For example, assembly teams at "Electric Components" maintain their own team measures of quality, productivity, cycle time, and on-time delivery. Each team has substantial influence over definitions of the measures and methods of collecting data, and it can supplement them with its own measures of other factors important to team performance. Management teams use summary measures that combine those from the teams into aggregated indicators.

Best practice for team measurement systems calls for balance between alignment of team performance with the organization's business strategy and involvement by teams in developing their own measurements. For teams to participate meaningfully in developing measures, however, they need basic business knowledge and financial information about their organizations. Team managers are usually responsible for making sure teams have the needed business training and current data on business operations and budget.

Well-informed teams participate in several phases of developing measurement systems: selecting measures, defining them to fit the team's work, choosing ways to count and collect data, deciding on the relative importance of different measures, setting performance standards, and setting team goals. Not every team has a hand in all of these, but it is important for members to participate in some of them, as with the Electric Components assembly team. Involvement of this kind creates the psychological ownership or buyin needed for teams to have an interest in finding ways to improve their work processes.

Because team effectiveness depends on meeting customers' expectations as well as business goals, measurement systems usually need to incorporate the customer's perspective. Production teams like the one at MotorCo serve customers inside the organization, such as the next assembly team or shipping department, while service teams deal with external customers. For both, it is important for team performance measures to reflect customers' expectations on such things as response time, turnaround time, quality, on-time delivery, and satisfaction. Best practice calls for involving customers directly in development of team measures.

Once the measurement system can provide feedback, support for team effectiveness calls for constructive use of the measurement data to improve performance. Ideally, team members receive regular, timely data on all of the team's performance measures. For production teams, data may be more or less continuous for some measures of quality and productivity. Other types of teams may have longer intervals between reports on their performance measures and might receive them from the team leader.

The team leader's role calls for coaching on constructive use of feedback from team measures (Chapters Four and Six), and for modeling appropriate responses to feedback. Among other things, this means focusing on team performance more than individual performance, celebrating successes, sharing credit for successes, constructively analyzing failures without personalizing them, and problem solving to find ways of improving the group's work practices. The difficult part is doing this while building individual team members' confidence and self-esteem, for instance by working toward a series of small successes rather than on a longer campaign to achieve the same success in one step.

•

Best Practices Checklist 11.6: Team Measurement and Feedback Systems

☐ Team manager: take action to ensure team performance measures reflect the organization's business strategy, key performance indicators, and business priorities.

☐ Team manager: make sure team members have the business knowledge needed to participate in developing and using team measures, and if not, arrange the necessary training.

☐ Team leader: help the team identify business and customer needs, team performance dimensions and their importance, measures for each dimension, and standards for the measures.

☐ Team leader: involve the team's customers directly in choosing performance dimensions and measures, and in establishing standards for the measures.

☐ Team leader: establish and model norms for constructive feedback, and provide coaching on collaborative problem solving.

•

Best Practices for Team Reward Systems

Team effectiveness depends on reward systems that give members incentive to commit their time, effort, and best ideas to their teams (Chapter Seven). However, traditional reward systems built around individual jobs do not necessarily aid team effectiveness and can even interfere with it. Team-based organizations need nontraditional reward systems, like the one developed at Solectron. Such systems succeed by paying individual employees for their knowledge, skills, and expertise, and by rewarding collective performance more than individual performance.

Unfortunately, incentive pay for team performance can be counterproductive. Where teams are interdependent, as in many manufacturing plants, rewarding them independently discourages interteam cooperation.[31] This happened in Motorola's unsuccessful team-based rewards for interdependent production teams (see Chapter Seven). Rewards for team performance are best suited to teams that work independently, including some project teams and performing groups. Among interdependent teams, the preferred approach involves pay for performance by the whole unit on site, for example through gain sharing.

Reward systems for teams can draw from several types of rewards and combine them into a profile tailored to the team and the organization's strategy and technology. Types of rewards available for teams include job-based pay (seldom a good idea); skill-based and knowledge-based pay; individual merit pay; team performance pay; and pay for organization-level performance based on gainsharing, profit sharing, or shares of company stock. Also, team reward systems sometimes make effective use of nonmonetary recognition to reward performance, such as awards and privileges. These are especially useful in parallel teams.

For most production and service teams, well-designed reward systems include substantial skill-based pay components. Early successes with manufacturing teams relied on pay for skill.[32] As outlined in Chapter Seven, reward systems for project and action teams also include pay based on individual members' expertise. Decisions about the elements of the reward system and how they are combined depend on the situation (Checklist 11.7).

●

Best Practices Checklist 11.7: Reward Systems for Teams

☐ Executive team: use a reward system with multiple pay components tailored to the organization's strategy and technology, and to the type of team.

☐ Team managers: use skill-based or knowledge-based pay for members of teams whose work calls for cross-training, cross-functional knowledge, or specialized, individual expertise.

☐ Team managers: use gainsharing bonuses, profit sharing, or stock plans tied to performance of whole sites or divisions to generate cooperation among all teams involved.

☐ Team managers: consider team-based performance incentives where a team's work requires coordination and integration of team members' individual efforts, as in some project teams.

☐ Team managers: use team-based performance incentives for teams whose work is relatively independent of other teams, and pay only for performance that is under each team's direct control.

☐ Team managers: for management teams, determine the kinds and levels of cooperation required, and consider team-based incentives for those cooperative responsibilities.

●

Best Practices for Team Information Systems

Interactive, networked information technologies have evolved concurrently with team-based organizations, as described in Chapter Eight. Information is an essential ingredient of teamwork, and it can be a principal team output. Because information is crucial to organizational effectiveness, executives are well advised to ensure development of flexible, open-ended information systems and encourage teams to adapt them for their work.

Digital Evolution's CDMS (car dealership management system) project team illustrates the importance of a responsive information system in a team whose product is itself an information system (Chapter Eight). The project requires awareness of fast-breaking software developments, so members use networked computers daily to monitor Microsoft's Web page. The same computers give access to Digital Evolution's database of programming resources and allow members to quickly exchange data with each other and report their progress to their managers.

The CDMS project team illustrates a key management practice: support and encouragement of participative redesign of open-ended team information systems with active involvement by all user groups. Digital Evolution's president expects and encourages employees to adapt the organization's information system to project needs, as the CDMS team did by creating a procedure for electronic progress reporting to managers. The team involved client representatives early in designing and testing the client's information system, incorporating the practice of collaborative design.

•

Best Practices Checklist 11.8: Information Systems for Teams

☐ Executives: ensure development of flexible, open-ended information systems for the organization, and encourage teams to modify them to accommodate the teams' work.

☐ Team managers: involve team members or prospective team members, along with other anticipated users, in designing and installing the team's information systems.

☐ Team managers: arrange team information links with company and external databases relevant to team tasks, such as customer data, programming libraries, and training resources.

☐ Team managers: ensure that teams have interactive information links with key counterparts, including managers, customers, suppliers, peers, staff, and others.

☐ Team managers: give teams communication links among team members and with nonmember counterparts consistent with the time-urgency of their work.

☐ Team managers: arrange temporary co-location of teams with customers (outstationing) where electronic media are insufficient for the interaction demanded by the work.

•

The CDMS project team uses another helpful practice: co-location of teams with their customers where the work requires frequent, collaborative decisions and close, time-urgent coordination with the client. The CDMS team needed face-to-face interaction for exchanges for on-the-spot decisions about redesigning the CDMS, testing the software, and fitting it with the client's existing systems. Even today's sophisticated electronic media do not allow this kind of close, personal cooperation, so the team opted to work at the customer's site. Such outstationing requires cooperation by the team's manager with counterparts in the client organization. Besides negotiating temporary quarters for the visiting team, managers at the client organization need to designate contact persons and establish policies for access to the client organization's information. Depending on how the client organization handles its part of the collaboration, the outstationed team may become an "interorganizational team," as described in the section on future trends in this chapter.

Teams may need special information systems to accommodate time-urgent work. Chapter Eight gives the example of a firefighting team whose members use compact intercoms for instant voice communication among team members and with support personnel. Other kinds of action teams use similar intercom systems, such as football teams, rescue teams, and expeditions. Similarly, service teams whose members work on the telephone with customers, as in insurance and mail-order businesses, may have similar needs for fast voice links.

Best Practices for Communications Technology

New technologies for communication allow teams to collaborate from different cities or continents. As described in Chapter Nine, these tools enable organizations to rely on virtual teams whose members rarely or never meet in person. Related communication technologies also support other kinds of work teams in today's information-intensive organizations.

A helpful management practice is to design the team's work first and then, based on a needs assessment, assemble the communication technology to support the team. (To buy the technology first in hopes of using it as a template for redesigning the team's work is to invite trouble.) Because new communication tools take time to master, it is best to start with easy tasks and relaxed deadlines, with ample time for trial-and-error, beginning with team leaders.

New communication technologies support four forms of team inter-action: (1) face-to-face meetings at the same time and place; (2) meet-ings at the same time from different places, such as videoconferences; (3) communication at different times through the same place, for example, in a team whose members work different shifts in a power plant control room; and (4) communication at different times from different places, as in exchanges of e-mail.

Support for same-time, same-place (STSP) meetings comes in the form of group support systems (GSSs), often in special meeting rooms equipped with networked computer workstations; software for anonymous brain-storming, polling, and joint decision making; multimedia displays; and keypads for electronic voting. As described in Chapter Nine, project teams at IBM used such high-tech facilities for generating ideas, report-edly with greater efficiency than in traditional rooms. (One reason for improved efficiency: meetings that use GSS comfortably accommodate more participants than traditional meetings can.) The World Bank sent action teams to client nations with their portable GSS hardware and soft-ware, and reported success with GSS on the road. Best management prac-tice for GSSs calls for collection of data to evaluate whether teams actually save time or produce higher-quality work with them.

Support for same-time, different-place (STDP) "virtual meetings" often involves videoconference facilities like those in "FirstGlobal" (Chapter Nine). Among best practices for videoconferences discovered at Ford, Hewlett-Packard, and elsewhere: (1) use separate audio and vi-sual channels, (2) use a separate process channel for communicating about meeting management, and (3) use a trained facilitator familiar with the technology and its capabilities.

Electronic support for different-time, same-place (DTSP) communi-cation applies to teams whose members work in shifts or take turns run-ning a facility like a control room or service center. An example is an airplane maintenance team of four workers who use the same team room for their round-the-clock operation.[33] Team room supports include work stations, display areas, shared databases, shared storage, and re-ception areas as needed.

The principal form of technological support for different-time, dif-ferent-place (DTDP) communication is e-mail. To help personalize the relationships in a team whose members only communicate in writing, it is useful to distribute photos and biographies of team members.

•

Best Practices Checklist 11.9: Communication Technology for Teams

☐ Team manager: design the work first and then, based on an assessment of team needs and with participation by the members, assemble the communication technology to support the team.

☐ Team managers: use meeting facilities with GSS for important face-to-face meetings or for meetings of relatively large groups.

☐ Team managers: collect data on meeting efficiency and performance to evaluate GSS.

☐ Team managers: for virtual meetings via videoconference, use separate channels for meeting content and process; use a facilitator to guide the meeting and make clear transitions.

☐ Team managers: for teams using the same place at different times, provide a team room with workstations, display areas, shared databases, shared storage, and reception.

☐ Team managers: For teams that communicate primarily via e-mail or other different-time, different-place technologies, distribute members' photos and biographies.

•

Best Practices for Facilities for Teams

As described in Chapter Ten, long-lived teams with stable memberships tend to perform best with members co-located in a shared work area. In a new product development team, for instance, co-location appears to be ideal, as in the case of the "Eagle team" that designed a prototype computer in record time. The team had its own laboratory available to members even late at night.[34] Co-location creates opportunities for informal, face-to-face interaction and intensive collaboration that is difficult to do from a distance. Evidence shows that cohesion often develops in groups whose members share the same work location.

Unfortunately, co-location of team members is not always practical. Members may work on different floors, in different buildings, or—more and more often—in separate cities. Ideally, each team member has a workstation equipped for electronic communication. Where team members work in the same building complex, two facility-related practices improve informal, face-to-face interaction. One is to locate convenient gathering places with beverages, vending machines, mailboxes, copier, library, cafeteria, or comfortable seating near thoroughfares. Another is to design circulation patterns with walkways and corridors that converge, for example in a lobby or atrium. Both practices increase the likelihood that team members meet by happenstance or have places to meet on purpose.

Teams of all kinds need access to conference rooms: conveniently located, easily reserved, and properly equipped for meetings. A minimum conference room has a large table; comfortable chairs; and a visual display such as a chalkboard, whiteboard, flipchart, or overhead projector.[35] For virtual teams, facility support includes basic electronic communication tools: telephone with conference-call capabilities, computers or terminals with access to e-mail, and sometimes other tools (Chapter Nine).

Best Practices Checklist 11.10: Facilities for Teams

☐ Facility manager: provide well-designed, temporary or permanent workstations.

☐ Facility manager: give teams access to convenient, well-equipped conference rooms.

☐ Team managers: co-locate members of long-lived, stable teams in clustered workstations with shared team workspace, including team display or reception area if needed.

☐ Facility manager: create convenient gathering places, such as coffee areas, mailboxes, copier areas, and vending areas.

☐ Facility manager: use layouts with converging pathways to promote informal interaction.

In all, the checklists suggest fifty-nine best management practices for supporting work team effectiveness. Fortunately, they apply to many different roles in the organization (though most belong to team managers and team leaders). Some practices are well supported by research, as detailed in the chapters from which they are drawn. Others are so new that researchers have not had time to evaluate them, especially the new communication and information technologies.

Complementary Team Support Systems

In your organization, some team support systems may be better developed or more responsive than others, and you may even have to do without some of them. Fortunately, most team support systems have at least one naturally complementary system that can serve the same objectives.

TEAM STRUCTURE VERSUS LEADERS' ROLES. Teams thrive on just enough structure to capitalize on members' expertise for establishing team work processes and roles (Chapter Two), consistent with the principle of "minimum critical specification."[36] Where multiple teams cooperate, as on the Boeing 777 in Chapter Four, the framework for team structure may come from a design team or steering group. However, where a team's structure cannot easily be specified in advance or emerges as the work unfolds, the team leader becomes the primary arbiter and facilitator of team structure. As in the CDMS project team (Chapter Eight), the team leader may help develop a team structure compatible with requirements for reporting to the team's manager and working with the team's customers. The less the team's structure is specified in its charter, the more it depends on a strong leader role to help negotiate an emerging structure.

CO-LOCATION VERSUS VIRTUAL COMMUNICATION. A team co-located in the same facility handles much of its need for communication via face-to-face conversation. Virtual teams whose members work in geographically separate locations interact electronically instead—via phone, e-mail, videoconference, and networked computers. For some purposes, such as routine announcements, e-mail and voice mail are more efficient than face-to-face meetings. Other purposes demand personal meetings, though the electronic substitute may have to do. In general, a team facility and communication technologies complement and substitute for one another as support systems.

STAFFING VERSUS TRAINING. Of the primary vehicles for bringing knowledge, skills, and abilities to a team, staffing (Chapter Three) is critical because it includes screening and selection of members who have the requisite ability to learn. Learning ability allows team members to take advantage of the training (Chapter Five) for new knowledge and skills integral to the work of all teams. Where staffing is predetermined or options for group composition are limited, training becomes the primary support system for remedying skill deficiencies and instilling new knowledge and skills. Each system substitutes for the other.

INFORMATION TECHNOLOGY VERSUS LEADER'S ROLE. In traditional, hierarchical organizations, a work group's leader has often constituted its main information system. Some organizations even have strong prohibitions against any formal communications outside the chain of command. As teams become more self-managing and take more responsibilities that were once the province of managers and supervisors, they increasingly manage their own information. Team members' use of information systems lightens some of the load on the leader's external liaison role and the manager's role as the team's source of information from management. On the other hand, leaders' roles must compensate for deficient information systems.

REWARD SYSTEM VERSUS TEAM STRUCTURE. Motivation is essential for an effective work team, and the primary source of motivation is a well-designed reward system in which members' pay depends directly on contributions to team performance. Ideally, members' salaries and continuing contracts depend on their team-related expertise, or on results achieved by the whole team, or both. Where salary does not provide motivation, recognition by way of awards and kudos might suffice. Lacking these, a manager must depend on team structure, which can complement a reward system in at least two ways. First, where team members are interdependent, they motivate one another through peer pressure. For example, service teams whose members cover for one another reinforce mutual assistance and make it uncomfortable for those who do not back up their teammates. Second, where the work is intrinsically interesting or integral to members' self-identities, motivation can come from the work itself. This is seen in its purest form in Olympic teams and volunteer organizations. A well-crafted team charter can go a long way toward compensating for a stingy reward system.

SUPPORT FOR DIFFERENT TYPES OF TEAMS

Previous chapters explain how to tailor support systems to various kinds of teams. Each type has a few needs that make certain support systems critical to its effectiveness; some types need more kinds of support than others. This section identifies support systems most central to each kind of team.

Management Teams

Management teams call for cooperation among managers who may at the same time be competing for scarce resources, such as budget, personnel, or space. Members of many management teams have inherently conflicting goals, such as the intrinsic divergence between operations and new product development.[37] Without incentives to cooperate, managers can easily fall into empire building and turf disputes.

A well-designed reward system in a management team engenders co-operation toward organizationwide goals. Feasible rewards for management teams include stock options and gain sharing (Chapter Seven). For example, a Canadian packaging company offers an annual bonus to plant management teams (and other employees at their sites) based on a gainsharing formula with multiple performance indicators. The bonus can add one-third to a manager's salary, but it requires cooperation among the managers.

A reward system necessitates a complementary measurement system, which ideally lets team members monitor performance in all areas of team responsibility. Without good performance measures, management teams lose track of what project, service, or production teams are doing, which allows them to go separate ways. Only with timely performance measurements can managers keep team efforts aligned. Also, managers need access to performance of their peers' departments; the sales manager needs to know immediately, for example, if an operations manager's unit falls behind schedule. At the packaging company, managers use networked computers to exchange data collected by purchasing, production, sales, maintenance, and shipping teams. Measures include plant output, equipment uptime, accidents, raw material utilization, energy costs, overtime, absences, and other factors. Production teams keep charts on the wall showing their week-by-week performance, and the management team receives plantwide summaries. Each manager uses the company's computerized information system to compare other plants' performance data and information about company suppliers, such as price lists and back orders, as well as customer data, such as order turn-around times and on-time deliveries.

Cooperation among managers can call for frequent conferences, so management teams depend on communication technology and facility support. At the packaging company, managers at each site meet daily in small conference rooms near their offices. Plant managers in different cities travel monthly to corporate headquarters for face-to-face meetings. All stay in touch by e-mail and phone. Teams hold videoconferences when travel is impractical.

Production Teams

Good performance measurement is crucial for a production team. Production work depends on the quality of the output as seen by customers. Effectiveness for a production team calls for attention to details of the output and adjustment to customers' requirements. This in turn requires feedback from measurements, as outlined in Chapter Six. A productivity expert once summed up the situation by saying, "What you measure is what you get!"

Because measurement is so critical for manufacturing, many organizations have adopted total quality management. A key feature of TQM is having dependable, customer-oriented measures of product quality that front-line employees can use in managing their work processes.[38] Manufacturing companies using TQM include Eastman Chemicals, Hewlett-Packard, Motorola, Saturn, and Xerox.[39]

Other challenges in supporting production teams depend on whether they are located in new factories or in existing facilities. In a new facility, managers have the luxury of designing a coherent sociotechnical system[40] and of selecting the staff before starting production. At an established factory the organizational structure, facility, staff, and reward system are already in place, and the managers face the challenge of changing an existing system to meet new business demands.

PRODUCTION TEAMS IN NEW ("GREEN-FIELD") FACTORIES. In a new factory, as with the Saturn case, support systems that are important at first include the facility, team structure, reward system, and staffing. Ideally, these are developed together by a design team: a new building is designed for the manufacturing processes (Chapter Ten) with a complementary team structure for the work (Chapter Two) supported by a reward system (Chapter Seven) that provides incentives for performance. Workers are recruited and selected to meet the work requirements (Chapter Three). For start-up, training (Chapter Five) is crucial: orientation for workers, plus training to support leaders' roles (Chapter Four) in clarifying expectations and reinforcing the employee involvement essential in fine-tuning new work processes.

PRODUCTION TEAMS IN ESTABLISHED FACTORIES. To support a transition to teams at an existing factory like the one at MotorCo (Chapter Two), crucial support focuses on leaders' roles, employee training, and rewards. Leaders' roles are critical because the transition is an organizational change. As in the Phelps Dodge case of Chapter Five, leaders must establish the need for change, create a vision of the future organization, develop a strategic plan, and unify the workforce around the plan.

For a transition to teams in an established workforce, training is the main vehicle for instilling new knowledge and skills. Workers unaccustomed to teamwork need training on teamwork, as at MotorCo and Phelps Dodge.

Employees with teamwork skills still need motivation to make the effort to produce effective teams. Motivation might come from the greater variety of work and autonomy in teams,[41] or from fear of layoffs if the plant closes. In the long run, though, the most dependable source of motivation is compensation. At an established plant like Phelps Dodge–El Paso, the existing reward system may already give enough incentive for team performance through site-based gainsharing. If employees share the financial benefits of improved productivity, and if they see that teams boost productivity, they have the needed motivation. Where teams require cross-training, workers may also need skill-based pay to prompt learning of new skills (see Chapter Ten).

Using team structure or facilities to support teams is limited at an established factory. The inertia of existing roles and relationships adds to the time and cost of changing the structure. The company can rely on existing natural teams, each composed of supervisor and supervisees, or it can invest in restructuring. Similarly, the organization can either use the existing facility, as at Phelps Dodge, or invest in plant renovation. Where an existing factory is redesigned and renovated, for instance when shifting to manufacturing cells or "lean production technology,"[42] the transition takes on the challenges of a green-field site while retaining many limitations of an established plant.

Service Teams

Service teams need customer-oriented information and measurement systems to be effective. Because their performance requirements center on repeated transactions with external customers, they need feedback on their success in meeting customers' expectations. For example, service teams at Eastman Kodak in Rochester, New York,[43] monitor measures of customer satisfaction as well as service accuracy and call length.

Needs of many service teams derive from their delivery of services by workers who interact one-to-one with clients as their clients' main point of contact with the organization. At Eastman Kodak, each customer service worker takes calls individually. Service team members cooperate by supporting one another's delivery of service through collaboration on scheduling, shift coverage, backup coverage, case consultation, and work procedures.

To support one another's client transactions, members of service teams rely on both information systems and communication technology. At Eastman Kodak, as in many customer service operations, each worker uses a computer terminal to gain access to the organization's huge client database. While calling up and entering client data, the worker uses other databases to retrieve relevant technical information. The worker uses a sophisticated telephone system to consult with teammates about clients' questions. The information system's flexibility, responsiveness, and speed largely determine how well service workers meet customers' service expectations and managers' productivity goals.

Teamwork on service teams depends on staffing systems to ensure that members have the needed abilities. Many kinds of service teams have specialized roles for different kinds of service handled by the same team. At Eastman Kodak, one team member might specialize in service questions about a certain product. Coverage of members' absences requires cross-training and coaching within the team. To the extent that teams are composed of people with needed teamwork skill, learning ability, and coaching skills, they may be able to manage their own cross-training. Where the staffing system leaves deficiencies in these skills, the burden of support goes to the training system.

Service teams work most work most effectively when co-located in a facility that allows face-to-face interaction for mutual support. In the human services team described in Chapter Ten, for example, members' workstations surrounded a team conference area convenient for impromptu meetings for case discussions, coverage of breaks and absences, work assignments, workload equalization, and policy questions.

Project Teams

Supporting a cross-functional project team calls for aligning members' diverse expertise and divided loyalties while steering the project through shifting demands from external customers and stakeholders. In the past, a project team could assume its mandate and budget represented a done deal, and the team could focus on getting the work on time, on budget, and on spec. Now a project team might have to respond to a shifting mandate, a shrinking budget, a shortened time line, a change in membership, a new leader, or a shift in expectations from customers or stakeholders.

Leaders' roles play a crucial part in the effectiveness of a project team. Because most project teams consist of experts who know more about their specialties than their managers do, the leader's challenge is to give team members sufficient control over the details of their work. This might mean resisting well-intended offers of direction from outside the team. From the outset, the leader's role is to protect the team,[44] and give members the discretion they need to organize their talents for the task. The "Eagle team" that developed a prototype computer is a good example; the leader often served as its advocate and worked to preserve its autonomy and resources.[45]

Because cross-functional project teams depend on members' specialized expertise, their effectiveness hinges on team composition and the staffing decisions behind it. Staffing for project teams often involves selecting members from existing professional staff. Fortunately, selection from within the organization takes account of the prospective team member's record of past performance. Unfortunately, the manager's choices may be constrained by demands for staffing from concurrent projects.

Project teams increasingly rely on interactive information systems to manage their external exchanges. At one time this task belonged more to the team's project manager and functional managers, who often served as the main external communicators. However, expectations of project teams have changed: responsibility for external liaison has migrated from managers to the teams themselves. No longer can project teams rely on managers as their primary interfaces; teams must develop on their own such roles as "ambassador" and "scout."[46] Project teams particularly need to keep stakeholders and customers informed of their progress, solicit customer information, and demonstrate early prototypes and designs. Like the CDMS team, today's project teams need to manage their own access to company databases, customer information, industry developments, and other information.

Project teams depend on support from the physical facility. Co-location allows use of a team room, like the one the CDMS team had, enabling members to cooperate closely and maintain work in progress, displays, materials, tools, and shared resources. Virtual project teams operate at a disadvantage; without a shared physical workplace the members must maintain contact via e-mail, phone, videoconference, and perhaps occasional face-to-face working sessions. In virtual teams, the leader has to work to keep members' attention on their long-distance work more than on pressing, local demands.

A reward system helps keep the attention of project team members on their work. Rewards might best be tied to site performance (Chapter Seven). Projects increasingly depend on cooperation from other teams in the organization. Team-based rewards may generate interteam conflict, while gainsharing encourages interteam cooperation.

Action and Performing Teams

To be effective, action and performing teams need staffing that ensures a composition of individually skilled specialists who work well together. From string quartets to military tank crews, team effectiveness hinges on selection of individual members with skills needed for their specialized roles on the team.

Training is critical to action teams because they generally have to practice between engagements to maintain and develop their concerted skills. For airplane cockpit crews, practice calls for access to sophisticated flight simulators. For firefighting crews, practice requires a facility where crews can fight actual fires in a controlled environment.

Action teams require well-designed practice facilities, staging areas, and performance facilities. Some kinds of action teams travel with their equipment to engagements and must maintain both a home base and a mobile base. Others have stringent requirements for performance facilities, such as musical groups and legal teams.

Action teams need state-of-the-art information technologies to stay in close communication with support personnel and with one another during engagements. For example, the firefighting crews described in Chapter Eight used an intercom system for real-time voice communication among firefighters and their support crew.

Action and performing teams demonstrate high effectiveness under a wide range of reward and recognition systems. Military, police, and firefighting teams have relatively low job-based pay, in contrast to relatively high job-based pay for airline cockpit crews, performance-based pay for legal teams, and high skill-based and performance-based pay for professional sports teams. Even so, a well-designed reward system is expected to benefit the effectiveness of an action team.

Parallel Teams

Parallel teams require the least support among the six kinds of teams. Because they are temporary, part-time, and relatively independent of the organization's operations, they have comparatively few needs. Their most important requirements are a charter that spells out their duties, deliverables, time line, and resources (Chapter Two); and a well-defined leader's role (Chapter Four). Also, to be effective they need support for conferences, either a meeting room or an electronic substitute for one. In addition, a parallel team benefits from a reward system that gives incentives for members to divert time from their primary responsibilities on the group's behalf. As outlined in Chapter Seven, a site-based gainsharing plan suffices.

Summary: Key Support Systems for Six Kinds of Teams

Exhibit 11.1 summarizes the key support systems for the six kinds of teams. It identifies the support systems that should receive priority when planning, designing, implementing, and managing the type of team.

Exhibit 11.1. Key Support Systems for Six Kinds of Work Teams.

Team support systems	Production Green-field	Production Established	Management	Service	Project	Action	Parallel
	Kinds of work teams						
Team structure	X			X			X
Leaders' roles		X	X		X	X	X
Building and facility	X		X		X		X
Staffing system	X			X	X	X	
Communication technology				X	X	X	
Measurement and feedback	X	X	X	X	X	X	
Information system	X	X	X	X	X	X	
Training and development		X	X			X	
Reward system	X	X	X		X		X

CHALLENGES AHEAD: SUPPORTING TEAMS IN ORGANIZATIONS OF THE FUTURE

The examples and trends described throughout this book point to rapid organizational change in a dynamic business environment. Teams are becoming more common, as outlined in Chapter One, and show signs of becoming more so. The challenges of supporting team effectiveness—defining teams, building support systems, and tailoring support systems for kinds of teams—will also continue. Trends in the nature of teams and in their support systems promise to complicate those challenges and add others. This section describes the trends, discusses the challenges they create, and offers advice for meeting the new challenges.

Team Trends

Against a backdrop of increasing use of teams, several trends can be seen today: teams for more kinds of work, more virtual teams, more interorganizational teams, more outstationed teams, more fast-start teams of strangers, and more multiteam efforts. Each trend poses management challenges.

TEAMS FOR MORE KINDS OF WORK. As organizations use teams for a wider range of purposes, the manager's challenge is to organize work for which teams are better suited than individuals are. An example is customer service in a mail-order company. Individual workers take customer calls, even when organized into teams. Though managers might want them to function as service teams, they do not cooperate while delivering the service. They can cooperate in support of one another's delivery of service. Collective responsibilities of this kind of service team include work scheduling, coverage of absences, workload equalization, consultation on service techniques, cross-training, and matching client types with service workers best suited to them. In considering whether to form a team for a new work function such as customer service, the key question is, What specific work would team members do cooperatively? Then, as outlined in Chapter Two, managers can use a participative process to design the work for teams.

VIRTUAL TEAMS. The rise of virtual teams, whose members communicate electronically from separate cities, may lead one to ask, "How can team managers promote cohesion like that found in teams that work in the same place?" One answer is that it is only necessary to foster enough communication to get the job done. The challenge for virtual team managers is to create conditions for motivated, distant collaboration.

To build personal relationships in a virtual team, experts suggest an early face-to-face meeting if possible.[47] Where a team cannot meet in person, new technologies allow fast, convenient exchange of photos and biographies. Communication via phone, e-mail, and videoconference may not be sufficient, however. For work done best in face-to-face meetings, such as contract negotiations and conflict resolution, team support may call for help and resources for traveling to a conference facility.

INTERORGANIZATIONAL TEAMS. Organizations increasingly use teams as vehicles for partnerships with other organizations, including customer, supplier, and peer organizations. Members of interorganizational teams represent the interests of their organizations and work toward the common interests represented by the partnership. For example, WalMart and Procter & Gamble formed customer-supplier partnership teams responsible for coordinating P&G's production, scheduling, and distribution of certain products with WalMart's purchasing, warehousing, and distribution of those products.[48] Besides the usual issues involved in supporting cross-functional teams, these teams bring the added management challenge of helping members cooperate across organizational boundaries while keeping confidential their companies' proprietary information not involved in the partnership. For interorganizational teams, the team structure and charter (Chapter Four) are more complicated and more important than for teams in just one organization, and the risks associated with ambiguous team charters are greater. Such teams will probably become more common as organizations master the best practices for using them.

OUTSTATIONED TEAMS. Today there are teams from one organization working full-time in other organizations' buildings. These outstationed teams deliver services such as tool-crib operation, procurement, travel support, retail sales, food service, and maintenance. In light of trends toward organizational consolidation around core competencies and subcontracting of ancillary business, these teams appear likely to grow ever more common.

Outstationed teams work in two cultures at once: their employer organization's and the client or partner organization's. They need clear team structures; managers must give specific guidance concerning disclosure of proprietary information to the other organization's employees; requirements for regulatory compliance, reporting, and accounting procedures; and safety requirements. An outstationed team must uphold the values and practices of its employer organization while organizing and operating in ways consistent with the client or partner's culture. As a result, the crucial supports for outstationed team are a clear team structure; a strong, well-defined leader's role; and careful team staffing.

In outstationed teams, the possibility exists that employees might be assimilated by client cultures as team members adopt clients' practices. The employer organization can turn this situation into an opportunity for learning. Helpful practices include short tours of duty in client organizations, interspersed with assignments at the home organization; best practices conferences; and routine recertification of team members' skills.

FAST-START TEAMS. More and more teams of expert specialists who are strangers to one another must cooperate immediately on time-critical tasks. Examples include surgery teams, disaster relief teams, and cockpit crews. Members of such teams tend to be highly trained in their specialized roles and in cooperating with specialists in counterpart roles. A cockpit crew, for instance, usually consists of pilot, copilot, and navigator, who have the requisite number of flight hours learning standard procedures for their roles. They spend hours in flight simulators learning crew procedures for handling many kinds of situations. Their training on standard procedures prepares them in advance to cooperate with anyone who happens to occupy the well-defined counterpart roles, because the team roles and norms are standard for the profession.[49]

The management challenge for supporting fast-start teams is to provide training to prepare expert specialists in new and emerging specialties for the fast-start teams. Training can involve simulations, like those used with police, firefighters, and soldiers, as well as computer-based tools such as flight simulators, as outlined in Chapter Eight.

MULTITEAM EFFORTS IN "FLAT" ORGANIZATIONS. Events of the past decade point to more large-scale efforts involving multiple teams, as in the Boeing 777 project in Chapter Four. They will probably take place in increasingly "flat" organizations with fewer hierarchical levels and wider spans of control than are seen even in the 1990s.

The support challenge is to coordinate multiple teams while preserving enough independence to allow for creativity. The Boeing 777 project called for coordination of ten thousand employees and five hundred suppliers. When the existing management hierarchy could not handle the job quickly enough, Boeing introduced a new kind of management team, called an *integration team*. Each consisted of twelve to fifteen representatives of cross-functional teams working on separate components, such as the passenger ventilation and emergency oxygen systems. Integration teams had the task of resolving conflicts between component teams. When two teams wanted to locate components in exactly the same place in the passenger compartment, the relevant integration team brought the component teams together to find a solution. Within a few hours, they discovered a way to accommodate both the ventilation outlet and the emergency oxygen supply in the same location. Integration teams proved faster at resolving such conflicts than having the teams work through Boeing's layers of management.[50]

Tomorrow's organizations are likely to expect management teams to serve the same function as Boeing's integration teams: cross-functional communication, conflict management, and integration of multiteam efforts.

Team Support: Emerging Challenges

Team support systems have evolved with teams and team-based organizations. In light of current trends, you can expect team support systems to continue to change. This section discusses emerging challenges for future team support systems.

TEAM STRUCTURE: TOWARD ROLE CLARITY FOR FLUID TEAMS. Team boundaries are blurring as people affiliate with more teams, as virtual teams become more common, as teams encompass more contractors and members of other organizations, and as shifting team membership becomes the norm. Teams show signs of becoming ever more fluid.

The management challenge is to clarify the roles of a fluid team, particularly in chartering one (Chapter Two). Managers negotiate clear team charters if they work from equally clear strategic plans. As companies spread across geographical boundaries, it becomes more important to integrate diverse elements. As demonstrated in such organizations as Solectron (Chapter Seven) and Boeing (Chapter Four), executive strategy lays the foundation for a management team structure that integrates many kinds of teams at many levels.

As teams become more fluid, their effectiveness increasingly depends on a culture of employee involvement. One reason for introducing teams in the first place is to give members the authority to make decisions on matters about which they have the best information. Team members have the best available information about an increasing range of details of their work. In the effective organizations of the future, team structure will be more and more responsive to team members' analysis of the demands of the work, as in the CDMS project team of Chapter Eight. A growing role for employees in defining team structure calls for a culture of involvement.

LEADERS' ROLES: MORE LIAISON AND COACHING. As described in Chapter Four, today's leader roles emphasize liaison as organizations increasingly treat divisions and work units as separate businesses. Leaders' roles have evolved toward being ambassadors, agents, and scouts. With the rising time-urgency and complexity of work, the task of coordination involves growing networks of peers, suppliers, customers, contractors, and regulators. At the same time, leaders belong to teams of peer managers dealing with the expectations of "team players" on management teams and boards of directors.

Leaders' roles in relation to team members are evolving toward coach, facilitator, and mentor, and away from boss, commander, and director.[51] As described in Chapter Four, today's leaders are expected to delegate authority and responsibility while establishing needed direction and accountability. Leader role expectations increasingly include helping team members develop their own capabilities. Organizations continue to flatten, creating wider spans of control and essentially forcing leaders to give up supervising the details of employees' work. Instead, leaders spend their time creating conditions that enable team members to take responsibility for their own work.

The emerging challenge is to define and clarify increasingly complex leaders' roles. In light of the rapid pace with which managers change jobs, it helps to specify as much as possible each leader's role counterparts and liaison duties. Leader roles increasingly focus on performance metrics: choosing selection indicators consistent with the organization's business strategy, coaching teams in developing and collecting local indicators, managing the performance database, reporting results of measurements, and facilitating team improvement projects. Facilitation promises to become more complex with the increasing functional variety of subordinates and increasingly diverse workforce. The future role of leader seems likely to call for speedier development of facilitator, coach, and mentor relationships with supervisees.

FACILITIES FOR TEAMS: FOCUS ON CONFERENCES. As outlined in Chapter Ten, facilities for teams serve members of varied origins: full-time employees, contractors who work out of home offices, part-time employees who share workstations, temporary employees, consultants, and visitors from different cities.

For face-to-face conferences, the challenge is to support teams having fluid membership in conference facilities equipped with full-service, networked computer workstations. Team members are likely to come and go during extended working sessions that include full-team meetings, subgroup conferences, and individual work. Likely configurations of facilities for team support consist of team rooms with multiple workstations and few walls. Such facilities might resemble the room used by the CDMS team in Chapter Eight or the office used by the CRSS Strategic Services Group (Chapter Ten).

As team conferences increasingly incorporate temporary members and consultants, teams call for resources to make the most of their time. This means rising demand for special meeting facilities with group support systems (Chapter Nine). A typical one has linked computer work-stations with group-decision software and large display screens with multimedia capability. Where these facilities exist today, they are already much in demand.

For increasingly common "virtual meetings," tomorrow's team needs more videoconference centers. As the technology advances, it seems likely to become commonplace and taken for granted by teams in much the same way that today's teams expect meeting rooms to have flipcharts.

TEAM STAFFING: MORE COMPLEX AND COLLABORATIVE. As teams grow more common, so do job applicants with experience in teams. This apparent blessing lets staffing managers focus on applicants' technical skills and the fit with the team's mix of skills. As organizations increasingly call for use of technical skills in collaborative projects, however, the emerging challenge is to adequately assess work skills in the context of team interaction.

Prospects of assessment for future teams appear likely to improve with changes in the employment relationship. Today's organizations rely increasingly on part-time employees, temporary workers, and contractors (or so-called temps), and this trend promises to continue. Temps provide a natural pool of prospective applicants whose performance can be assessed directly on the job, often in the same type of work they might do as full-time employees. Staffing systems capitalize on this by hiring promising workers as contractors, and by using actual job performance as a basis for hiring them as full-time employees, as is done now at some large computer software companies. In effect, the organization of the future is increasingly becoming a large assessment center, and contract work an arena for assessing prospective team members' performance.

An emerging challenge for team staffing is to ensure the fit between prospective team members and both the organization's values and the team's mix of skills and traits. Fit with organizational values gains importance as company leaders seek to articulate the values of their cultures and build consensus around them. In some organizations, managers hesitate to recruit outside the company for any but entry-level positions, to avoid hiring people whose values differ from their culture. At the same time, specialized skill requirements of high-tech teams create difficulty in filling openings. It may be difficult to find people in the organization who meet the dual tests of values congruent with the culture and skills needed for the work of the team.

Increasing attention to the compatibility of new employees with prospective teammates adds pressure for staffing systems to collaborate with the managers and teams they serve. Managers and teammates are sure to take on a growing role in defining requirements of openings. The role of staffing manager may evolve into that of expert internal consultant, as more responsibility for selection moves to teams and their managers. Team leaders may take a more active part in the recruit-screen-assess-select cycle described in Chapter Three, particularly in the final selection.

ELECTRONIC COLLABORATION TOOLS: MORE INTEGRAL TO TEAMWORK.
Use of electronic communication technologies to support teams appears to be expanding, with no end in sight. Sophisticated team meeting rooms with group support systems are appearing in more and more organizations as their leaders read reports of the value of GSS in improving group performance. At the same time, increasingly global organizations must rely on videoconferences for long-distance meetings and continue to learn how to capitalize on the improving technology for videolinks. Expect today's electronic communication tools to improve and become more integral to teams of the future. To support team effectiveness, a manager needs to keep learning about these tools, and organizations have to invest in continuous upgrades of equipment, software, and expertise in their application as the technologies improve.

MEASUREMENT SYSTEMS FOR TEAMS: MORE DIVERSE AND INTEGRATED.
Several trends are likely to drive organizations to improve their team measurement systems. Technology for measurement is becoming faster, more sensitive, and more responsive. Possibilities for collecting and using data from measurements are multiplying. Organizations are integrating their measurement systems around strategic plans and key performance

indicators, and learning how to align and link measures up and down the hierarchy and across work processes. More organizations are learning to use tailored, local measures for team performance (Chapter Six).

Current trends suggest that future measurement systems for teams will be more diverse and more integrated. One challenge for team managers centers on alignment. As measures and data proliferate, setting priorities and facilitating development of local indicators of performance variables is no doubt more difficult.

The team leader's role is complicated by the increasing need for direct, active participation by team members in developing their measurement systems. Products and services are getting more complex, and the features that matter to customers more numerous and subtle. Distinctions between products and services are blurring, as part of a product's appeal is the associated service, and part of service is the associated information. Team members directly involved in production, service, performance, and development are also in the best position to design the fine-grained measurements needed to monitor the quality of tomorrow's complex products.

INFORMATION SYSTEMS FOR TEAMS: EMERGING SPECIALIST ROLES. As described in Chapter Eight, information systems for teams depend on up-to-date technologies customized by teams to suit their particular tasks. The increasing speed and capacity of information technology allow flexibility, which becomes more important as the work of teams becomes more time-urgent and responsive to customers' expectations. A challenge for supporting teams is to put them in a position to customize their information systems to suit customers and other stakeholders.

In light of the complexity of new technologies and the speed with which they are evolving, teams probably need more specialists to configure and troubleshoot new systems and guide the team in use of the equipment. Expect teams to evolve roles such as information specialist, network coordinator, or "computer wizard." Support for team effectiveness means providing such specialists as permanent members or as visiting or consulting members.

TRAINING FOR TEAMS: MORE SPECIALIZED, LESS CENTRALIZED. As the workforce collectively gains skill and experience in teamwork, training needs become more advanced and specialized. You can expect to see classroom training in basic teamwork skills—of the kind used at Phelps Dodge, for example—to grow less common in organizations as it becomes more available at community colleges and universities.[52] Training in organizations can then focus on specific teamwork skills, such as peer appraisal and feedback, in particular types of teams. Where members cross-train, as in service and production teams, training can focus on peer coaching skills and specific technical skills needed for team point roles. Where members are expert specialists, training is likely to involve simulations.

As teams assume more management duties, the initiative for training is likely to shift to teams. If so, training departments can expect more diverse requests for training. High-tech teams like the CDMS project team (Chapter Eight), for example, might ask for training on new computer programs or regulatory policies. Training requests may come on short notice as emerging demands of the work become less predictable. Training support may take the form of quick train-the-trainer sessions for team members, who later train their teams. Or the training department might send trainers to help teams quickly design and deliver custom sessions.

Although future training will probably continue to involve classroom instruction, the mix of training methods should include more customized consultation to teams on location, as at MotorCo (Chapter Two). Training support seems likely to evolve toward onsite, on-call, technical assistance focused on narrowly defined topics. If these trends continue, they call for training departments to be more flexible in their offerings, decentralized in their delivery, and intrapreneurial in dealing with teams.

TEAM REWARD SYSTEMS: MORE OPTIONS, MORE CUSTOMIZATION. Today's organizations are making performance incentives out of features of the employment relationship once taken for granted. One is employment itself. As temporary contractors supplant lifetime employees, contract awards become significant incentives for performance. Many companies already reward contractors' performance with renewed or expanded contracts.

Other rewards formerly taken for granted include benefits such as medical insurance, retirement plans, child care, paid vacations, paid travel, paid attendance at conferences, and access to such facilities as fitness centers, cafeterias, and libraries. As organizations rely more on temporary employees and contractors, such benefits move to the menu of performance incentives.

The likely consequence of supporting team effectiveness through reward systems is that managers will have more options in designing reward systems for new teams. New information technologies promise to make managing these complex, tailored reward systems easier, but they make the learning curve for team managers even steeper.

CONCLUSION

In conclusion, managers face a daunting series of challenges in supporting the work teams that increasingly dominate today's organizations. The nine support systems are all complicated, and they vary in importance for the different types of teams. Tailoring support systems to each team's needs means taking account of many details that may be changing before your eyes. Fortunately, you can meet these challenges by relying on teams to do what they have shown they can do very well: design and manage organizations. If you are a manager, the first team to support in being effective is your own.

APPENDIX:
TOOLS, MANUFACTURERS, AND URLS

Category	Meeting cell	Team type	Product	Company	URL
Group support systems	STSP, *STDP*	Management, project, *parallel*	GroupSystems	Ventana Corporation	http://www.ventana.com/
			Council	CoVision	http://www.covision.com/
			MeetingWorks	Enterprise Solutions	http://www.entsol.com/
Electronic whiteboards	STSP, STDP, *DTSP, DTDP*	Project, *parallel, service*	TeamBoard	TeamBoard Inc.	http://www.teamboard.com/
			SmartBoard	Smart Technologies	http://www.smarttech.com/
			SoftBoard	Microfield Graphics	http://www.softboard.com/
Keypad voting systems	STSP	Project, parallel	OptionFinder	Option Technologies	http://www.optionfinder.com/
			Audience Response System	Reactive Systems	http://www.reactivesystems.com/
Presentation support systems	STSP	Management, project, *parallel*	PowerPoint	Microsoft	http://www.microsoft.com/
			Freelance Graphics	Lotus	http://www.lotus.com/
			Corel Graphics	Corel	http://www.corel.com/
Audio conferencing	STDP	Management, project, action, *parallel*	SoundStation	Polycom	http://www.polycom.com/
Video conferencing	STDP	Management, project, *parallel*	Concorde 4500	PictureTel	http://www.picturetel.com/
			Hermes, Supernova	Aethra	http://www.aethra.com/
Desktop video conferencing	STDP, *ATAP*	Management, project, *parallel*	Live 200p	PictureTel	http://www.picturetel.com/
			ProShare Conferencing Video System 200	Intel Corporation	http://www.intel.com/
			NetMeeting	Microsoft	http://www.microsoft.com/
			CUSeeMe	White Pine	http://www.wpine.com/

Document conferencing projector	**STSP, STDP**	GroupView	PictureTel	http://www.picturetel.com/
Application sharing	**STDP**, *STSP*	GroupShare	PictureTel	http://www.picturetel.com/
		NetMeeting	Microsoft	http://www.microsoft.com/
Screen sharing	**STDP**, *STSP*	PublicSpace 1.1	Teamwave Software	http://www.teamwave.com
		Eshare	Eshare Technologies	http://www.eshare.com/
		NetMeeting	Microsoft	http://www.microsoft.com/
Distributed GSS	**STDP**, *DTDP, STSP*	Facilitate.com	Facilitate.Com	http://www.facilitate.com/
		Consensus@anyWARE	Soft Bicycle	http://www.softbicycle.com/
		3-2-1 IntraNet	Internet Media Inc.	http://www.iminet.com
Internet chat (real-time conferencing)	**STDP**, *DTDP, ATAP*	Ichat	Acuity	http://www.ichat.com/
		WebBoard	O'Reilly & Associates	http://www.oreilly.com
		Caucus	ScreenPorch	http://www.screenporch.com/
Integrated tools	STDP, DTDP, ATAP	Workplace 2.0	Teamwave Software	http://www.teamwave.com
		NetMeeting	Microsoft	http://www.microsoft.com/
		Eroom	Instinctive Technology	http://www.instinctive.com/
Document management repositories	**DTDP, ATAP**	BSCW	GMD	http://bscw.gmd.de/
		Eroom	Instinctive Technology	http://www.instinctive.com/
		Notes	IBM/Lotus	http://www.lotus.com/

Category	Meeting cell	Team type	Product	Company	URL
Group calendars	DTSP, DTDP, ATAP	Management, project, production, service, parallel	CaLANdar	Microsystems Software	http://www.microsys.com/calan/
			Netscape Calendar	Netscape	http://www.netscape.com/
			Exchange	Microsoft	http://www.microsoft.com/
			Organizer	IBM/Lotus	http://www.lotus.com/
E-mail	DTDP, DTSP	All teams	Eudora	Qualcomm	http://www.eudora.com/
			CCMail	IBM/Lotus	http://www.lotus.com/
Computer conferencing (non-real-time conferencing)	DTDP	Management, project, parallel	Caucus	Screen Porch LLC	http://www.screenporch.com/
			TeamTrax	Trax Softworks	http://www.webcom.com/~traxsoft/
			Eshare	Eshare Technologies	http://www.eshare.com/
Workflow management systems	DTSP, DTDP, *ATAP*	Production, service	InTempo	JetForm Corp	http://www.jetform.com
			Metro Autopilot	Action Technologies	http://www.actiontech.com/
			Flowmark	IBM	http://www.software.ibm.com/ad/flowmark/
			TeamBuilder	NetStart	http://www.netstartinc.com/
Enterprise groupware environments	All categories	All teams	Notes	IBM/Lotus	http://www.lotus.com/
			Groupwise	Novell	http://www.novell.com/groupwise
			Exchange	Microsoft	http://www.microsoft.com/exchange
			Collabra Server	Netscape	http://www.netscape.com/
Message pad	ATAP	Management, *action, service*	Palm Pilot	3com	http://palmpilot.3com.com/
			HP660LX	Hewlett Packard	http://www.hp.com/

Notes:

1. The specific products mentioned are representative of many products in each category. Mention herein does not constitute an endorsement in any way.

2. This chart is accurate as of February 1998. Product models change quickly; Websites change occasionally. Over time, this table will lose its accuracy.

3. Many of the products in this chart actually fall into a variety of categories, as category lines are not tightly drawn and many vendors design multipurpose products. Products have been placed in a principal category (or two). Do not presume that this choice reflects the only features of the product.

4. The team-type column should not be treated as following hard-and-fast rules. Teams of each type might use any type of tool. However, the teams listed in column three offer a good guideline.

5. In columns two and three, boldface type denotes primary and italic secondary.

CHAPTER NOTES

CHAPTER ONE

1. Peters (1987), p. 396.
2. Gronstedt (1996).
3. See, for example, Daft (1995); Kiechel (1993); Mohrman and Mohrman (1996); and Womak, Jones, and Roos (1990).
4. See, for example, Byham (1990); Wellins, Byham, and Wilson (1991); and Kirkman and Rosen (1997).
5. See, for example, Orsburn, Moran, Musselwhite, and Zenger (1990); Katzenbach and Smith (1993); and Cohen, Ledford, and Spreitzer (1996).
6. See, for example, Hoerr (1989); Dumaine (1990, 1994); Wellins, Byham, and Wilson (1991); and Wellins, Byham, and Dixon (1994).
7. Lawler, Mohrman, and Ledford (1992, 1995).
8. Sundstrom, DeMeuse, and Futrell (1990), p. 120. We use the terms *work team* and *work group* interchangeably in this book, though some writers argue they differ, because features used to define one term have often been used to define the other. See Guzzo and Dickson (1996), pp. 309–310, for a discussion. See Katzenbach and Smith (1993) for an argument favoring separate definitions.
9. Katzenbach and Smith (1993), p. 45.
10. For discussions of the defining features of a group, see Cartwright and Zander (1968) and McGrath (1984). For features that define work teams, see Guzzo and Shea (1992).
11. For an example of military tank crews, see Tziner and Eden (1985); for examples of cockpit crews see Foushee (1984) and Ginnett (1990). See also Shea and Guzzo's discussion (1987) of "task interdependence."
12. See McGrath (1984). Campion, Medsker, and Higgs (1993) review the concept of goal interdependence.
13. See, for example, Dumaine (1990); Wilson, George, and Wellins, with Byham (1994); and Zenger, Musselwhite, Hurson, and Perrin (1994).
14. Sundstrom (1986). See also Gifford (1987).
15. Aviel (1994).
16. For example, Katzenbach and Smith (1993). See also McGrath (1984).
17. George (1996).
18. Goodman and Leyden (1991).

19. See, for example, Hackman (1990) and Guzzo and Shea (1992).
20. See Sundstrom, DeMeuse, and Futrell (1990) for a definition of team viability; see also Hackman and Oldham (1980).
21. Hackman (1987).
22. See Pritchard and Watson (1991) and Pritchard (1992) for a discussion.
23. See Moran, Musselwhite, and Zenger (1996).
24. Argote (1993).
25. Bandura (1986); see also Guzzo, Yost, Campbell, and Shea (1993).
26. See, for example, Fisher (1993); Kozlowski, Gully, Salas, and Cannon-Bowers (1996); Nygren and Levine (1996); and Wilson, George, and Wellins, with Byham (1994).
27. See Wellins, Byham, and Wilson (1991) for a list of responsibilities that a self-managing team might have or share with managers.
28. Borman, Hanson, and Hedge (1997).
29. Henkoff (1993) and Gronstedt (1996).
30. Bassi, Cheney, and Van Buren (1997).
31. See, for example, Pritchard and others (1988).
32. Hackman and Wageman (1995).
33. See Lawler (1990); Lawler and Cohen (1992); and DeMatteo, Eby, and Sundstrom (1998).
34. See Mankin, Cohen, and Bikson (1996).
35. A review of training industry trends by Bassi, Cheney, and Van Buren (1997) identified computer skills training as the current top priority expressed in a survey of human resource development executives, and one of the top two priorities for the next three years.
36. See, for example, Bostrom, Watson, and Kinney (1992) and Post (1992).
37. See, for example, George (1996) and Lipnack and Stamps (1997).
38. Mankin, Cohen, and Bikson (1996).
39. See Sundstrom (1987).
40. For discussions of kinds of work teams, see Sundstrom and Altman (1989); Sundstrom, DeMeuse, and Futrell (1990); Hackman (1990); Lawler and Cohen (1992); Dumaine (1994); and Cohen and Bailey (1997).
41. Hackman (1987).
42. See, for example, Hackman (1990), Ancona (1990), and Ancona and Caldwell (1992).
43. Lawler and Cohen (1992) and Wellins, Byham, and Dixon (1994).
44. Dumaine (1994).
45. Kidder (1981).
46. Ancona and Caldwell (1992) and Cohen and Bailey (1997).
47. George (1996).
48. Wellins, Byham, and Wilson (1991).
49. Sundstrom and Altman (1989).
50. For example, Gladstein (1984).

51. See Hackman (1990) for case examples of all of these kinds of service teams.
52. Sundstrom, DeMeuse, and Futrell (1990).
53. Murnighan and Conlon (1991).
54. Ginnett (1990).
55. Lawler and Cohen (1992).
56. Quality circles consist of frontline employees who meet to identify ways to improve the quality of products or services and to recommend changes. See Marks, Mirvis, Hackett, and Grady (1986) and Lawler, Mohrman, and Ledford (1992).

CHAPTER TWO

1. Katzenbach and Smith (1993); Ray and Bronstein (1995); Lawler (1992); Ketchum and Trist (1992); Sundstrom, DeMeuse, and Futrell (1990); and Orsburn, Moran, Musselwhite, and Zenger (1990).
2. Weisbord (1987).
3. Miller (1959).
4. Pava (1983).
5. Mohrman, Cohen, and Mohrman (1995).
6. Among the best of the many standard meeting agendas we've seen is the one in Ketchum and Trist (1992), pp. 152–153.
7. Herbst (1974).
8. Hackman (1987).
9. Orsburn, Moran, Musselwhite, and Zenger (1990); Weisbord (1987); Emery (1993); and Ketchum and Trist (1992).
10. Schuster (1984).
11. Tichy and Devanna (1986).
12. Bridges (1991).
13. Orsburn, Moran, Musselwhite, and Zenger (1990).
14. Weisbord and Janoff (1995).
15. Wheelright and Clark (1992) have thoroughly described a design process for complex product development teams.
16. Pasmore (1988) and Lytle (1991a, 1991b).
17. Mohrman, Cohen, and Mohrman (1995); Rummler and Brache (1990); Lytle (1991a); and Pava (1983).
18. Zenger, Musselwhite, Hurson, and Perrin (1994); and Fisher (1993).
19. Moran, Musselwhite, and Zenger (1996); Montebello (1994); Bendaly (1996).
20. Ketchum and Trist (1992).

CHAPTER THREE

1. Caudron (1994).
2. The teamwork KSA test is in Stevens and Campion (1994).

3. See Schneider and Schmitt (1986) for details on preparing and administering these assessment tools.
4. Morgan and Smith (1996).
5. Katz and Kahn (1978).
6. Wellins, Byham, and Wilson (1991).
7. Louis and Faraj (1997).
8. Besser (1996).
9. Kinshuk Sinha (personal communication, Aug. 1996).
10. Wellins, Byham, and Wilson (1991).
11. Austin, Klimoski, and Hunt (1997).
12. Austin, Klimoski, and Hunt (1997).
13. Wellins, Byham, and Wilson (1991).
14. Validity should be considered; see Cascio (1993) for more on validity.
15. Mumford, Costanza, Connelly, and Johnson (1996).
16. Schneider and Schmitt (1986).
17. Schuler and Harris (1991).
18. Wellins, Byham, and Wilson (1991).
19. Stevens and Campion (1994).
20. "Uniform Guidelines on Employee Selection Procedures" (1978).

CHAPTER FOUR

1. Nygren and Levine (1996), p. 75.
2. Rawles (1996), p. xvii.
3. Lane (1996a, 1996c).
4. Lane (1996a).
5. Lane (1992).
6. Dumaine (1994).
7. Fisher (1993).
8. Dumaine (1994).
9. Dumaine (1994).
10. Dumaine (1994), p. 88.
11. Katz and Kahn (1978).
12. Dumaine (1994).
13. Dumaine (1994).
14. Lane (1996d).
15. See exceptions by Hackman and Walton (1986) and Kozlowski, Gully, Salas, and Cannon-Bowers (1996).
16. Fleishman and others (1991); Hackman and Walton (1986); Lord (1977); Mumford and others (1993); and Roby (1961).
17. Hackman and Walton (1986), p.75.
18. Fleishman and others (1991); Mumford and others (1993); and Zaccaro, Marks, O'Connor-Boes, and Costanza (1995).
19. Ancona (1987) and Ancona and Caldwell (1988).

20. Roby (1961).

21. Marks and Zaccaro (1997).

22. Jacobs and Jaques (1987).

23. Locke and Latham (1990) and Mohrman, Cohen, and Mohrman (1995).

24. Locke and Latham (1990).

25. Shamir, House, and Arthur (1993).

26. Mohrman, Cohen, and Mohrman (1995).

27. Locke and Latham (1990).

28. Fleishman and others (1991).

29. Hackman and Walton (1986).

30. Mumford and others (1993).

31. Jesuino (1996).

32. Zaccaro, Blair, Peterson, and Zazanis (1995).

33. Zaccaro (1996) and Zaccaro, Blair, Peterson, and Zazanis (1995).

34. Bandura (1982, 1986).

35. Gist and Mitchell (1992) and Kozlowski, Gully, Salas, and Cannon-Bowers (1996).

36. Bass (1985) and Burns (1978).

37. See Bass (1985), House (1977), and House and Shamir (1993) for a delineation.

38. House and Shamir (1993).

39. Burns (1978), House and Shamir (1993), and Jesuino (1996).

40. Kozlowski, Gully, Salas, and Cannon-Bowers (1996).

41. Kozlowski, Gully, Salas, and Cannon-Bowers (1996).

42. Zaccaro, Marks, O'Connnor-Boes, and Costanza (1995).

43. Marks (1997).

44. Hinsz, Tindale, and Vollrath (1997) and Kozlowski, Gully, Salas, and Cannon-Bowers (1996).

45. Kozlowski, Gully, Salas, and Cannon-Bowers (1996).

46. Flavell (1979), p. 906.

47. Sternberg (1985) and Davidson, Deuser, and Sternberg (1994).

48. Katz and Kahn (1978).

49. Kraut, Pedigo, McKenna, and Dunnette (1989) and Luthans, Rosenkrantz, and Hennessey (1985).

50. Lane (1996b).

51. Katz and Kahn (1978).

52. Kotter (1982).

53. Lane (1996b, 1996d).

54. Lane (1996a, 1996c).

55. Baehr (1992) and Paolillo (1981).

56. Jacobs and Jaques (1987).

57. Lane (1992, 1996b) and Lim (1996).

58. Lane (1992, 1996b).

59. Hooijberg and Quinn (1992) and Jacobs and Jaques (1987).

60. McCauley, Eastman, and Ohlott (1995).
61. See Bass (1985), Yukl (1994), and Zaccaro (1996) for reviews of this literature.
62. Locke and Latham (1990).

CHAPTER FIVE

1. Wellins, Byham, and Wilson (1991).
2. Henkoff (1993).
3. Goldstein (1991).
4. From *Phelps Dodge Mining Corporation Corporate Newsletter,* Jan. 1997.
5. In addition to the refinery operation, Phelps Dodge–El Paso also has a rod mill with about two hundred employees. It was built adjacent to the refinery in 1969 and its employees were represented by a separate union. Although it was not included in the refinery's 1985 decertification election, the rod mill did have its own successful decertification election in 1997.
6. The order of emphasis is important: safety is always viewed as the first priority at Phelps Dodge–El Paso.
7. Campion, Cheraskin, and Stevens (1994).
8. Campion and Stevens (1991).
9. Stevens and Campion (1994).
10. Hogan and Hogan (1991).
11. Stevens and Campion (forthcoming).
12. Goldstein (1993).
13. Wellins, Byham, and Wilson (1991).
14. Filipczak (1992).
15. Hammer (1996).
16. Meyer and Davis (1992).
17. Conn and Rieke (1994) and Russell and Karol (1994).
18. Stevens and Campion (forthcoming).
19. Rahim (1983).
20. Glenn and Pood (1989).
21. Harris and DeSimone (1994).
22. Goldstein (1991), p. 557.
23. Wellins, Byham, and Wilson (1991).
24. Goldstein (1991), p. 509.

CHAPTER SIX

1. Pritchard (1990, 1995).
2. Jones and others (1993); Jones, Powell, and Roberts (1990); and Jones, Hein, and Payne (1994).

3. Pritchard (1990).
4. Teams on Track is available from Steve Jones at (615) 898-5937.
5. Hay Group (1997).
6. Pritchard (1990).
7. Katzenbach and Smith (1993).
8. Katzenbach and Smith (1993).
9. Katzenbach and Smith (1993), p. 160.
10. Zander (1994).
11. Feldman (1984).
12. Pritchard (1990).
13. Katzenbach and Smith (1993).
14. Don Schilling (personal communication, Feb. 28, 1997).
15. Hitchcock and Willard (1995).
16. Hitchcock and Willard (1995), p. 134.
17. Deming (1986), p. 102.
18. The team scorecard is based on Boyett and Conn (1988) and Schilling and Valera (1996). Although it shares part of the name of the Balanced Scorecard (Kaplan and Norton, 1996), it was developed independently. (Goal Tracker software is also available for the Team Scorecard; contact Don Schilling at (360) 587-4571).
19. Riggs and Felix (1983).
20. Heninger (1994).
21. Craig Heninger may be contacted at (541) 758-5436.
22. Zigon (1995, 1996).
23. Jack Zigon may be contacted at (610) 891-9599 (or at the Website www.zigonperf.com).
24. Kaplan and Norton (1996).
25. Meyer (1994).

CHAPTER SEVEN

1. Lawler, Mohrman, and Ledford (1995) and Lawler (1998).
2. Lawler (1996).
3. Lawler, Mohrman, and Ledford (1995) and Lawler (1998).
4. Lawler and Cohen (1992); Mohrman, Cohen, and Mohrman (1995); and Wageman (1995).
5. Seaman (1997).
6. Zingheim and Schuster (1997a, 1997b).
7. Seaman (1997).
8. Seaman (1997).
9. Lawler (1990).
10. Lawler (1990).
11. Lawler (1978, 1986).
12. Jenkins, Ledford, Gupta, and Doty (1992).

13. Mohrman, Cohen, and Mohrman (1995).
14. Lawler, Mohrman, and Ledford (1995).
15. Kerr (1975) and Heneman (1992).
16. Kohn (1993).
17. Cameron and Pierce (1997).
18. Lawler (1990).
19. Lawler (1990).
20. Schuster and Zingheim (1992) and Zingheim and Schuster (1997b).
21. Wageman (1995).
22. Lawler (1986).
23. Lawler (1990).
24. Frost, Wakeley, and Ruh (1974).
25. Mohrman, Mohrman, and Lawler (1992).
26. Abosch and Reidy (1996).
27. DeMatteo, Rush, Sundstrom, and Eby (1997).
28. McAdams and Hawk (1994).
29. Zingheim and Schuster (1997a).
30. DeMatteo, Rush, Sundstrom, and Eby (1997).
31. Mohrman, Cohen, and Mohrman (1995).

CHAPTER EIGHT

1. Van der Spiegel (1995).
2. Ciborra (1991).
3. Mankin, Cohen, and Bikson (1996).
4. Mankin, Cohen, and Bikson (1996).
5. Mankin, Cohen, and Bikson (1996).
6. Stasz and Bikson (1986) and Stasz, Bikson, Eveland, and Mittman (1990).
7. Woodward (1965).
8. Mankin, Cohen, and Bikson (1996).
9. Berry and Parasuraman (1997).
10. Gutek (1997).
11. Mankin, Cohen, and Bikson (1996).
12. Berry and Parasuraman (1997).
13. Mankin, Cohen, and Bikson (1996).
14. Hambrick (1998).
15. Mankin, Cohen, and Bikson (1996).
16. International Atomic Energy Agency (1997b).
17. International Atomic Energy Agency (1997a).
18. Granovetter (1973).
19. Feldman (1987).
20. Mankin, Cohen, and Bikson (1996).
21. Bikson and Eveland (1996).
22. Bikson (1996).

23. Ciborra and Patriotta (1996).
24. Bikson, Stasz, and Mankin (1985).
25. Brown and Duguid (1991) and Ciborra (1991).
26. For more information on these new change processes, see Mankin, Cohen, and Bikson (1996) and Mankin, Cohen, and Bikson (1997).

CHAPTER NINE

1. CyberAtlas (1998).
2. Campbell and Levitt (1997).
3. Nunamaker (1991).
4. McGrath and Hollingshead (1994).
5. Johansen (1992).
6. Coleman (1997).
7. Grahowski, McGoff, Vogel, Martz, and Nunamaker (1990).
8. Jones (1996) and Ventana Corporation (1997).
9. Nunamaker, Briggs, Mittleman, Vogel, and Balthazard (1996–97).
10. Microsoft (1997).
11. Smart Technologies (1997).
12. Sprout (1995).
13. Fontana (1997).
14. Exxon (1998).
15. Sprout (1995).
16. PictureTel Corporation (1997a).
17. PictureTel Corporation (1997b).
18. Blundel (1997).
19. LiveWorks is no longer marketing the LiveBoard. However, the SmartBoard by Smart Technologies and the SoftBoard by Microfield Graphics are similar.
20. Anderson (1998).
21. Anderson (1997).
22. DeSanctis, Poole, Desharnais, and Lewis (1991).

CHAPTER TEN

1. Frances, Dressel, MacArthur, and Neathammer (1986); Lawrence (1989); Sullivan (1990); and Wilson (1985).
2. American Productivity Center (1984) and Brill, with Margulis and Konar (1984).
3. Brill, with Margulis and Konar (1984).
4. Polley and Stone (1993).
5. Allen (1977).
6. See Sundstrom (1986), Wineman (1986), and Vischer (1996) for a review.
7. See Springer (1986) for a review.

8. Polley and Stone (1993).
9. Allen (1977), Pelz and Andrews (1966), and Shilling and Bernard (1964).
10. See Sundstrom (1986) for a review.
11. Allen (1977).
12. Allen (1977) and Fernald (1986).
13. Hackman (1987).
14. See Becker (1981), pp. 104–111, for a review.
15. Szilagyi and Holland (1980).
16. Sundstrom, DeMeuse, and Futrell (1990).
17. Sundstrom, DeMeuse, and Futrell (1990).
18. Sundstrom and Altman (1989).
19. Herman Miller (1990).
20. Polley and Stone (1993).
21. Herman Miller (1990).
22. Adams and Parham (1995).
23. Smith (1994).
24. "Brave New Work" (1995).
25. Becker (1990).
26. Becker (1990).
27. "Brave New Work" (1995).
28. Becker (1981).
29. Spaulding (1978).
30. For a review see Lang (1987) and Allen (1977).
31. For further discussion, see Hillier and Hanson (1984).
32. Richards and Dobyns (1957).
33. Allen (1977) and Baker, Siegmann, and Rubinstein (1967).
34. Peters and Waterman (1981).
35. Allen (1977).
36. Fernald (1986) and Allen (1977).
37. Becker and Steele (1995).
38. Sundstrom, DeMeuse, and Futrell (1990).
39. Alderfer (1987).
40. Friedlander (1987).
41. Ketchum (1981).
42. Sundstrom, DeMeuse, and Futrell (1990).
43. Lawrence and Lorsch (1969).
44. Sundstrom, DeMeuse, and Futrell (1990).
45. Sundstrom and Altman (1989).
46. Sundstrom (1986).
47. Sundstrom and Altman (1989).
48. Herman Miller (1990).
49. T. Scarbrough, Strategic Services Group, CRSS International, Atlanta, Ga., personal communication, Aug. 1997.

50. Sundstrom and Altman (1989).
51. Allen (1977).

CHAPTER ELEVEN

1. See, for example, Wellins, Byham, and Wilson (1991); Wellins, Byham, and Dixon (1994); and Moran, Musselwhite, and Zenger (1996).
2. See Schneider (1987a) for a discussion of defining and measuring organizational culture.
3. See Lawler (1986, 1992) and Lawler, Mohrman, and Ledford (1992, 1995).
4. Xerox (1990).
5. Walton (1982).
6. Ketchum and Trist (1992).
7. Galagan (1997).
8. Reid (1990).
9. Kaplan and Norton (1996).
10. See Schein (1986, 1993) and Schneider (1987a).
11. See, for example, Lawler (1986, 1992).
12. Lawler (1996).
13. Senge (1990).
14. Reid (1990).
15. Walton (1982) and Ketchum and Trist (1992).
16. Wellins, Byham, and Wilson (1991).
17. Mohrman, Cohen, and Mohrman (1995).
18. Wellins, Byham, and Dixon (1994).
19. Beckhard and Harris (1987).
20. Locke and Latham (1990).
21. Schwarz (1994).
22. Ree and Earles (1992) and Ree, Carretta, and Teachout (1995).
23. For example, Kabanoff and O'Brien (1979) and Tziner and Eden (1985).
24. Campion, Palmer, and Campion (1997).
25. Likert (1961).
26. Wilson, George, and Wellins, with Byham (1994).
27. Wellins, Byham, and Dixon (1994).
28. Xerox (1990).
29. Andrews, Waag, and Bell (1992).
30. Cannon-Bowers, Tannenbaum, Salas, and Volpe (1995).
31. DeMatteo, Rush, Sundstrom, and Eby (1997).
32. For example, Galagan (1986) and Wagel (1987).
33. Denison (1990).
34. Kidder (1981).
35. Sundstrom (1986).
36. Herbst (1974).

37. Katz and Kahn (1978).
38. Lawler, Mohrman, and Ledford (1995) and Hackman and Wageman (1995).
39. Gronstedt (1996).
40. See, for example, Pava (1983) and Cherns (1976).
41. Hackman and Oldham (1980).
42. Womak, Jones, and Roos (1990).
43. Wellins, Byham, and Dixon (1994).
44. See Ancona and Caldwell (1992) and Ancona (1990).
45. Kidder (1981).
46. Ancona and Caldwell (1992).
47. Geber (1995).
48. Goodman and Wilson (1997).
49. Ginnett (1990).
50. Dumaine (1994).
51. Wilson, George, and Wellins, with Byham (1994).
52. Bassi, Cheney, and Van Buren (1997).

REFERENCES

Abosch, K. S., and Reidy, D. B. "Supporting Teams Through Rewards Systems." *ACA Journal,* 1996, *5*(4), 72–81.

Adams, H. L., and Parham, D. W. *Repositioning the Office Building: Reinventing Real Estate.* Washington, D.C.: Urban Land Institute, 1995.

Alderfer, C. P. "An Intergroup Perspective on Group Dynamics." In J. Lorsch (ed.), *Handbook of Organizational Behavior* (pp. 190–210). Upper Saddle River, N.J.: Prentice-Hall, 1987.

Allen, T. *Managing the Flow of Technology.* Cambridge, Mass.: MIT Press, 1977.

American Productivity Center. *White-Collar Productivity: The National Challenge.* Grand Rapids, Mich.: Steelcase, Inc., 1984.

Ancona, D. G. "Groups in Organizations: Extending Laboratory Models." In C. Hendrick (ed.), *Group Processes and Intergroup Relations* (pp. 207–230). Thousand Oaks, Calif.: Sage, 1987.

Ancona, D. G. "Outward Bound: Strategies for Team Survival in the Organization." *Academy of Management Journal,* 1990, *33*(2), 334–365.

Ancona, D. G., and Caldwell, D. F. "Beyond Task and Maintenance: Defining External Functions in Groups." *Group and Organization Studies,* 1988, *13*(4), 468–494.

Ancona, D. G., and Caldwell, D. F. "Bridging the Boundary: External Activity and Performance in Organizational Teams." *Administrative Science Quarterly,* 1992, *37*(4), 634–665.

Anderson, J. R. "Praise and Contempt." *Navy Times,* Sept. 29, 1997, p. 14.

Anderson, J. R. "Hunter Warrior: Testing New Ideas/Exercise Will Pit Speed, Stealth Against Armor." *Navy Times,* Jan. 5, 1998, p. 10.

Andrews, D. H., Waag, W. L., and Bell, H. H. "Training Technologies Applied to Team Training: Military Examples." In R. W. Swezey and E. Salas (eds.), *Teams: Their Training and Performance.* Norwood, N.J.: Ablex, 1992.

Argote, L. "Group and Organizational Learning Curves: Individual, System, and Environmental Components." *British Journal of Social Psychology,* 1993, *32*(1), 31–51.

Austin, J. T., Klimoski, R. J., and Hunt, S. T. "Dilemmatics in Public Sector Assessment: A Framework for Developing and Evaluating Selection Systems." *Human Performance,* 1997, *9*(3), 177–198.

Aviel, D. "Flying High on Auto-Pilot." *Wall Street Journal,* Nov. 14, 1994, p. A10.

Baehr, M. E. *Predicting Success in Higher-Level Positions: A Guide to the System for Testing and Evaluation of Potential.* Westport, Conn.: Quorum/Greenwood, 1992.

Baker, N. R., Siegmann, J., and Rubenstein, A. H. "The Effects of Perceived Needs and Means on the Generation of Ideas for Industrial Research and Development Projects." *IEEE Transactions on Engineering Management,* 1967, *11,* 158–162.

Bandura, A. "Self-Efficacy Mechanism in Human Agency." *American Psychologist,* 1982, *37*(2), 122–147.

Bandura, A. *Social Foundations of Thought and Action: A Social Cognitive Theory.* Upper Saddle River, N.J.: Prentice-Hall, 1986.

Bass, B. M. *Leadership and Performance Beyond Expectations.* New York: Free Press, 1985.

Bassi, L. J., Cheney, S., and Van Buren, M. "Training Industry Trends 1997." *Training & Development,* Nov. 1997, pp. 46–59.

Becker, F. D. *Workspace: Creating Environments in Organizations.* New York: Praeger, 1981.

Becker, F. D. *The Total Workplace: Facilities Management and the Elastic Organization.* New York: Van Nostrand Reinhold, 1990.

Becker, F., and Steele, F. *Workplace by Design: Mapping the High-Performance Workscape.* San Francisco: Jossey-Bass, 1995.

Beckhard, R., and Harris, R. *Organizational Transitions: Managing Complex Change.* Reading, Mass.: Addison-Wesley, 1987.

Bendaly, L. *Games Teams Play: Dynamic Activities for Tapping Work Team Potential.* Toronto: McGraw-Hill Ryerson, 1996.

Berry, L. L., and Parasuraman, A. "Listening to the Customer: The Concept of a Service-Quality Information System." *Sloan Management Review,* 1997, *38*(3), 65–76.

Besser, T. L. *Team Toyota: Transplanting the Toyota Culture to the Camry Plant in Kentucky.* Albany: State University of New York Press, 1996.

Bikson, T. K. "Groupware at the World Bank." In C. Ciborra (ed.), *Groupware and Teamwork.* New York: Wiley, 1996.

Bikson, T. K., and Eveland, J. D. "Groupware Implementation: Reinvention in the Sociotechnical Frame." In *Proceedings of the Conference on Computer-Supported Cooperative Work,* Association for Computing Machinery, New York, Nov. 1996.

Bikson, T. K., Stasz, C., and Mankin, D. "Computer-Mediated Work: Individual and Organizational Impact in One Corporate Headquarters." (R–3308-OTA). Santa Monica, Calif.: RAND Corporation, 1985.

Blundell, D. "Collaborative Presentation Technologies: Meetings, Presentations, and Collaboration." In D. Coleman (ed.), *Groupware: Collaborative Strategies for Corporate LANs and Intranets* (pp. 269–317). Upper Saddle River, N.J.: Prentice-Hall, 1997.

Borman, W. C., Hanson, M. A., and Hedge, J. W. "Personnel Selection." *Annual Review of Psychology,* 1997, *48,* 299–337.

Bostrom, R. P., Watson, R. T., and Kinney, S. T. *Computer Augmented Teamwork.* New York: Van Nostrand Reinhold, 1992.

Boyett, J. H., and Conn, H. P. *Maximum Performance Management.* Macomb, Ill.: Glenbridge, 1988.

"Brave New Work." *Details,* Feb. 1995, pp. 94–98.

Bridges, W. *Managing Transitions: Making the Most of Change.* Reading, Mass.: Addison-Wesley, 1991.

Brill, M., with Margulis, S., and Konar, E. *Using Office Design to Increase Productivity, Vols. I and II.* Buffalo, N.Y.: Workplace Design and Productivity Inc., 1984.

Brown, J. S., and Duguid, P. "Organizational Learning and Communities-of-Practice: Toward a Unified View of Working, Learning, and Innovation." *Organization Science,* 1991, *2*(1), 40–57.

Burns, J. M. *Leadership.* New York: HarperCollins, 1978.

Byham, W. *Zapp! The Lightning of Empowerment.* New York: Harmony Books, 1990.

Cameron, J., and Pierce, W. D. "Rewards, Interest, and Performance." *ACA Journal,* 1997, *6*(4), 6–16.

Campbell, I., and Levitt, M. "The Pervasive Internet." Intentional Data Corporation Technical Report #14581, Nov. 1997.

Campion, M. A., Cheraskin, L., and Stevens, M. J. "Career-Related Antecedents and Outcomes of Job Rotation." *Academy of Management Journal,* 1994, *37*(6), 1518–1542.

Campion, M. A., Medsker, G. J., and Higgs, A. C. "Relations Between Work Group Characteristics and Effectiveness." *Personnel Psychology,* 1993, *46*(4), 823–850.

Campion, M. A., Palmer, D. K., and Campion, J. E. "A Review of Structure in the Selection Interview." *Personnel Psychology,* 1997, *50*(3), 655–702.

Campion, M. A., and Stevens, M. J. "Neglected Questions in Job Design: How People Design Jobs, Influence of Training, and Task-Job Predictability." *Journal of Business and Psychology,* 1991, *6*(2), 169–91.

Cannon-Bowers, J. A., Tannenbaum, S. I., Salas, E., and Volpe, C. E. "Defining Competencies and Establishing Team Training Requirements." In R. Guzzo, E. Salas, and Associates (eds.), *Team Effectiveness and Decision Making in Organizations.* San Francisco: Jossey-Bass, 1995.

Cartwright, D., and Zander, A. (eds.). *Group Dynamics.* (3rd ed.) New York: HarperCollins, 1968.

Cascio, W. F. "Assessing the Utility of Selection Decisions: Theoretical and Practical Considerations." In N. Schmitt and W. C. Borman (eds.), *Personnel Selection in Organizations* (pp. 310–340). San Francisco: Jossey-Bass, 1993.

Caudron, S. "Team Staffing Requires New HR Role." *Personnel Journal,* 1994, *73*(5), 88–94.

Cherns, A. B. "The Principles of Sociotechnical Design." In W. Pasmore and J. J. Sherwood (eds.), *Sociotechnical Systems: A Sourcebook,* pp. 61–95. San Diego: University Associates, 1976.

Ciborra, C. "From Thinking to Tinkering: The Grassroots of Strategic Information Systems." *Proceedings of the International Conference on Information Systems,* Association for Computing Machinery (ACM), New York, Dec. 1991.

Ciborra, C., and Patriotta, G. "Groupware and Teamwork in New Product Development." In C. Ciborra (ed.), *Groupware and Teamwork.* New York: Wiley, 1996.

Cohen, S. G., and Bailey, D. E. "What Makes Teams Work: Group Effectiveness Research from the Shop Floor to the Executive Suite." *Journal of Management,* 1997, *23*(3), 239–290.

Cohen, S. G., Ledford, G. E., and Spreitzer, G. M. "A Predictive Model of Self-Managing Work Team Effectiveness." *Human Relations,* 1996, *49,* 643–679.

Coleman, D. "Electronic Meetings as Today's Presentations." In D. Coleman (ed.), *Groupware: Collaborative Strategies for Corporate LANs and Intranets* (pp. 183–191). Upper Saddle River, N.J.: Prentice-Hall, 1997.

Conn, S. R., and Rieke, M. L. *The 16PF Fifth Edition Technical Manual.* Champaign, Ill.: Institute for Personality and Ability Testing, 1994.

Cooper, M., Shiflett, S., Korotkin, A. L., and Fleishman, E. A. "Command and Control Teams: Techniques for Assessing Team Performance." (ARRO Final Report.) Washington, D.C.: ARRO, 1984.

CyberAtlas. "How Many People on the Net?" [http://www.cyberatlas.com/market/size/index.html]. Jan. 13, 1998.

Daft, R. L. *Organization Theory and Design.* (5th ed.) Minneapolis/St. Paul: West, 1995.

Davidson, J. E., Deuser, R., and Sternberg, R. J. "The Role of Metacognition in Problem Solving." In J. Metcalf and A. P. Shimamura (eds.), *Metacognition: Knowing About Knowing.* Cambridge, Mass.: MIT Press, 1994.

DeMatteo, J. S., Eby, L., and Sundstrom, E. "Team-Based Rewards: Current Empirical Evidence and Directions for Future Research." *Research in Organizational Behavior,* 1998, *20,* 141–183.

DeMatteo, J. S., Rush, M. C., Sundstrom, E., and Eby, L. T. "Factors Related to the Successful Implementation of Team-Based Rewards." *ACA Journal,* 6(4), 1997, 16–28.

Deming, W. E. *Out of Crisis.* Cambridge, Mass.: Center for Advanced Engineering Study, Massachusetts Institute of Technology, 1986.

Denison, D. R. "Airline Maintenance Group." In J. R. Hackman (ed.), *Groups That Work (and Those That Don't).* San Francisco: Jossey-Bass, 1990.

DeSanctis, G., Poole, M. S., Desharnais, G., and Lewis, H. "Using Computing to Facilitate the Quality Improvement Process: The IRS-Minnesota Project." *TIMS Interfaces,* 1991, 21(6), 23–26.

Dumaine, B. "Who Needs a Boss?" *Fortune,* May 7, 1990, pp. 52–60.

Dumaine, B. "The Trouble with Teams." *Fortune,* September 5, 1994, pp. 86–92.

Emery, M. *Participative Design for Participative Democracy.* Canberra: Australian National University, 1993.

Exxon. "Refining and Marketing." [http://www.exxon.com/exxoncorp/where_we_are/map_cu_right.html]. June 1998.

Feldman, D. "The Development and Enforcement of Group Norms." *Academy of Management Review,* 1984, 9(1), 47–53.

Feldman, M. S. "Electronic Mail and Weak Ties in Organizations." *Office Technology and People,* 1987, 3, 83–101.

Fernald, L. W. "Breaking Barriers: Overcoming Four Communication Obstacles." *Management World,* Sep.–Oct. 1986, pp. 28–29.

Filipczak, B. "What Employers Teach." *Training,* 1992, 29(10), 43–55.

Fisher, K. *Leading Self-Directed Teams: A Guide to Developing New Team Leadership Skills.* New York: McGraw-Hill, 1993.

Flavell, J. H. "Metacognition and Cognitive Monitoring: A New Area of Cognitive-Developmental Inquiry." *American Psychologist,* 1979, 34(10), 906–911.

Fleishman, E. A., and Zaccaro, S. "Toward a Taxonomy of Team Performance Functions." In R. Swezey and E. Salas (eds.), *Teams: Their Training and Performance* (pp. 31–56). Norwood, N.J.: Ablex, 1992.

Fleishman, E. A., and others. "Taxonomic Efforts in the Description of Leader Behavior: A Synthesis and Functional Interpretation." *Leadership Quarterly,* 1991, 2(4), 245–287.

Fontana, J. "Chrysler Saves Big Online — Using the Internet and Notes, the Automotive Giant Links with its Wide Range of Suppliers to Slash Billions in Costs." *Internet Week.* Apr. 28, 1997, issue 660.

Foushee, H. C. "Dyads and Triads at 35,000 Feet: Factors Affecting Group Process and Aircrew Performance." *American Psychologist,* 1984, 39(8), 885–893.

Frances, J., Dressel, D. L., MacArthur, S. A., and Neathammer, R. D. *Office Productivity: Contributions of the Physical Setting.* U.S. Army Corps of Engineers, C.E.R.L. Technical Report P–86/13, Sept. 1986.

Friedlander, F. "The Ecology of Work Groups." In J. W. Lorsch (ed.), *Handbook of Organizational Behavior* (pp. 301–314). Upper Saddle River, N.J.: Prentice-Hall, 1987.

Frost, F., Wakeley, J. H., and Ruh, R. A. *The Scanlon Plan for Organizational Development: Identity, Participation, and Equity.* East Lansing: Michigan State University Press, 1974.

Galagan, P. A. "Work Teams That Work." *Training and Development Journal,* Nov. 1986, pp. 33–35.

Galagan, P. A. "Strategic Planning Is Back." *Training & Development,* Apr. 1997, pp. 32–37.

Geber, B. "Virtual Teams." *Training,* 1995, *32*(4), 36ff.

George, J. A. "Virtual Best Practice: How to Successfully Introduce Virtual Team-Working." *Teams,* Nov. 1996, pp. 38–45.

Gifford, R. *Environmental Psychology.* Needham Heights, Mass.: Allyn & Bacon, 1987.

Ginnett, R. C. "Airline Cockpit Crew." In J. R. Hackman (ed.), *Groups That Work (and Those That Don't).* San Francisco: Jossey-Bass, 1990.

Gist, M. E., and Mitchell, T. R. "Self-Efficacy: A Theoretical Analysis of Its Determinants and Malleability." *Academy of Management Review,* 1992, *17*(2), 183–211.

Gladstein, D. L. "Groups in Context: A Model of Task Group Effectiveness." *Administrative Science Quarterly,* 1984, *29*(3), 499–517.

Glenn, E. C., and Pood, E. A. "The Listening Self-Inventory." *Supervisory Management,* 1989, *8*(1), 12–15.

Goldstein, I. L. "Training in Work Organizations." In M. D. Dunnette and L. M. Hough (eds.), *Handbook of Industrial and Organizational Psychology (vol. 2).* Palo Alto, Calif.: Consulting Psychologists Press, 1991.

Goldstein, I. L. *Training in Organizations.* (3rd ed.) Pacific Grove, Calif.: Brooks/Cole, 1993.

Goodman, P. S., and Leyden, D. P. "Familiarity and Group Productivity." *Journal of Applied Psychology,* 1991, *76*(4), 578–586.

Goodman, P., and Wilson, J. "Exocentric Groups: Effectiveness, Leaders, and Linkages." Presentation at Interfaces of Leadership and Team Processes in Organizations, conference sponsored by George Mason University, Fairfax, Va., Sept. 1997.

Grahowski, R. B., and others. "Implementation of Group Support Systems at IBM," *MIS Quarterly,* 1990, *14*(4), 369–383.

Granovetter, M. "The Strength of Weak Ties." *American Journal of Sociology,* 1973, *78*(6), 1360–1380.

Gronstedt, A. "Integrated Communications at America's Leading Total Quality Management Corporations." *Public Relations Review,* 1996, *22*(1), 25–42.

Gutek, B. A. *The Dynamics of Service.* San Francisco: Jossey-Bass, 1997.

Guzzo, R. A., and Dickson, M. W. "Teams in Organizations: Recent Research on Performance and Effectiveness." *Annual Review of Psychology,* 1996, *47,* 307–338.

Guzzo, R. A., and Shea, G. P. "Group Performance and Intergroup Relations in Organizations." In M. D. Dunnette and L. M. Hough (eds.), *Handbook of Industrial and Organizational Psychology, Vol. 3.* (2nd ed.) Palo Alto, Calif.: Consulting Psychologists Press, 1992.

Guzzo, R. A., Yost, P. R., Campbell, R. J., and Shea, G. P. "Potency in Groups: Articulating a Construct." *British Journal of Social Psychology,* 1993, *32*(1), 87–106.

Hackman, J. R. "The Design of Work Teams." In J. Lorsch (ed.), *Handbook of Organizational Behavior.* Upper Saddle River, N.J.: Prentice-Hall, 1987.

Hackman, J. R. *Groups That Work (and Those That Don't).* San Francisco: Jossey-Bass, 1990.

Hackman, J. R., and Oldham, G. R. *Work Redesign.* Reading, Mass.: Addison-Wesley, 1980.

Hackman, J. R., and Wageman, R. "Total Quality Management: Empirical, Conceptual, and Practical Issues." *Administrative Science Quarterly,* 1995, *40*(2), 309–342.

Hackman, J. R., and Walton, R. E. "Leading Groups in Organizations." In P. S. Goodman and Associates, *Designing Effective Work Groups.* San Francisco: Jossey-Bass, 1986.

Hambrick, D. C. "Corporate Coherence and the Top Management Team." In D. Hambrick, D. A. Nadler, and M. L. Tushman (eds.), *Senior Leadership and Corporate Transformation: CEOs, Top Management Teams, and Boards in Turbulent Times.* Boston: Harvard Business School Press, 1998.

Hammer, A. L. *MBTI Applications: A Decade of Research on the Myers-Briggs Type Indicator.* Palo Alto, Calif.: Consulting Psychologists Press, 1996.

Harris, D. M., and DeSimone, R. L. *Human Resource Development.* Orlando: Dryden Press, 1994.

Hay Group. *The Hay Report: Compensation, Benefits, and Human Resources Strategies for 1997 and Beyond.* Wellesley, Mass.: Center for Management Research, 1997.

Heneman, R. L. *Merit Pay.* Reading, Mass.: Addison-Wesley, 1992.

Heninger, C. *Performance by Criteria Matrix.* Corvallis, Oreg.: Heninger, 1994.

Henkoff, R. "Companies That Train Best." *Fortune,* Mar. 22, 1993, pp. 62ff.

Herbst, D. *Socio-Technical Design: Strategies in Multi-Disciplinary Research.* London: Tavistock, 1974.

Herman Miller. *Facilities for Project Teams: A Research Summary from Herman Miller, Inc.* Zeeland, Mich.: Herman Miller, June 1990.

Hillier, B., and Hanson, J. *The Social Logic of Space.* Cambridge, England: Cambridge University Press, 1984.

Hinsz, V. B., Tindale, R. S., and Vollrath, D. A. "The Emerging Conceptualization of Groups as Information Processors." *Psychological Bulletin,* 1997, *121*(1), 43–64.

Hitchcock, D. E., and Willard, M. L. *Why Teams Can Fail and What to Do About It: Essential Tools for Anyone Implementing Self-Directed Work Teams.* Burr Ridge, Ill.: Irwin, 1995.

Hoerr, J. "The Payoff from Teamwork." *BusinessWeek,* July 10, 1989, pp. 56–62.

Hogan, R., and Hogan, J. "Personality and Status." In D. G. Gilbert and J. J. Conley (eds.), *Personality, Social Skills, and Psychopathology.* New York: Plenum, 1991.

Hooijberg, R., and Quinn, R. E. "Behavioral Complexity and the Development of Effective Managers." In R. L. Phillips and J. G. Hunt (eds.), *Strategic Leadership: A Multiorganizational Perspective* (pp. 161–175). Westport, Conn.: Quorum/Greenwood, 1992.

House, R. J. "A 1976 Theory of Charismatic Leadership." In J. G. Hunt and L. L. Larson (eds.), *Leadership: The Cutting Edge.* Carbondale: Southern Illinois University Press, 1977.

House, R. J., and Shamir, B. "Toward an Integration of Transformational, Charismatic, and Visionary Theories." In M. Chemers and R. Ayman (eds.), *Leadership Theory and Research: Perspectives and Directions* (pp. 81–107). New York: Academic Press, 1993.

International Atomic Energy Agency (IAEA). *A Manager's Guide.* Vienna, Austria: IAEA, 1997a.

International Atomic Energy Agency (IAEA). *Resource Management in the International Atomic Energy Agency.* Vienna, Austria: IAEA, 1997b.

Jacobs, T. O., and Jaques, E. "Leadership in Complex Systems." In J. A. Zeidner (ed.), *Human Productivity Enhancement (Vol. 2)*, pp. 7–65. New York: Praeger, 1987.

Jenkins, G. D., Jr., Ledford, G. E., Jr., Gupta, N., and Doty, D. H. "Skill-Based Pay: Practices, Pay-Offs, Pitfalls, and Prescriptions." Scottsdale, Ariz.: American Compensation Association, 1992.

Jesuino, J. C. "Leadership: Micro-Macro Links." In E. Witte and J. H. Davis (eds.), *Understanding Group Behavior: Small Group Processes and Interpersonal Relations (Vol. 2).* Hillsdale, N.J.: Erlbaum, 1996.

Johansen, R. "An Introduction to Computer-Augmented Teamwork." In R. P. Bostrom, R. T. Watson, and S. T. Kinney (eds.), *Computer Augmented Teamwork: A Guided Tour,* pp. 5–15. New York: Van Nostrand Reinhold, 1992.

Jones, N. "Using GroupSystems V in Africa: The World Bank's Experience with Stakeholder Consultations." In *Defining Meetings for the 21st Century,* seventh annual GroupSystems Conference Proceedings, Tucson, Ariz., Mar. 25–29, 1996.

Jones, R. G., and Lindley, W. D. "Issues in the Transition to Teams." *Journal of Business and Psychology,* 1998, forthcoming.

Jones, S. D., Hein, M. B., and Payne, S. L. "Measuring Team Performance with Self-Directed Teams: A Description of the Process with Examples from Manufacturing and Knowledge Work Teams." *Proceedings of the Fifth Annual International Conference on Work Teams* (pp. 94–108), Denton, Tex., Sept. 1994.

Jones, S. D., Powell, R., and Roberts, S. "Comprehensive Measurement to Improve Assembly Line Work Group Effectiveness." *National Productivity Review,* 1990, *10*(1), 45–55.

Jones, S. D., and others. "Work Group Performance Measurement and Feedback: An Integrated Comprehensive System for a Manufacturing Department." *Group and Organization Management,* 1993, *18*(3), 269–291.

Kabanoff, B., and O'Brien, G. E. "Cooperation Structure and the Relationship of Leader and Member Ability to Group Performance." *Journal of Applied Psychology,* 1979, 64(5), 526–532.

Kaplan, R. S., and Norton, D. P. *The Balanced Scorecard.* Boston: Harvard Business School Press, 1996.

Katz, D., and Kahn, R. *The Social Psychology of Organizations.* (2nd ed.) New York: Wiley, 1978.

Katzenbach, J. R., and Smith, D. K. *The Wisdom of Teams: Creating the High-Performance Organization.* New York: HarperCollins, 1993.

Kerr, S. "On the Folly of Rewarding A, While Hoping for B." *Academy of Management Journal,* 1975, 18, 769–783.

Ketchum, L. "How to Start and Sustain a Work Redesign Program." *National Productivity Review,* 1981, 1, 75–86.

Ketchum, L., and Trist, E. *All Teams Are Not Created Equal: How Employee Empowerment Really Works.* Thousand Oaks, Calif.: Sage, 1992.

Kidder, T. *The Soul of a New Machine.* New York: Avon, 1981.

Kiechel, W. III. "How We Will Work in the Year 2000." *Fortune,* May 17, 1993, pp. 38ff.

Kirkman, B. L., and Rosen, B. "A Model of Work Team Empowerment." *Research in Organizational Change and Development,* 1997, 10, 131–167.

Klimoski, R. J. "Predictor Constructs and Their Measurement." In N. Schmitt and W. C. Borman (eds.), *Personnel Selection in Organizations* (pp. 99–134). San Francisco: Jossey-Bass, 1993.

Kohn, A. *Punished by Rewards.* Boston: Houghton Mifflin, 1993.

Kotter, J. P. *The General Managers.* New York: Free Press, 1982.

Kozlowski, S.W.J., Gully, S. M., Salas, E., and Cannon-Bowers, J. A. "Team Leadership and Development: Theory, Principles, and Guidelines for Training Leaders and Teams." In M. M. Beyerlein, D. Johnson, and S. T. Beyerlein (eds.), *Interdisciplinary Studies of Work Teams.* Vol. 3: *Team Leadership.* Greenwich, Conn.: JAI Press, 1996.

Kraut, A. I., Pedigo, P. R., McKenna, D. D., and Dunnette, M. D. "The Role of the Manager: What's Really Important in Different Management Jobs." *Academy of Management Executive,* 1989, 3(4), 286–293.

Kuhn, T. *The Structure of Scientific Revolutions.* Chicago: University of Chicago Press, 1970.

Lane, P. "Conduit at Boeing Controls: New President Aims to Pilot Company Through Turbulent, Competitive Times." *Seattle Times,* Nov. 22, 1992.

Lane, P. "Conduit: Boeing Needs to Take Some Risks—President Cautions, 'You Can't Stay Static.'" *Seattle Times,* Feb. 27, 1996a.

Lane, P. "New Boeing Chief Faces the Challenge of Continuing 'Work in Progress.'" *Seattle Times,* Apr. 28, 1996b.

Lane, P. "Shrontz Reviews His 10 years as Boeing CEO—and Looks Ahead." *Seattle Times,* Mar. 29, 1996c.

Lane, P. "The Shrontz Years: Boeing Leaders' Push for Change Has Left the Company Headed for a Strong Future." *Seattle Times,* Apr. 14, 1996d.

Lang, J. *Creating Architectural Theory.* New York: Van Nostrand Reinhold, 1987.

Lawler, E. E. III. "The New Plant Revolution." *Organizational Dynamics,* 1978, 6(3), 2–12.

Lawler, E. E. III. *High-Involvement Management: Participative Strategies for Improving Organizational Performance.* San Francisco: Jossey-Bass, 1986.

Lawler, E. E. III. *Strategic Pay.* San Francisco: Jossey-Bass, 1990.

Lawler, E. E. III. *The Ultimate Advantage: Creating the High-Involvement Organization.* San Francisco: Jossey-Bass, 1992.

Lawler, E. E. III. *From the Ground Up: Six Principles for Creating New Logic Organizations.* San Francisco: Jossey-Bass, 1996.

Lawler, E. E. III. *Strategies for High-Performance Organizations.* San Francisco: Jossey-Bass, 1998.

Lawler, E. E. III, and Cohen, S. G. "Designing Pay Systems for Teams." *ACA Journal,* 1992, 1(1), 6–19.

Lawler, E. E. III, Mohrman, S. A., and Ledford, G. E. *Employee Involvement and Total Quality Management: Practices and Results in Fortune 1000 Companies.* San Francisco: Jossey-Bass, 1992.

Lawler, E. E. III, Mohrman, S. A., and Ledford, G. E. *Creating High-Performance Organizations: Practices and Results of Employee Involvement and Quality Management in Fortune 1000 Companies.* San Francisco: Jossey-Bass, 1995.

Lawrence, P. "Building Design: More Than Meets the Eye." *Journal of Business Strategy,* July/Aug. 1989, pp. 15–19.

Lawrence, P. R., and Lorsch, J. W. *Developing Organizations: Diagnosis and Action.* Reading, Mass.: Addison-Wesley, 1969.

Likert, R. *New Patterns of Management.* New York: McGraw-Hill, 1961.

Lim, P. "Conduit to Take Boeing Reins." *Seattle Times,* Feb. 27, 1996.

Lipnack, J., and Stamps, J. *Virtual Teams: Reaching Across Space, Time, and Organizations with Technology.* New York: Wiley, 1997.

Locke, E. A., and Latham, G. P. *A Theory of Goal Setting and Task Performance.* Upper Saddle River, N.J.: Prentice-Hall, 1990.

Lord, R. G. "Functional Leadership Behavior: Measurement and Relation to Social Power and Leadership Perceptions." *Administrative Science Quarterly,* 1977, 22(1), 114–133.

Louis, M. R., and Faraj, S. *The Migration of Boundary Work to the Team Level: Features of a Team's Environment That Make a Difference.* Paper presented in symposium at the annual meeting of the Academy of Management, Boston, Aug. 1997.

Luthans, F., Rosenkrantz, S. A., and Hennessey, H. W. "What Do Successful Managers Really Do? An Observational Study of Managerial Activities." *Journal of Applied Behavioral Science,* 1985, 21(3), 255–270.

Lytle, W. *Socio-Technical Systems Analysis and Design Guide: For Linear Work*. Plainfield, N.J.: Block-Petrella-Weisbord, Inc., 1991a.

Lytle, W. *Socio-Technical Systems Analysis and Design Guide: For Non-Linear Work*. Plainfield, N.J.: Block-Petrella-Weisbord, Inc., 1991b.

Mankin, D., Cohen, S. G., and Bikson, T. K. *Teams and Technology: Fulfilling the Promise of the New Organization*. Boston: Harvard Business School Press, 1996.

Mankin, D., Cohen, S. G., and Bikson, T. K. "Teams and Technology: Tensions in Participatory Design." *Organizational Dynamics*, 1997, 26(1), 63–76.

Markowitz, J. "Using Meetingware and Facilitators: Guidelines and Case Studies." In D. Coleman (ed.), *Groupware: Collaborative Strategies for Corporate LANs and Intranets* (pp. 255–265). Upper Saddle River, N.J.: Prentice-Hall, 1997.

Marks, M. A. "Creating Adaptive Teams: Investigating Antecedents of Effective Team Performance in Dynamic Environments." Unpublished doctoral dissertation, George Mason University, 1997.

Marks, M. A., and Zaccaro, S. J. "Leader-Team Dynamics in Hierarchical Decision Making Teams." Paper presented at the meeting of the Academy of Management, Boston, Aug. 1997.

Marks, M. L., Mirvis, P. H., Hackett, E. J., and Grady, J. F., Jr. "Employee Participation in a Quality Circle Program: Impact on Quality of Work Life, Productivity, and Absenteeism." *Journal of Applied Psychology*, 1986, 71(1), 61–69.

McAdams, J. L., and Hawk, E. J. "Organizational Performance and Rewards: 663 Experiences in Making the Link." Scottsdale, Ariz.: Consortium for Alternate Reward Strategies Research, American Compensation Association, 1994.

McCauley, C. D., Eastman, L. J., and Ohlott, P. J. "Linking Management Selection and Development Through Stretch Assignments." *Human Resource Management*, 1995, 34, 93–115.

McGrath, J. E. *Groups: Interaction and Performance*. Upper Saddle River, N.J.: Prentice-Hall, 1984.

McGrath, J., and Hollingshead, A. *Groups Interacting With Technology*. Thousand Oaks, Calif.: Sage Publications, 1994.

Meyer, C. "How the Right Team Measures Help Teams Excel." *Harvard Business Review*, May–June 1994, pp. 95–103.

Meyer, P., and Davis, S. *The California Psychological Inventory Applications Guide*. Palo Alto, Calif.: Consulting Psychologists Press, 1992.

Microsoft. "Ford Motor Company: Case Study." [http://www.microsoft.com/netmeeting/corp/]. Apr. 1997.

Miller, E. J. "Technology, Territory, and Time: The Internal Differentiation of Complex Production Systems." *Human Relations*, 1959, 12, 245–272.

Mohrman, S. A., Cohen, S. G., and Mohrman, A. M. *Designing Team-Based Organizations: New Forms for Knowledge Work.* San Francisco: Jossey-Bass, 1995.

Mohrman, S. A., and Mohrman, A. M. "Fundamental Organizational Change as Organizational Learning: Creating Team-Based Organizations." *Research in Organizational Change and Development,* 1996, *10,* 197–228.

Mohrman, A. M., Mohrman, S. A., and Lawler, E. E. *The Performance Management of Teams: Performance Measurement, Evaluation, and Incentives.* Boston: Harvard Business School Press, 1992.

Montebello, A. *Work Teams That Work: Skills for Managing Across the Organization.* Minneapolis: Best Sellers, 1994.

Moran, L., Musselwhite, E., and Zenger, J. *Keeping Teams on Track: What to Do When the Going Gets Rough.* Burr Ridge, Ill.: Irwin, 1996.

Morgan, R. B., and Smith, J. E. *Staffing the New Workplace.* Milwaukee, Wis.: ASQC Quality Press, 1996.

Mumford, M. D., Costanza, D. P., Connelly, M. S., and Johnson, J. F. "Item Generation Procedures and Background Data Scales: Implications for Construct and Criterion Related Validity." *Personnel Psychology,* 1996, *49*(2), 361–398.

Mumford, M. D., and Stokes, G. S. "Developmental Determinants of Individual Action: Theory and Practice in Applying Background Measures." In M. D. Dunnette and L. M. Hough (eds.), *Handbook of Industrial and Organizational Psychology.* Palo Alto, Calif.: Consulting Psychologists Press, 1992.

Mumford, M. D., and others. *Cognitive and Temperament Predictors of Executive Ability: Principles for Developing Leadership Capacity.* Technical report #977 (AD#A267 589). Alexandria, Va.: U.S. Army Research Institute for the Behavioral and Social Sciences, 1993.

Murnighan, J. K., and Conlon, D. E. "The Dynamics of Intense Work Groups: A Study of British String Quartets." *Administrative Science Quarterly,* 1991, *36*(2), 165–186.

Nunamaker, J. F., Jr., and others. "Electronic Meetings to Support Group Work." *Communications of the ACM,* 1991, *34*(7), 40–61.

Nunamaker, J. F., Jr., and others. "Lessons from a Dozen Years of Group Support Systems Research: A Discussion of Lab and Field Findings." *Journal of Management Information Systems,* 1996–97, *13*(3), 163–207.

Nygren, R., and Levine, E. L. "Leadership of Work Teams: Factors Influencing Team Outcomes." In M. M. Beyerlein, D. Johnson, and S. T. Beyerlein (eds.), *Interdisciplinary Studies of Work Teams* (pp. 67–104). Vol. 3: *Team Leadership.* Greenwich, Conn.: JAI Press, 1996.

Orsburn, J., Moran, L., Musselwhite, E., and Zenger, J. *Self-Directed Work Teams: The New American Challenge.* Burr Ridge, Ill.: Irwin, 1990.

Paolillo, J. G. "Managers' Self-Assessments of Managerial Roles: The Influence of Hierarchical Level." *Journal of Management*, 1981, 7, 43–52.

Pasmore, W. *Designing Effective Organizations: The Sociotechnical Systems Perspective.* New York: Wiley, 1988.

Pava, C. *Managing New Office Technology.* New York: Free Press, 1983.

Pelz, D. C., and Andrews, F. M. *Scientists in Organizations: Productive Climates for Research and Development.* Ann Arbor: Mich.: Institute for Social Research, 1966.

Peters, T. J. *Thriving on Chaos: Handbook for a Management Revolution.* New York: Knopf, 1987.

Peters, T. J., and Waterman, R. H. *In Search of Excellence: Lessons from American's Best-Run Companies.* New York: HarperCollins, 1981.

PictureTel Corporation. "PictureTel Applications: Industry: Discrete: Owens Corning." [http://www.picturetel.com/apps/applications/owens.html#Heading2]. Nov. 1997a.

PictureTel Corporation. "3M Application Story." [http://www.picturetel.com/apps/applications/3M.html]. Nov. 1997b.

Polley, R. B., and Stone, P. J. "Flexspace: Making Room for Collaborative Work." In L. M. Jessup and J. S. Valacich (eds.), *Group Support Systems.* Old Tappan, N.J.: Macmillan, 1993.

Post, B. Q. "Building the Business Case for Group Support Technology." In J. Nunamaker and R. Sprague (eds.), *Proceedings of the Twenty-Fifth Annual Hawaii International Conference on Systems Sciences.* Los Alamitor, Calif.: IEEE Computer Society Press, 1992.

Pritchard, R. D. *Measuring and Improving Organizational Productivity.* New York: Praeger, 1990.

Pritchard, R. D. "Organizational Productivity." In M. D. Dunnette and L. M. Hough (eds.), *Handbook of Industrial and Organizational Psychology,* Vol. 2. (2nd ed.) Palo Alto, Calif.: Consulting Psychologists Press, 1992.

Pritchard, R. D. *Productivity Measurement and Improvement: Organizational Case Studies.* New York: Praeger, 1995.

Pritchard, R. D., Jones, S., Roth, P., Stuebing, K., and Ekeberg, S. "Effects of Group Feedback, Goal Setting, and Incentives on Organizational Productivity. *Journal of Applied Psychology,* 1988, 73(2), 337–358.

Pritchard, R. D., and Watson, M. D. "Understanding and Measuring Group Productivity." In S. Worchel, W. Wood, and J. A. Simpson (eds.), *Group Process and Productivity.* Thousand Oaks, Calif.: Sage, 1991.

Rahim, M. A. "A Measure of Styles of Handling Interpersonal Conflict." *Academy of Management Journal,* 1983, 26(2), 368–376.

Rawles, D. "Foreword." In M. M. Beyerlein, D. Johnson, and S. T. Beyerlein (eds.), *Interdisciplinary Studies of Work Teams.* Vol. 3: *Team Leadership.* Greenwich, Conn.: JAI Press, 1996.

Ray, D., and Bronstein, H. *Teaming Up: Making the Transition to a Self-Directed Team-Based Organization.* New York: McGraw-Hill, 1995.

Ree, M. J., Carretta, T. R., and Teachout, M. S. "Role of Ability and Prior Job Knowledge in Complex Training Performance." *Journal of Applied Psychology,* 1995, *80*(6), 721–730.

Ree, M. J., and Earles, J. A. "Intelligence Is the Best Predictor of Job Performance." *Current Directions in Psychological Science,* 1992, *1*(2), 86–89.

Reid, P. C. *Well Made in America: Lessons from Harley-Davidson on Being the Best.* New York: McGraw-Hill, 1990.

Richards, C. B., and Dobyns, H. F. "Topography and Culture: The Case of the Changing Cage." *Human Organization,* 1957, *16*, 16–20.

Riggs, J. L., and Felix, G. H. *Productivity by Objectives.* Upper Saddle River, N.J.: Prentice-Hall, 1983.

Roby, T. B. "The Executive Function in Small Groups." In L. Petrullo and B. Bass (eds.), *Leadership and Interpersonal Behavior.* Austin, Tex.: Holt, Rinehart & Winston, 1961.

Roethlisberger, J., and Dickson, W. *Management and the Worker.* Cambridge, Mass.: Harvard University Press, 1939.

Rummler, G., and Brache, A. *Improving Performance: How to Manage the White Space on the Organization Chart.* San Francisco: Jossey-Bass, 1990.

Russell, M. T., and Karol, D. L. *The 16PF Fifth Edition Administrator's Manual.* (2nd ed.) Champaign, Ill.: Institute for Personality and Ability Testing, 1994.

Schein, E. H. *Organizational Culture and Leadership.* San Francisco: Jossey-Bass, 1986.

Schein, E. H. "How Can Organizations Learn Faster? The Challenge of Entering the Green Room." *Sloan Management Review,* 1993, *34* (Winter), 85–92.

Schilling, D., and Valera, A. "Building Business Measurement Systems to Drive Performance." Workshop presented to the eleventh annual conference of the Society of Industrial and Organizational Psychology, San Diego, Apr. 1996.

Schneider, B. *Organizational Culture and Climate.* San Francisco: Jossey-Bass, 1987a.

Schneider, B. "The People Make the Place." *Personnel Psychology,* 1987b, *40*(3), 437–453.

Schneider, B., and Schmitt, N. *Staffing Organizations.* Glenview, Ill.: Scott, Foresman, 1986.

Schuler, R. S., and Harris, D. L. "Deming Quality Improvement: Implications for Human Resources Management as Illustrated in a Small Company." *Human Resources Planning,* 1991, *14*, 191–207.

Schuster, J. R., and Zingheim, P. K. *The New Pay.* San Francisco: Jossey-Bass, 1992.

Schuster, M. *Union-Management Cooperation: Structure, Process, and Impact.* Kalamazoo, Mich.: W. E. Upjohn Institute for Employment Research, 1984.

Schwarz, R. M. *The Skilled Facilitator: Practical Wisdom for Developing Effective Groups.* San Francisco: Jossey-Bass, 1994.

Seaman, R. "Rejuvenating an Organization with Team Pay." *Compensation and Benefits Review,* 1997, 29(5), 25–30.

Senge, P. *The Fifth Discipline.* New York: Doubleday, 1990.

Shamir, B., House, R. J., and Arthur, M. "The Motivational Effects of Charismatic Leadership: A Self-Concept-Based Theory." *Organization Science,* 1993, 4(4), 577–594.

Shea, G. P., and Guzzo, R. A. "Groups as Human Resources." In K. M. Rowland and G. R. Ferris (eds.), *Research in Personnel and Human Resources Management (Vol. 5).* Greenwich, Conn.: JAI Press, 1987.

Shilling, C. W., and Bernard, J. W. (1964). "Informal Communication among Bio Scientists." Report 16A-64. Washington, D.C.: Biological Sciences Communication Project, George Washington University, 1964.

Smart Technologies. "Smart Technologies Inc., Customer Profile: Team Collaboration at Hewlett-Packard." [http://www.smarttech.com/userpro6.htm]. Nov. 1997.

Smith, B. (1994). "Welcome to the Virtual Office." *HR Focus,* 1994, 71(11), 16.

Snow, C. C., and Snell, S. A. "Staffing as Strategy." In N. Schmitt and W. C. Borman (eds.), *Personnel Selection in Organizations* (pp. 448–478). San Francisco: Jossey-Bass, 1993.

Spaulding, W. "Undiscovered Values in Meetings." *Journal of Systems Management,* 1978, 29(6), 24–27.

Springer, T. *Improving Productivity in the Workplace: Reports from the Field.* St. Charles, Ill.: Springer Assoc., 1986.

Sprout, A. L. "The Internet Inside Your Company." *Fortune,* Nov. 27, 1995, pp. 161–168.

Stasz, C., and Bikson, T. K. "Computer Supported Cooperative Work: Examples and Issues from One Federal Agency." Proceedings of the Conference on Computer-Supported Cooperative Work, Association for Computing Machinery (ACM), New York, Dec. 1986.

Stasz, C., Bikson, T. K., Eveland, J. D., and Mittman, B. "Information Technology in the U.S. Forest Service: An Assessment of Late Stage Implementation." (R-3908-USDAFS). Santa Monica, Calif.: RAND Corporation, 1990.

Steiner, I. *Group Process and Productivity.* New York: Academic Press, 1972.

Sternberg, R. *Beyond IQ: A Triarchic Theory of Human Intelligence.* New York: Cambridge University Press, 1985.

Stevens, M. J., and Campion, M. A. "The Knowledge, Skill, and Ability Requirements for Teamwork: Implications for Human Resource Management." *Journal of Management,* 1994, 20(2), 503–530.

Stevens, M. J., and Campion, M. A. "Staffing Work Teams: Development and Validation of a Selection Test For Teamwork Settings." *Journal of Management,* forthcoming.

Sullivan, C. "Employee Comfort, Satisfaction, and Productivity: Recent Efforts at Aetna." In S. Sauter, M. J. Dainoff, and M. J. Smith (eds.), *Promoting Health and Productivity in the Computerized Office: Models of Successful Interventions.* New York: Taylor and Francis, 1990.

Sundstrom, E. *Work Places: The Psychology of the Physical Environment in Offices and Factories.* New York: Cambridge University Press, 1986.

Sundstrom, E. "Work Environments: Offices and Factories." In D. Stokols and I. Altman (eds.), *Handbook of Environmental Psychology.* New York: Wiley, 1987.

Sundstrom, E., and Altman, I. "Physical Environments and Work-group Effectiveness." In L. L. Cummings and B. Staw (eds.), *Research in Organizational Behavior (Vol. 11), pp. 175–209.* Greenwich, Conn.: JAI Press, 1989.

Sundstrom, E., DeMeuse, K., and Futrell, D. "Work Teams: Applications and Effectiveness." *American Psychologist,* 1990, *45*(2), 120–133.

Szilagyi, A. D., and Holland, W. E. "Changes in Social Density: Relationships with Functional Interaction and Perceptions of Job Characteristics, Role Stress, and Work Satisfaction." *Journal of Applied Psychology,* 1980, *65*(1), 28–33.

Tichy, N., and Devanna, M. A. *The Transformational Leader.* New York: Wiley, 1986.

Tziner, A., and Eden, D. "Effects of Crew Composition on Crew Performance: Does the Whole Equal the Sum of the Parts?" *Journal of Applied Psychology,* 1985, *70*(1), 85–93.

"Uniform Guidelines on Employee Selection Procedures." *Federal Register,* 1978, *43,* 38290–38315.

Van der Spiegel, J. "New Information Technologies and Changes in Work." In A. Howard (ed.), *The Changing Nature of Work.* San Francisco: Jossey Bass, 1995.

Ventana Corporation. "GroupSystems Success Stories: Stakeholder Consultations." [http://www2.ventana.com/html/stakeholders.html]. Nov. 1997.

Vischer, J. C. *Workspace Strategies: Environment as a Tool for Work.* New York: Chapman and Hall, 1996.

Wagel, W. H. "Working (and Managing) Without Supervisors." *Personnel,* Sept. 1987, pp. 8–11.

Wageman, R. "Interdependence and Group Effectiveness." *Administrative Science Quarterly,* 1995, *40,* 145–180.

Walton, R. E. "The Topeka Work System: Optimistic Visions, Pessimistic Hypotheses, and Reality." In R. Zager and M. P. Rosow (eds.), *The Innovative Organization: Productivity Programs in Action* (pp. 260–287). New York: Pergamon Press, 1982.

Weisbord, M. *Productive Workplaces: Organizing and Managing for Dignity, Meaning, and Community.* San Francisco: Jossey-Bass, 1987.

Weisbord, M., and Janoff, J. *Future Search: An Action Guide to Finding Common Ground in Organizations and Communities.* San Francisco: Barrett-Koehler, 1995.

Wellins, R. S., Byham, W. C., and Dixon, G. *Inside Teams: How Twenty World-Class Organizations Are Winning Through Teamwork*. San Francisco: Jossey-Bass, 1994.

Wellins, R. S., Byham, W. C., and Wilson, J. M. *Empowered Teams: Creating Self-Directed Work Groups That Improve Quality, Productivity, and Participation*. San Francisco: Jossey-Bass, 1991.

Wheelright, S., and Clark, K. *Revolutionizing Product Development: Quantum Leaps in Speed, Efficiency, and Quality*. New York: Free Press, 1992.

Wilson, J. M., George, J., and Wellins, R. S., with Byham, W. C. *Leadership Trapeze: Strategies for Leadership in Team-Based Organizations*. San Francisco: Jossey-Bass, 1994.

Wilson, S. *Premises of Excellence*. London: Building Use Studies, 1985.

Wineman, J. (ed.). *Behavioral Issues in Office Design*. New York: Van Nostrand Reinhold, 1986.

Womak, J. P., Jones, D. T., and Roos, D. *The Machine That Changed the World*. New York: HarperCollins, 1990.

Woodward, J. *Industrial Organization: Theory and Practice*. London: Oxford University Press, 1965.

Xerox. "Xerox Forum on the National Quality Award Presentation Slides." (Accompanying reports: "Xerox Corporation: 1960–1980"; "Xerox Corporation: 1980–1983"; and "Xerox Corporation: 1983–1989.") Fairport, N.Y.: Xerox National Quality Communication and Promotion Office, 1990.

Yukl, G. *Leadership in Organizations*. (3rd ed.) Upper Saddle River, N.J.: Prentice-Hall, 1994.

Zaccaro, S. J. "Social Contextual Considerations of Efficacy Beliefs: Defining Multiple Forms of Social Efficacy." Keynote address presented at the annual meeting of the Association for the Advancement of Applied Sport Psychology, Williamsburg, Va., Oct. 1996.

Zaccaro, S. J., Blair, V., Peterson, C., and Zazanis, M. "Collective Efficacy." In J. Maddux (ed.), *Self-Efficacy, Adaptation, and Adjustment* (pp. 305–328). New York: Plenum, 1995.

Zaccaro, S. J., Marks, M., O'Connor-Boes, J., and Costanza, D. "The Nature of Leader Mental Models." Alexandria, Va.: U.S. Army Research Institute for the Behavioral and Social Sciences, 1995.

Zander, A. *Making Groups Effective*. (3rd ed.) San Francisco: Jossey-Bass, 1994.

Zenger, J., Musselwhite, E., Hurson, K., and Perrin, C. *Leading Teams: Mastering the New Role*. Burr Ridge, Ill.: Business One Irwin, 1994.

Zigon, J. *How to Measure the Results of Work Teams*. Media, Pa.: Zigon Performance Group, 1995.

Zigon, J. "How to Measure the Results of Work Teams." Workshop presented at the Seventh International Conference for the Study of Work Teams, Dallas, Sept. 1996.

Zingheim, P. K., and Schuster, J. R. "Best Practices for Small-Team Pay." *ACA Journal,* 1997a, 6(1), 40–49.

Zingheim, P. K., and Schuster, J. R. "How to Pay Members of Small High-Performance Teams." (In "Team Pay Case Studies," *Compensation and Benefits Review.*) New York: American Management Association, 1997b.

INDEX

A

Accountability: measurements needed for, 33. *See also* Measurement and feedback systems

Action (performing) teams, 20–21, 23; communication technologies for, 267, 344, 346; facilities for, 290, 292–295; information system for, 230–233, 242; leaders' roles in, 119–120; measurement and feedback system for, 178–179, 180; recruiting for, 80; structure for, 51–52; support systems for, 330–331, 332; tools for assessing applicants for, 87; training for, 153–154

Aetna, productivity at, 273

Agendas, for feedback review sessions, 172–173, 173–174

Andersen Consulting, communication technologies at, 266

Anytime, anyplace (ATAP) meetings, 263–264, 270

Assessment of applicants: sources of data for, 85; tools for, by types of teams, 87; when staffing teams, 71, 72, 81–86, 87, 91. *See also* Training needs assessment

AT&T, 3

Authority, as team boundary, 35

B

Balanced scorecards, 179, 181

Baldrige Awards, 3, 189

Bell Labs, pay system at, 198

Best practices, 302–325; for communication technologies, 268–270, 320–322; by executive team, 303–306; for facilities, 296–297, 322–323; for information system, 229, 241, 242, 319–320; for leaders' roles, 123–125, 311–312; for measurement and feedback systems, 184–186, 315–317; for reward systems, 317–319; for team staffing, 90–91, 308–311; for team structure, 60–62, 306–308; for training, 154–155, 313–315

Boeing, 3, 8, 19

Boeing 777 project, 304, 335–336; case study of leaders' roles with, 97–101, 113, 121, 324

Bonus pay plans, 201, 202, 204; and measurement and feedback systems, 182–183, 186

Boundaries: authority as, 35; function of managing, 74–75; modulation of, and facilities, 286–288, 290, 297; resources as, 35–36; responsibilities as, 34–35; scope as, 34; as team charter element, 54; as team structure element, 33–36

Brown-field situations: production teams in, 327, 332; recruiting in, 79; training as essential in, 156

Buyin, and measurement and feedback systems, 167–168, 184